No Law Against
MERCY

Jailed for Sheltering a Child From the State

BARBARA LYN LAPP

RACHEL B. LAPP

Hand of Hope Press   Cassadaga, New York

Published by Hand of Hope Press
Post Office Box 101
Cassadaga, New York 14718

ISBN 0-9653547-0-9

Library of Congress Catalog Number 96-094579

10 9 8 7 6 5 4 3 2 1

For the innocent and the helpless.

For all the Billy Stefans in the world.

■ CONTENTS ■

APPENDIX A: Sources of Learning
APPENDIX B: Fully Informed Jury Association—The Yellow Flier
APPENDIX C: Jailhouse Poetry
APPENDIX D: Jailhouse Freelancing
APPENDIX E: Letters to the Editor—Conflict of Views
APPENDIX F: Mayville Five Songs

■   A C K N O W L E D G M E N T S   ■

Many hands and minds contributed to the making of this book. Its message is not complete without these individuals' names.

David Belmondo who said, "I want the first copy," before the book was conceived.

Beverly, Mary, Tony, Scott, Marc, Ruth, Jim and Alvina, who photocopied and typed our two thousand pages of jail journals, some of which became part of this book.

The Donald Stefan family, for their cooperation in obtaining court and medical records, invaluable in substantiating our writing.

Jen and Jule, who came for editing sessions, even in a snowstorm.

Our parents, brother, sisters, and in-laws, who milked the cows, were patient with us when we put the book before farm work, and even critiqued our writing.

Nancy Whitelaw, who taught us the origin of the word "deadline," and helped us meet it.

Professor Sandra Cookson, who said the work was good, but made it better.

Frank Parlato, Jr., whose editing talent, and his willingness to work day and night, helped to shape the entire book.

Bill West, who generously allowed his skilled photography to be included in this book.

Hannah Lapp, who assisted in editing and developed the photo section of this book.

Jon Swerens, who offered professional advice on photo selections and layout.

Miriam and Michael, who didn't complain when Mom wrote at night, and wasn't there to see their needs.

Everyone we haven't named who shared our labor.

■ F O R E W O R D ■

By Jacob Lapp

No Law Against Mercy represents but another page in the ages-long struggle between the forces of those who wish to dominate others and those who want to earn their own living and honor.

When I was in jail with my son-in-law Joe and two daughters, Rachel and Barbara Lyn, some found it hard to understand why we defied the government, courts and police. Why did we go to such an extent to rescue Billy, the fifteen-year-old boy who had been institutionalized by the state?

A more pointed question is in order here: Why would anyone *not* help Billy? Why would everyone else stand by while Billy is being tormented, ruined?

The answer is: People believe government can do no wrong. Or if it is wrong, it is still somehow needed. Anarchy is a bad word in most people's minds. Today monopoly government is held in esteem, just as in ages past the divine right of kings was held in esteem. As Rose Wilder Lane points out in her book, *The Discovery of Freedom*, the kings, though crippled, diseased, imbecile or insane, were, by their birth and nature, a superior human being.

Without this belief in monopoly government, everyone would have been outraged at what the Family Court judge and his minions were doing to Billy.

People have asked if it was our religious beliefs that caused us to disobey authority. Yes, and no. The Bible says, "Pure religion and undefiled before God and the Father is this: to visit the fatherless and widows in their affliction, and to keep himself unspotted from the world." (James 1:27.) And, "Whoso shall offend one of these little ones…, it were better for him that a millstone were hanged about his neck, and that he were drowned in the depth of the sea." (Matthew 18:6.)

Certainly, our religion includes mercy toward helpless children. It is true also, that I have long feared God rather than man. Thirty-five years ago when I perceived inconsistencies in my former church (Amish), I, along with my wife, left that church, denouncing tradition disguised as Biblical principle. We then intensified our quest for the true will of God.

So yes, our deep religious convictions may well have played a part in our radical pursuit of justice for Billy. However, we also join ranks with people of all races, religions and creeds who have searched for secular justice in all ages.

We have been influenced by such deep thinkers as Henry David Thoreau, who wrote on the duty of civil disobedience. "Must the citizen ever for a moment, or in the least degree, resign his conscience to the legislator? Why has every man a conscience then?" And, "Under a government which imprisons any unjustly, the true place for a just man is also a prison."

And by Lysander Spooner, a nineteenth century lawyer/philosopher who thought our secret ballot voting system was a cowardly and irresponsible way of delegating authority. He wrote that we would be likely to continue experiencing our present problems with government usurpation, "until men are ready to say: We will consent to no constitution, except such an one as we are neither ashamed nor afraid to sign; and we will authorize no government to do any thing in our name which we are not willing to be personally responsible for."

The reader will find in *No Law Against Mercy* that we occasionally asserted the Constitution in defense of our actions. Constitutional scholar Andrew Melechinsky had taught us the value of the freedom guarantees in the Bill of Rights. Having since studied historical freedom principles more deeply, we would now differentiate between the statute law of the main Constitution and the natural law in the Bill of Rights. There is a contradiction between the two. To combine them in one document invites confusion. And that is perhaps why justice has declined since the days of fiercely independent, freedom-loving colonial America.

■ INTRODUCTION ■
By Barbara Lyn Lapp

The first chapter of this book begins with happenings in the spring of 1993. The story's setting, however, must be gathered from earlier dates and circumstances.

Rachel's and my parents were raised Amish, in a society where telephones, electricity and automobiles were shunned. Dress codes such as black hats for the men and long, plain dresses for the women were deemed as important as their church standards of pacifism and non-involvement in worldly affairs.

In 1961, the year I was born, my father and mother left the church, abandoning traditional Amish directives. However, they did not give up Biblical teachings of simplicity and modesty. They raised my eleven siblings and me with emphasis on principles of honesty, community sharing, and hard work—an integral part of our heritage. We were home-schooled, and together as a family, made our living tilling the soil and milking cows.

Appreciation for my own upbringing inspired me to adopt two youngsters who had been brutally abused by their biological parents. Both children came from Belize, Central America, where members of my family were stationed for a church outreach project.

It was the spring of 1985 when I adopted my first child, a tiny five-year-old girl who had been abandoned at a Belizean hospital—severely malnourished and abused. In 1987 her older brother, physically and emotionally scarred by abuse at the hands of an alcoholic father, also joined my family.

In 1989, behavioral difficulties with my adopted son resulted in charges of child neglect against me. Although I was later vindicated of the charges, I was troubled by what I viewed as reckless intervention and inept investigative practices by the Child Protective Services agency that handled my case. I resented the confidentiality laws that shrouded the agency's unscrupulous actions, and vowed to speak out against injustices in the Family Court system.

In 1990, I started a local chapter of Victims of Child Abuse Laws (VOCAL), a national organization that rallies around the rights of parents and children. With help from my family and other concerned members of the community, I organized public meetings, documented cases involving improper actions by Child Protective Services (CPS), and made frequent appearances at legislative hearings.

Families in trouble with CPS disclosed their court records to me, invited me to their homes to talk with their children, and asked me to attend court hearings and meetings with their case workers and lawyers.

I started a publication, *Family Alert,* and worked with local news reporters to publicize cases which I believed were unjustly handled by the Family Court system.

In December, 1992, our county commissioner of Social Services publicly voiced his contempt for my involvement. "I'm about at the limits of my patience with the grotesque and irresponsible claims that have been made, and by the way in which these claims have continued to be promoted by the media," he said at a December 8 meeting of the county legislature. "This is a circus. My staff and my attorneys have had to restrain me personally from being more aggressive than I am naturally inclined to be. I am about at the limits of letting them restrain me."

The book begins four months after that date, when I had been president of the Chautauqua County chapter of VOCAL for three years. Through a hotline in my home, I had heard complaints from more than five hundred people beleaguered by child protective agencies.

❋   ❋   ❋

Much of the writing in this book originated in a jail cell. In creating the book, Rachel and I used diaries we wrote during our incarceration, to establish an accurate running account of the story. The original diaries have been abridged, and are interspersed with narrative when needed for clarification. On several occasions, we combined dates or otherwise altered the diary format to improve readability. All major incidents, court appearances, and information with important relevance to a particular date are in chronological order. Every part of this book has been factually recorded to the best of our ability. Names of inmates have been changed to protect their identity. All other names are true.

Our journals, as well as other parts of this book, were enhanced in accuracy by adding verbatim dialogue from court documents and video/audio recordings of dramatic incidents.

■ CHAPTER 1 ■

Billy

By Rachel

It was the third phone call I'd gotten since I sat down to eat a late supper. This call came in on the VOCAL hotline, which my sister, Barbara, operated from a tiny office off our dining room. She wasn't home tonight.

"Is Barbara Lyn Lapp there?" The caller, Donald Stefan, told me he had heard through an acquaintance that Barbara was someone he could trust. "Right now it's hard for me to trust anyone," he said.

Barbara had started a chapter of VOCAL (Victims of Child Abuse Laws) four years earlier, and frequently advised families in trouble with child welfare agencies. I admired her outreach, but was occasionally annoyed that she wasn't doing her share of the work on our family's farm anymore. Tonight, she was out at one of her monthly VOCAL meetings.

Donald Stefan told me Social Services had forcibly taken two of his teenage sons a year before, after he was accused of abusing them. He said he was innocent. The younger of his sons was in a boys' home, where Don was rarely allowed to see him. "The place is like a prison to him," Don said. "I'm afraid he'll lose his mind if he's there much longer."

I listened to Don's story, and promised him Barbara would speak to him. We arranged for him to call the following night.

The desperation in the man's voice, and his son's plight, stayed in my mind long after he hung up. I made notes for Barbara, then scrapped the cold food that was left on my dinner plate.

By Barbara Lyn

Rachel told me about the call as soon as I got home at 10:30 that night. "Are you going to see to it that you're here when he calls?" she asked as she showed me her notes. "It sounds like an unusual case."

Donald Stefan called the following night, on April 9, 1993. He told me that his two youngest sons had been taken from him during an acrimonious separation from his wife. He had been charged with assaulting and molesting his youngest son, Billy, who was now in a boys' home in Bradford, Pennsylvania.

"I never molested my son, and I never beat him," Don said. "I know I can't expect you to believe me. I don't know why I'm even talking to you. But I don't know where to turn."

Don told me that another son, Tom, was living with his grandmother, and by order of the Family Court judge, he could see him only on supervised visits.

"How old are your boys?" I asked.

"Billy is fifteen and Tom is sixteen."

"Do they want to come home?"

"Of course they do! But the judge won't let them testify," Don said. "When they tried to run back home, Social Services put them in a psychiatric ward and gave them drugs. I'm at the end of my rope." He continued, "I'm about ready to take my shotgun down to the county building, and put an end to those people. They're destroying my sons!"

"Don't do that, Don," I said. "You need to take control of this situation—both for yourself and your sons. They're old enough to have some say in this."

"What's the legal age when they can get away from Social Services?"

"It's usually sixteen. There could be exceptions."

"Tom's almost seventeen—they still say he has to stay away from me."

"That's ridiculous. Why don't you just let him come home?"

"Couldn't I get in trouble?"

"I don't think so. But I'd like to see the court papers. I'd like to talk to your boys, too. Could you come for a visit—and bring the papers?"

The following day I met Don Stefan. He came to our farmhouse with his son Tom, a husky sixteen-year-old legally in the custody of Social Services, and an older son, Kevin. Don's sister, Diane, also accompanied him.

We sat around our family dining room table.

"Tom's not supposed to be with you, is he?" I asked.

"Not really," Don said, "but after we talked on the phone yesterday, I decided there's no sense in this court order. He's gonna be seventeen next week."

I turned to Tom. "What do you think?"

"I'm old enough to talk for myself," Tom said. "They can't force me to stay away from Dad."

The Stefan family's primary concern now was Billy. Almost a year had passed since police and child protective workers had taken him from his father's home. Don showed me a recent court order stating Billy was to remain at the Bradford Children's Home, in custody of the Department of Social Services, for an additional year.

"I can't take another year of this," Don said. "They've had Billy in five different hospitals. Sometimes they drugged him so heavily he hardly knew us when we visited."

Don and Diane explained that Billy was "a few years behind" his age level mentally. And they told me of the incident that led to his removal from his father's home. Don said he had spanked Billy with a belt, to discipline him for using a vulgar word. Billy fought back. Struggling to bring him under control, Don said, he accidentally scratched Billy's face. Billy also sustained a bruise on his back when he fell against a kitchen counter.

A few minutes after the incident, Billy's mother, Linda Stefan, came home and found Billy upset. Hearing what happened, she told him to report it to the school. The next day Billy told the school nurse about the incident. Shortly afterward, two Child Protective Services (CPS) case workers and a policeman brought Billy home from school. Don was at work.

"They talked to Billy's mom for over an hour," Diane told me, "but they spent only five minutes questioning Billy and the other boys."

One of the CPS workers, Chuck Talbot, wrote a report stating that Billy had multiple scratches and bruises on his face, arms and back. Diane, who had seen Billy at the time, said the report was greatly exaggerated.

When Don came home he was arrested and taken away in a police car. Then the CPS case workers took Billy, his mother, and brother, Tom, to a domestic violence shelter.

Don Stefan was charged with assault and child endangerment, taken to the town justice, and released on his own recognizance.

As we spoke, Diane showed me letters and court documents pertaining to Don's case. I was impressed with her involvement, and what I perceived as a genuine motherly sentiment for the boys.

"Are you the boys' favorite aunt?" I asked.

Don answered. "She was like a second mother to them."

"Their mother, Linda, has had mental problems," Diane explained. "I live just a few miles away. The boys would come to me when things got rough."

Don said during his twenty-year marriage with Linda, family disputes were frequent. Linda left him repeatedly, leaving the boys in his care. She sought psychiatric counseling off and on, and once received inpatient treatment at a mental health ward. Don's son Kevin, a high school senior and signed up for college, told me his mother "constantly screamed" at him and his brothers, and sometimes tried to turn them against their father.

Tom, who had lived with his mother and Billy after CPS took them from their father, said he believed his mother lied to the case worker, to "get Dad in trouble." He said the case worker wouldn't listen when he told him his father was not abusive.

Diane had with her a letter that Tom and Billy had sent to the Family Court judge who signed the order to take them from their father. She gave me a copy of the letter.

> Dear Judge Nenno,
> Hi. My name is Thomas Stefan and my brother's name is Billy (William Stefan).
> We are writing to find out if we can talk to you alone. And we want you to know that we want to talk to you badly about the lies that have been told.
> We would like you to talk to my brothers also, because they know a lot and we want you to know the truth....
> Our mom and dad and grandma have a court date about us on 12-22-92, and we would like to be there and we're worried about it.
> > Please talk to us. We need your help.
> > Thank you.
> > Thomas Stefan
> > Billy

"The boys were never allowed to testify," Diane said. "Social Services refused to talk to anyone from Don's side of the family."

"Don't they have to investigate before they break up a family?" Don asked.

I shook my head. "It's a closed court system, and they get away with shoddy investigations. I've been hearing hundreds of stories like this since I started the VOCAL chapter here."

※   ※   ※

I learned more of Billy's troubled story in subsequent visits with the Stefan family, and through court, police, and hospital records I obtained from them.

Six days after Billy had been taken from his father, his mother took him to the emergency room of the Olean General Hospital. The hospital intake notes say Billy "became very angry because his mother says he can't see his father," and "said he was going to kill himself." Billy told the hospital social worker, "If my mother keeps on pushing me or if the judge does not let me see my father, I will do it."

On Billy's physical examination chart, none of the injuries reported by Chuck Talbot from Child Protective Services were noted by his doctor, except an "abrasion on cheek—about one week old."

Billy stayed in the hospital for three days. During his stay Chuck Talbot came to interview him. Nurses' notes indicate Billy and his mother accompanied Talbot to a private room, where they stayed for more than an hour. When they emerged, Talbot notified hospital staff that Billy had disclosed he was molested by his father. Talbot ordered an immediate sexual abuse examination.

Within hours, a hospital staff physician came to see Billy. In his notes, he wrote that Billy would not answer his questions "about sexual behavior in the family." He reported there were no signs of sexual abuse. However, he noted that "a normal pelvic examination does not rule out sexual abuse."

The next day Don Stefan was again arrested, the second time in eight days. This time the charges were much more serious: "Sodomy in the third degree," allegedly committed against Billy six months earlier. Don stayed in jail for several days, until a business associate bailed him out.

I later acquired Chuck Talbot's hand-written report of his interview with Billy. According to Talbot, Billy gave a graphic description of being molested by his father and brothers. The statement was signed by Billy, Chuck Talbot, and Linda Stefan.

This statement, and the corresponding notes in Billy's hospital records, raised some questions on Talbot's competency—if not his motives. Permitting Linda's presence during his interview with Billy, then using her as the only other witness to a statement that would incriminate a man she hated, was highly improper. Talbot's bias became even more clear as I listened to other members of the Stefan family.

Diane said Talbot ignored her argument that Linda had a history of sexual perversion, and occasionally had attempted to "buy off" the boys into taking her side during marital disputes. Tom, who was questioned by Talbot immediately after Billy, said he was pressured repeatedly to make a statement against his father. "I told him Dad didn't do any-thing," Tom said. "But he said, 'You must be lying—Billy already told us.'" Don's two older sons, Kevin and Ron, said Talbot "badgered" them for statements, and treated them rudely when they refused.

As I read more of the records, and listened to Don and his family discuss the horrible crimes he had been accused of committing, I was confronted with the same question I had dealt with countless times in the past four years: How can a person prove his innocence?

In the middle of the turmoil was Billy—holding the key to the knowl-edge of his father's guilt or innocence. But he was cut off from con-tact with most of his family. When Billy got out of the hospital, he went to live in a motel room where Social Services had temporarily placed him with his mother and Tom. After several weeks in the mo-tel, Linda allowed the boys to visit at the home of their paternal grand-mother, Effie Stefan. During the visit Billy talked with his cousins. Diane said they told her Billy retracted his story, saying he had lied about his father molesting him.

Social Services' records, however, gave a different story. Dr. Craig Zuckerman, a psychologist hired by Social Services, reported Billy maintained his statement, and was "spontaneous" in his descriptions of being molested. Dr. Zuckerman recommended to the Family Court that Billy's contact with has father and brothers be "brief and very strictly supervised."

As the story became more complex, my search for answers revolved around two considerations: common sense and due process. If Don were guilty, would he ask for a thorough investigation in open court? Would he beg, as he did, that I take time to question his boys, pri-vately and individually? I examined the legal processes. If police and CPS believed Don were guilty, why didn't they take the case to a grand jury, as the district attorney, Larry Himelein, had originally intended? But nothing troubled me so much as the court's blatant refusal to hear Billy and Tom. Did the fact that they were minors preclude them from constitutionally guaranteed due process rights?

Billy and Tom had become prisoners in a motel room. Once, when their older brothers tried to visit, Linda called Chuck Talbot, com-plaining that they were harassing her. However, Linda permitted a fifteen-year-old friend of Tom's to visit, and sometimes, to stay over-night. Tom told me of one night when he awoke to find his mother engaging in sex with the teenage boy.

A few days later, Billy tried to run away. His mother forced him to return to the motel room, resulting in a violent confrontation between them. Police and Chuck Talbot assisted Billy's mother in subduing him, and took him to the emergency room. He was admitted to the psychiatric ward of the Olean General Hospital, and medicated with a drug called Ativan, which, according to his doctor, was administered "to reduce hostile behavior."

The hospital admission record reported that Billy had run out onto the road in front of the motel, trying to wave down cars so he could hitch a ride to his father. The staff psychiatrist noted: "There is a court order that he cannot see the father, and the patient has had a great deal of difficulty in dealing with this." He concluded his report: "There is also a question whether or not his allegations of sexual abuse are valid."

During his stay at the psychiatric ward, Billy's progress notes indicate, he became very outspoken about his desire to go home to his father. He told nurses and doctors that his father did *not* molest him. He did admit that he and some of his brothers had experimented with sexual activity among themselves. He claimed his mother knew about this.

Billy told hospital staff, "If my mother takes me, I will run away."

After two weeks in the hospital Billy became even more agitated and aggressive, accusing staff of "kidnaping" him, and threatening to run away. Day after day, his medical notes show that he was confined to "seclusion" and injected with Bendryl, a sedative. Ativan was also prescribed. When he refused to take it orally, they administered it by injection. His psychiatrist noted repeatedly that Billy expressed "feelings of anger at not being allowed to be with his father."

After reading hundreds of pages of Billy's psychiatric records, I began to realize I might never have the benefit of all the answers. From my previous research and experience with false child abuse charges, particularly in divorce/custody settings, I knew that hostile parents and CPS workers sometimes coerce children into making statements about molestation. Billy, with mental abilities somewhat limited, may well have become confused during the initial questioning. Yet why did he, in retracting his statement, first indicate he had lied in his statement against his father, then later deny making the report? He stated to one of his doctors, "I did not say my father. It was my brother...."

These questions led to an even more plaguing consideration. At what cost is the state justified in forcing separation between child and parent—even in questionable circumstances? It seemed to me that any reasonable effort at protecting children from abuse should include careful examination of whether a child's life would be made better, or worse, by intervention.

While Billy was confined to the mental hospital, his brother, Tom, also tried to run home to his father. He was picked up by police, who had some question on whether they could legally intervene because of his age. He was already sixteen. But after conferring with Chuck Talbot and Linda, police took him to the hospital in handcuffs, where he was sedated with shots.

As Billy and Tom languished in two different adult psychiatric wards, their aunt, Diane, was making daily phone calls to lawyers, doctors, social workers and other professionals involved. "These boys were never in trouble before their mother took them—they were never on medication before." She begged that they be allowed to go home.

Don's attorney, William Mountain, contested Linda's court-ordered custody of the boys. He asserted that an investigation and trial would prove that Billy "made the [sexual abuse] accusations… under pressure of [Linda] and the Department of Social Services." He also stated that the boys would suffer "irreparable damage" if they continued to be denied contact with their paternal family, who were the stabilizing factors in their lives.

On July 31, after nearly four weeks in the psychiatric ward, Billy was again returned to his mother, who now was living in an apartment complex in Salamanca. By court order, Billy and Tom still could not visit their father.

The Stefan case was scheduled for trial on September 22, almost four months after Don was first charged. Don told me he had been ready with witnesses, and was confident that his sons' testimony would vindicate him. But before the trial began, Don's attorney, Mr. Mountain, informed him he could avoid criminal prosecution if he would just admit to having physically abused Billy. In exchange for the admission, the district attorney, Larry Himelein, would agree to drop the sexual abuse charges.

"I didn't abuse my boy!" Don said he told his lawyer. "I'll never admit to that!"

Mountain warned Don he could not regain custody of his sons if he didn't make the admission. Don finally consented to a compromise. He agreed to state for the court record that he had hit Billy.

In court, however, the judge required Don to answer the question of whether he had "assaulted William with his hands and a belt, resulting in physical pain, numerous bruises and lacerations." Don told me he was horrified, and didn't reply—until his attorney told him to answer yes. As promised, the sexual abuse charges were dropped, and the criminal case against Don was closed. His admission, however, resulted in what the Family Court defined as a "finding of abuse." Upon this "finding," Judge Nenno ordered that the boys remain in their mother's custody and have no contact with their father except as directed by the Department of Social Services. Don felt betrayed—and angry.

Billy, living with his mother in the apartment—thirty miles from his father's home—knew nothing of Judge Nenno's ruling. But he was also angry. On November 8, he was again taken to the hospital by police, this time restrained in an ambulance. Linda told the hospital staff that Billy had hit her twice, threatened suicide, and tried to break windows. "Behavior disorder," the intake notes said. "Mother unable to cope."

The physician's note said: "He wants parents reunited." A physical examination of Billy revealed "multiple welts, abrasions to extremities and back."

According to hospital notes, Billy told nurses that his mother's boyfriend "threw him around this morning." Billy was admitted to the hospital's psychiatric ward, and injected with Bendryl to calm him down.

A week later Billy was transferred to Buffalo, to the juvenile psychiatric ward at BryLin Hospitals. Diane told me she went to visit him there, and Billy showed her the red and blue marks that remained on his back. He described to her the incident which had resulted in his third hospitalization since being taken into Social Services custody seven months earlier. Billy told her he had been beaten "all over" with a belt that day, by a brother of his mother's new boyfriend. His brother, Tom, had tried to intervene, but the man struck him also, with the belt. Billy tried to use the phone, but was prevented. He ran into a nearby woods, but was soon apprehended by police and taken to the hospital in the ambulance.

Both boys told Diane that Chuck Talbot from Child Protective Services had investigated, and photographed their injuries. The next day Don tried to press charges against the man who had beaten his sons. But Child Protective Services withheld their records, and contradicted his sons' contention that they had photos. Without CPS cooperation, police refused to investigate.

"They took my son from me, for spanking him," Don said later. "I even went to jail. Now he gets beaten—I mean *beaten up*—and CPS won't do a thing!"

After three weeks at BryLin, Billy was discharged. The psychiatrist who wrote his discharge summary noted: "Mother is apparently intellectually limited and unable to provide adequate parental guidance." The court then placed Billy in the temporary custody of his grandmother, Effie Stefan. Tom was also placed with her. Don and his family were happy to finally be progressing toward their goal of being reunited.

Uncertainties were looming, though. Social Services had objected to this arrangement and promised to continue in their efforts to find an "appropriate therapeutic placement for William." The placement with his grandmother was to be "considered temporary."

When Billy came to live with his grandmother he was taking regular dosages of Lithium Carbonate, an antidepressant. Diane described him as "nervous, jumpy and pale, with a lot of pent-up anger." With the consent of Billy's doctor, Effie gradually took him off medication. Both boys went to school, and received good reports from their teachers. They made new friends, played with their cousins, and obeyed their grandmother. Don was allowed to spend Christmas Day with Billy and Tom, at their grandmother's house.

Although things were going well, Social Services was still looking for a "therapeutic placement" for Billy. Effie told me Billy was anxious. He would come home from school each day, do his homework perfectly, then ask, "Now can I stay, Grandma? Because I'm doing good."

On February 16, a Family Court hearing was held to determine whether Billy could continue residing with his grandmother. During out-of-court negotiations with Social Services attorneys, Don and Effie told me, their attorneys urged them to "cooperate" with a plan by Social Services to place Billy at the Bradford Children's Home in Bradford, Pennsylvania. At the children's home, visitation would be allowed, and Billy would not be at risk of being placed back with his mother. Don said his lawyer told him if he didn't cooperate with Social Services he might not see Billy until he's eighteen.

Effie said that during the negotiations she had presented Billy's school reports, in which his teachers noted his good grades and expressed opposition to him being moved. Her attorney refused to look at them, she said.

Fearing total loss of contact with Billy, Don and Effie reluctantly consented to the Social Services placement. They followed the attorneys into the courtroom and listened as Judge Nenno read the ruling. Billy's continued residence in the home of his grandmother would be "contrary to [his] best interest," Nenno said. Billy was to be placed in the Bradford Children's home for a period of one year. Nenno said the decision was based on "inquiry into the facts and circumstances…, and upon agreement of the parties."

On February 23, Billy's family drove him across state lines to Bradford, almost a hundred miles away.

"Billy was so scared," Effie told me. "He couldn't understand why he had to leave." She tried to assure him he could someday come home again.

For Billy, life in the boys' home was misery. He was now afflicted with involuntary muscle tremors—possibly prolonged side affects from the drugs he was given at previous institutions. When he slept, his legs would repeatedly hit the wall. The noise angered his roommates. Billy said one night they threatened to kill him. Once when they went swimming, two big boys tried to drown him. He reported it to the staff, he said, but they didn't believe him, and he was punished.

In a letter that Diane showed me, Billy wrote: "I tried to tell staff that my dad wasn't a child molester, but they said that Dad was."

❋   ❋   ❋

At the time of my first visit with the Stefans, Billy had been at the Bradford Children's Home for almost two months. He had just turned fifteen.

As we sat at my family's dining room table discussing Billy's ordeal, Don said, "I can't let him get hurt for another whole year. How can we get this investigated before it's too late for Billy?" Don was fighting back tears.

"I could help you file a petition for writ of habeas corpus," I said. "We have not been successful with petitions in the past. Family Court bypasses due process. But we could try."

"How long would it take?" Don asked.

"Probably several weeks—maybe months."

"That's too long. When I saw Billy on his birthday, he cried and kept asking, 'Dad, when can I come home?'"

I felt indignation rising in me. Memories flashed through my mind—my own encounter with Child Protective Services four years earlier, and their refusal to do a proper investigation; the torment my daughter had endured with the threat of being removed from me; my promise to her that I wouldn't allow it to happen, and my vow to help other families entangled with state intervention.

Across the table from me, Don leaned forward, looking for an answer.

"If that were my child, Don, I'd bring him home," I said.

Diane and Don looked at each other.

"We've thought of it," Diane said. "We could pick him up at a family visit."

Tom and Kevin joined the discussion, offering suggestions for a possible getaway.

"What would happen? Could I be charged with kidnaping?" Don asked.

The court order lay on the table in front of us. On the first page, in capital letters, it read: "Willful failure to obey the terms and conditions of this order may result in commitment to jail for the term not to exceed six months."

"I don't think they'd keep you that long," I told Don. "If they arrest you, the case will have to go to public court. They wouldn't be able to hide behind all this family court confidentiality."

"I'd rather be in jail than have my son's mind destroyed," Don said.

"I doubt that they'll arrest you," I said. "Billy is almost of age. But if they do, I'll help your boys get their story out."

The family told me they had a visit with Billy scheduled for April 20—a week and a half away. As they left the house, I wished them well. "And please let me know what happens," I said.

It was the night of April 20. Rachel and I were out at a meeting, and we arrived home late. As we walked into the kitchen, I noticed a note by the phone that read, "They got Billy." Tingling with excitement, I picked up the phone and called Diane.

"Barbara, we got him!" she said. Billy's psychologist had given them permission to take him out to lunch at a restaurant, and the getaway was simple. "Don is hiding away with Tom and Billy, out of the county—"

"Don't tell me where!" I interrupted. "I don't want to know."

Diane said she had already called the Bradford Children's Home and informed them that Billy's dad had taken him, and would not be back. They advised her they would notify Social Services.

"Billy should write a letter to the Bradford home, and let them know he's okay," I told Diane. "They might not even look for him."

On our 375-acre farm, spring planting had begun. Farm activities were keeping every member of our three-generation household busy. My father was on his tractor, plowing, from dawn to dusk. My brother planted oats, corn and alfalfa. My mother, sisters, and thirteen-year-old daughter helped me milk our sixty dairy cows. My sisters' children—after school—helped us plant peas, strawberries, lettuce, and other crops we raised for our fresh fruit market that would open in the summer.

Two weeks had passed since Billy's escape from Bradford. I remained hopeful that authorities would not pursue him. Then, on May 5, I received a call from Kevin Stefan, Don's eighteen-year-old son. He told me his father had just been arrested and jailed, and their house searched. The police hadn't found Billy, since he and Tom were still hiding in another county.

After speaking with Kevin, I called Diane. She asked me to come see Billy. We arranged to meet at the home of one of the Stefan's friends, so I would not find out where he was hiding.

That night at 10:30 I met Billy for the first time, in a small house at the end of a dead-end street. As I walked in with Diane and Kevin, Billy eyed me with suspicion. I reached out for a handshake. His eyes danced nervously, glazed with mistrust.

"I'm not a social worker," I said, holding on to his hand.

Billy smiled a little.

We gathered around a table with Billy's family and friends. Billy gradually became less nervous, as we talked about his father, his escape from Bradford, and his feelings about being in hiding. Billy spoke freely of the spanking incident that led to him being removed from his home. He sheepishly described his misbehavior that day. "Dad had the right to spank me," he said.

Finally, after talking almost two hours, I asked Billy, "Why did you tell the caseworker that your father molested you?"

"I lied—my mom paid me ten dollars to say that lie."

Billy was very concerned about his father. "Are you gonna get him out of jail?" he asked, fidgeting painfully.

I promised Billy I'd do my best, and would visit his father in jail.

The next day, May 6, Don was taken to court in Olean. I went to attend his hearing, along with several of my friends and a half dozen members of the Stefan family. We were not permitted to enter the courtroom.

Through court transcripts, I later learned what transpired inside. Judge Nenno had begun by asking Don if he wanted an attorney.

"Barbara Lapp is out there to help me right now," Don said.

"I'm sorry, but she's not an attorney."

"I want her though…. I should also have the right to have some of my family members in here with me so I am not alone."

"This is a private proceeding under the Family Court Act that limits it to the parties involved and you're the only party involved in this. I know Mr. Mountain had represented you in the past, and he can be available this afternoon."

"No, he didn't do his job for me."

"Well, do you wish to be represented by any other attorney?"

"No. Just Barbara Lapp."

"I told you Ms. Lapp is not permitted to be in this courtroom…. She's never appeared before in this courtroom and she isn't going to start…. Do you understand that?"

"No. I read it in the Constitution where I have the right to counsel of my choice."

"Counsel means attorney…. Let's get to the point here."

"I guess I'd like to get this to open court."

"This is open—as open as you're going to get."

"With a trial by jury."

"You don't get a jury here. Mr. Stefan, where is your son William?"

Don was silent.

"I direct you to answer," Judge Nenno said.

"I stand on the Fifth Amendment."

"…You do not have the availability of the Fifth Amendment because you can not incriminate yourself…. What you say cannot be used against you. Do you understand that?"

"I heard you."

"Then I'll ask you again, where is your son, William Stefan?"

Don was again silent.

"I direct the sheriff's department… to remove Mr. Stefan to the county jail, and that he remain there until he either notifies the court that he is willing to advise the court of the whereabouts of his son, William, and/or in the alternative bring [Mr. Stefan] back in on the morning of May 13th at 9:30."

The following day Diane and I visited Don at the Cattaraugus County jail in Little Valley. He told us that the police search on his house had been without a warrant, and he was not shown a warrant for his arrest. Don asked us to find out about bail. But most important to him was his son not going back to state custody. "Don't let them find Billy," Don pleaded as we left. "I can handle being in jail as long as I know Billy's safe."

I went with Diane directly to the sheriff's office, and asked to talk to the officer in charge of Don's case, Lt. Ernest Travis.

We walked into his small office. Lt. Travis was seated behind a desk. "Have a seat," he said. Diane and I sat down on chairs in front of his desk.

"I'd like to know what's going on with my brother," Diane said. "Where is the warrant?"

"He was arrested on a valid warrant signed by Judge Nenno—"

"Could we see the warrant?"

Travis looked at me, then at Diane. "There's a fifteen-year-old kid involved here, and until I find that kid, I'm not going to give anyone anything. My name's Lt. Travis… and if I find that kid, somebody's gonna be in a lot of trouble—I can tell you that right now. You've got a lot of nerve fooling around with a fifteen-year-old kid."

"He's safe and happy," Diane said.

"It doesn't matter if he's safe or not, he's a ward of the court, and until we get him, you're not gonna get any cooperation. How's that?"

"How long is Don going to be in here?" Diane asked.

"That's not for me to determine…. The officers were acting on a valid warrant."

"But where is that warrant?" I asked.

"Are you an attorney?" Travis demanded.

"No, my name is Barbara Lyn Lapp."

"Are you related to the missing child?"

"No. Is the warrant in family court?"

Travis tossed his head, then turned to Diane. "You keep trying to get information, and I'm sure the court's gonna deal with you when the time comes. You don't recognize the courts of the United States? Or of Cattaraugus County?"

"I recognize the constitutional rights," Diane said.

"*What* constitutional rights?"

"Don never had a trial by jury, the family was never heard, a complete investigation was never done, the boys were never heard, they begged the judge to listen to them—he refused. They wrote him twice…."

"Do you suppose what you're teaching the kid now, to not obey the law, is helping him? Back up and leave it up to the court. I have nothing to do with what Social Services does…."

"How do you make Family Court listen to the family?" Diane asked.

"Get yourself an attorney."

"He had Mountain—" Diane began.

"No he didn't!" Travis yelled. "Your brother *fired* Mountain and wanted some *woman* to represent him in family court."

"No, no. He had Mountain when we went to court the first time—"

Travis interrupted. "The conversation's over! The conversation's over with!"

"Mountain sold him," Diane said.

"Get an attorney."

I began to speak, but Travis interrupted.

"You are not a family member, I don't wanna talk to you."

Travis' phone rang. Diane and I got up to leave. We waited until he got off the phone. Diane asked, "So we're not allowed a copy of the warrant?"

"Not from me you're not. Get it from the court!"

"Do your officers, as a matter of policy—" I began.

"Who are you?" Lt. Travis demanded.

"I'm Barbara Lyn Lapp."

"Who's that? Are you an attorney? Do you have a licence to practice law in the state of New York?"

"Oh no, no. This isn't about law, it's just about policy. We want to know whether a person who's being arrested has a right to see the warrant for his arrest."

"Who are you talking about?"

"Don Stefan. He said he didn't see a warrant."

Travis looked at me squarely. "Are you the woman that tried to represent him in court?"

"I didn't try to represent him," I said.

"Are *you* the woman he said he wanted to represent him?" Travis' voice was escalating. He leaned forward on his chair, coming closer.

"I don't think he said that."

"Are *you* the woman he said he wanted to represent him in Family Court yesterday?" Travis demanded.

"He wanted me present as a witness."

Travis jumped from his chair, raising his hands in front of him. "Conversation's over. See ya!"

"Okay," I said. Diane and I backed up a step, then turned and walked out of his office.

Several days later Diane called me. She was worried that too many people had seen Billy and Tom at the place they were staying. "We need a safer place for them," she said.

"I know someone a few miles from here who might take them," I said. "This county might be best for them anyway."

The next day Billy and Tom were brought to Chautauqua County. They came in the night, curled up between the front and back seats of a friend's mini-van. Lynn Carroll Bedford, secretary of our VOCAL chapter, and her husband, Barry, welcomed the boys into their log cabin situated in a pine forest, six miles from my home.

On May 10, several dozen people picketed the Cattaraugus County jail where Don was still being held. They displayed protest signs denouncing the injustice of Don's incarceration. "Father jailed for protecting sons," one sign read.

After the rally, a reporter from *News Channel 7,* a Buffalo TV station, asked me if we had any pictures of Billy. I promised to get one to him before his news deadline at 5:00 PM.

As soon as I got home, Hannah, one of my sisters, accompanied me to Billy's secret location. We videotaped him and Tom, then quickly delivered the tape to the TV station, fifty miles away—just before news deadline.

That night Billy was on TV. "Topping *Eyewitness News* at six," the anchorman began. "An impassioned plea from a son caught in the middle of a bitter legal battle."

On the screen, Billy and Tom were shown standing in a wooded area. "Both boys are in hiding," the announcer said. "We don't know where this video tape was shot. It was delivered to *News Channel 7* by a member of VOCAL late this afternoon."

"I love my dad and hope he gets out," Billy said on TV.

"Both boys are adamant that their father did not abuse them," the announcer said.

The day after the newscast, two sheriff's deputies came to Lynn and Barry's home and asked if the boys were there.

"Do you think I'd tell you if they *were* here?" Lynn asked one of the deputies.

As soon as the officers left, Lynn called me. I went right over. Within a few hours the Stefan boys were transported to my home, in a neighbor's windowless van.

Several days later Tom, who was no longer sought by authorities because of his age, returned to his father's home. He lived with his older brothers, and helped to maintain Don's welding and farm equipment business.

Meanwhile, I was working on making Billy's plight known to the general public, while keeping his whereabouts secret. A reporter from *The Buffalo News* agreed to a clandestine interview with Billy and other members of the Stefan family. The resulting front page news story said, "Billy Stefan is in hiding—somewhere in the Chautauqua-Cattaraugus Counties area." The article detailed Billy's plight. It included pictures of him with his brothers—and a letter he had written to Judge Nenno, pleading to be reunited with his father.

With the publicity, I felt that the Stefan boys were receiving a belated, well-deserved public hearing. The news stories on the Stefans, read and seen by hundreds of thousands of Western New York residents, promised to be a major step toward Billy's freedom.

On May 13, Don was again taken to court.

"Mr. Stefan, are you prepared to provide the court with information as to the whereabouts of your son, William Stefan?" Judge Nenno asked.

"I've asked that Barbara Lapp be my advisory and I have been denied," Don said

"The court explained to you before that... we do not allow non-attorneys to participate.... It's a misdemeanor in the State of New York.... Maybe [it] would be appropriate to have her come in and she could be arrested for that."

"I want a trial by impartial jury," Don said.

"I'm asking you whether you understand your right to counsel."

"Open trial, sir."

"This is not a trial matter. This is a matter where you are instructed to inform the court as to where William Stefan is. Are you prepared to do that today?"

"Judge, I cannot tell you. I promised these boys that I will protect them under all circumstances. I'm not going to break my promise—they trust me. So it could go on for months and months, judge."

Don appeared weekly in front of Judge Nenno. Each time I went to the courthouse along with Don's family members, and each time friends and VOCAL members picketed along the highway in front of the courthouse.

At one hearing, Don pleaded with the judge. "I've got two boys at home.... My one boy wants to go to college—I've got him signed up.... I'd hate to see him lose that opportunity. Being self-employed and a business to run, these boys at home do need me."

"As far as I'm concerned," the judge said, closing the proceeding, "until you inform the court as to where [William is], you're going to spend your time in jail.... If you have a change of heart... all you have to do is notify the sheriff and they'll notify me and we'll set up a time and get you released. So it's in your hands, Mr. Stefan."

Don was returned to jail. There was no end in sight to the stalemate with Cattaraugus County officials.

In an effort to get Don's case moved to public court, I consulted a constitutional expert, Andrew Melechinsky from Connecticut. I had known Andy for several years, and his experience with legal arguments, based strictly on the Bill of Rights, intrigued me. He recommended filing a writ of habeas corpus for Don. The writ's origin dates back to the Magna Carta, and in current law, is used to test the legality of a person's detention.

With Andy's assistance, I drafted a petition for writ of habeas corpus, claiming that Don was unlawfully detained by the warden of the Cattaraugus County jail. We cited the sheriff's failure to produce a warrant for Don's arrest. We claimed that the Family Court order was invalid, because it had deprived Don and his sons of their liberty, without due process.

Kevin Stefan and I filed the writ in the county's Supreme Court. Judge George F. Francis signed an order to have the sheriff bring Don out for a hearing the following day—in open court. As petitioner for the writ, I was prepared to make the arguments for Don's release.

At the hearing, Judge Francis twisted the writ's historical intent. Instead of requiring the sheriff to prove that Don was legally detained, he insisted that Don show why he should not be detained. "The burden of proof is on you," Judge Francis told Don.

Judge Francis did not allow me speak, and Don was left without a legal argument. However, he spoke to the judge, telling of the extreme circumstances that led to him hiding his sons. "I did what any father would do to protect his kids," he said, speaking through tears. "I tried for a year to prove my innocence. Why can't they prove I'm guilty?"

The county attorney was there to defend the sheriff's position. He claimed it was Don's fault that he was incarcerated. "Mr. Stefan holds the keys to the jail in his own hands," he said. "All he has to do is tell the judge where his child is, and he will be free."

Judge Francis ordered Don returned to the custody of the sheriff.

After the hearing, I shed tears with the Stefan family—and dreaded going home to face Billy.

What had I done wrong? Petitioning on behalf of Don was perfectly legal, and the judge, as far as I could determine, had no right to deny me arguing my own petition. I had thoroughly researched the historical purpose, as well as current usage of the writ of habeas corpus. The judge also had no right to shift the burden of proof to Don.

The law (Civil Practice) clearly states it is the sheriff who must "show cause."

My father, Jacob Lapp, was not as surprised by the outcome of the hearing as I was. He had been an avid student of historical freedom principles for a number of years. "What else can you expect," he said, "when myriad laws support these lawyers and judges in ignoring time-tested rules of justice?" He was also not discouraged. "Common law is on our side," he said. "If the officials don't listen, let it be heard by the people."

We began to make plans for a "Citizens' Common Law Court," a public hearing with historical basis in common law. Andrew Melechinsky agreed to come from Connecticut to serve as judge. I would represent Don. A neighbor of ours was assigned the duty of court clerk, and helped me mail subpoenas to the officials involved. We posted public notices for the event, announcing that twelve ju-rors would be selected from the first twenty volunteers to arrive the night of the hearing—scheduled for June 28, 5:00 PM at Jamestown Community College.

Two days before the scheduled hearing, Cattaraugus County offi-cials acknowledged to the media that they had received the subpoe-nas. However, the county attorney advised the officials not to attend, on the grounds that the Citizens' Court "has no jurisdiction."

On the night of June 28, twelve jurors, empaneled from the first twelve volunteers, listened attentively to evidence presented regarding the legality of Don Stefan's detention. Common Law Judge Melechinsky allowed the jurors to ask questions during the trial, and conferred openly with them when questions of law arose. The court clerk marked exhibits and swore in the witnesses. A man in a tan uniform performed the role of a bailiff. He kept watch near the door, but did not deny entrance to anyone. A court reporter we had hired sat between the judge and jurors, typing. In the auditorium, sixty spectators sat in tiered rows that reached all the way to the high ceiling. They leaned forward in their seats, faces solemn.

Television media called it a "mock trial." But to many observers it was a real trial—a trial of last resort—its purpose to demonstrate the true meaning of justice.

The only part of the trial that was "mock" was the gentleman who played devil's advocate for the three officials named in Don's com-plaint. He objected to proceeding in the absence of the officials. As counsel for Don, I argued that they had been duly served and showed a clause in their subpoena that read: "On your failure to appear, as herein directed, a default judgment may be granted for the relief of [Donald Stefan]."

Five members of the Stefan family testified. Billy, our top witness, made his first public appearance, after four weeks of hiding. He was brought to the courtroom flanked by the bailiff and about a dozen supporters. He testified of his painful separation from his father while in Social Services custody, and affirmed that his mother had convinced him to lie about his father abusing him.

As Billy spoke, a cameraman from *News Channel 4* was filming.

After his testimony, I asked for a brief recess, "to help ensure the safety of the witness." A large number of courtroom participants hastily surrounded Billy and escorted him to a waiting car. He was transported back to hiding at my home, two vehicles following.

At 10:15 PM, the jury delivered a unanimous written verdict. The foreman stood and read it aloud.

> We have every reason to believe that Don Stefan was arrested without valid warrant....
>
> We furthermore believe that upon public demand to see a warrant, a warrant was manufactured after the fact.
>
> Furthermore, the home of Don Stefan was searched without valid warrant, as the only warrant produced was dated two days after the fact.
>
> Furthermore, William and Tom Stefan were abducted and wrongfully detained by the Department of Social Services and the Sheriff's Department, and denied due process under the Constitution of the United States....
>
> We therefore demand the release of Don Stefan and the immediate surcease of the Sheriff's Department to apprehend and harass Don, William and Tom Stefan.

I mailed copies of the verdict to Cattaraugus County Sheriff Jerry Burrell, Family Court Judge Michael Nenno, Supreme Court Judge George Francis, and the county attorney. Participants of the Citizens' Common Law Court realized the verdict would have limited legal bearing. But we believed it would be honored as a strong voice from common citizens.

The day after Billy's appearance in the Common Law Court, a white Bronco repeatedly drove up and down our quiet country road. We had previously seen a vehicle like this driven by Sheriff Jerry Burrell.

Each time the white Bronco came down the road, Billy ran for cover inside the house. As the vehicle drove past, the driver watched the house.

I discussed with Diane and Don the idea of publicly revealing Billy's whereabouts. We agreed it was likely that officials already knew he was with us. Then I spoke to Billy about it. "We can't keep it secret for always, Billy. I think it would be better for us to tell the sheriff you're here."

"What if they'd take me back to Bradford?" he asked.

"I don't think they'll do that, Billy. After all the newspaper and TV stories about you, they'd be ashamed to hurt you again."

"If they take me, will they keep me long?" Billy's face quivered with fear. "How do you know they won't take me?"

"I can't be sure, Billy. But it's just a matter of time before they find you here. If we're honest now, the police won't be as likely to pick you up. And your dad can get out of jail if he tells."

Finally Billy consented. I agreed to deliver a letter he had written to the sheriff. In his letter, he begged the sheriff to leave him alone. "Don't look for me," he wrote. "I want my father to have custody of me and not the state."

On the morning of July 7, I took Billy's letter and headed for the town of Little Valley—to the jail where Don had been held for the past two months. We had arranged a news conference for 9:00, at which time Don was scheduled to disclose Billy's whereabouts.

■ CHAPTER 2 ■

Standoff

By Barbara Lyn

Clad in orange prison uniform, Don was surrounded by news reporters, cameras, the sheriff and deputies. "My son is hid with Barbara Lyn Lapp," he said, speaking from a conference room at the Cattaraugus County jail.

I was in the jail waiting room as Don spoke.

"And your son is there now?" asked the sheriff.

"Yep. He's right there, right now," Don said.

In the room where I was seated, a heavy wooden door opened. A large middle-aged man in a white shirt and tie entered, and walked up to me. Extending his hand, he said, "I'm Sheriff Jerry Burrell. Barb, why don't we step outside to have a word."

I followed him out through the double glass doors of the jail entrance. We stood on the sidewalk facing each other.

"I've spoken with Don," Sheriff Burrell began. "He disclosed that his son Billy is at your residence." He paused. "Is that so?"

"Yes, that's true."

The sheriff looked me in the eye. Neither of us spoke.

"If you would like to talk to Billy to confirm he's there, we could arrange that," I said. "But you can't take him."

"Why is that?" he asked. He looked surprised, and was smiling a little.

"Billy is terrified of being taken back to the Bradford boys' home," I said. "We can't let him down."

"You do know there is a legal order involved here?"

"I can't take part in forcing him to go where he doesn't want to be. He trusts me."

"Okay," the sheriff said, nodding.

We went back inside. Sheriff Burrell returned through the wooden door, and I sat down on a bench in the waiting room. The press conference with Don was still going on.

A friend who was waiting with me offered to make a phone call home. He stepped outside to use the pay phone, and returned a minute later.

"Barbara, they want you home right away," he said, his voice urgent. "The police are there."

"But—I promised the news people I'd be here to talk with them—"

"You better go," he said. "I'll talk to them when they come out."

I ran to the parking lot, got in my car, and headed home. The thirty-five-mile drive had taken almost an hour on my way over.

The road was winding and hilly, leading through three towns and villages. I sped along, missing a stop sign, nearly oblivious to the rolling countryside. Rounding a curve, I saw a vehicle that appeared to be an unmarked police car, parked along the road. I cruised past at a reasonable speed, shuddering at the thought of being stopped before I reached home.

A small green sign along the road marked the county line: "Chautauqua County." Almost home, I thought. Will Billy be okay until I get there? I remembered his anxiety as I had left the farmhouse in the morning.

Rigid with fear, I topped the final hill to our farm. In the valley below, vehicles lined both sides of our narrow road. I could tell who most of the cars belonged to—friends and relatives. Several television news crews were already there. Parked across the road from our house was a white, late-model Chevy Caprice Classic. I recognized it as an unmarked sheriff's car from Cattaraugus County. Two officers stood outside the car.

I parked behind the line of vehicles and headed straight for the officers. They stood with their backs against their car. One was wearing a police uniform, the other a white shirt, dark tie, and grey pants. Pistols protruded from their belts.

"What are you people here for?" I asked.

"Why are we here? Because we're instructed to pick up Billy," said the officer in uniform. He spoke in a calm, deliberate tone.

"What do you think you want with *him?*" I asked.

As we spoke, two television cameramen approached, cameras focused on the officers. Behind me, a dozen friends had gathered on the road.

"Mr. Stefan, uh—uh—did make a statement today that he was here at this residence, and we have come over here to make a demand for William Stefan. And uh—if he's not here, fine, or if you're not going to turn him over, then we're going to leave."

"Whether he's here or not, *I'm* not going to have any part with turning him over to someone he doesn't want to be with," I said. "I know the boy well enough to know he wants to be with his dad. And it would be a crime for me to have any part in turning him over."

The officers listened attentively.

Pointing to the side of the road where their car was parked, I said, "Of course this is not our property here. We can't force you to leave. But I think you might as well leave."

"All right," said one of the officers. They looked at each other. "Have a good day," said the other one. They got in their car and drove away.

More than thirty people stood in the front yard of my home—the two-story, century-old farmhouse that had been Billy's sanctuary for the past four weeks. Among them were Billy's relatives, members of my family, and friends.

As I walked up the driveway, I was greeted with cheers.

"Do you think they'll stay away?" Billy's cousin asked.

"They probably went to get help," answered someone.

"You cooled down now there, Miss Lapp?" a woman asked, laughing.

"Well, yes. I just got a little mad—the sheriff delayed the press conference for an hour and a half, probably just to get officers here before I got back."

At the edge of the lawn, several teenage boys kept an eye on the road. Our Australian Shepherd dog lay on the driveway, alert.

"Did anyone tell Billy he can come out?" asked Nathan, my 24-year-old brother. Billy's cousin found him in an upstairs bedroom beside his bed, where he had been huddled for the past hour.

As Billy emerged from the house, the crowd clapped and cheered. I ran toward him. "It'll be okay," I said, throwing my arms around him. "We sent them packing, Bill."

"They couldn't take more!" a lady jeered.

The crowd burst into laughter. Billy was smiling.

"Barbara, who never raises her voice!" someone giggled.

The television cameramen and news reporters converged on me.

"Have you heard when Don will be released?" a reporter asked.

"The sheriff told me he could be released as soon as a judge signs an order for his release," I said. "The judge who signed the order for his detention is on vacation, and won't be back for the rest of the week."

I stood with Billy in the shade of a maple tree in the front yard. "Is Dad gonna come home now?" he asked. "The judge promised. He wouldn't lie, would he?"

The mood of the crowd was relaxed. Women stood in small groups, chatting. Fathers and mothers served lunch to their children at our picnic table near the porch. Counting children, our group had grown to fifty. Even Billy looked happy.

Suddenly someone yelled, "A white car coming back! You got a white car coming down the road!"

"Go, Billy!" his cousin said.

Billy spun around and ran for the house, picking up speed as his cousin's tone of voice escalated: "Go, go, *GO!*"

The car pulled up and parked in the same spot it had been before—just off the pavement, across the road from our house. The same two officers got out. I approached them, holding a mini cassette recorder in my hand.

"What do you wish?" I asked.

"Our instructions are, we're not to leave," the uniformed officer said.

"Okay," I said, and walked back to the people in the yard.

Several more news reporters arrived with their cameras. Neighbors and friends continued to drop in, joining us on the lawn. Men, women and children formed a line on the edge of the lawn, facing the road.

"They could get enough officers in here to overpower us," a woman said quietly, her voice tense.

A grassy bank and the road separated the group from the officers who stood leaning against their car, ten yards away. Nathan was operating our video camera.

"Nathan, is there someone else who could take the camera?" I asked. My voice lowered to a whisper. "You and Kevin could take off to the woods with Billy."

Billy's relatives and members of my family huddled together, talking.

"I think he's safer here," Diane said. "He'd get real scared on the run."

Others in the group disagreed. "He has to leave while there's still a chance," someone said. "They could surround us with officers any minute. How could you forgive yourself?"

Rachel was adamant. "He can't go away from here. If they catch up with him anywhere else, they'll get away with taking him in secret."

"He has to stay," I concluded. "I told the sheriff and media he's here."

In front of the house, children bounced on a large inner tube from a tractor tire, shrieking gleefully. The sound of song sparrows chirping filled the air. A lively breeze rustled the leaves of the four tall maple trees bordering our lawn.

Black and white Holstein cattle grazed on a hill south of our house. A hundred feet west of our house stood a 150-foot-long cement block structure—home of our sixty dairy cows. Two feed storage silos towered above the gambrel roof of the barn. Directly across the road, where the officers stood by their car, was a large grey barn. Almost a hundred years old, it was the only building besides our house that had been here when my father purchased the property two decades earlier. A chicken house, a tool shed, a dog kennel, and two calf barns completed the array of small buildings that dotted the flat bottom of our valley.

"Can we talk to Billy?" asked a television cameraman.

"He doesn't want to come out when the officers are here," I said. "But you're welcome to come into the house."

A half dozen men and women with cameras and notebooks filed into the house. We found Billy in the living room, peering through a crack in the curtain. The sheriff's deputies stood by their car, only forty feet from the window.

Billy looked back over his shoulder, eyeing the media crew suspiciously.

"Must be kind of frightening, huh?" a newsman asked him.

"Yeah, I want to be left alone and go home with my father."

"How many cars are out front, Billy?"

"A lot of people." Billy smiled. "Good people."

A dark red Chrysler sedan, equipped with tall antennas, pulled into the drive by the old barn, near the white sheriff's car. Two men in business suits got out and stood alongside the white car, conversing with the officers.

I recognized the men from a distance. "Chautauqua County sheriffs!" I said. I took my mini-cassette recorder and walked out to them. My parents and Rachel followed. It was almost 1:00.

"Hi," I said, extending my hand to one of the officers, a tall dark-haired man. "You're from Chautauqua County?"

"Rex Rater," he said as we shook hands. "You're Barbara Lapp?"

"Yes, um—why are you here?"

"I'm here because this is in our jurisdiction—Chautauqua County," Rater said. "I understand that you have someone who the court has ordered to be turned over to Cattaraugus County so the family court judge can talk with him. And I understand you're going to have a news conference and then you were going to turn that individual over."

"Which individual?" I asked, looking up into his eyes. His six-foot frame had him standing a half foot above me.

Rater pulled a color photo of Billy from an inside pocket of his suit, and displayed it for me to see. "William Stefan," he said.

I looked at the photo. "William Stefan is *not* going to be turned over," I said.

Rater looked down, studying the photo he held in his hands. Eyes narrowing, he slowly lifted them until they met mine. His lips tightened, and he said nothing.

Media cameras closed in around the four officers and me standing next to the white car. Several family members and friends stood close behind me. The group of people on the lawn fell silent.

"Do you have a warrant?" I asked.

"No, I don't."

"Why are you on our property, then?"

"Uh—I'm not. I'm on the roadway."

"Didn't you park your car right here?" I pointed to his car in the driveway.

"Yes, I did. Would you like me to move it?"

"We would like you to get off the property, yes."

"Okay," Rater said, then paused. "Could you tell me what the— uh—occurrence is today—what's going to happen?"

"What's going to happen? Well, nothing's going to happen on my part."

"You just called a news release." Rater stared at me, his chin jutted.

"The news release was in Little Valley at the jail when Mr. Stefan informed the sheriff and the media that his son William was staying at our house," I said.

"The news media is here today. Is that for any particular reason?"

"That's because of the commotion that started here when the sheriffs arrived. Also, we were going to give the news media, as well as the sheriff, the opportunity to come up and see that William is here."

TV cameras on all sides of him, Rater kept his gaze on me. "And that's the reason for this today?"

"That's right."

"And is William here today?" Rater drew out the photo of Billy again, and held it toward me with both his hands.

"Yes. I've told the Cattaraugus County sheriff. I told Sheriff Burrell myself."

"He is here now?" Rater asked, his index finger tapping the photo.

"Yes," I said. "But he's not going to be released to you."

Rater looked down with a smirk on his face.

I remembered Rater's recent photo in the newspaper—with a group of Child Protective Services workers. "Are you on the Chautauqua County Child Abuse Team?" I asked him.

"I'm a member of that, yes," he said coldly.

"How do you feel about putting a child through this kind of abuse?"

"Well, I'm not here to discuss philosophy or anything else," Rater said. "What I'm here for specifically is to see if I can assist in any way."

"I'm just wondering if you're going to take any responsibility for the suffering that's been caused this child. He's terrified."

"I'm not familiar with this case," Rater said quickly. "It didn't originate in Chautauqua County."

"Well, I think it would be better for you not to be involved if you're not familiar with the case."

"Well, if I'm going to do anybody any benefit, then isn't it my responsibility to find out some information first?" Rater said, his voice rising. He tossed his head. "I'll move my car." He walked off abruptly, parked along the road for a short time, then drove off.

A cameraman from *News Channel 4,* a Buffalo TV station, approached me. "How long is this going to last?" he asked.

"As long as it takes for these people to leave us alone," I said.

"You're not prepared to give up the boy under any conditions?"

"Certainly not."

"What are you going to do if they come with a warrant?"

"Um—I don't believe they will arrest this many people."

"You're telling me that the people would actually block the way?"

"Yes. If they would arrive with a warrant I believe their problem would be bigger than ours."

The cameraman chuckled. "How is that?"

"If they would start arresting people—there would be a very low public opinion of that. There's no one here who has harmed anybody, and Billy has clearly stated he wants to be left alone. We're only protecting his wishes."

"So the people here would try to block the sheriff from coming in?"

"We would certainly block the way. But we're not violent people."

The cameraman laughed. "Just trying to get this straight," he said.

"I just hope they back off before things go further," I said.

A dozen children, ranging in age from four to fourteen, lined up along the edge of the yard, holding signs we had prepared for demonstrations in the past weeks. "Child Protective Services is dangerous to children," one sign read. "Judge Nenno: Number one child abuser," read another. Bright orange day lilies growing on the bank along the road swayed in the breeze in front of the signs.

The Stefan family's van was parked across the road, near the sheriff's car. Painted on the back window was this message: "Family court violates the family."

Now and then a vehicle would pass on the road. Billy's brothers and several of their cousins, and my brother Nathan, carefully watched each approaching car. "That one's okay," Nathan would tell the other boys when he recognized the vehicle.

"There's Rex Rater again!" someone called.

This time Rater parked his car a hundred feet down the road, near a drive by the dairy barn. Another vehicle approached.

"What's that gray car?" a lady asked. "Isn't that the one that passed through earlier?"

"Pennsylvania license plate!"

"I'll bet it's somebody from the Bradford Children's Home."

"Look at that! He turned around!"

The car was a late model Pontiac Trans Am, with windows so heavily tinted we could not see its occupants. It cruised past, pulled up alongside Rex Rater's car, stopped a moment, then sped on.

Rater and his companion walked up to the Cattaraugus County officers, who were standing outside their car. The four of them conversed in low tones.

I went out to talk to them. "Could you tell me what you're waiting for?" I asked.

"We were just told to wait," the uniformed officer said.

"Told to wait for what?"

"We don't know what. We were just told to stay here—'till we're relieved."

"Would you like to see Billy, to confirm that he's here? Is that a concern to you?"

"No. That's all right. I just heard you tell Investigator Rater that he's here. I believe it. I have no reason to doubt you."

"Do you have any idea how long you're going to be here?"

"Not the *foggiest* clue."

By mid-afternoon radio stations across Western New York were announcing news of the incident. They called it a "standoff." On the phone with one of the news reporters I explained it isn't what I would call a standoff. "They haven't even tried to enter our property—and we're not armed. We don't believe in hurting anyone."

The gray Trans Am went past again, then parked along the road on the eastern side of our valley. Several newsmen approached the car with their cameras. Through the windshield, two men could be seen. The driver grabbed a pair of sunglasses from the dashboard, put them on, and sped away, barely slowing down for the crowd of people who were on the road.

A reporter from *The Post-Journal*, using our kitchen phone, called the director of the Bradford Children's Home and confirmed our suspicion that the gray car was from that facility. Two staff members from the children's home were in the area, prepared to take Billy back, the director said.

A few minutes later, both sheriffs' cars left.

Soon Billy came out of the house again. "Are they going to take me?" Billy asked Nathan. "Are they going to come back and get me?" His eyes darted from Nathan to the road.

"I don't think so, Bill," Nathan said. "We'll take care of you."

A half hour after the sheriffs' cars left, several members of the television media were in the house, talking about returning to their stations in time for evening broadcasts.

"They're just waiting until the media leaves to get Billy," said someone from the crowd.

A cameraman from *News Channel 7* heard the comment. *"I'm staying,"* he said.

"My boss said I have to be back by four," complained a cameraman from another station. He checked his watch and paced the floor. "Could I use your phone?" On the phone, he quickly got permission to stay.

Everyone was gravely concerned about Billy. "I think you should move him out of here," a news reporter told me quietly.

We devised a strategy for helping Billy escape through the back door of the house, then blocked all our driveways with trucks, tractors, and farm equipment. Police would now have to enter our property on foot, and the house could not be surrounded quickly.

Billy relaxed, and played with the children in the yard. Adults sat on chairs and picnic benches. My father bounced the little children up and down on the inflated tractor tire tube. Several more children swung on the branches of our lilac bushes, bubbling with laughter.

We served watermelon slices and cold drinks. Our half-acre strawberry patch, fifty feet from the house, was frequented by adults and youngsters, stooping in search of ripe fruits.

It was about 3:30 when the officers in the white car returned again. They stood outside, leaning against their car, arms folded. I went out to talk to them, for the fourth time.

"I have a question," I said. "Were either of you at the press conference there in Little Valley?"

"No, Ma'am."

"What has Sheriff Burrell told you?" I asked. "Did Don make it clear to the sheriff that it's his desire to have Billy protected here?"

"No. Miss Lapp, when we were sent up here—okay—it was our understanding and belief that after the press conference Donald was going to call this residence and authorize for the child to be turned over to us," said the uniformed officer who had identified himself as Lt. Buchhardt. "That's why we're here."

"When I talked to Sheriff Burrell I told him that the child was not going to be released. Weren't you aware of that?"

"No, we didn't get that message. The only person we have talked to is our undersheriff. We went to call him just a minute ago to find out what our function is. And our function is to stay here until we're told not to stay here, and that was the end of the phone call."

"Well, I'm going to suggest to Don that he talk to the undersheriff," I said.

"That would be fine," Lt. Buchhardt said, nodding.

"This doesn't make sense," I said. "We're not going to release Billy, and Don knows we're not going to."

Buchhardt laughed amicably.

The other officer joined the conversation. "See, we were just two officers that were the closest to here—"

Laughing heartily, Buchhardt added, "And we just happened to be at the office at the wrong time—and got to the wrong place!"

I went to the house and got a call through to Don, at the jail. "Did you make it clear to the sheriff that you didn't intend for Billy to be released to them?" I asked.

"I said my son is at the home of Barbara Lapp in Cassadaga. I told them exactly what the court required me to tell," Don said.

"They've been here all day, Don," I said. "But we're not going to force Billy to go."

"I know Billy's in good hands," Don said. "But please be careful. The undersheriff's real mad about what's happening out there. He told me they're gonna get a warrant, and if you people try to stop them, people *will* get hurt."

News of the standoff spread throughout the nation. Our three phone lines were ringing continuously as the afternoon wore on, with calls coming in from as far away as California and New York City. Several local news stations who were not able to stay on the scene, called for live interviews every hour. "What is happening now?" they would ask me. "What will happen if they come with a warrant?"

Late in the afternoon one officer drove off, leaving Lt. Buchhardt standing by the roadside. On the lawn, we were serving sodas and ice cream to everyone. Even media personnel, who earlier in the day had declined to take food, joined us.

I walked across the road to Lt. Buchhardt—for the first time, approaching him without my tape recorder. "Would you like something to drink, or a piece of watermelon?" I asked.

"No thanks, I'm fine," he said.

I turned to leave. "Barbara?" Buchhardt called, stepping toward me. "I want you to know this is nothing personal," he said softly. "We don't mean to be causing you a problem." I nodded, and returned to the group in the yard.

At about 4:30 it began to rain. Buchhardt was still alone, with no vehicle. I went out to him again. "Could I get you a raincoat or something?" I asked.

"That's okay. It's been hot all day—this feels good."

"What about your equipment?" I asked, noticing his radio, pistol, and a string of silver ammunition hanging around his belt.

"It's okay. Thank you."

Soon the white car returned, and the officers again stood outside it, facing the house.

Someone from the crowd told me the officers wanted to talk to me. I got the little recorder and went.

"Ma'am?" Lt. Buchhardt said as I approached.

"Yes, sir."

"Barbara, we just got a call, a radio call from our office that told us to return to our office, so we're leaving. We have no idea what is going on. We do apologize for causing any great alarm. We're *not* here to cause you a problem."

"I understand that, and I hope it won't continue to be a problem," I said. "I would be more than happy to talk to anyone who could help resolve it. The only thing I'm interested in is that the child is safe— that's the only objective I have in this thing."

"We understand," Lt. Buchhardt said.

"With good faith, we just wanted to tell you that we are going," the other officer added.

"And no word about returning?" I asked.

"I really doubt that they would call us all the way back to Little Valley and have us come back here again," Buchhardt said. "Okay?"

"Okay. Thank you."

It was 5:00 PM—six hours after the standoff began.

We remained watchful as we milked the cows and served dinner to the crowd. Billy rode his bike, and joined in a water fight with the rest of the children. Several news reporters stayed, expressing concern that police would return when they left—or worse, after dark.

A friend brought a portable TV set to our living room, and we watched the news, seeking clues to the authorities' next possible move. But the news broadcast at 6:00 revealed more about our position than that of authorities.

> *Channel 4, WIVB TV:* All is quiet here now in this Chautauqua County Community. The Cattaraugus County sheriffs left about an hour ago, and Billy Stefan is still here, the supporters here still on guard at Barbara Lyn Lapp's house. They say that they are prepared to take any nonviolent means to keep Billy free, and that includes being arrested.

By 9:00 all except one of the news reporters had left, as well as most of our supporters. Nathan, with a half dozen other men and boys from the group, took Billy for a swim in our pond. Then they trekked through a deep woods to arrive at my sister and brother-in-law's home, a mile and a half from our farm. Billy stayed there to sleep, escaping the fear of police returning to our valley after dark.

At 11:00, we gathered to watch the news again.

> *Channel 7, WKBW TV:* Police say they aren't coming back for Billy now. They say it is not in the child's best interest.

> *Channel 4, WIVB TV:* Chautauqua County Sheriff's deputies say no action will be taken tonight to remove William Stefan from the Lapp farmhouse. They say it is not in the child's best interest to argue the matter in his presence.

■ CHAPTER 3 ■

Ambush

By Barbara Lyn

On July 12, five days after Don had disclosed Billy's whereabouts, he was scheduled to appear before Judge Nenno in Family Court. According to previous promises by the judge, he would be released.

Anxiety tormented me as I made the 65-minute drive to Olean to be at Don's hearing. What if Billy would be captured by police when I wasn't home? Will Don be released? How could I face Billy again if his father did not get out?

My brother, Nathan, and several members of the Stefan family walked with me into the Cattaraugus County Courthouse at 1:30.

"Here, take the keys," I told Nathan, handing him my car keys. "In case something happens to me." I laughed when I saw the look of alarm on Nathan's face.

In the courthouse hall, we waited for Don's hearing to begin. Reporters for *The Post-Journal* and *News Channel 4* arrived. Diane asked the bailiff if we could get into the courtroom.

"Not everyone," he said. A moment later he motioned toward me and said I could go in. Don's niece and Nathan followed.

"Did you notice how eager the officer was to let us in?" I commented to the others as we sat down. We conversed quietly for several minutes. Then a side door opened, and Lt. Buchhardt stepped into the court waiting room. "Barbara, I'd like to talk to you for a moment," he said.

I hesitated. "Can I have someone with me?"

"Sure, you can have anyone you want."

Nathan and I followed Lt. Buchhardt into a hallway. The door closed behind us. I noticed three officers in a room just off the hallway. One of them was Lt. Travis. He glared at me.

Buchhardt spoke. "Barbara, we have a warrant for your arrest." Several officers stepped out in front of me.

"Uh-huh," I said, concealing my shock. I glanced across the hall-way where another small room was packed with officers. They were watching.

Buchhardt explained there were actually two warrants, one for "Custodial Interference in the Second Degree," and one for "Unlawful Imprisonment in the Second Degree."

I looked at him as he spoke. I wondered what it meant to be under arrest. Would they give me an appearance ticket?

Buchhardt continued. "We're transferring you to Chautauqua County."

"It doesn't seem to me you should be doing this," I said. "I haven't harmed anybody. I haven't committed any crime."

"We have a valid warrant here, signed by Judge Ward," Buchhardt said.

A young deputy who stood only a few feet from me held the warrants up high, displaying one in each hand. "See, there are two!"

"But you don't have jurisdiction," I argued.

Buchhardt laughed nervously. "We have been authorized by Chautauqua County to make the arrest. We're just following orders—doing our job."

Nathan spoke. "Isn't that exactly what Hitler's boys did?"

Beside us, Lt. Travis jumped from his chair. "Take her now!" he said.

A small lady officer approached, handcuffs open. "Put your wrists together," she said.

I stood silent for a moment, my arms folded. "I can't cooperate with this kind of lawlessness," I said.

"You're gonna have to go, Barbara," Lt. Buchhardt said, stepping up close. The lady officer pulled my arms out in front of me, and one of the other deputies helped her fasten the handcuffs.

"Let's go," an officer said, wrapping his hand around my elbow. Then a half dozen more of them moved tightly against me, forcing me to walk.

We went down the hallway. I saw Don Stefan in a room, waiting for court. "Good luck, Don," I said. He didn't seem to notice that I was in handcuffs.

The police woman who handcuffed me and a male officer took me to a sheriff's car. They opened the back door and told me to get in. I stopped and faced them. "I just can't do this," I said. "I can't volunteer to get into that car."

"Well, you got to get in," the police woman said. Then they pushed me into the back seat. My hands bound, I couldn't use them to get out of the twisted sitting position in which I had landed.

❊   ❊   ❊

Don entered the courtroom. Others present were Don's mother Effie, his estranged wife, Linda, and four attorneys.

"Mr. Stefan, do you wish to be represented in these proceedings, other than by Ms. Lapp?" Judge Nenno asked.

"You're not going to allow her to represent me then?"

"I can't…. [S]he's not an attorney, she cannot appear in this courtroom and cannot represent anybody. It's also my understanding that she's not available in any event."

Judge Nenno then asked Stephen Riley, the Social Services attorney, for his recommendation on the case.

"Your Honor, I believe… that the court is empowered to sentence the defendant up to six months in jail. It's the Department's position at this time that Mr. Stefan should be sentenced to a term of incarceration for six months."

Riley continued. "Mr. Stefan, I realize, last week announced where his child was located. It's my understanding that Mr. Stefan was previously told he would remain incarcerated until he did tell us where the child was. This is a distinct and separate proceeding. This is a violation proceeding. What we're asking for is that even though he may have served close to two months in jail… that he be additionally sentenced to [a] six month period under this order.

"The reason for that is, again, Mr. Stefan has led us on a goose chase, he has made this into a media madhouse. I think they've abused the child again by doing this. And I feel that only six months more will let the message get through to Mr. Stefan that when this court gives an order… and then he violates that, that the court can't put up with that. I think that the only way Mr. Stefan is going to learn not to do this again is to have some time to think about it in the Cattaraugus County Jail."

Don spoke up. "I'd do it a hundred times over…. I did what was right. [Billy] was unlawfully taken away from me…. That woman over there, Linda Stefan, is the abuser and neglector and molester, and I have witnesses that can prove it…."

Linda's attorney responded: "…[W]e would categorically deny Mr. Stefan's allegations regarding my client. It was he that was charged, not her. It was he that was found in violation, not her. No charges have been brought against her. We do believe that Billy should be brought to a hospital and examined, both for physical and mental problems...."

Billy's law guardian concurred, stating that Billy, "after he is returned," should be evaluated by health professionals.

Don spoke up again. "Now you said I'd be released if I told you where I hid him. That I've done. You failed—you're going to fail to keep your end of the bargain."

"No, no—" Judge Nenno began.

"You are going to release me?" Don asked.

"We're here on a different proceeding, Mr. Stefan. We're here on the violation.... You admitted the violation when you were in court."

After a few more exchanges the judge began to read his ruling. "It's the determination of the court that disposition shall be as follows: That Mr. Donald Stefan, having admitted the violation of the order—"

"I haven't admitted anything," Don interrupted.

Nenno started to speak again, but Don continued. "Also, those four boys need a father out there. I got four children out there."

"Did you not say you'd do it all over again?" asked Nenno.

"To keep him protected and safe from the Social Services—these people—children's home in Bradford," Don answered. "You don't see that?"

Finally Judge Nenno completed his ruling: "Mr. Stefan will be held in Cattaraugus County Jail for a period of six months from this date." Regarding Billy's custody, Nenno said that would be decided as soon as Social Services got him back.

Don was furious. "I promise you he's going to be safe," he told the judge. "If I have to protect him from *you*, also."

"Well, that can be," said Nenno. "This concludes today's proceedings."

"Which is void," answered Don. "All constitutional rights have been flushed down the toilet."

❉   ❉   ❉

In the police car, we drove along the expressway toward the Mayville jail. The two officers in the front chatted about the previous night's ball game. I sat speechless in the back seat. "Lord, give me strength to put aside my fear," I prayed.

After a while I asked the officers for the warrants. The woman slipped them through a crack in the wire mesh barrier between us. Each warrant was a single sheet of paper, with a court seal on it. Several papers called "informations" were attached to the warrants, and outlined the complaints against me. Social Services Commissioner Ronald B. Hackett was the complainant. Included in the evidence against me was a *Buffalo News* story which told of my efforts to help the Stefans.

I glanced down at my hands on my lap, locked together with chains. Never before had anyone, even in my childhood years, deemed me so unmanageable that I needed to be physically restrained. I would have been glad to talk to Commissioner Hackett, or any of the officers. Why did they use force on me instead of talking? I blinked away tears.

After driving about forty minutes we arrived at the county line. The police car stopped in a U-turn area of the expressway, where we waited for a Chautauqua County Sheriff's car. An officer arrived in an unmarked car. It was Lt. John Runkle, who happened to be an acquaintance of our family. The police woman removed my handcuffs, and Lt. Runkle asked me to follow him to his car. "I don't need to handcuff you, if you cooperate," he said.

I walked a few steps toward his car, then stopped to consider my position. I wanted to please Runkle, as I would any other neighbor. But should I give an appearance of consent by cooperating? "I guess I can't volunteer to go with you," I said, "since this is an unlawful arrest."

"I understand you are a peaceable person," Runkle said, pleading, "and I'm trying to be as peaceable as possible too."

I made no move. He reached for his handcuffs.

"Are you going to have a part in this unwarranted use of force?" I challenged him.

"I have to follow the judge's orders—I have no choice," Runkle said. He seemed distressed. "I can't just let you go free right here. You pay your taxes, just like everyone else—to help keep the peace, enforce laws. That's all I'm doing."

"I have not done anything to disturb the peace, and I don't think you should either."

"I don't—usually," he said. "C'mon now, Barbara. Won't you get in the car so I don't have to handcuff you?"

"It is my position that I cannot cooperate with these lawless actions. I'm sorry."

Runkle motioned to the Cattaraugus County officers, who were still waiting by their car. They came over and urged me to get into his car. "We don't want a confrontation here," the police woman pleaded. A moment later Runkle handcuffed me, then took my arm and pulled me toward the car as the other officers pushed me to the open door. The woman officer bent my knees, while the two men bent my neck and shoved me downward. I landed in the back seat of the car, my skirt entangled awkwardly around my legs.

It took about a half hour more to get to Mayville. At the jail, an officer opened the car door, and told me to get out. I suspected they would try to take me to court before anyone from my family could find out where I was. "Can I make a phone call home?" I asked, remaining seated.

"After the arraignment you can," an officer said. "Come on, Barbara, get out now."

I didn't move. "I need to call my family."

"Okay, if you cooperate, and go along in, you can make the call."

"Before court?" I asked.

"Yes."

I walked in. On the phone in the jail booking room, I spoke briefly to Mom. She told me Hannah, my sister, was already on the way to Mayville and would be here in time for my arraignment. A radio news reporter was at the house to get information about my arrest. He got on the phone. "Barbara Lyn, where are you now?" he asked.

"I just arrived at the jail in Mayville. I'm sitting in a small room, in handcuffs, with four or five uniformed men standing close around me. It's all very strange—"

An officer nudged me. "Hurry up!" he said. "The judge is ready for you."

A large middle-aged officer seemed in charge. His name tag said "Lt. Lawrence." He politely asked me to walk with them across the street to court. I started walking, but then I saw they were taking me to an underground tunnel. I stopped. "This is not right," I said.

Lt. Lawrence's gentle manner quickly changed. He grabbed my upper arm with one hand and my forearm with his other hand. Another officer on my right did the same, and they forced me along. We entered a long, dimly lit hallway, about six feet wide. At the end of the tunnel we took several steps up, then went in an elevator to a second floor courtroom.

In a small waiting room outside the courtroom the officers took off my handcuffs and allowed me to go to the sink for a drink. Soon the judge called for me, and the officers told me to come.

"I cannot voluntarily enter that courtroom," I said.

"Come on!" Lt. Lawrence demanded. Both officers quickly took my arms and forced me in. My daughter, Miriam, and a friend were there.

Judge Larry M. Himelein was on the bench, elevated on a platform several feet above floor level. He sat on a chair with a high back, leaning forward onto a counter that formed a semi-circle around him. The officers walked me to the bench. I looked up at the judge.

"Are you Barbara Lyn Lapp?" Judge Himelein asked. He glanced at the papers on the counter in front of him, then down at me.

"I don't believe I need to answer that question," I said.

He chuckled. "That is probably true, but I can't arraign you if you don't tell me who you are."

"Well, you don't have any right to have me here right now, sir. You don't need to arraign me."

"Okay, take her out," he said abruptly, to the officers.

Outside the courtroom, Lt. Lawrence put my handcuffs back on. "You'll need to go down in a cell now, and stay there 'till you're ready to cooperate. You understand?"

I didn't answer.

"We can't set bail if you don't stand for arraignment—you're giving up your chance of getting released on your own recognizance."

The officers walked me down to the booking room, where they seated me across the desk from a lady officer. She got out some forms and asked my date of birth.

"I don't want to give information to you," I said.

"You'll need to, in order to get processed," she said. "It's just standard procedure."

I sat in the chair, silent.

"You'll need to change into jail clothes too."

"I can't cooperate with that. At least not until I've consulted with counsel."

The officers conferred. "You had a phone call already," one of them said. "You're entitled to only one." I was silent. After a while they let me use the phone.

I called home. While I was on the phone an officer interrupted to tell me that bail had been set at $5,000. When I got off, he said, "Barbara, you won't get out with or without the $5,000 if you don't cooperate." Turning to another officer he asked, "Didn't the judge mention anything about contempt charges? She didn't even answer his questions."

A very heavy officer in a white shirt sat across the desk from me, at his computer. "What name and number do you want to give as an emergency contact?" he asked.

"I guess you'll have to figure that out yourself," I said, "I'm not giving any information. I'm sorry."

"I'm sorry too," he said.

Several more officers came. "You said you would cooperate if we give you a call home," one said. "We've given you every privilege we can."

"I appreciate your generosity, but the bottom line is, you shouldn't have me here."

"We can't help that the judge ordered it," he said. "We have to do our job."

"The issue involves more than a job," I said. "This is immoral."

The lady officer was on the phone. "Do we have to change her?" she was asking. "It will be very difficult—she's being very difficult."

From a nearby room I could hear the noise of women inmates. A high-pitched cry faded into a moan. Loud voices blended with laughter. Heavy metal music thundered in the background.

Behind me, officers were speaking together in low tones. Finally, because I wouldn't change into jail clothes, they decided to isolate me in a cell within the women's cellblock.

"You'll need to remove your hair barrettes—any jewelry—your watch," the lady officer said.

I didn't move. A male officer grabbed my wrist and took off my watch, while the lady took out my barrettes. My hair tumbled over my shoulders. Then two officers lifted me up by my arms and walked me through a narrow door, a curtain, a gate, and into a cell. "I'm sorry, Barbara," said one, as the cell door locked behind me.

The officers left. Several women inmates came up to my cell. They were in a larger area, outside the cells.

"What are you here for?" one of them asked, speaking to me through the bars.

"I have a boy at my house that ran away from Social Services custody, and—"

"What's your name?" she interrupted. "Are you the woman that was in the paper?"

More inmates gathered outside my cell gate. "I read about her!" one exclaimed.

"She's the one that didn't let the cops get that boy," another girl said.

The lady officer, whom the girls called Doreen, came back, bringing me a towel, toothbrush, and comb. The inmates gave me rubber bands for my hair, writing paper and snacks. One of them offered to call home for me, as they had access to a phone.

At 6:00 PM the news of my arrest came on TV. Doreen moved the screen so I could see it from my cell, and we all watched.

"Don Stefan thought he was going to get out of jail today," said the news announcer. "Barbara Lyn Lapp was helping him try to make that happen. Tonight they are both behind bars.

"For the past two months Don Stefan has been told to tell authorities where he hid his son, and he can go free. Last Wednesday from the Cattaraugus County Jail he revealed that his son, William, has been living here at the Chautauqua County home of Barbara Lyn Lapp....

"Lapp is held on $5,000 cash or $10,000 property. She says she will *not* post it."

When the newscast was over the inmates clapped and cheered.

At 8:00 a crowd of family, friends and supporters gathered outside the jail. I could hear them when I stood close to my cell window. "Keep it up, Barbara Lyn!" they were chanting. Then they sang, "Brighten the Corner." A heavy plastic canopy over the window kept me from seeing them, but I could hear the words:

"Do not wait until some deed of greatness you may do,
Do not wait to shed your light afar,
To the many duties ever near you now be true,
Brighten the corner where you are."

Shouts arose from the cellblock as inmates cheered. "You *go*, Barbara!" They pressed close to the window and called to the demonstrators. "You *go*, Barbara's fans!" More shouts and whistling followed, as male inmates on the upper floors joined the cheering. There was so much noise inside, it seemed the jail shook.

As Doreen, the Corrections Officer (CO) was leaving her shift at 11:00 PM, she asked if there was anything I needed for the night.

"Is there a Bible available?" I asked. She said yes, and brought a Gideon Bible.

The CO on the next shift was Brenda Van Vlack, one of our fruit stand customers. She walked up to my cell. "Hi, Barbara! A once in a lifetime experience, huh?"

"Hopefully a one and only," I said.

"I know one thing, you have good produce."

I read several chapters in the book of Esther, where my Bible had fallen open. Then I sat at a small metal table and jotted down the events of the day.

At midnight the TV was finally turned low. I took the well-worn mat provided by the jail and placed it on the bottom bunk of the solid metal bed. There was no pillow. I climbed in, closed my eyes and mentally summoned power to endure—and to feel love for my enemies.

Tuesday, July 13

A new CO, Sue Melson, came in. She seemed nice, but more stern than the others. She began to hand me the morning newspaper, *The Buffalo News*. "There's something in here you'll want to read," she said. Just as I reached out to take it through the bars, she pulled it back. "I'd better read it first, to see if there's anything that might upset you." As she read, the other inmates looked over her shoulder, and excitedly told me that I was on the front page.

After Sue read the paper, she handed it to me. "Lapp Arrested on Charges of Unlawful Imprisonment," the headline read.

I passed the morning cleaning my cell, writing, and conversing with other inmates. Lunch came early. I couldn't eat much. My stomach felt knotted. It seemed all the emotions I had contained for the past twenty-four hours were about to explode. I silently shed tears, and prayed.

CO Sue unlocked my door to allow me a phone call. I called home and talked to Susan, my youngest sister. Her voice was tense. "A sheriff's car just came," she said. "They're asking if we'll hand over Billy—I have to go—"

"Stay calm, Susie," I said. She hung up. CO Sue locked me back in.

For the next half hour I felt sick with anxiety. I knew my family would protect Billy as well as they could. But would the police use force?

CO Sue came up to my cell. "Come on, Barbara, you're going to see the judge," she said, unlocking my gate. I followed her to the booking room. Sgt. Rex Rater and Lt. Lawrence were there. Rater was looking at me with a bold stare, his chin jutted out as usual. He stepped toward me, handcuffs clacking.

"I don't want to go," I said. "Do I have to?"

"Yes, you do," Rater said.

"Are you going to force me?"

"Yes."

Rater grabbed my hands and fastened the handcuffs.

"Let's go, Barb," Lt. Lawrence said, directing me toward the hallway to court. I walked with both officers close behind, nudging me whenever I hesitated. We got to the courtroom.

"Good afternoon," I greeted Judge Himelein.

"This time I'll assume you are Barbara Lyn Lapp," he said, smiling. "I asked them to bring you over again because I want to make sure that you understand what the charges are and what rights you have."

"Do I have the right to have counsel here?" I asked.

"Yes. That's one of the rights I'm going to explain to you right now. You have the right to an attorney at all stages of these proceedings...." He read a lengthy statement about my right to counsel, then continued. "There are two charges here. In both of them the complainant is—"

"Excuse me," I interrupted. "Didn't you say I have the right to counsel at all stages? I do not wish to proceed without having somebody here."

"I'm not going to do anything substantive," he said, "other than explain what the charges are and what your rights are—okay? I'm going to enter a not guilty plea on your behalf."

"I object to any plea being entered, on the grounds that this court does not have jurisdiction."

"Okay. Well, your objection is noted, but let me just explain the charges. They are both class A misdemeanors which carry a maximum penalty of one year in the local jail.... The factual allegations claim—"

"Well, judge, I do not choose to be here," I said. "I won't stay here." I turned and started to leave.

The officers caught me by my arms. "Just stay there for a moment," Lt. Lawrence said. "Then we'll go back down." He gently pushed me back toward the judge, attempting to turn my body so I would face him. I resisted, and stood facing away from the judge.

The judge began to speak again. "The second charge... alleges that you restrained another person, again one William Stefan...."

"You have the right to an attorney... and if you can't afford a lawyer you have the right to have counsel assigned to you. Do you understand that?"

Looking down at the floor, I didn't answer.

"Okay," the judge said. "The record should reflect that the alleged Ms. Lapp is not answering, and is standing with her back to the court...." He looked at the officers. "She has refused to let the department fingerprint her?" he asked.

"That's correct."

"I will make it a condition of bail that she cannot be released until she has been fingerprinted and photographed." He then instructed the officers to take me to the Town of Charlotte Court.

"Is there anything you would like to say or do, Ms. Lapp?" he asked.

"I am not a part of this proceeding."

The officers took me out of the courtroom. A lawyer from the public defender's office approached me, offering legal services. I told him I was not interested. He tried to persuade me to accept assistance, and finally went back into the courtroom. I could hear him talk to the judge. They were both laughing.

Lt. Lawrence walked me back to my cell. "Five thousand dollars and some black blotches on your fingers will get you out of here," he said.

In the cellblock, Sue allowed me to call home again. The family told me that the police had left without Billy. I informed them of my schedule to appear in Town of Charlotte Court at 5:30.

We were still talking when CO Sue called. "Barbara, the lieutenant wants to talk to you."

"What should I do?" I asked the family. "They're calling me to see the lieutenant, and I don't want to talk to him alone."

"Barbara, if you don't stop that right now, and get out here, you're not going to have any more phone privileges at all!" Sue yelled. "She's trying to ask advice on the phone," she complained to the officers outside the cellblock.

"Guess I have to go," I told my family.

I went to the booking room with Sue, where I met Lt. Lawrence.

"I don't appreciate you calling me out without witnesses or counsel present," I said.

"It'll take just a minute," Lawrence said. Then he and another large man suddenly took me by the shoulders, turned me around, and pushed me into a corner next to the fingerprinting apparatus. "We're going to fingerprint you," he explained. "So if Judge Newton decides to release you on your own recognizance tonight, you'll be ready to go."

"I don't think you people should lie like that," I said as they held me for fingerprinting. "If you wanted me to come out here to be fingerprinted, you should have told me so."

"We didn't intend to deceive you," Lt. Lawrence said.

"When I talk to you, I tell you the truth," I continued. "You should do the same."

Lt. Lawrence spoke kindly. "This is standard process. You are still innocent until proven guilty. You have a good record, Barb—nothing criminal on file."

They held me tightly, pressing each finger on ink, then on a card. When they were done Lawrence showed me the fingerprint card. "You probably don't want to sign this?"

"No."

Back in my cell, I sat down to write.

"Barbara, you have a visit," CO Sue called.

I followed her up a stairs to the visiting room on the first floor. Lydia, my sister, had brought Miriam to see me. Miriam looked scared. Even my hug didn't make her smile. We sat down on opposite sides of a long, narrow table with a wooden barrier across the top. "Mom, I saw you in court yesterday," Miriam said. "Mom, were those officers hurting you?"

We were allowed a half-hour visit. Then I was returned to the booking room, where I waited for a CO to put me into my cell. A guard standing there asked, "Not the nicest place in the world to be, huh?"

"It's pretty strange to be in a pen," I said.

He nodded.

"I put my dogs in pens, and my cows sometimes—never imagined being in a pen myself."

Back in the cellblock, the CO left my cell door open, allowing me to share the day room with inmates from all four cells. The extra freedom was refreshing, and I could use the phone at my convenience. One of the inmates fixed my hair for court, in a French braid.

Just after 5:00, I was called to leave for court. The inmates cheered as I went out. Even the officers wished me well. In the office, I asked for a copy of my warrant. Lt. Lawrence told me I wasn't entitled to it. He and another officer took me out, and we got into an unmarked car.

A few miles down the road, Lawrence turned to me. "I've heard you do good business at your fruit stand. Lots of hard work, huh?"

"Keeps us busy, yes."

"Do you grow all your own fruits and vegetables?"

"Most of them. Some things we buy from other farmers."

"Who does all the work—you?"

"My sisters take care of that end of the business. I manage the dairy, milk the cows."

It was a half-hour drive to court. Ten minutes before we arrived, one of the officers made a call on his car phone. When he got off the phone he said, "They say there are already thirty people there." There was a hint of alarm in his voice.

After a silence, Lawrence spoke. "Barbara, I know you have to do what you think is right, but we'd really appreciate it if you could help us keep this as low key as possible." He paused. "It's okay to have support. Just please keep in mind there are only two of us, and we did this in confidence that things would go relatively smoothly."

"My people have always been non-violent," I said.

"I know. But any group can have those few who are not rational," he said. "It would be helpful if you would cooperate."

I sighed. "I want you to know it is not my pleasure to be uncooperative. It has been very, very hard for me to take this noncompliant position."

"Barbara, you don't know what we're used to dealing with," Lawrence said. "You were a queen."

He made another phone call. When he got off the phone he said, "Better do your hair, Barb—you're gonna be on TV again!"

A message came through their radio: "Drive right up, and just walk her in."

We drove up to a rural highway department building that served as town hall in my home township of Charlotte. There were dozens of cars in the parking lot. A neighbor's John Deere tractor was parked near the road, with a large sign mounted on it. It read: "Barbara Lyn, you are our hero!"

Lt. Lawrence opened my door. "Barbara, could you step out?"

I remained seated. My brother-in-law, Joe, came up close to the car. The officers stepped in front of him. Joe grabbed my hand for a handshake.

"Wait a minute, please," one officer said to Joe as they pulled me out of the car. Family members and friends crowded around me for hugs and kisses. I tried to hug, but couldn't because of the handcuffs. The officers escorted me in to the courthouse.

Judge Newton sat behind a table in the small town hall that served as a courtroom. He asked the officers to keep the crowd out until after he'd read my paperwork. The officers took off my handcuffs, seated me in front of the judge, and stood nearby.

Outside the window about fifty people had gathered, some holding signs that read, "Keep it up, Barbara Lyn!" Two television news reporters were there, too.

When the judge opened the courthouse door, more than thirty people entered. They could barely get into the small courtroom. An occupancy limit of twenty was posted on a fading sign on the wall. Miriam stood behind my chair, arms wrapped around my neck.

"Miss Lapp, you are charged with custodial interference," Judge Newton began. He read both my charges.

"Do you wish to get an attorney?" he asked.

"Judge, this court does not have jurisdiction," I said. "There is no injured party, there's no one been harmed. Therefore, I'm a free person. And I'm not agreeable to be part of this proceeding."

"That still does not answer my question whether you wish to obtain counsel," Judge Newton said.

"Sir, I have no part in this proceeding."

"At this time, I want to adjourn it until the 29th of July...," the judge said, "and if I release you on your own recognizance now, will you affirm that you would be here on the 29th?"

I didn't answer.

The crowd of people around me seemed to have stopped breathing. Miriam, with her arms still wrapped around me, bent forward and looked into my face. Outside, TV cameras were pressed against the window. But my voice would not say yes, because deep inside I knew this was all wrong.

The silence was broken when several spectators began to speak. Judge Newton brought down his gavel. "No! I'm talking to her. Everybody's supposed to be quiet here."

Finally I spoke. "Sir, I'm a free person until it has been proven by a jury of my peers that I am not free."

"If I release you on your own recognizance you are a free person. Except, that I want the condition that you will guarantee to appear back here and also stay out of trouble while you are released this way," Judge Newton said.

"I've always stayed out of trouble. I've always complied with the law. That I will affirm."

"You will affirm that you will be here then on the 29th?"

"I will comply with any lawful order."

"This is a lawful order then. You'll be here on the 29th—"

"Well, at this point, I'm the same free person I was yesterday and the day before. I will exercise my freedom to leave here," I said, rising from my chair. I walked out, Miriam in front of me, as the crowd broke into applause.

"Yea!" several people yelled in unison. "You're a hero!" The judge and two officers stayed motionless in the courtroom, as the rest of the group scrambled to follow me out.

"Stay close around her—tight circle!" Hannah told the crowd.

Cameramen and reporters broke through the protective circle of family and friends. "How do you feel?" they asked. "Where are you going from here?"

"Going home—to milk the cows!"

The Post Journal—July 14, 1993:

Ms. Lapp's surprise departure abruptly ended the arraignment.... Neither the judge nor the officials from the Chautauqua County Sheriff's Department attempted to stop Ms. Lapp, whose family quickly drove her to the family farm on Cassadaga Road where she is today. Ms. Lapp made no commitment to return to the Town Court on July 29, as ordered by Judge Newton."

In the weeks after my arrest I was inundated with phone calls, media inquiries, and requests for help from other families in trouble with Social Services. I made visits to Don Stefan at the Cattaraugus County jail, and plotted phone contacts between him and Billy, who was becoming increasingly disturbed about the prolonged separation from his father. Miraculously, Don's release date was set for September 1, four months earlier than expected. Apparently the Cattaraugus County jail ignored the court's stipulation that Don's six-month term be served in addition to the two months he had served before sentencing. Besides that, they deducted two months for "good behavior," as is customary.

Meanwhile, our crops were ripening. Family members, from six-year-old nieces and nephews to my 66-year-old parents, were caught up in a flurry of summer farm activities—picking peas and corn, making hay, and trucking melons and tomatoes from southern states, for our fruit stand.

In my spare time I picked raspberries with Miriam and her cousins—and worked on legal papers for my defense. Andy Melechinsky assisted me in drafting a four-page document entitled, "Jurisdictional Challenge, Counter Complaint and Claim for Damages." It outlined violations of due process in my case, charged officials with unlawful arrest, and required them to "provide substantial proof that further and similar malicious acts under color of law will not be perpetrated against harmless citizens." I went to law libraries, studied historical writings on the Bill of Rights, and searched my soul for answers to the moral questions surrounding my legal dilemma.

"*Will* you appear?" a Buffalo TV program director asked me during a live interview, a few days before the court hearing scheduled for July 29.

＊　　＊　　＊

More than a hundred people convened in the parking lot of the Town of Charlotte Court. A half dozen members of the media were there too. It was July 29, 6:45 PM—almost time for my hearing to begin.

Black clouds rolled overhead, darkening the balmy summer evening. Standing beside my car, I spoke to the crowd through a public address system. I showed them three documents the court had filed against me, each entitled, "The People of the State of New York vs. Barbara Lyn Lapp."

"These three papers have abused the name of the people," I said. "Not a single person— not one soul—in the State of New York has come forward with a personal complaint against me. Tell me, where is the crime?"

"There is none," said a woman from the crowd.

I continued. "I don't know if the judge is here yet. When he comes, I'm not going in to see him." I held up the jurisdictional challenge papers. "My sister will deliver this to the judge…. When he set this calendar call date, I promised him I would appear tonight if he issued any lawful order. The only thing I received from him was a handwritten notice that said, 'please appear.'

"The law, under the Constitution of the United States; the law, under all time-tested rules of honor and justice; and the law, by any simple standard of common sense and human decency, dictates that no person shall be deprived of liberty without due process. I have agreed to abide by the law, and I'm only asking Judge Newton to do the same."

Someone in the crowd spoke up. "Barbara, were there ever any orders to hand over Billy, or stop keeping him at your home?"

"I have not violated any orders—written or verbal," I said. "There have been no demands made to me by either the sheriff's department, the judge, or the parents involved in the case. The only order I know of was directed to the sheriff—not to me."

Just as I finished speaking, a violent thunderstorm hit. People fled for shelter—some to the courthouse, others to their cars. Newsmen scrambled to get their cameras under cover. The courtroom and the short hall leading up to it filled with people, but there was not room for everyone. Some of them stood with me under the eaves of the building. My shoes were soaked with water that poured from the roof.

"This court's never seen so many people," an attorney said as he squeezed through the hall leading to the courtroom.

I gave Hannah the legal papers, and she went in. Susan followed with our video camera.

"Out with that!" the judge yelled, waving his hand. "Out with the TV!"

Susan backed up. I moved into the hallway. The door to the courtroom was open. Judge Newton sat at the table with the assistant district attorney, Paul Andrews. Hannah handed the papers to the judge.

"This is *her* case," he said, his voice shaking. "When she is sitting there, I'll take the paperwork."

"She is available only if there is a lawful grand jury order," Hannah told the judge.

"Have her come in—the order is right here," he said.

"I guess I'm not in charge of bringing her in," Hannah said.

"She's in charge of bringing herself in!" Judge Newton yelled. "This case is *not* going to proceed until she is in here!"

Paul Andrews tried to calm him. "Judge, judge—wait, we don't play games. Let's just adjourn these proceedings," he said. "These people are now turning this into a circus. I don't think it's proper. We've got cameras right outside the window, taking pictures in here. We've got people playing games. It's a media circus."

A woman spectator spoke up. "What is the game we're playing? We're fighting for our Constitutional rights. Is that a game?"

Andrews said, "I think, judge, I'm not going to get into arguing with a mob—"

"A mob? I'm a mob?" the woman asked.

A clap of thunder hushed the proceedings for a moment.

From the hallway, I put my head inside the courtroom. "Judge, it is your lawful duty to throw these charges out. They came from the dirt, and should be thrown back into the dirt."

"If you want to speak, get in here!" the judge said.

Protests erupted from the crowd.

"This is not justice!"

"Throw it out!" rang a chorus of voices.

"We want the real justice! We want the Constitution of America upheld!" a woman outside the courtroom yelled at the top of her voice.

"What are you, a criminal?" someone challenged the judge.

"Criminals!" others shouted.

"The people say, throw it out!"

Judge Newton, still sitting at his desk in the courtroom, called to the crowd. "You people go! We have more business."

Hannah came out to the hall. "He's refusing to take the papers," she told me.

"Tell him we won't go until he takes them," I said.

She went back to the courtroom, and returned quickly. "He took them. Let's go!" she said.

It was still raining heavily. Members of the crowd who had been unable to get into the courtroom were soaked.

A radio reporter in a rain suit approached me. "Barbara Lyn, are you going to make a statement for us?" he asked.

Someone from the group opened a door into an adjacent highway equipment garage, to accommodate the crowd. Standing by the doorway of the garage, I began to read aloud a copy of the jurisdictional challenge that had just been submitted to the court. "Be it known to all concerned that this court does not, and lawfully cannot have jurisdiction over Barbara Lyn Lapp because, one, there is no victim; two, no private person has sworn under oath that harm has been done to person or property; three, there has not been a probable cause finding by a probable cause grand jury; four, the complainant and its state-paid judge are in a conflict of interest position with the U.S. Constitution, Article three, Section two...."

"In this regard, questions of law to be answered by the prosecuting attorney and/or presiding judge are: Can the U.S. Constitution and its mandates, especially those in Amendments four, five, and six, be ignored or violated by any judge or other official?"

I read the remainder of the document, which named individual officials in Cattaraugus and Chautauqua counties, alleging violations of law by each of them.

When I finished reading, the people started clapping. Whistles and screams rose above the applause, echoing through the garage and courthouse.

"Long live justice!" a man shouted.

"What happens from here?" asked someone from the media.

"I will try to stay out of court until this jurisdictional challenge is answered," I said. "Then I will cooperate."

More questions came from the crowd. I continued. "The government is holding captive the most vulnerable members of society—our children. Just as the liberation of nineteenth century slaves depended on people who helped them escape, the liberation of children held captive by the state now depends on responsible adults standing up for them."

A half hour had passed since court was adjourned. Some members of the group were leaving. A radio reporter asked me quietly, "Barbara, what should the news say about Billy's whereabouts?"

"He is still at our place, and it's no secret," I answered.

Two days after the Town Court hearing I received a letter from the district attorney's office. It said the Chautauqua County Grand Jury had indicted me on charges of "Obstruction of Governmental Administration," "Conspiracy," and "Custodial Interference." In the letter, Paul Andrews, the assistant DA, advised me to appear in County Court on August 16 for arraignment. "Failure to appear at this time will likely result in a warrant for your arrest," he wrote.

August 3, 1993—WJTN Radio:

ANNOUNCER: The president of the Chautauqua County chapter of VOCAL has been secretly indicted by a county grand jury..., but Lapp is questioning that indictment.

LAPP: They know very well that I've been demanding lawful process throughout, and just the fact that they didn't give me the opportunity to speak with the grand jury tells me they have violated yet another lawful process....

JAMES SUBJACK, DISTRICT ATTORNEY: I don't care how just her cause is, how strongly she believes in it, there's laws by which she has to abide. And if she doesn't abide by them—if she violates the law, she needs to be prosecuted like anyone else.

CHAPTER 4

Melee

By Barbara Lyn

On August 16, 1993, the day I was ordered to appear in court, a convoy of over a dozen cars crossed the hills and valleys that spanned the fourteen miles between our homestead and Mayville, New York—home of the county courthouse. I was in the second vehicle, riding with Lynn Carroll Bedford in her little Datsun pickup. Miriam sat between us.

"Lynn, if I get arrested, don't let anything happen to Billy," I said. "His dad gets home in just two weeks."

One of the cars in the caravan was our blue Subaru station wagon. It was loaded with protest signs we had prepared for a rally outside the courthouse.

Beside me, Miriam looked up, her dark eyes piercing into mine. "But Mom, they won't arrest you today, will they?" she asked.

"I don't think so, Miriam," I said. "They'll probably wait for a chance when there aren't as many people around."

One by one the cars in the caravan pulled into a large parking lot behind the courthouse. Dozens of people were gathered. Besides Miriam, family members present were my father and mother, four of my sisters, my brother Nathan, two brothers-in-law, and five nieces and nephews. Others in the group were neighbors who had known my parents since I was a little girl, customers of our fruit stand, a former legislator, and even a number of people I didn't recognize. Two gentlemen who came, Richard Tripp and Charles Gardiner, I had become acquainted with through concerned citizens groups. They had driven in from more than a hundred miles away. Tom and Kevin Stefan were in the group, as well as other teenagers and children whose families had contacted our VOCAL hotline. Three television crews were there, also.

I handed Rachel my jurisdictional challenge to County Court, and instructed her to deliver it to the court clerk, on the second floor of the courthouse. Then I spoke through a microphone to the gathered crowd. "I'm here to make it clear I will not submit to a court system that can throw a child in a garbage dump, then throw in jail anyone who tries to help that child live again," I began. Giving my reasons for not cooperating with the court, I said, "As far as I'm concerned there hasn't been any legally valid notice for me to be here today.... I got a letter from the district attorney's office stating that I'd been indicted. It was not a summons, nor was it signed by a magistrate....

"That type of secret indictment is clearly invalid in a free country. If we are going to submit to secret proceedings and court systems that don't abide by any rules, we might as well go back to the sixteenth century Star Chambers....

"I have prepared my jurisdictional challenge for the court, telling them that at such time as they agree to abide by the rules of law, I will cooperate. I want to make it clear, once again, that I'm more than willing to do that at any time the court begins to demonstrate some loyalty to the laws of our nation."

Richard Tripp, dressed in a business suit, stepped up and took the microphone. An advocate for reform of Family Court, Richard had lost custody of his own son through false child abuse allegations. "Who is the victim of Barbara Lyn Lapp's actions of trying to reunite Billy Stefan with his father?" he began. "Which of you has the cruelty, as Family Court did, to restrain a child crying for his parent, then jail the parent for trying to comfort his child? The criminals in this case are the people within the Family Court system....

"When a law is unjust, when families are senselessly torn apart," Richard continued, his voice rising in fervor, "it is not only our right to stand here in defiance, just as we stand today—it is our duty...."

After he ended his speech, members of the group selected protest signs from the back of our station wagon and lined up in the parking lot. Some signs read, "Honor the Constitution—it's the law;" "Barbara Lyn—persecuted for caring;" "Justice in—lynch law out."

Rachel returned from the courthouse and informed the group that the papers had been received and stamped by the court.

My sister, Susan, was leading the rally. "Let's take a walk down the road, and through the park," she told the crowd. "I'll remind everybody not to block sidewalks. Respect the traffic, respect pedestrians—we're going to be quiet and peaceable. I'm going to lead, and you can follow. Put about ten feet between each person."

"Are we going to be quiet and peaceable only until they try to drag Barbara away?" Hannah kidded.

"We'll each use our own judgment on that," Susan said, smiling.

"We'll form a circle, right?" asked Nathan.

The crowd, with some late arrivals, had grown to about sixty. Susan in the lead, we formed a line on the sidewalk, moved slowly past the courthouse, then continued around the block, past the jail.

Ken Bellet, an older man who walked with a cane, came up beside Rachel and me as we walked single file. A few years earlier Ken had lost a battle with Social Services involving his own grandchildren. He had also participated in war protests in Washington during the sixties, and was the only one in our group besides Charlie Gardiner who was experienced with organized protests. He carried a copy of the Constitution in his shirt pocket. From another pocket, he pulled a pair of handcuffs. "See this?" he said to Rachel, holding up the handcuffs. "If they take her, they're taking me with her." Ken explained that he would fasten one cuff to his hand, and one to mine. He laughed when he saw I was frowning. "It's not like I'll stop your arrest," he said. "It's up to them if they want both of us."

For two hours, the group walked around the streets of Mayville. Charlie and a few others stood on street corners, handing leaflets to passersby. Families with children stopped to rest on the grass along the road, signs turned toward traffic. Motorists stared as they passed our block-long lineup, some honking their horns and raising thumbs in support.

Seventy-five feet back from the road was the courthouse. A stately, historic building, its entrance was marked by a two-story high portico rising above a forty-foot width of concrete steps. Above the portico was a majestic white dome, studded with tall, narrow windows.

A news reporter for the *Evening Observer*, Jim Fox, came out of the courthouse. "Your case is coming up," he told me. "Are you going to go in?"

"Not unless the judge has somebody come and haul me in," I said.

"He probably will," Jim Fox said as he wrote in his notebook. Then he walked back into the courthouse.

"Do you think he talked to the judge?" asked Hannah.

"I don't know," I said. "But I still don't think they'll come out here with all these people around."

"We could sit in a tight circle, holding hands," suggested Richard

Tripp. "Gandhi style. How about that, Barbara? You could be in the middle."

"I guess not," I said. "I don't think we should try to block them."

Miriam and I crossed the street to a Yellow Goose convenience store and bought soda pop. We came back and sat down on the courthouse lawn, near the sidewalk. Ken Bellet joined us on the grass, laying his cane beside him. Mom walked toward us, carrying a protest sign. "End the cruelty," it read. She looked tired.

"Mom, why don't you sit down with us?" I asked. She sat down, smoothed out her long gray skirt, and propped her sign against her chest. The courthouse was directly behind us, twenty-some yards away.

As noon approached, some of the crowd began to leave. Those who were staying conferred about lunch, and we decided to order sandwiches from the Mayville Diner, right across the street. A waitress came over and took our orders. "Lunch should be ready shortly after twelve," she said. "We'll bring it over."

It was 11:35. We were waiting for lunch when two officers in plainclothes, Sgt. Rex Rater and Sgt. James Tyka, came out of the courthouse. A dozen members of the group hurriedly came near me. Television cameramen hoisted their cameras onto their shoulders. I stayed seated on the lawn, now surrounded by a circle of supporters.

Coming close, Sgt. Tyka stooped, peering through the legs of the people. "Hey Barb? The judge says he will be calling your case just momentarily, okay?"

"Okay," I said. Both men turned and went back to the courthouse.

People in the group began to speak together in hushed tones. Some predicted the officers would be back, others wagered they wouldn't.

"If they do come for me, you should follow to the courtroom," I said.

Twenty minutes passed. Charlie Gardiner, who had gone into the courtroom to watch the proceedings, came out. He anxiously announced that Paul Andrews, the assistant DA, had made a request to Judge Himelein for a bench warrant for my arrest.

"Maybe you should go home now," Hannah said to me.

"No. Might as well face them square," I said, as confidently as I could.

"They'll probably come out and get you right here, don't you think?" Rachel asked.

By Rachel

It was almost noon. I had to leave the rally to pick up a load of apples and plums in Ripley, then get back to the fruit stand by two.

"I feel bad about leaving," I told Barbara. "They might come for you when I'm not here."

"There's nothing you can do about it anyway," she said.

I started walking toward my truck. Then I heard someone say, "There they are!" I looked back and saw two men in dark business suits coming down the walkway from the courthouse, toward Barbara. I hurried back and stood beside her. The two men approached at a brisk stride.

"That's Rex Rater and Lt. Lawrence," Barbara said. Sgt. Peter Pett, in a beige suit was close behind.

Several dozen people from the crowd quickly formed a circle around Barbara. Displaying their signs, the crowd began to chant, "Just give us justice!" Mom put her arms around Barbara. Standing on her other side, I did the same.

"Barb!" called Lt. Lawrence. The crowd quieted for a moment to listen. "Excuse us," he said, pushing aside several people at the outside of the circle. "Come, Barbara, I need to talk to you."

Some of the people began to chant again, while Dad, walking along the outer circle of the crowd, came toward the officers. "Take care of your own crimes," he told them as he met Sgt. Rater heading for Barbara. A protest sign in his right hand, Dad stretched his left hand forward, blocking him. But Rater continued forward at a fast pace, and Dad's hand collided with his chin. Rater's head jerked back.

"That's it! You're under arrest," said Sgt. Pett. He grabbed Dad's arm from behind, pulled his hands back, and handcuffed him.

Dad looked back in surprise. "What kind of arrest is this?" he asked.

Meanwhile, Sgt. Rater and Lt. Lawrence were pushing themselves into the crowd, their hands stretched toward Barbara.

"Leave her alone!" yelled the people. My brother-in-law, Joe Torres, who had been eating lunch on the courthouse steps with his wife and children, ran toward us.

Hannah went up to Lawrence, with a video camera on her shoulder. "Sir, could you identify yourself?" she asked.

Lawrence, barging forward, didn't stop to look at her. "I'm from the Sheriff's Department," he said, breathing hard. Tom Stefan moved in front of him. Lawrence shouted, "Knock it off!" He put his arm around Tom's neck and pinned him against his chest. Tom stumbled and fell free.

Ken Bellet, walking with his cane, had managed to get inside the circle, right behind Barbara. As the people jostled around us, he and Nathan struggled to attach Ken's handcuff to her.

Lawrence reached through the crowd and grabbed Barbara's other hand.

"If she goes, I go too," Ken said. "You're gonna take me with 'er!"

By Barbara Lyn

Lt. Lawrence's grip on my hand sent shivers through me. At that moment, even the touch of all the loved ones around me offered no consolation. Next will be handcuffs, I thought. Then jail again. Why was I so foolishly confident this wouldn't happen today?

Lawrence pulled hard. Rachel and Mom, their arms around my waist, were jolted forward. "Barbara, I think we're going to fall," Mom said, her voice barely audible amid the loud cries of protest from the crowd.

By Rachel

Ken held onto Barbara with one hand. His cane had fallen, his handcuff plan aborted. Sgt. Rater came up behind Ken and yanked on his belt. Joe Torres and a neighbor, Dick Daniels, came in on each side of Rater, and tried to pull his hands off Ken. Rater swung around to face Dick, who was wearing a straw cowboy hat, and grabbed his arms. Dick responded instantly, grabbing Rater's arms. They glared into each other's eyes and shook each other vigorously. The cowboy hat fell to the ground as the pair rocked back and forth.

"Knock it off!" Rater said, his voice shaking. "You're under arrest!"

"Under arrest for *what?*" asked Dick. "I'm just standing here, man!"

Arms still locked, Rater barged forward and pushed Dick back several yards. His wife, Donna, tugged on Rater's arm. "Get your hands off my husband!" she yelled. Both men dropped their grip on each other and drew a fist. Then Rater suddenly turned and darted toward Barbara.

"Don't hurt those ladies!" said Donna.

"Nobody's gonna hurt anybody," Rater responded.

"I don't believe you!" she said. "You don't just force your way into a crowd of people."

Meanwhile, Lt. Lawrence, inside the circle, had let go of Barbara. He went after Ken, and yanked him away from her. Ken fell backward. Two women stumbled and fell with him. Almost losing my balance, I dropped to my knees and wrapped my arms around Barbara's left leg. I held tightly, thinking: When they've cleared everyone else away from her, I'll still be here.

Rater had broken through the crowd. He and Lawrence advanced toward Barbara, trampling Ken, who lay on the ground.

"Be careful, you're hurting the old man!" Mom yelled.

Lt. Lawrence nearly had Barbara's hand again when Joe Torres came up and grabbed his arm. Lawrence shouted, "Knock it off, pal!" He shook himself free from Joe's grip. Instantly, Sgt. Pett came up behind Joe, threw his arm around his throat, and locked his head to his chest. Joe twisted free, then moved back into the crowd. Pett reached to his belt and took out his handcuffs. "Put your hands behind your back," he said to Joe, his face red and menacing. "You're under arrest!"

"Leave us alone," Joe said, backing away,

Joe's wife, Nancy, gathered their children. "Stand back here!" she said hurriedly as she escorted them away.

Meanwhile, a few people had slipped in between Lawrence and Barbara. Tom Stefan again stood in front of Lawrence. This time Lawrence threw Tom to the ground, then struck Hannah across her midsection with the back of his arm, sending her reeling.

"Watch it!" a woman shrieked, as Hannah landed at the foot of a tree, her video camera and glasses beside her.

Several more officers arrived, and stood outside the circle. Inside, Lawrence lunged forward and grabbed Barbara's left hand again, which was draped over Mom's shoulder. "You're under arrest," he said. Holding her wrist, he attached a handcuff. The other cuff dangled on its silver chain close to my head, as I knelt by her side.

"This isn't justice!" someone shouted.

"She's done no harm."

"Where's your warrant?"

Rater reached for Barbara's other hand, but Dick Daniels blocked him. Rater dropped his hands to his sides. "Listen, listen!" he said, raising his right hand. He could barely be heard above the noise of the crowd.

By Barbara Lyn

Minutes had passed since anyone had spoken to me.

"Barb, come on now," Lt. Lawrence said as he held my hand, handcuff attached. "Why don't you stop this? Just tell these people to leave, Barb. Someone's gonna get hurt if you don't."

Almost smothered by the crowd, I was vaguely aware of more officers around me. Physical struggles seemed to be escalating, and there was a lot of yelling.

I considered Lawrence's request. But to speak would be futile. It was too late to remedy the near-panic reaction of the crowd, after the police had used irrational force on them. The noise was too great, emotions too strong.

I remembered my previous discussion with Lawrence regarding my position on passive noncompliance. Why does he think I would cooperate now?

"I've spoken to you before," I told Lawrence. "You know better than doing this. You know I haven't harmed anyone." As he pulled on my hand, Rachel held my leg. Mom and Nathan had their arms around me, too. I struggled to keep my balance.

By Rachel

As Lawrence was speaking to Barbara, Rater addressed the crowd. "The judge has issued a warrant," he said.

"She has not done anything wrong," Nathan said. "That warrant is toilet paper!"

"Show who she hurt," a woman said.

"Where's your legal cause?"

"What's your name?" someone demanded.

Nathan answered, "It's Mr. Rater."

"Mr. Rater, Mr. Rater!" the crowd began to chant.

"She *has* to go in," Rater said.

"Mr. Rater, you're *wrong!*" a woman said.

Rater looked away, his lips drawn tightly. Joe squeezed in beside him, one hand on his arm. Rater turned abruptly. "Don't get arrested!" he said, shoving Joe with his shoulder.

"Careful, there are pregnant women in here," someone said.

One of the officers pulled out his radio and called into it. A moment later, the sheriff, John R. Bentley, and a half dozen uniformed officers ran down the courthouse steps, across the lawn, and surrounded the crowd. Lawrence and Rater were still in the middle with Mom, Barbara and me. For a moment, no one moved. Officers looked from side to side, and glanced at each other across the crowd. A large, balding officer gave a nod. Then Lt. Lawrence, who had lost his hold on Barbara for the second time, raised his chin and shouted, "Pull 'em back!" A long, sharp whistle followed. Suddenly the officers plowed forward, overpowering the lines of people, shoving some to the ground.

A chorus of protests erupted. "Oh-h, no-o!" a woman moaned. Some of the people who had been shoved aside, jumped right back and tightened around us. Hannah hurriedly gave her video camera to Susan and ducked under an officer's elbow, into the group.

"Pull 'em off of us!" shouted Lawrence.

A half dozen more officers arrived, coming from the courthouse, the jail, and even from the diner across the street. From all sides they assailed the crowd, grabbing and throwing people aside. "You're one! You're two! You're three!" shouted one uniformed deputy as he sent bodies flying backwards.

"What are you doing?" someone yelled.

"This is crazy!"

"Kidnappers!"

"Creeps!"

Lawrence and Sgt. Pett plunged forward and grabbed Barbara's arms. They jerked her violently, pulling her to the ground. Barbara landed face down, on top of Mom.

"Get her out of here!" an officer hollered. "Drag her out of here!" They began to drag Barbara down the slope toward the road.

Jack Crate, a senior citizen from our group, followed Lawrence. "Easy, easy," he said, tugging on Lawrence's arm. Just then Tom Stefan stumbled backwards out of the crowd, falling onto the arms of Lawrence and Pett. They lost their grip on Barbara and fell on their seats, then jumped up, regained their hold, and pulled Barbara to the curb. Mom and I, still hanging onto Barbara, were dragged along with her. Our skirts were displaced, exposing our legs.

A woman who stood watching screamed in terror, "My God!"

Susan, filming with our video camera, yelled, "Stop it! Stop it!"

"Next they'll pull guns and shoot us!" said an older lady, clutching her arms to her chest.

Deputy Gary Giambrone, uniformed and wearing a black hat, plunged through the crowd, throwing three men and a woman head-long to the ground. The woman lay on the grass, face down, groaning. Jack Crate, one of the men who had fallen, jumped back up and turned to face Giambrone. "Look what you did!" he shouted. "Who do you think you are?"

"I'll show you in a minute!" Giambrone said. Moving up against Jack with arms raised, he lifted his knee, shouting, "Back off! Back off!"

Several officers hovered over Barbara, trying to get her hands. Her right hand was trapped under her body, her left hand, still in cuffs, wrapped around Mom.

"Barbara, come off!" an officer said.

"She's my daughter!" Mom cried. "She's my daughter!"

An officer tried to pull my arm off Barbara's leg.

"Don't do that," I said. I pulled Barbara's skirt down to cover her legs.

"Look what you've done," said Joe, his hand stretched toward Sgt. Rater. "Look what you've done here!"

Nathan came and knelt beside Barbara, his arm over her shoulder. Sgt. Rater pulled him into a sitting position and pushed his head down to the ground.

"You're breaking my back!" Nathan screamed.

"Help!" Mom called. "Nathan, why don't you help us? They're stepping on us!"

Nathan broke free and darted to Mom's side. Two officers gripped him by his head and jabbed their fingers under his jaw. Pulling Nathan by his neck and shoulders, they dragged him head first over Barbara and Mom. Nathan stumbled to his feet, panting, his face and throat red.

"Nathan, be careful! They'll have you arrested," said Marilyn Danielson, a poised older woman from our group. Richard Tripp, who was trying to calm members of the crowd, put his arm around Nathan and escorted him away.

By Barbara Lyn

A half dozen officers leaned over me, where I lay on the ground with Rachel and Mom. My handcuffed hand with Mom's weight on it was hurting so much I was getting faint. I took long, deep breaths. It seemed as if a lot of time had passed. I couldn't understand why the officers weren't taking me.

Suddenly one of them yanked my arm out from under Mom. Then he rolled her onto her back, lifted his foot and punched the heel of his boot under her ribs. "There!" he said.

Mom gasped.

My hands were free again. Rachel, with her arms still around my leg, asked me if I was okay. "I'm alright, but I'm worried about Mom," I said. "I think it's enough. I want to get up."

Mom had somehow managed to get her arms around me again. Rachel lifted her head to look at her. "Mom's okay," she said.

The disgraceful position I was in was almost unbearable. I wanted the whole thing to end. But Rachel's and Mom's bodies against me offered a small barrier to the hands, shoes and pant legs of officers who pressed in on me. Mom had stopped talking. What if she wouldn't make it, I thought. Still face down on the ground, I turned slightly and wrapped my left arm tightly around her.

By Rachel

Sgt. Rater, straddling Barbara, reached for his handcuffs and leaned forward. His coat fell upward and snagged on his pistol in its holster.

"Leave her alone," people screamed.

"You're hurting them!" said Terry Mayer, a blond lady who stood several yards back from us. Dozens of others also remained on the outside of the circle, some still holding their protest signs high. On the sidewalk behind them was Dad, where the police had left him, standing in handcuffs. He was turned toward the crowd, watching in silence. Three TV cameramen and Susan circled the group, filming.

Closer to Barbara, Mom and me, there was constant turbulence, as officers warded off those who kept trying to get to us. Supporters all around us reached out hands to help those who had been pushed down. Frustrated officers were grabbing people and yelling, "You're under arrest! You're under arrest!" But they were hindered by Nathan, Hannah and several others who would pull on their arms whenever they tried to handcuff people.

Sgt. Rater, still straddling Barbara and attempting to handcuff her, could scarcely keep his balance. He teetered backwards, and came within inches of sitting on me.

Ken Bellet, who had given up his attempt to attach himself to Barbara, walked back into the group. Rater gave him a push, which sent him flying backwards down the slope. Ken tumbled off the curb and landed flat on the street between two parked cars, his cane lying beside him.

Rater put his handcuffs back under his coat and stepped off of Barbara. Then he and several other officers pulled upward on her arms. "Okay, Barb, come on," said one of them gruffly.

"*Look* at this!" another officer said. They paused and stared at our tangle of arms and legs, the three of us still embracing each other as we lay on the ground. One of them bent down close to my face. I could see only his eyes. "Let go!" he said.

"Get out of here!" I said.

Nathan squeezed in between two officers who knelt over us. They rose to their feet. "I've *had* it with you!" said one. Both of them put a hand on Nathan's chest and sent him flying backwards.

It took Nathan several seconds to recover. "I've had it with *kidnappers!*" he yelled.

"A bunch of pigs!" a lady said, her voice throaty. "Pigs! Pigs! Pigs!"

A teenage boy walked up behind an officer who was bending over us, and put his hand on the officer's pistol. Sheryl Christy, a young woman with long brown hair, grabbed his wrist. "We don't need that," she told the boy.

Joe Torres had been trying to get past the wall of officers around us. He finally pushed his way in and stood by my feet. Two officers grabbed his arms and sent him sprawling. He landed on the grass, close to his wife and three small daughters. Nancy knelt beside him, their daughters clinging to her long maternity jumper.

"Stay back!" Joe told Nancy, as two officers struggled to handcuff him. They wrestled Joe onto his stomach and pulled his hands behind him.

Joe's eight-year-old daughter looked into his face. "No, no!" she screamed, then bolted out into the busy village street. Betty Howard, a petite young woman standing nearby, restrained her. A neighbor of ours, Steve Goot, picked up her two younger sisters and held them. Dangling from the three-year-old's hands was a cardboard poster that read, "Honor our families."

Nancy was weeping. "No, don't take my husband," she said.

"We're just taking him for an appearance ticket," said an officer. "He's coming right back."

An officer pulled Mom to her feet and held her arms back. Mom began to run. The officer held on, running behind her.

Marilyn Danielson approached Sheriff Bentley, who stood outside the crowd, directing his deputies. "John! John!" she pleaded. "Stop this!"

"You're gonna hurt somebody! You're gonna hurt somebody!" Jack Crate said to the sheriff.

"Stay back!" Sheriff Bentley replied. He turned to face Susan, who stood behind him with the video camera. "I've had it with you!" he said. He slapped her camera, knocking it off her shoulder. Susan looked up at the sheriff, startled. Then she put the camera back on her shoulder and resumed filming.

I lay beside Barbara, clinging to her. Two officers pried my arms off Barbara's thigh. Two others pulled her to her feet. I still had her ankle locked between my knees. She stumbled. As she fell, our skirts flew up. I felt an officer's hands on my bare legs. Then one of them covered my face with his hand and pushed my head down on the grass.

"You can't do that to them!" a bystander screamed.

"You criminal bastards!" said another.

"Criminal a - - h - - -!"

Lynn Carroll Bedford, who had just come from the courthouse, ran toward us, hands outstretched, palms up. "Stop!" she screamed at the officers, her voice rising above the protests of the crowd. "Those aren't animals—they're human beings! You can't do this to people!" Lt. Lawrence came up from behind her. Jabbing two of his fingers into her eyes, and two into her nose, he pulled her head and body forcefully backwards.

Lynn screamed.

"They're poking her eyes out!" cried Kevin Stefan.

Dick Daniels walked up to Lawrence and grabbed his wrist. "That's not necessary," he said.

An officer ran up behind Dick and grabbed his arms. "You're under arrest!" he said, his handcuffs ready. But when he tried to attach them, the handcuffs fell to the ground. Dick's wife snatched them up and gave them to another woman in the crowd. When the officer turned to look for them, he couldn't find them. He let Dick go, and went back to the rest of the group.

In the meantime, Mom came running back to Barbara and me, her loose red blouse fluttering behind her. Barging in between the officers kneeling beside us, she yanked on the shoulder of one of them who was holding onto our bare legs. The officer she had just escaped from lunged for her. He lost his balance, his right leg swinging up behind him. But he caught Mom around her throat with his arm, pulled her back, and held her. Her glasses dangled from his hand.

Two officers grabbed my feet and legs below the knees. Another gripped my right knee. They started moving apart, spreading my legs.

"My God! Look what they're doing!" a woman cried.

The protests of the crowd turned into unintelligible, high pitched screams.

"I've got her now," Lawrence said as Barbara's foot slipped from my grip.

I got up quickly. An officer held my arms. "Let me go," I said, wriggling free.

Sgt. Rater and Lt. Lawrence pulled Barbara to her feet and locked their arms around her elbows. Nathan, who had just escaped a third attempt by officers to arrest him, came up to Lawrence and grabbed his arm. Two officers yanked him away from Lawrence and hurled him against a woman standing behind him. Nathan and the woman spiraled down the slope into each other, and struck a parked car with a crash.

Regaining his footing, Nathan ran back, again toward Barbara. This time officers caught him and pulled his hands behind his back. "You're done!" one of them said. "You're under arrest!" He pushed Nathan's head down and grabbed his collar at the throat, yanking downward. Buttons popping, Nathan's shirt flew open.

Richard Tripp rushed up to the officers. "Please don't take him," he pleaded, laying his hand on an officer's back. "He's the farmer. They can't run the farm without him."

The officers slowly relaxed their hold, and Nathan walked away.

By Barbara Lyn

After pulling me free from Rachel, Sgt. Rater, Lt. Lawrence, and five other officers walked me briskly to the courthouse. One of my shoes fell off, but I was too stunned to care. I looked over my shoulder, and couldn't understand why none of my family or supporters were following. I didn't want to leave them behind in despair. In a final burst of strength, I called back, "We won! We still won. We have the truth!"

"I can't believe you did this to us!" Lt. Lawrence said as he and Sgt. Rater pushed me through the door of the courthouse. "Jesus!" he said through his breath.

They walked fast. Lawrence was still scolding. "Is this what you wanted to happen? Is this what you really wanted, Barbara?" He was talking so fast he could hardly breathe. "I thought you said your supporters are non-violent. What happened to that?"

I didn't answer.

"I'm going to write up more charges," he went on. "Riot in the second, attempted escape, obstruction."

He turned to the other officers. "Go back and make some more arrests—the man with the lavender shirt, that Puerto Rican guy, the girl in the tan skirt—we can make room in the jail for everybody—we got lots of camera on this—we'll have a strong case."

We went down a stairs to the basement of the courthouse, then walked through the long tunnel to the county jail.

By Rachel

As Barbara disappeared into the courthouse, Marilyn Danielson again confronted the sheriff. "There aren't many decent people," she yelled, waving her hands. "And you take a girl in that's done nothing wrong! What did she do? She was protecting a child!"

People and officers were all over the courthouse lawn, their voices rising and falling with the noise of village traffic. Crumpled protest signs, hats and leftover lunches cluttered the area. Under a tree lay a sign that read, "The court system is incredibly corrupt."

Across the sidewalk I saw Miriam crying hysterically. A friend stood behind her, arms supporting Miriam's upper body as she rocked with screams.

"Miriam!" I called, running toward her. "Miriam!"

Suddenly I saw Mom being led toward the courthouse by two officers. I turned and ran to her.

"Get Miriam over here!" Mom yelled, her voice hoarse. I went to Miriam and brought her to Mom, putting my arms around both of them.

Sheriff Bentley grabbed my arm. "Please let them go," I said, bending forward and looking up into Bentley's face.

"You're an animal!" a woman screamed at the sheriff. "Criminal animals!"

Clinging to her grandmother, Miriam was wailing, "I want my mom, I want my mom!"

"She's going wherever I go!" Mom said to the officers. "Look what you're doing to this child! Let me take my granddaughter to the car to comfort her."

The officers who held Mom dropped their hands to their sides. They looked distressed.

"Let her go comfort the little girl," I said to them, my hands still on Mom and Miriam. Suddenly Mom turned and hurried away, sheltering Miriam in front of her. Donna Daniels put her arm around Mom's shoulder, walking with them.

An officer strode up to Donna. "You can't take my prisoner," he said. "She's under arrest." Mom and Miriam, with the officer behind them, ran to our car parked along the road and got in. My brother-in-law, Tony, was waiting at the wheel, and quickly drove them away.

Sheriff Bentley was still beside me, holding my arm.

"Do you want her?" asked an officer in front of me.

"Yes, take her!" the sheriff said, waving his hand.

Two officers closed in on me. They clutched my arms, bent my elbows, and pushed my wrists inward forcefully. The pain was numbing.

Just ahead, I saw Dad in handcuffs. Lynn Carroll Bedford walked up beside Dad and put her arms around him. "What are you doing to him?" she asked the officers. "He didn't do anything wrong!" Her voice was so loud it drowned out every other sound. "Where's your grand jury indictment?"

An officer said to Lynn, "Let go!" Two of them pulled her from Dad. One twisted her hands behind her back, and bent her wrists and fingers.

"O-ow!" Lynn screamed. "You're breaking my wrists!"

"No, we're not," the officer said, still wrenching her fingers. Lynn continued to scream out in pain.

As they took Dad toward the courthouse, Nathan ran up to him and held his arm. "What are you trying to do?" Nathan asked the officers.

"Take him in there," Deputy Giambrone said, gesturing toward the courthouse, "give him an appearance ticket, and he can leave!"

Susan went up to Nathan, who was still holding onto Dad. She put her hand on Nathan's shoulder. Nathan turned to her. "What should I do?" he asked.

"I think you should stay away from them," Susan said, pulling his buttonless shirt together. "We need you at home."

A few feet away, I was wedged between two officers, as they whisked me up the courthouse steps. The officer on my left swore, using an obscene word.

Looking at him for the first time, I said, "That's pretty nasty language. I'm not used to words like that."

"I didn't say anything," he said. Both of the officers laughed.

I was escorted inside the courthouse, where they handcuffed me, pulling my arms behind my back. Then, twisting my handcuffs until I nearly blacked out in pain, they took me up a flight of stairs, through the courtroom, and into a small waiting room just outside it. There were several wooden chairs in the room, and on one side, an elevator door. An officer in street clothes sat slumped in one of the chairs, elbows on his knees. His hair was damp and disheveled.

The man looked familiar. "What are you doing here?" I asked. "Are you helping to use force on me, too?"

"Give me a break," he said.

"You come to our fruit stand, don't you?"

"No," he said, not looking up. He left and did not return.

I stood waiting, my hands so tightly cuffed they were numb.

By Barbara Lyn

In the jail booking room, Corrections Officer (CO) Louise White was in charge of booking me. She looked at me coldly. "So much for pacifism," she said. She got out jail intake forms.

"Date of birth?" she began.

"I've been here before," I said. "You know I won't cooperate an inch with this process."

At a nearby desk an officer said, "It's going to be different this time, Barbara."

"In what way?"

"You're gonna be put in jail clothes. You *will* cooperate."

"Oh," I said.

CO Louise went on questioning me. "Social security number?"

"I don't want to answer those questions."

"Any health problems? Taking any medications?"

"How many times do you expect me to tell you I won't answer?" I turned in my chair and looked at the wall.

"Have you ever tried to hurt yourself?"

I laughed involuntarily. "This is ridiculous," I said. "You people are ridiculous!" I got out of the chair and stood facing the wall. Two officers caught me and forced me to sit down, facing CO Louise.

"Do you feel suicidal now?" she asked.

I didn't answer.

"I'm going to refer you to Mental Health," she said.

Officers took me by the arm, lifted me up, and walked me into a cell—the same one I'd been in a month ago. The clock in the cell-block said 12:25.

By Rachel

I was still waiting in the small room, when several officers carried Lynn Carroll Bedford in. They set her down on the floor, hands bound behind her. She sat hunched forward, her feet in front of her. Her face looked red and swollen.

The room was filled with officers. A young one standing near me had a name tag that said, "Anderson."

"What are you doing? Are you preventing my freedom?" I asked him. "I haven't harmed anyone—"

He interrupted. "I don't have anything to do with this."

"You have nothing to do with this? Then I will leave." I walked toward the door.

He blocked the doorway.

"You're keeping me from leaving. You said you have nothing to do with this."

He looked like he was trying not to smile. "What I mean—I'm only following orders."

"Do you follow all orders?"

"Yes."

"Even if they're bad?"

"Yep. Good or bad, I follow them all."

"That's pretty base. Even as a child I was taught to discern between good and bad, and choose the good," I said.

Soon he stepped aside and sat down in a chair beside the doorway.

"I guess I'll leave now," I said. "You said you have nothing to do with this."

He grabbed my handcuffs, twisted them, and pulled me backwards into a chair.

"You're worse than a child," he said. "You're worse than my two-year-old. You're making me babysit you."

"Hitler's men followed orders too," I said.

"These are entirely different circumstances," he said. "This is a free country, and we have courts to settle things."

Lynn was seated on the floor where the officers had put her. I knelt down beside her. "Are you okay, Lynn?" I asked. She told me her hand felt like it was broken.

Anderson stooped down, and asked if he should loosen my cuffs.

"Yes," I said.   "It hurts."

He adjusted them. "Is that better?"

"I think so," I said, wriggling my fingers. "My hand is numb—yes, it feels better. Thank you."

I asked if I could call home.

"Not now, " Anderson said.

"My family is expecting me. I was supposed to be at the fruit stand when my hired girl leaves."

"Tough."

Hours passed. I sat in a chair for awhile, then stood gazing out the window.

"Now she's making a statement," an officer mocked. "She's saying a prayer."

Lynn was sitting on the floor, very still.

"She must be sound asleep," an officer said.

"She's not snoring yet," said another.

Anderson opened the zipper to my purse, which was locked into the handcuffs behind me. I looked back, watching him. "What do you want in there?" I asked, as he leafed through the contents. "That's my dog book. Do you want to read it?"

Smiling, he opened another zipper and found cash. "What's that, bail money?" he kidded.

"No, I was on my way to Ripley to buy apples."

By Barbara Lyn

In my cell, locked in, I sat at a little metal table and leaned my head into my hands. Several women inmates came up to the bars. I asked one of them to call home for me. On the phone with my family, she relayed to me that Rachel, Dad, Joe and Lynn had been arrested. I felt nauseated. Was I the cause of all this?

At 3:00 I was called for arraignment. Lt. Lawrence and Sgt. Rater took me through the tunnel to court. I still had only one shoe. As we walked, Lt. Lawrence began to scold me again. "You said you would cooperate if there was a grand jury. Now you're going back on your word."

"I don't consider secret court processes acceptable under American law," I said.

In the holding area we met Rachel, Dad, Joe, and Lynn—all handcuffed with hands behind their backs. At least four officers were in the room.

Not wanting the officers to hear what we were saying, I spoke in Spanish to Joe, and "Deutch" (Pennsylvania Dutch) to Dad and Rachel. With Lynn, we spoke in English.

"Can you believe what happened?" Rachel asked.

Dad shook his head. "They do anything they want," he said.

Suddenly we heard songs coming from the adjoining courtroom. It was the voices of our family and supporters. We joined them in singing some verses of "Brighten the Corner," and, "My Country 'tis of Thee."

Then I was called to the courtroom. Judge Larry Himelein arraigned me only on my previous charges of custodial interference, conspiracy and obstruction. He did not mention any new charges resulting from the events of the day.

The officers took me back down to the jail booking room. A different CO, Carole Martin, was there. "Are you staying overnight?" she asked kindly. Handing me a stack of dark green clothes, she said. "You'll need to change into these."

"She won't do it," Lawrence said. "There are more coming in, and it's gonna be a problem."

"Don't they have to be fingerprinted?" CO Carole asked.

"Absolutely!" Lawrence said. "Not one of them is getting out of here without being fingerprinted and photographed." He was holding on to my arm, walking me from one part of the room to another. It seemed he didn't know what to do.

By Rachel

I had been waiting for three hours in the small waiting room. Finally, the officers took off my handcuffs and led me to court. The judge referred to me as "Jane Doe," as I hadn't given my name. Judge Himelein told me I was charged with two crimes, "Riot in the Second Degree," and "Obstruction of Governmental Administration," both of them misdemeanors. He informed me that these charges would be heard in Town of Chautauqua Court tomorrow at 1:30, and set bail at one thousand dollars for each of the charges. After my arraignment, the officers took me back to the waiting room. Then they came for Dad.

"This is not a court of law," Dad told them, "I won't go in voluntarily." Two officers carried him in. They left the door to the courtroom open. Dad was in front of the judge, dangling from the arms of the officers that were on each side, holding him.

Then I heard Dad's voice. "This is a big joke!" he said. "It's supposed to look like an honorable court. This is a court of dishonor." The officers were trying to lift him up by his arms, but couldn't make him stand. "I have no intention of standing up," Dad said.

The officers, stooped over Dad, tried to look at the judge as he detailed Dad's charges—obstructing, resisting and riot. "You could be sentenced to up to one year on each of these charges. All of them allege that you and others attempted to forcefully prevent the arrest of Barbara Lapp—"

"Let me out of here!" Dad interrupted. "I have no business in here. This is a *crazy* court! You know what started this? A child was being helped, and now all this. Why, this is crazy! You guys should have a heart for the children that Barbara was helping. This is not a lawful court at all. You're breaking the law—all kinds of laws. I don't want to be a part of this."

The judge ignored Dad's statement and continued, reading his right to an attorney. He entered a not guilty plea on Dad's behalf, and set bail at three thousand cash. After Dad was brought back out of the courtroom, Lynn and Joe were arraigned. Then we all were crammed into an elevator and taken to the ground floor. Lynn and I were put into the "trap," a temporary holding cell just outside the booking room. We waited for three hours.

At 7:00 PM CO Carole took us through a side door of the office, into the ladies' cellblock. There were four cells in the block—two on each side of a small room. I saw Barbara already locked in one of them. Carole opened the gate. Barbara welcomed Lynn and me as we walked in, and Carole locked the gate behind us.

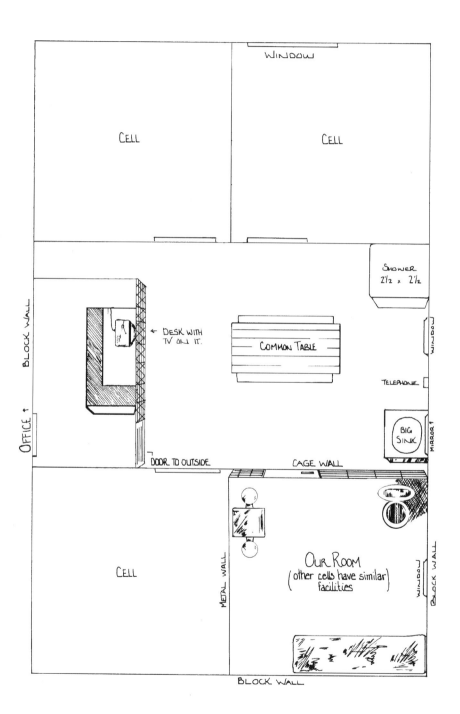

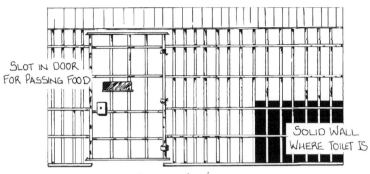

SLOT IN DOOR
FOR PASSING FOOD

SOLID WALL
WHERE TOILET IS

CAGE WALL

DOOR INTO CELLBLOCK   ↑ CAGE WALL

SINK

TOILET

SOLID
STAINLESS STEEL
CONSTRUCTION   (1 UNIT)

TABLE 2ft x 2ft

CELL SIZE
9ft x 12ft

BARBARA'S MAT ON FLOOR
MAT 2ft x 6ft

WINDOW TO OUTSIDE

BUNK BED
BED 6ft x 2ft
(RACHEL SLEEPS HERE)

■ CHAPTER 5 ■

In Jail

August 17, 1993

By Rachel

I slept on a mat on the floor last night, wearing the same clothes I had on when I was arrested yesterday. Lynn and Barbara were on the metal bunk bed, with their mats. All three of us were restless. My muscles hurt all over, and my right hand is still numb from the handcuffs. I woke a number of times during the night, but didn't allow myself to start thinking.

I can't believe I can't get out to pick vegetables and open the fruit stand this morning.

The struggle yesterday left us dirty, and sticky with sweat. But we are locked in, with no access to a shower. When CO Sue came in, I asked if we could shower.

"Are you going to cooperate now?" she asked. "Give your name and change into greens?"

After a pause I said, "Since I was brought in here without cause, I won't offer personal information."

"If you don't cooperate, you won't get a shower," Sue said.

By Barbara Lyn

One of my ankles was injured during the arrests yesterday. It got swollen and painful overnight. I told CO Sue about it this morning, and asked if the jail nurse could look at it. She said she'd ask, and a half hour later returned to say there was no nurse or doctor available, but one of the COs who is an EMT (Emergency Medical Technician) would take a look. I went out to the office with her, and the CO wrapped my ankle with an ace bandage.

While in the office, they allowed me to use the phone to call home.

I discussed with the family our upcoming arraignment, which is supposed to be at 1:30 this afternoon.

I was called out to the office at 1:15. Lt. Lawrence handcuffed me, took me down the hall, and left me with Sgt. Rater and a bunch of other officers while he went back for Rachel and Lynn. I leaned against the wall, silent, forcing back thoughts of yesterday.

Rater, standing across the hall from me, asked, "How are you this afternoon, Barbara?" His voice was even, almost taunting.

"I'm fine," I said cheerfully. "It takes a lot to break my spirit."

"I'm not trying to break your spirit—nobody here is trying to break your spirit," Rater said. "We could care less about what happens to your spirit."

By Rachel

Officers handcuffed Lynn and me, then walked us down a hall lined with uniformed men, where we joined Barbara. We entered the long underground tunnel. Three television cameramen were in the tunnel, filming and firing questions as we walked.

At the elevator, Lynn and Barbara went in with several officers. Waiting for the next trip up, I looked around at the four officers who were squeezed in the corner with me. The absurdity of it all struck me. "What are you doing here?" I asked, facing them. "Are you here to keep me from being a free person?"

A few of them nodded, without looking up. The TV cameras pushed forward.

"Four guys it takes to hold one little woman?" I asked.

"Yup," one officer said.

I spoke to them about Billy. "He had no family to care for him, and we let him live with us. You're helping to abuse this child—all of you."

The elevator opened, and we entered.

"I think I'll get another job," an officer said. He sighed.

"I think you should," I said. "There are jobs of integrity to be had. I'm a farmer."

"Are you hiring?"

"I might give you a job, but I may have to ask you a few questions first."

We stepped into the waiting room. Rex Rater was seated there, guarding Barbara.

"What are you doing here today?" I asked him.

"I am, within the scope of my duty, attempting to help enforce the law," Rater said.

"You got rather violent out there yesterday," I told him. "You threw me down, handcuffed me, injured my wrists. That wasn't nice."

"Anyone watching that video would have to be blind not to see who was violent," Rater shot back. "You know, your father pushed my head back. He even admitted it—he apologized to me."

Someone from the courtroom called Rater and he left quickly.

By Barbara Lyn

My name was called. I walked into the courtroom, an officer on each arm. Judge Himelein was on the bench again. Red-haired and mustached, he had a boyish, almost kind expression.

Himelein said he had read my jurisdictional challenge. "That's certainly an issue you can raise, but there are procedural ways to raise the issue. The grand jury has charged you with three crimes. And whatever your feelings are about the jurisdiction of this court…. this is where those cases will be tried."

He advised me of my right to an attorney, as well as my right to go on without a lawyer. "The down side of that is that most people who represent themselves are not successful," he said.

"Excuse me," I said. "You seem to be ignoring the fact that there is not a valid proceeding in front of this court right now."

"Well, you and I are going to have to agree to disagree about that."

"I don't want to be a part of this proceeding. You have the right to your opinion, and I have the right to my opinion. I have the right to my freedom, too." I turned and began to walk away. Officers blocked me and grabbed my arms.

I remained with my face to the people in the gallery as the judge continued. He said he would enter a not guilty plea on my behalf, appoint the Public Defender's Office to represent me, and schedule a jury trial. "You don't have to participate in that trial, either," he said. "But if you don't, there would be a good chance that you would be convicted on the charges. And the maximum sentence on those charges would be two years in the county jail."

Himelein asked if I wanted him to set bail. I had my back toward him, and did not answer.

On the three new charges—resisting, obstructing, and riot—he set bail at a thousand dollars each. He said those charges would be referred to the Town of Chautauqua Court, and there would be an arraignment next Monday.

Himelein again urged me to get an attorney. "I would hate to see you spend two years of your life in jail," he said. "I mean, if you feel like you want to be a martyr, that's your decision. I'm not going to try to dissuade you from that. But to me, trying to be a rational person, that's two years out of my life that I wouldn't want to spend, no matter what the cause was that I believed in."

I challenged Himelein about the validity of the secret indictment. He said grand jury proceedings have always been in secret.

"What gives you the right to deprive me of liberty…?"

"If you ask for bail, I will set it."

"That's not liberty…. You have the right to throw me in jail, have officers stomp over me like an animal and deprive me of liberty to be at home with my business right now… without first proving I have done anybody any wrong?"

"I don't think I would phrase it quite like that."

"Phrase it however you want."

"I would say I have the right to set bail in your case, and I will set bail if you ask me to…. [And] you would be able to post that bail and be released pending this trial."

"And you could deprive me of my property without first proving that I have harmed anybody?"

"Yes."

"…You can take my liberties without proving anything?"

"Yes."

"…Well, it might as well be the Star Chamber of England in 1550."

"Thank you," Judge Himelein said. The proceeding ended.

By Rachel

When Barbara came out, officers led me to the courtroom. On my left, the gallery was packed to capacity with our family and supporters. Their faces were etched with concern. I turned to them as I walked in. "Hello, everyone! I'd like to be with you, but they have me in jail. They got violent yesterday. They threw me down, stomped on me, handcuffed me. I wasn't threatening anyone. I wasn't harming anyone."

People in the gallery were staring at me. Some of them nodded. Two officers took my arms and turned me toward the judge, on my right. "Let's go," one of them said.

"No, I'm a free person," I said.

"Take her out," the judge said.

The officers tried to turn me, but I braced myself with my feet. "No, I'm talking with them," I said. "I'm not going. You'll have to force me. Show who you are. Show your true colors."

More officers came. They tried to push me forward, but I hung back harder. Several of them carried me out and set me down on the floor of the waiting room.

"That's another charge—obstruction!" an officer said as they handcuffed me.

"Brute beasts!" I said.

The officers were out of breath, chests heaving. Sgt. Rater stood by the wall, visibly shaking. An officer who was waiting with us began to rant. "If you people had it the way you say, people would be out there shooting each other! There'd be no law at all!" He was pacing as he spoke.

"We don't hurt people. We are peaceable," I said.

He went on puffing and talking. "When you had trouble at your fruit stand we came up to take care of it, and this is what we get!"

I felt truly sorry for him. Earlier in the summer we had appreciated their attention when vandals had taken letters from our roadside sign. How could I explain to this fellow human that we do respect their work? He had his back turned to me. I wished I could speak to him.

By Barbara Lyn

Lt. Lawrence took Lynn and me down on the elevator. He was still out of breath from carrying Rachel out of the courtroom. "What's wrong with your sister, acting like that?" he asked. "She could at least act decent like you do—she could go up and challenge the court's jurisdiction like you do. There's no need to act like she did." He patted me on the shoulder.

By Rachel

I went into the elevator with four officers. At the basement floor, the door opened. I didn't move. The officers mumbled something about the media, then began to plead with me to cooperate. "Please, Rachel," said Sgt. Braley, a shorter, balding officer who looked kind. "Come on, please." They pulled me out of the elevator. I could see media cameras up ahead in the tunnel.

For a moment I wondered whether resisting was worth the distress I was causing the officers, and my own embarrassment in being physically handled. I began to walk. But it all seemed so wrong. I thought of Billy. I stopped and turned to the officers. "Why are you doing this to me?"

They began to push and pull me along. I went limp. They carried me down the hall, grunting and swearing under their breaths. In the booking room, near the door to our quarters, they let me down. I lay on the floor, on my back.

Sgt. Braley was still pleading. "Rachel, you're just making it harder for yourself—please, Rachel."

"This is an outrage," I said. "It's outrageous that this happens in America."

Then CO Louise and another officer picked me up by my ankles and wrists, and carried me into the cell.

At about 7:00 this evening we asked CO Carole if we could get out to shower. Carole, a middle-aged lady who seems understanding, explained that inmates in double lock usually get out for an hour at 8:00, after the other inmates are locked in for the night. She stood in front of our gate, contemplating whether she could let us out early. A teenage girl who knew Barbara from the other time she was here, stepped in front of Carole. "You're ordered to open that door right now!" she said in mock authority. "They're just as good as the rest of us. Stick that key in there right now!" Carole complied, laughing.

We called home, and discussed with the family today's court hearings, and the possibility of getting bail. Barbara and I don't feel we should accept bail, at least not for now. We want to stay out of the court process as far as possible. But Monday seems very far away. I can't imagine Mom and Susan managing the fruit stand for a whole week.

After our call, we showered, putting our dirty clothes back on. Then we were locked back into our cell. I asked Carole for jail greens to sleep in, so we could wash our soiled clothing. She brought us each a set of coarse, dark green pants and slip-over shirts. The other inmates lent us each a large T-shirt. Lynn, Barbara and I put on the jail clothes, then washed our own clothes in the tiny sink in our cell, using cold water and a bar of Ivory soap. We hung them on the bars to dry.

August 18

By Barbara Lyn

I had just changed back into my dress this morning, when CO Sue walked up to our cell. "What's the matter, Barb, didn't you like your greens?" she teased. Rachel and Lynn were still in greens.

"I just wore them to sleep," I said. "I really don't mind wearing them in here with the ladies."

An hour later CO Louise came in. "I have orders from the sheriff to get you changed into greens," she said. "We've been easy on you for a few days."

I couldn't believe they would force me to change. I had never worn pants in public. Wouldn't there be legal protections for religious beliefs on dress code? I asked Louise if I could use the phone.

"Not until after you change," she said. She started taking the clothes we had hung on the bars to dry. Lynn scrambled to get into her skirt, while Louise attempted to prevent her by stepping on it. Next Louise pulled at a blouse Rachel held in her hands. Rachel soon relinquished it, but rebuked Louise for using force. "It's not right that we're being kept here," Rachel told her.

"This is my job!" Louise said angrily. "You're trying to deprive me of my livelihood!"

"Louise, is money more important than integrity?" Rachel asked.

Louise moaned. She went out, and came back with four male officers. "They're making things hard for me," she complained to the officers.

A kindly, older officer came into our cell, to the table where I was writing. "I understand what you're standing for," he said. "I've heard about your cause—and I'm almost on your side. But I think this is going a little too far." He talked for a long time, urging me to cooperate. I listened, but did not answer. As he spoke to me, Rachel stood by our bunk bed, explaining our position to two young officers.

"We've been through this whole thing before!" Louise fumed. "They have no respect for me, or anyone in here! They're trying to put my job in jeopardy."

"We're not here to argue the case with you," an officer told Rachel. "We're under orders and only doing our job."

"Do you follow all the orders you're given, even if they're not good orders?" Rachel asked them.

"Yes, we don't make that judgment."

"If you were given the order to shoot me, would you follow that order?"

"No."

"You see, you have to draw the line somewhere." Rachel also told them about Billy. "Would you refuse a child help? I really think you would have done the same thing."

"You're probably right," one of the officers said.

Louise interrupted the conversation. "I'm leaving these greens here with you," she told me. "I'll give you fifteen minutes. If you don't have them on when I get back, we'll do it." She and the other officers left.

A half hour later Louise came back in. I still hadn't changed. "You need to come out and talk to the sergeant," she said.

I followed her to the office and sat on a chair, facing Sgt. A.J. Melson.

"We have orders from the sheriff to get you changed into greens," he said. "If you don't take the clothes and change yourself, I'll have my men here do it." He motioned to five officers who had come into the room. Among them was a CO who is a neighbor.

"Your men aren't going to touch my body, are they?" I asked.

"It's your choice—either you go with Louise into that room, and do it yourself, or these men will. Besides that, if any of my men get injured, if you hit anyone, I'm going to charge you with assault in the second. And *that's* a felony."

I sat listening, stunned. After a while I said, "I've never injured anyone intentionally, and I don't ever intend to."

"Are you ready to go in and change now?" Sgt. Melson demanded.

"I want to make a phone call before I will agree," I said. "I need advice on this."

"You're gonna change first," Melson said. "After that you can use the phone. If you don't agree with this, you can argue it later. We have a system of law, and it works. I believe in this system. You can take it all the way to court if you think it's wrong."

"After you've violated me."

"We're not violating you. We're just obeying the law. Now go with her."

Louise came over, the greens in her hand. "Come on now, Barbara, come this way," she said. I followed, thinking she'd take me to my cell. But she went in another direction.

"Why are we going that way?" I asked.

"You're going to go in there and change your clothes."

"No, I didn't volunteer to do that."

Two men grabbed me and pushed me into a room.

"You're being silly," Louise scolded. "You're going to embarrass these guys. They're all married men with families at home."

Louise and another officer shoved me into a chair. Four more officers stood around us. Louise unbuttoned my dress and pulled it down to my waist. I closed my eyes. Louise put the jail shirt over my head, then pulled my limp arms through the short sleeves. "Stand up," she said. I didn't respond. One of the men helped her lift me out of the chair, and she finished dressing me with pants.

Louise returned me to the cell, dressed in greens. I said to Rachel and Lynn, "They've changed me on the outside, but they can't change me inside." A little later Louise came back, and without a word, unlocked our cell. We could now share the day room with the rest of the inmates.

"Thank you for letting us out," Rachel told Louise.

"Sure," she said sarcastically. "Thanks for changing into greens."

At 10:00 AM I was called out to the office again, this time to see a psychologist. It was Tom Rhodes, from Mental Health. "You know why I'm here?" he asked.

"Apparently they thought I was crazy because I wasn't answering their questions," I said. "But I don't need any help." I laughed a little. "It's ludicrous that it should be thought someone is ill simply for standing up for principles."

Our visit was short. Rhodes said he knew my family through colleagues. He asked only a few questions, which I answered to his satisfaction.

By Rachel

Now that we're not double locked, we're allowed to go to the jail gym, along with the other girls. Barbara wasn't able to go today because of her ankle, but Lynn and I went, and spent the hour jogging and playing basketball.

In the gym upstairs, I had a chance to say hello to Joe. His cell has a window high up on the gym wall. When the officers heard us exchange greetings, they closed the shutters on Joe's window so we couldn't talk more.

Tonight at 6:00 our family and friends came to demonstrate outside the jail. Officers gathered outside our cell. We could see only their feet and legs, because of a heavy plastic canopy covering most of our basement window. Through the canopy, I could barely distinguish the forms of a dozen or so supporters, standing about fifty feet from our window. Then voices as of angels drifted into our cell as they sang, "Brighten the Corner," and, "Come, Thou Fount of Every Blessing." I felt so drawn to them, it seemed I was moving toward them. Or were they moving toward me? But the officers outside were increasing in number, and some of them were walking toward our supporters. I felt brief feelings of anger toward these gunmen in uniform, standing guard against our loved ones. Then I thought, God will provide.

One of the inmates called to the officers outside the window and asked how many demonstrators were up there.

"One or two," one of them answered. It seems lies are nothing to these people.

August 19

By Rachel

It must have been close to midnight when a loud, boisterous male voice just outside our cellblock awoke me. The words he was using can't be repeated, they were so filthy, and he referred to "those little boys and girls." I thought he was drunk. Then Brenda, the young female CO in charge of our cell last night, laughed loudly with him, and I realized the man was an officer, too. Next they said some prisoners' names and laughed as they talked about "raping someone in an elevator." The male officer said something about "Barbara Lyn," and immediately their voices lowered.

We already distrusted these people. Now we almost fear them.

In our phone call home this morning Mom told us she's concerned about Dad. His asthma is bothering him, but he is adamant he won't post bail. I told her she should visit him. She's afraid, since they heard through the media that Sheriff Bentley has threatened to arrest anyone else who can be identified as having had a part in the melee on Monday.

I expressed my worries to the family about them doing all the vegetable picking, and taking care of my dogs. They said they're managing okay. "We're getting on our feet," Mom said. "Some things come from a strength we can't explain."

Lynn got out on bail. Barbara and I now share a cell alone.

This afternoon Barbara helped settle an argument between several girls about who gets to choose the TV channel. She made a written agreement with time slots that satisfied everyone, and all eight of us inmates signed. When CO Sue inspected the agreement, she appeared pleased. She laughed when she saw that the only request Barbara and I had for TV time was for the 6:00 news.

August 20

By Barbara Lyn

I was called out to meet Scott Humble, a lawyer who had passed his card to me several days ago. Mr. Humble said he wanted to represent me. He asked whether I was willing to face two years in jail. I told him there's one thing more significant to me than the pain of imprisonment, and that is upholding honesty and principles. "I'm afraid an attorney would defeat my position on this," I said. I also told him that I felt an attorney would want my cooperation in working with the court system, and I would be impossible to satisfy. "I realize I'm taking an unusual position," I said, "and I want to be personally responsible for it."

He said my jurisdictional challenge is fascinating, and so rare it has "those people up there" scrambling to find case law.

I asked him some questions about court processes. "I would like to present my case to a jury," I said, "but I don't trust the judge to properly inform them of their right to judge according to conscience."

"Do you plan to post bail?" he asked.

"No. My problem with posting bail is that I'd be volunteering to come back for trial."

"And you'd be agreeing to give the court jurisdiction," he said. "Unless you'd skip."

"I wouldn't do that. That would be breaking a promise."

By Rachel

In the gym today, I met CO Doug Christian, the officer who had been wearing street clothes when I came in on Monday. Today he wore a uniform.

"You were here the day I came in," I said casually.

"No," he said.

"You were in the small room by the court."

"Yes."

"You look familiar," I said. "I know I've seen you." I remembered he had denied being a fruit stand customer when I asked him about it on Monday.

"I come to your fruit stand," said Christian.

After rec, while we waited for the elevator, he stood beside me.

"How do you feel about us being here?" I asked.

"I don't." He shrugged and spread his hands. "That's between you and the courts. I've worked here for fourteen years. *Anyone* comes in here." The elevator opened, and we were taken back to our cell.

An hour later Barbara and I were called for a visit with a friend. Doug Christian sat behind us, in the guard's chair. After my visitor left, I was waiting to be taken back down. Christian began to talk about his horses.

"Have you ever trained horses?" he asked.

"Just a little," I said, not feeling like taking on the conversation. After a pause I said, "You know, I really don't have anything personally against any of you here. But the biggest grief is to see there are people in power who don't know, and don't care."

"We can't," he answered quickly.

August 21

By Rachel

This morning a new girl, Sonya, who is double locked in her cell, started to argue loudly with another girl. CO Brenda came in and told them to quiet down. Sonya kept on shouting and swearing.

Barbara and I were in our cell, trying to ignore the hateful language. Still in my night shorts, I began to clean the toilet. Brenda went out, then suddenly came back in with CO Doug Christian, who was carrying handcuffs and shackles. I grabbed a towel to cover myself.

"Sit back on the bed until we have this taken care of," Brenda told me tensely.

Christian went up to Sonya's cell with the shackles and told her she had better cool it or this is what she'll get. Sonya stopped yelling.

On their way out Christian stopped at our cell. "How are you? Keeping busy?" he asked.

"Yes," I said, barely able to answer. The whole incident had the effect of making me teary. The argument was frightening. Then that guy came in without warning, as if our privacy is nothing. Then he said hello, like it's all appropriate.

It's evening now—Saturday night—and the jail has been busy today. CO Louise came in to let out another girl, the second release in a half hour. Overpopulation, she said. New inmates are coming in, apparently men, and the jail is running out of sleeping mats and linens. We hear that there are 171 inmates tonight. They released a woman who came in drunk, and has slept most of the past two days. "I'm getting a six-pack as soon as I get out!" she said loudly as she left.

By Barbara Lyn

At night when I fall asleep my arms go numb, and I keep waking up. It's hard to get comfortable on a thin mat on a cement floor. My whole body still feels sore. Besides physical discomfort, it's hard to sleep with the office radio running all night. And the TV in our block doesn't get turned off until midnight. All day it has those dreadful MTV songs running, and at night, movies.

I had a lovely visit with Miriam and the family today. Joe also got a visit from Nancy and their children. A kind officer arranged for Joe and me to sit side by side. He even allowed us to have our children on the prisoners' side of the table for five minutes of the half-hour visit. We sit across from our visitors, but we can see only half their faces because of the wooden barrier that runs across the top of the table.

Back from our visit, CO Brenda searched me, as they do each time before returning inmates to their cells. She told me to take my shoes off, then moved her hands all over my body. As she took me into the cellblock she said to the rest of the inmates, "Barbara tried to bring in cigarettes, but I confiscated them."

The girls laughed at her joke. "Why did you let her take them?" they asked me, groaning in mock disappointment.

"Shame on you, Brenda," I said with a smile.

Later Brenda came over to me. "I hope it doesn't bother you I kidded you like that."

"No, that doesn't bother me," I said. "Not at all. It just bothers me that I'm in here." I turned away because of unexpected tears.

"I know," Brenda said.

I read until past midnight to finish a book the family had mailed, *The Ordeal of Edward Bushell.* It's about the trial of William Penn in England, in 1670, when he was charged with preaching in public, in open disobedience to the laws of the land. Bushell and the other jurors on Penn's trial defied the court and the law by refusing to bring a guilty verdict against Penn. The judges were enraged, and punished the jurors severely. But the jurors stood their ground, and in so doing, gained religious freedom for countless people, over many ages.

I fear that the book has instilled in me an irreversible spirit of rebellion to tyranny.

CO Carole asked us tonight how we have been doing. I told her the longer we stay here, the more convinced we become we're right. "Rachel and I just aren't a bit penitent," I said. "We call home and tell the family we're just getting more firm in our stand."

"That's a lot to be said, after being here for five days," she said.

August 22

By Rachel

CO Carole gave us a copy of *The Post-Journal* this morning. It had several articles about our case, starting on the front page, and filling most of the second page. "Lapp Family Perseveres Through Ordeal," one of the titles said. It gave me a strange feeling to learn about home through the newspaper—Mom and Susan picking vegetables, Nathan caring for the cows and crops.

The article also told of Joe's family. "I'm very proud of him," Nancy was quoted as saying. "He comes from El Salvador where there was no law, where people were shot and killed for no reason…. On the phone, he tells me he did this for our children. If no one stands up for what is right, then someday this country might be like El Salvador."

We called home. The family said volunteers are helping out at the stand, relieving the strain of their workload. Susan said she finally got some rest today.

"Rachel, you have a visit," called CO Carole.

It's exciting to be called for a visit. I never know who my visitor will be. But it's somebody for me, someone that's not in jail garb. Visitors make me feel closer to physical freedom.

"Does it seem you've been here longer than you really have?" Carole asked, walking beside me down the hall to the visiting room.

"Well—sometimes."

"What do you think will happen in court tomorrow? You think you'll be going home?"

"I don't know," I said.

Barbara and I don't confide in anyone here. With Carole, you almost could.

At the foot of a flight of stairs, Carole unlocked a gate and we walked up to the first floor. A guard unlocked another gate and motioned for me to enter the visiting area. I found Joe waiting for his visitor, too.

"How's your courage?" I asked Joe.

"Good! How's yours?"

"Sit down there in the corner," the guard told Joe. "You're getting a visit with five children."

Officers brought Dad from his quarters. He walked as if tired, in bare feet, almost limping. But his face, framed in his small gray beard, looked bright.

"Dad!" I exclaimed. He took a chair beside mine. Dad and I talked as we waited for our visitors. He said jail staff had taken his shoes, and gave him shower slippers. But he couldn't wear them because both were for the same foot. "Last night I was desperately cold," he said. "I thought I might die. I felt as though I could just let go, and fall asleep." Dad's eyes glimmered with tears. "But then I decided it wouldn't be right to my family, so I forced myself to stay awake. Finally an inmate brought me an extra blanket."

The guard opened the gate, and our family filed in—Tony (my brother-in-law) and his son; Drusilla (my sister) with her two daughters. Then Nancy and her five children. We prisoners greeted each of them, reaching across the high narrow table for hugs and kisses. Lelia

(Joe and Nancy's two-year-old) laughed and chattered, "Daddy, Daddy!"

When our half-hour visit was almost over, Drusilla said, "How about singing, 'This is the Day?'" Together, we started softly: "This is the day that the Lord hath made, we will rejoice—"

The guard, CO Lawton, interrupted. "I'm telling you, and I'll tell you just once, you are not allowed to sing!" he said loudly. "It's against the rules. If there's any more, the visit is over."

We stopped and watched him speak. Then Dad started to sing again, and Drusilla and a few children joined him.

"Jacob, the visit is over, this is it," Lawton said. He called on his radio, and five other officers came in. Lawton unlocked the gate.

Joe's children looked frightened. Their oldest daughter was on the verge of tears. "It's okay, Naomi," I said as officers escorted me out of the room. Joe and Nancy remained seated, holding hands over the table. They were allowed to continue visiting.

CO Carole came to take me down. She looked puzzled. "What happened?" she asked as we walked down the hall.

"We were singing a little song," I said, then sighed. "I just can't get used to being in a place where people have no feelings."

"Well—they try to make themselves believe they don't," Carole said slowly. Opening the door to my cell she added, "Maybe they're afraid they'll learn something from you."

I got another visit this afternoon, this time from a friend of Dad's. He looked worried when I greeted him. "Tell me, what were you singing?" he asked, then added quickly, "Don't sing it, please!"

The visiting room was full and noisy. We had to bend close to hear each other.

"We were just singing one verse of a song," I said. "There was no one here except my family, and when they were almost ready to leave, we sang."

"Oh," he said, appearing relieved. "When the officers brought me in, they told me, 'Be careful—she sings.'"

I burst out laughing.

He showed me a Psalm on a piece of paper. One of the verses said something about not fretting. "You don't look like you're fretting," he said. "They're the ones that are fretting."

August 23

By Barbara Lyn

Every morning the CO on duty brings cleaning supplies to the cellblock for us—mop, bucket, a plastic brush and cleaners. We each clean our cells, and all the inmates take turns cleaning the common area. This morning it was Rachel's and my turn. We thoroughly scrubbed the shower, the sink, the metal table, dusted the book caddy, then swept and mopped the floor.

After cleaning I tried to take a nap, but couldn't sleep. There were too many things on my mind. We go to court tonight. I know Rachel and the others could be released. But not me, because of my two sets of charges, and the indictment.

I called home and talked to the family about arranging a jailhouse visit with Andrew Melechinsky, our constitutional advisor who drove in from Connecticut to see us. Shortly after lunch, he came and visited Rachel and me for more than an hour. Jail staff didn't limit our time because it was a "legal visit," though Andy is not a licensed attorney.

We talked about how to handle the arraignment coming up tonight, and the possible consequences of our noncooperation. During our visit CO Doreen came in and gave me a letter she'd just gotten from County Court. It was a notice from Judge Himelein, saying he had found case law that showed he was wrong in not setting bail at my arraignment last week, despite my refusal to apply for it. Bail was now set at twelve thousand—cash or insurance bond only. That's in addition to the three thousand on my charges in Town Court.

Escorted back from our visit, we walked past some inmates who were mopping the floor in the hallway. "Good luck tonight, Barbara!" one of the men said. "Give 'em h - - -!"

Later this afternoon CO Doreen called me for an interview with a gentleman from *Inside Edition*. She took me to the jail classroom, where I met a television news team. The gentleman in charge said he spent time at our farm yesterday, learning about me and my family. "Your mom was out in the field, working hard," he said. "It's tough for the family with all of you in jail."

The interview was harrowing, as it seemed he intentionally questioned me on details that would make me tearful, or angry. "Don't you think that defiance of the law conflicts with your religious beliefs?" he asked. "What would happen to Miriam if you spent two years in jail?" He told me he had talked to officials from both counties. "They say you're trying to manipulate the system, and you're good at manipulating the media," he said. "They say you love being on stage. Is that true?"

I answered his questions the best I could, but almost lost my cool.

6:00 PM. We were called for court. The arraignment, which was pertaining to the Town Court charges from August 16, was held in the county courthouse—the same place we were before, but with a different judge.

Judge Edward J. Mifsud, an older gentleman with a coarse voice, read off our charges and urged us to get attorneys. The hearing was short, because he did not allow us to speak. "You are to answer only yes or no," he said when I started to question the court's jurisdiction. Then he set another hearing date for all of us, for September 17— almost four weeks away.

CHAPTER 6

Habeas Corpus

Habeas Corpus—*(Compton's Encyclopedia) When a person is held prisoner against his will, a judge may… issue an order compelling the jailer or other custodian to bring the prisoner to court and explain why he is held captive. If no lawful reason is found the prisoner is released. This court order is called a writ of habeas corpus, often known as "the great writ of liberty."*

The principle of the writ is of English origin, for in Magna Carta King John was forced to promise that "no free man shall be taken or imprisoned except by the lawful judgment of his peers and by the law of the land."

August 24, 1993

By Barbara Lyn

For the first time, prolonged imprisonment hits me as reality. Miriam's needs strike me with overwhelming clarity, and I find myself expending my energy, almost to the point of exhaustion, just to open my heart far enough for the Good Spirit to show me that what God ordains is always good.

The last couple of days I've been working on habeas corpus petitions for Dad, Joe, Rachel and me. But the law books I need are not accessible to prisoners. Someone told me I have to ask Swanee, the recreation director, for them. Today I asked him. He just made a face. Later he asked which volume I needed, and said he'd have it by tomorrow.

11:45 is rec time. Rachel and I look forward to it, for the sake of good health, and for the chance to say hello to Joe. But we also dread it, because of being herded up and down the halls, walking past people who, only a little more than a week ago, threw us around without regard. And we hate wearing pants, especially when the officers watch us in action—playing basketball, jumping rope, or doing pull-ups.

Swanee stays in the gym all the while. Other officers come and go. Today a CO from the men's block was watching me from an upper floor window. I feel so used by these men, sometimes I feel like just staying in my cell. But Rachel says we must maintain our physical health if we are to remain mentally sharp.

CO Carole walked us back from rec. "What do you think is going to happen now?" she asked.

"I don't know. The judge said back to jail 'till September 17."

"I can't see you staying in here for three more weeks," she said. "Wouldn't it be better to post bail?"

"If we post bail, we agree to return to court, and the court has not established legitimate cause to compel us to appear," I said.

"What about your daughter?" Carole asked. "How can she take it?"

"We're still hopeful—Mom says she's doing pretty well." Fighting back tears, I said, "Carole, we have to look at the bigger picture. Our family tells us Billy Stefan and his brother are doing well—still staying at our farm part of the time."

I called home to give final instructions to Andy and Charlie, our legal advisors, on how to prepare the habeas corpus papers. I advised them to come to the jail for our signatures, then take the papers across the street to the courthouse. Two hours later they still had not come, and we were getting worried. Finally, in a phone call home, we found out they had been here, but the jail supervisor wouldn't allow them to see us.

August 25

By Barbara Lyn

We got letters today from Mom, several friends, and a lady I don't know who wrote that she had followed newspaper stories and wanted to express her support. As usual, all the envelopes had been opened and inspected by jail staff.

One of the letters was from Don Stefan. He expects to be released in one week. But a court order might prevent him from seeing Billy. At the end of his letter he wrote: "I feel hurt it was my family that put you in jail. I never thought the whole deal would be so big."

CO Doreen came into the cell block. "Barbara, get your greens on," she said.

I hurried to comply, pulling my green shirt over the T-shirt I was wearing. "You never know what they're calling for," I commented to Rachel.

Doreen took me out, and a sergeant walked me up to the visiting area. Andy and Charlie were outside the gate, habeas corpus papers in hand. The jail supervisor, Lt. Belson, stood behind them. "Here she is—now give her the papers," he said. He didn't open the gate.

Charlie pushed the folders containing our papers between the iron bars. "You and Rachel can sign them, and we'll be back this afternoon, during visiting hours," he said hastily.

At 12:30 we got a visit from the family, and returned our signed papers. Mom told us Dad doesn't want anything to do with the habeas corpus. He says he was brought in without a hearing, and they can let him out that way as well.

Now if the State Supreme Court judge signs the habeas corpus order, Sheriff Bentley will have to take Joe, Rachel and me for a hearing on the legality of our detention.

August 26

By Rachel

This morning after breakfast, CO Brenda found a spoon missing from our food cart, and got very upset. "I went through this whole thing last week, and I'm not putting up with it!" she yelled. "If that spoon doesn't show up, there will be no phone for you today!"

The other girls were angry about the threat. All of us tried to track down the spoon, to no avail. Then CO Carole, who had served our breakfast, came in. I heard her tell Brenda it wasn't the inmates' fault. Later on I asked Brenda what had happened with the spoon. She blamed the cooks and Carole for counting wrong, and said we could have the phone.

I asked one of the girls why the COs were so worried about the missing spoon. She said they're afraid of hard objects being used as weapons or tools. That's also the reason we get no silverware besides spoons.

I started reading the book, *The Ordeal of Edward Bushell,* about William Penn's trial. Barbara has been telling me I have to read it.

The first page put a fan to the fire within me. "Freedom is a do-it yourself job," it says. "Leaders may write a declaration of independence and a constitution, but their enforcement and vitality is the never-ending responsibility of the people restraining the government."

I was impressed by the emphasis William Penn and his followers placed on "God-given rights." We speak much of constitutional law, which is okay. But in England in 1670 they didn't have a constitution to refer to. The Quakers simply claimed that God's law was above the King's law.

August 27

By Barbara Lyn

I was up until 1:00 AM, making notes for our habeas corpus hearing today.

CO Louise came in at 10:00 AM and told us to get dressed for court. We were allowed to wear dresses that had been sent from home. They took Rachel to court first, brought her back, then came for me.

The booking room was full of officers when I got out. One stepped forward, handcuffs clacking. He approached fast, hardly giving me time to acknowledge him. It was Lt. Belson—generally courteous, stately, wearing a white shirt—because he's a lieutenant.

"I'd appreciate if you would do me the courtesy of not chaining me this time," I said. "I'm going voluntarily." As I spoke he had already grabbed my wrist and fastened one hand.

"They're not chains," he said. "They're handcuffs, and I'm putting them on as comfortably as I can." He helped me reposition my tablet and pen, which had become entangled in the chain between my wrists.

In the tunnel to court, we met television news crews. "I see you're in your street clothes–how does that make you feel?" one cameraman asked.

"Good," I answered. "It makes me feel a bit more free." The officers kept me walking at a fast pace. Cameramen ran ahead of us, then walked backwards with cameras perched on their shoulders, facing us. They questioned me about the habeas corpus proceeding, and whether we expected to be freed.

"How do you feel?" one of them asked again.

"Fine," I said. "I just don't like these shackles. I asked them not to put them on this time, but they did anyway."

We entered the elevator. "They're not shackles," Lt. Belson sputtered as the doors closed.

The court appearance was brief. The judge adjourned the hearing because he said he had to check out the credentials of our non-attorney consultants before we could proceed.

Back on the elevator, Lt. Belson let out a sigh. "Another circus on Monday," he said.

In the tunnel, we met the newsmen again. "What happened with the hearing?" one of them asked.

"The judge adjourned until Monday," I said. The officers were walking close, pushing me onward. I stopped, and turned to face the newsmen. "Why weren't you in the courtroom?"

"We put in a request to be there, but the judge denied it," one of the cameramen said. "He waited 'till the last minute—we didn't have time to contest the ruling."

Back in the cell, Rachel was sitting at our little metal table, head cradled in her hands. She was still wearing her clothes from home. We exchanged a few words about what had happened in court. Then I was called out for a news conference.

Returning to the cellblock, I walked with CO Louise, through the office.

"Get those girls to change their clothes," a male officer said loudly, "or it's going to be the same thing over again. And the men *will* help you."

In the cell with Rachel, Louise asked sternly, "Did you hear that? Did you hear what he said?" Neither of us answered. Louise said she'd give us a few minutes. "Believe me, I don't enjoy this any more than you do," she said as she left. "And you probably won't ever get your clothes back if you don't change now."

We changed into greens, and laid our clothes on the table. After a few minutes Louise came to pick them up. "Thank you, girls," she said.

Later, during a phone call home, we learned that Joe's habeas corpus petition was dismissed. The judge had denied Joe's request to have Nancy translate for him during the hearing. Instead, a Spanish inmate was brought in to serve as interpreter. Joe, unable to express the arguments in the petition, had a brief exchange with the judge and was ordered back to jail.

August 28

By Rachel

I'm excited with what I'm learning as I read the Edward Bushell book. One juror in the story said that the record of tyrants shows that if a person gives up one liberty, two more will be taken, until we are slaves. But when the people resist, tyranny is stopped and liberty lives.

The sequestered jurors in Penn's trial suffered much more cruelty than Barbara and I do. They were confined without food and bathroom facilities because they refused to give a guilty verdict as instructed by the judge. One juror died from the poor conditions. But they didn't give in, and Penn was freed.

This afternoon we had a round of aerobic antics with the girls here—tossing and juggling oranges, apples and socks. Every time the orange fell it got more battered, until, flying high, it got stuck between the bars above our door, dripping juice. Next we walked on our hands, and hung from the metal frames above our cell door.

When CO Louise came in, I was ashamed. The block was noisy, and in a mess. But she didn't seem to mind, and joined the girls in discussing our games.

"It's so crowded in here," one of the girls said to Louise. "Looks like no one's getting bail."

"If you're like me, you don't have money for bail," Louise said.

I sat at the common table, listening to the girls' comments about the difficulty of getting bail—and thinking of the many people who had offered to bail us out. "I'm not giving one dollar to this mess!" I said. "This place is too corrupt."

Louise looked surprised.

August 30

By Barbara Lyn

It is two weeks since we were caught and penned in. Today we go to court to plead our release.

Rachel and I both had a restless night. Around midnight I awoke and tried to see what time it was. I peered through the bars and the chain-link fence—to the clock that hangs on the wall outside the cellblock—but couldn't tell if it was 6:00 or 12:30. The hands are both the same length. The CO and other inmates were talking loudly, as if it were the middle of day. I turned over on my mat, but couldn't find a comfortable position. My shoulder hurt, then my ankle.

This morning I called home. It delighted me to hear Dad got to see part of our visit yesterday, through a crack in the wall of his cell. He has been double locked since he refused his TB test last week, and isn't allowed out for visits.

After cleaning, I tried to nap but couldn't fall asleep. I dragged myself out of bed. "Yucky jail! Yucky court! Yucky judge!" I said.

Rachel ordered me to eat part of her orange, and drink some grapefruit juice that was left from breakfast. "It will improve your mood," she said.

"It'll just make me meaner," I joked. "It'll rinse the apathy out of my brain nerves."

By Rachel

I felt unusually resigned as we prepared for court. Neither of us expected release. At 1:45 we were on our way. In the booking room we met officers, but not as many as usual. We greeted them cheerfully. After being handcuffed we walked single file, no one pushing us. CO Dorine accompanied us.

The judge, Willard W. Cass, looked kind as I approached him at the bench. He allowed me to speak with Charles Gardiner, my legal advisor, but insisted Charlie could not address the court. "As a matter of fact, it's a crime for him to appear and represent somebody," the judge said, quoting Judiciary Law of the State of New York.

"It's my right under the sixth amendment of the Constitution to have assistance of counsel," I said. "And the ninth amendment says all rights are mine, even those that aren't enumerated in the Constitution. So I believe it is my right to have him...."

"Well, he's not an attorney," Cass said, "therefore he has no right to represent you as counsel."

When the hearing finally began, two assistant district attorneys stood on my right, appearing on behalf of Sheriff Bentley. I talked to the judge, expressing my beliefs about freedom and responsibility. "Is it ever right to violently apprehend and injure a person that's peaceful and unarmed as they did me on August 16?" I asked. Then I spoke about Billy's plight, and the cause behind our protest.

"I realize I'm a crude person and I'm not much for formality," I said. "If you feel that I'm off the main stream with my comments and my actions, I remind you of Henry David Thoreau's words, 'If it seems as though someone is not keeping pace with his companions, perhaps it's because he hears the music of a different drummer.' I ask that you allow me to peaceably step to the drum of my own conscience, as I'm allowing you to do, and anyone who's present here to do also. I think individuality is American... and I wish you would honor that, and allow me to go home today."

Then the assistant DA spoke. "I'm not going to talk about the Billy Stefan issue because I don't think it has anything to do with the problems that Rachel Lapp has in this courtroom," he said.

"The response that she made... where she took certain action on behalf of her sister that they claim was not violent; was just the opposite—it was violent. It was committed in the presence of police officers... and they exercised their duty and arrested Miss Lapp."

The judge upheld the Sheriff Department's position and ordered me back to jail. I turned and started to speak to my friends in the gallery. "I wish I could be with all of you—"

"Come, Rachel," said CO Doreen, putting her hand on my back. Officers closed in on me, pushing and pulling.

Trying to keep myself stationary, I involuntarily grabbed Doreen's shirt, and continued my message to the crowd. "You can see, these men who call themselves officers of law are using violence on me again—"

The officers were pushing harder now. I braced my foot against the leg of a large wooden table in the courtroom, and held on to the tabletop with my hands, still speaking. "I appeal to the highest law of our land, and to the law of God, which holds me a human being, created as their equal, with equal rights—"

Officers lifted me by my arms, pulling my hands off the table. Two of them reached for my feet. I quickly pulled both feet under me, then walked slowly, finishing my message as they took me out: "Let the world be the judge as to whether society is a better place for the fact that I am in jail. If not, to what end are they attempting to enforce the laws that keep me in bonds?"

Officers pushed me through the door to the waiting room, and took Barbara in. Sgt. Braley put my handcuffs on and prepared to take me down to jail.

"I'd like to stay, to listen to Barbara," I pleaded. I was too exhausted to think of anything else.

"I don't think you'll be able to hear," one of them said. He closed the door to the courtroom.

I sat in a chair. Sgt. Braley came and took a chair across the corner from me. "What did the judge say, Rachel?" he asked in his soft-spoken manner.

I looked at him as he spoke, but couldn't think what to answer. Finally I said, "Lock and key."

"Why?" asked Braley.

"Maybe you know. I don't understand."

"What did he say? He must have given you a reason."

"Apparently he upholds the actions of this department on August 16."

Braley nodded. There was silence. Then I asked, "What do you think? What do you think about this case?"

"We don't really have a choice. There are laws we have to abide by. We have to do our job."

Another officer, rather heavy and bald, was in the room. He had a mean expression. A third officer came in.

"Do you believe all laws are good?" I asked Braley.

"No, but if we were the ones to decide which ones to enforce, there would be complete confusion," he said. "That's what the courts are for—to challenge laws and determine which ones are okay."

"Don't your actions have to have a purpose?" I asked Braley. "Don't they have to be for the betterment of society?"

Braley appeared uneasy. Soon he and the other officers began to talk about a man who had murdered someone. Turning to me again, Braley asked, "What do you think about that?" He explained the murder case briefly, then continued. "If you had a problem on your farm, like someone burning your barn, or kidnaping a child, you would *want* us to help."

I faced him. "Would that be an honorable thing to do? Kidnap a child? Kill somebody?"

"No."

"No, that wouldn't be a good thing to do—damaging property or harming someone," I said. "That would be wrong. You know what's right and wrong. That wouldn't be right by God's law or any rules of human decency."

Braley seemed embarrassed. He and another officer started explaining to me how the legal system works.

I listened, then began slowly. "We have an excellent foundation for justice in this country. The reason for our problems is that we've gotten away from it. Yes, legislatures can make laws, but if we don't like a law our actions challenge it, and a jury of our peers decides whether our actions are responsible."

An officer checked the time. They got up. "Come, Rachel," Braley said.

I remained seated. "I can't," I said, looking down. "It's not right."

They began to pull on my arms. My tablet and court papers fell.

"Don't lose your papers," Braley said, picking them up. He and another officer again started to lift me.

"You don't know how difficult this is for me," I said. "I enjoy following instructions, but I just can't do this."

They had stopped to let me talk. It was the first time any officer gave me time. But the force was inevitable. One on each side, they lifted me by my arms. I went limp.

They set me on the elevator floor. I leaned against the wall of the elevator, three officers around me. "If I cooperate, I put myself on your level—following bad orders," I said.

The door opened. Braley said, "We're going to get from here to there anyhow, Rachel. It just makes it harder for everyone if you resist." They pulled me to my feet, and I walked. Nearing the door of the office, Braley said, "Thank you for walking."

"We could be friends," I said, "if you'd treat me like a human being."

"We try," he said.

I entered our cell and lay on the bed. More than anything I needed time to think. One of the inmates came to my cell. "So how's it going, Rachel?" she asked.

"Not too good," I said. "Judge said back to jail."

Thoughts of refusing to change into jail clothes went through my mind. These are my clothes! They can rip them off me if they want. I'm a free person. Then I remembered the favor they did in letting us have our clothes for court. What benefit are they to me, anyhow? I'd get double locked, with no phone, no rec.

I changed, laid my clothing on our table, and went back to lie down. Barbara still had not come back from court. CO Sue came in. "Can I have these clothes?" she asked.

I looked away, silent. She came to my side. "Are you all right?" she asked.

"Yes."

She sat down on the bed. "Are you sure?"

"Yes, I'm sure."

CO Sue stroked my arm, then left with the clothes, locking the gate behind her. I lay still, allowing numbness to seep away, and reasoning to flow in. My will to resign myself to what must be, fought hand to hand with contempt for my situation. Human desires were met with the inevitable denial of their fulfillment. Court day was over. Profound relief stepped discordantly with repulsion, grief, defiance. Finally gratitude and resolution moved in. Surely, God, you helped me through this day. My Lord, I believe!

By Barbara Lyn

After Rachel, I was called to the courtroom. Before my habeas corpus hearing began, I asked Judge Cass why he had forbidden media cameras in the courtroom.

"That's discretionary with the court, and I made that determination," he said.

"By what reasoning?" I asked.

"Just my discretion."

"Do you have the ultimate authority in that?"

"That's correct. I made that determination, that no cameras would be in the courtroom."

I noticed a uniformed sheriff's deputy with a video camera. "When government cameras are in the courtroom... is that [film] available as public information?" I asked.

"No, it's not available as public information."

"So you're favoring the government above the private parties involved here?"

"I'm not favoring anybody. I'm just making a ruling that cameras cannot be in the courtroom, with the exception of the video camera that's taping these proceedings for the Sheriff's Department."

"You are allowing the government to videotape it, but you're not allowing the common people to do the same?"

"That's correct."

I told the judge I objected to his determination. Then, using my prepared notes, I began my statement for the habeas corpus petition:

> I bring this claim in defense of liberty, the basis being that no person shall be deprived of liberty without due process of law, according to Amendment five of the U.S. Constitution.
>
> For the past 14 days I've been locked behind iron bars in a small space…. I've been forced to be separated from my daughter who is of tender age and has no other parent…. Even my livelihood has been jeopardized.
>
> I was first arrested… on July 12, 1993… by consent of the Chautauqua County sheriffs. It is now seven weeks since that time, and I have been forced to appear in court six times, against my will. I still have not faced my accuser, nor have I had verification that these charges against me are valid.
>
> The accusations were of a nature that I couldn't know what law, if any, I violated. This youth, Billy Stefan, was staying at my home with his father's consent and the Cattaraugus County Department of Social Services was claiming custody of him against his and his family's wishes.
>
> To the best of my knowledge, there was no law violated in allowing Billy to stay at my home. There were never any orders requiring me to turn Billy into somebody else's care, yet I was accused of refusing to hand Billy over to law enforcement. There were no warrants issued, yet I was accused of not allowing Sheriff's deputies on my property. The ac-

cusation included that the media was at my place, yet in my knowledge, it's not against the law to have the media at your place. The accusation also included that there were 50 to 75 people outside my home…, yet, to the best of my knowledge there's no crime involved in that.

Also, since I don't own Billy, I have no right or authority to hand him around like so much merchandise. He's a young man of size and stature nearly equal to mine, and it wouldn't be in my physical capability to force him to go, while he steadfastly declared he wouldn't go.

To arbitrarily deprive this youth of liberty would be an act of lawlessness itself. If I should have taken part in such action, I would expect to be found guilty of coercion and cruelty, under the just laws of our nation, and I would surely stand condemned under God's law of mercy.

If a law is used against a person in hindering that person from free exercise of conscience, such law must of necessity be null and void. An honorable, free citizen can't be expected to obey that which is dishonorable.

On August 16, 1993, I was again unlawfully arrested. Two weeks prior to my arrest I received a letter from the district attorney's office which referred to a secret grand jury finding against me on three charges. There was no summons, no order issued by any magistrate or any officer of law directing me to appear on August 16.

In defense of liberty, I challenged the jurisdiction of the court that was to hear the fraudulent accusation against me. I presented myself on the sidewalk of the courthouse on that date, only in respect to the citizenry, since there was an indication, however unverified, that there were charges against me. Also, I was there to be available to the court in case the court should come forward with a valid order for my appearance. I fully believed, and still believe, that I was honoring the law.

The court chose to recklessly ignore the jurisdictional challenge, which was filed and received by the court prior to my arrest.

The copy of the so-called indictment the court provided does not verify, in any way, that there was an indictment against me. It shows no number, no date, no signature from the jury foreman. It was not even signed by the district attorney, and on the top it was entitled "secret." As far as I'm concerned, it's a useless piece of paper. How am I to know that there was an indictment? How do I know the DA didn't dream up charges, and get busy at his typewriter?

Based on the patent disregard for lawful process, the court that issued the warrant for my arrest, if there was any, cannot lawfully try me or issue orders against me.

My arrest on August 16, therefore, was not lawful. The officers had no right to forcibly remove me from an assembly of citizens who were merely exercising their right to assemble for their common good, in a peaceful protest.

I would bring that argument again on behalf of the other people that are incarcerated with me…. Any detention of those people is not lawful, based on the fact that they have never been a threat to society or hindrance to the peace and protection of the common people.

The assistant DA, Paul Andrews, rebutted my statement. "There is a misconception with respect to how Miss Lapp feels law enforcement agencies should act when they are given a court order," he said. "When people do not comply, when they take it upon themselves to tell us and tell society and tell members of the public how they feel…, when they couple that with absolute refusal to come in to discuss those allegations, then we are bound by our own procedures in making sure that somehow we arrive at a fair disposition.

"She is charged with these crimes. A complaint was heard in the lower court. A grand jury heard the complaint. I, as an officer of the court, directed her to appear to answer these allegations. She refused to appear. Her past tactics in dealing with the media and the followers, her followers… does not accord with all of the case law, and with the procedures that our state constitution in conjunction with the U.S. Constitution has provided…."

Concluding his argument, Andrews asked the judge to deny the writ. Judge Cass said he would first review my jurisdictional challenge, and render a decision tomorrow.

By Rachel

Barbara joined me in the cell. After supper, we sat on the bed discussing the day's happenings, and looked over our court papers. As we talked, we found ourselves trailing off and losing thoughts.

"We've got to do our writing," Barbara said. But she wasn't writing.

"We can't sleep until it's done!" She moaned.

I folded my mat and set it on the floor, against the wall. Then I tried to find a spot on my seat that didn't hurt to settle on, and took my pen in hand. Behind me, the TV was noisy—screams, laughter, dirty jokes. Then there was a rumble overhead. "It's thunder!" I exclaimed. Barbara and I looked at each other in delight. "The first since we're here!"

A flash of light, and a louder rumble followed. We could feel a strong breeze coming in the partially shuttered window of our cell. It was rich, invigorating, bearing the smell of rain. Then we heard the rain. Harder and harder it came, its dampness and the smell of moist earth flowing into our cell. Lightning flashed, thunder reverberated across the universe. It seemed to share our small room, speaking of God's power over the whole of humankind.

"Barbara, I love it!" I said. She and I began to prance around the cell. "It's for us!"

The day and its evil were over. Now the storm was over too. A light, clean breeze flowed in. I began to write, and kept it up until early morning.

August 31

By Rachel

9:30 AM. The peaceful morning silence was disturbed when CO Doreen entered and came to our cell. "I have orders from the lieutenant to double lock you," she said to me, "because of what happened in court yesterday. There's to be a hearing on it soon." She avoided looking at me as she spoke.

Doreen then asked Barbara if she wanted to come out and move into another cell. Barbara said she'd stay. Doreen closed our iron cell door and locked it.

"Why?" asked one of the young girls. "Why do they have to be in?" She and the other girls looked shocked. After Doreen left, they came to us and asked what happened.

I explained what had taken place in court yesterday. "These people don't like to be challenged," I said.

"It's not right to treat you like that!" one of the girls said.

I tensed when CO Brenda called me at 5:15 this evening. "I need you to put on your greens and come with me for a minute," she said.

After I dressed, Brenda took me out and explained I was to have a hearing on the double lock. "The sergeant will be talking to you about the incident, and you'll have a chance to say your side," she said. As we walked down the hall, Brenda continued. "Usually these hearings are when the girls get into really bad arguments with a CO." She led the way into a room where Sgt. Panfil, a heavyset man in a white shirt, was seated at a desk.

"You can have a seat," Panfil said in a friendly manner. "I know a little about your case," he continued. "I partly agree with you. But I'm just doing my job and have to make a living like everyone else does. Just like you, on your farm. I respect your way of making a living."

"I agree with you that individuals should be free to pursue what they wish," I said, "as long as their actions don't adversely affect others. I'm a firm believer in that."

Panfil looked down. "We didn't bring you in here," he said. "The courts brought you here, and obviously they are the ones to take care of this matter."

"The court did not bring me in here," I said.

"The officers brought you, on order of the court."

"Your department brought me here."

"Yes," he said. He began to talk about the struggle in court yesterday. "Apparently the officers had to carry you out."

"Well, they didn't actually carry me, but I did make resistance," I said.

He explained that according to their rules, I would be double locked for two weeks, for disobeying an order. Then he waited for me to answer.

I offered no rebuttal. "You have the guns," I said.

"We don't have guns."

"You have the chains, and you have the keys."

"Yes," he said, fidgeting.

He repeated the decision. CO Brenda took me back to my cell and locked me in.

7:00 PM. Confined to my cell, I've spent the day writing. A comfortable position to do this is much in demand. My seat feels completely bruised from sitting so much. The round metal seat attached to our table is awfully uncomfortable. It's too small, and is positioned so far back from the table that you have to sit on its sharp edge to write.

It hurts to be double locked. Not so much for lack of small comforts like phone access and room to walk. It hurts to be accused of disobeying orders when God knows it would be a hundred times easier to comply, to walk nicely to court (Please, God, make those men keep their hands off of me!) and honor the judge. I'd be praised for being agreeable and cooperative. But then I would be corrupt like they are. Poet Robert Frost said, "Conformity is the worst form of cowardice." I'd be a coward, too, then. Guess I'll take the double lock.

We got a letter from Dad today. Mailed from the first floor of the jail to our basement quarters, it was postmarked in Buffalo, fifty miles away. Dad wrote:

> Dear Daughters and Sisters in the Spirit,
> Barbara Lyn and Rachel,
>   Grace and peace be with you. I hope it is with you as it is with me—as desirous and firmly committed to press on 'till the heavenly goal is won as I ever was. The difference between that heavenly goal and any other goal seems to increase progressively, with one growing ever brighter, and the others, ever dimmer....
>   I don't have a handkerchief to blow my nose or wipe my tears as I write. The roll of toilet paper that I use is getting smaller.
>   Song number 86 in *Ausbund* (translated) says something like this: "All those who sow with tears, will reap with joy. They carry precious seeds along as they go forth with tears...."
>   There is always the danger that we put too much effort in winning alleviation for the temporal sufferings of our fellow citizens, and not enough in saving souls. I think there is one very effective and true way to check ourselves, and that is by the measuring rule of love. "Though I have all faith so that I could remove mountains, and have not charity, I am nothing. And though I bestow all my goods to feed the poor, and though I give my body to be burned, and have not charity, it profiteth me nothing." (I Corinthians 13:2,3)
>   Tonight I'm trying to figure out what to say when the COs ask me how I am. I have been saying, "good." But is it true? Is it proper to say to your captors you're okay when they have ripped you away from your duties such as earning your living and being a husband, father and grandfather? How can I be as nice to them as possible, without being hypocritical? Maybe I should ask them if they really care. Or maybe ask them which part of me they mean.

Actually, one part of me is better than ever. I'm elated that God has seen fit to let me suffer for His name's sake.

My chest is real good the last few days. I have no olive oil, no Vicks Formula 44D, and not one Halls since I'm in here….

From *The National Educator:* Five of the signers of the Declaration of Independence were captured by the British, treated as traitors, and were tortured before they died. Twelve had their homes ransacked and burned. Two lost their sons in the war. One, John Hart, was driven from his dying wife. Their thirteen children fled for their lives. A year later, he couldn't find any of them.

Let's build our hopes on things eternal,
Dad

September 1

By Barbara Lyn

Today is the day of Don Stefan's release from jail. I was awake long before it was time to get up this morning, with thoughts of gladness and sadness combined. Last night on TV the newsman said Don would risk going back to jail if he were to see Billy. First they were kept apart by imprisonment, now by court order.

But Billy looked good in the TV pictures taken around our farmhouse—speeding in the driveway on his bike, then hugging our dog. The news announcer said the case has "evolved into a community wildfire."

On the phone, Susan told me Don is planning to come to visit me as soon as he gets out of jail, and the media is asking for interviews with us, together.

After lunch, CO Doreen called me out for a press conference. She said Lt. Belson won't allow the media to film my visit with Don. She took me to the jail classroom, where I was interviewed by reporters from *WGRZ TV (News Channel 2)* and *The Buffalo News.*

At 1:00 Doreen called again.

"A visit?" I asked.

"*The* visit!" she exclaimed.

We walked up the hall toward the visiting room. "You've been waiting for this a long time, haven't you?" Doreen asked.

I shrugged and said yes, quietly. It seemed that Doreen herself was anxious for this visit, perhaps seeking to find me guilty of an ulterior motive.

I took a chair in the visiting room, and waited. Miriam came in with Don. I stood up and embraced Miriam, then Don—forgetting for a moment the prying eyes of COs all around us.

Don and I discussed the happenings that had landed both of us in jail. "I couldn't have imagined it would come to this," I said. "But I'm not sorry for the advice I gave you the first time we met."

Don told me of Judge Nenno's new order—issued just before his release—directing that he have "absolutely no personal contact" with Billy. "If I do, I'll be back in jail," Don said.

We calculated it would be six more months until Billy turned 16. "For Billy, that's a long time," I said.

"I have no choice but to stay away from him," Don said. "If I go back to jail, I'd lose my home and business—and Billy wouldn't have a home to come back to."

"At least he's not in an institution," I said. "And he can spend time with the rest of your family. Actually, we've come a long way!"

The usual clamor of the visiting room was noticeably absent, giving us little cloak for our conversations. The visits are video-taped.

The guards allowed Miriam to sit with me through the entire visit. She took my arm with her hands, and wrapped it around her petite shoulders. "I'd like to stay and live with you," she said, curling into my lap.

Back in our cell this evening, CO Brenda brought us a small box containing vitamins that were sent for us from home. "Double X," she read from the package. "What kind of vitamins are they?"

"They're to make us strong, so we never give up," I said.

September 4

By Barbara Lyn

Lunch came at 11:15. The girls complained bitterly, claiming that the pizza was burned, the French fries raw, and the oranges rotten. In protest, they all returned their plates to the food cart and called CO Dorine.

"We're not eating that sh - -! Take it back to the cook!" one of them said.

Dorine said the cook wouldn't replace it, and left, leaving the laden food cart behind. The fries were white, but not quite raw, and the small round pizzas were burned around the edges. Rachel and I ate our portions, and some of the others did, too.

I found an interesting book, titled, *P.S. You're Not Listening,* on our cellblock book caddy. The caddy has probably a hundred paperbacks on it, mostly useless novels. This one was a true story by Eleanor Craig, teacher of a special education class of five severely disturbed children. The children were intelligent but had bizarre behavior, due to poor home situations—mothers with numerous partners and no time for their child, or upper class parents whose child hadn't offered the satisfaction they'd anticipated. The saddest case was an adopted child who wasn't loved by her adoptive family, after having been rejected by her biological mother at age two.

When I finished the book, a thought stung me. This was the kind of reading which had, over the past decade and a half, drawn me into my outreach for troubled children. Is that why I'm in jail today?

After lunch I read five chapters in the Bible. Then, aching from sitting, I got up and started walking. The cell is small, and it made me dizzy to walk around in circles, so I went catty-corner—six steps forward, six steps backward–on and on, maybe a hundred times. Finally it felt a little like I was going for a walk, and my muscles relaxed.

Across the cellblock, several girls watched me, smiling.

"I'm not nuts!" I said.

After my walk I did pull-ups on the frame of our bunk bed, which is made of strong metal and bolted to the wall.

I felt distressed today, viewing myself as terribly unproductive. It didn't help when Rachel reminded me at 4:30 this afternoon that Lydia could probably use some help with supper preparation at home.

CHAPTER 7

Cellblock Songs

September 6, 1993

By Rachel

"Rise and shine!" CO Carole called for our 6:00 AM wake up.

I was drunk with sleep. In fact, for the past few days I can't shake the cloudy feeling. My neck and head hurt, and my eyes feel swollen. My back is sore too. I'm two weeks overdue for my chiropractic adjustment. I wish the chiropractic pillow I have at home could be sent in here.

It's 8:45 in the evening now, and I'm sitting in the common area, alone. I'm allowed out of my cell for an hour each evening, after everyone else is locked in for the night.

Now that I'm double locked and Barbara isn't, there are parts of the day when we're separated, and we are experiencing yet another new aspect to cell life—we have to pass things through the bars to each other. "Rachel, hand me my writing pad," or "Barbara, my comb, please." Both prisoners, but one more than the other?

By Barbara Lyn

This morning I picked a magazine from the bookshelf called, "Chautauqua Vacationlands." Browsing through it, I took special notice of business ads from our hometown.

"Do you think we'll ever go home, Rachel?" I asked. I thought of the compliments we've gotten about our beautiful valley and farm, and the many times we reminded each other not to love our earthly possessions, but use them in return service to God. God is showing us now that these things are not ours, but His gift to us.

It was cold in our cell this afternoon. Rachel and I hopped around to get warm. Jumping high, I hit the ceiling with the palms of both hands at once. In an odd mental state common to caged people, I got a thrill out of the bang my hands made on the metal ceiling panel.

Rachel couldn't hit the ceiling as well as I could because she's shorter. But she tried to outdo me by running across the nine-foot width of the cell, then, stopping short, she jumped and placed the soles of both feet solidly on the wall. As I continued with the ceiling stunt, Rachel began to sing a little jingle. "Get that panel right down and climb right out!"

The other girls gathered outside our cell to view our antics, and cheered us on. Then CO Sue came in to check out the noise. Feeling ashamed, I told her we had gotten cold and were warming up. She didn't give us the scolding we expected.

Tonight I called a gentleman, a stranger, who had sent me a letter asking what he could do for us and our family. On the phone, he said he had visited our farm and met Mom, Nathan, and Susan. He said he had offered to help with bail, and at first couldn't understand why we wouldn't accept it. Now he said he can see it's a principle we are protecting. He wants to help out on the farm, and also offered to send postage stamps and books for Rachel and me.

I just finished writing ten letters, one for each of my school-aged nieces and nephews. It seemed they were close to me, as I communicated with them, using colored pencils and pen. It helped to take away the hurt of not being there for them as they embark on a new school term.

September 9

By Barbara Lyn

We received twelve letters and three packages in the mail today. One of the packages, from a friend, contained postage stamps. It was a godsend, as we had just run out of stamps.

Notes from home are short, but sweet. We love them, and cry, then go on.

Despite the chilly air this afternoon, we're cozy—thanks to the sweat shirts that were sent to us by people who care. Small comforts mean a lot. Looking back at home life, I fear I was often unthankful. Perhaps just forgetful, because of our plenty.

Even in here we have much to be thankful for. A clean conscience with God and clear understanding of truth would be enough. Besides that, our basic physical needs are filled. The hard beds that caused so much discomfort in the beginning now offer nearly comfortable sleep at night.

At the gym, the sun was shining brightly through the three large windows. Rachel and I did a record workout—800 rope jumps each. I'm getting better at basketball, too—which I could detest. It's so unproductive compared to pitching hay and milking cows. Rachel is obsessed with a hand bar that protrudes from the gym wall, about seven feet up. She swings on it like a monkey, amusing the girls.

Today, as I jumped rope, I imagined different ones at home working hard. Ignoring my tiredness, I planted scenes of farm work in my mind–Nathan loading tomatoes; Mom moving baskets of peaches at the fruit stand; Lydia and the young girls scurrying to get lunch on time. The scenes became so vivid, I could see lines and sweat on people's faces, arm muscles bulging. I became so engrossed in imagination that I jumped rope until I nearly collapsed in exhaustion.

September 9

By Rachel

At 6:30 this morning, the TV in the office was running very high, with wild songs and people talking. Occasionally we heard loud outbursts of laughter by the officers.

The girls in here wanted the music down, as they go back to sleep after breakfast. They called CO Carole as loudly as they could, but there was no response.

The TVs here are a constant torment. The one in our cellblock is on all day and late into the night, usually with the volume high. When we go out through the office for visits or rec, the TV there often has soap operas running, with sergeants and COs standing around watching them. The same shows run here in the cellblock, all afternoon. The woman CO comes in and jabbers with the girls about what's on. I can't stand the soaps. They are basically insane, with people invariably ending up screaming, swearing, fighting and running off. I can't imagine living by that garbage, especially to have it running in a police office where people are supposedly busy at computers and telephones.

In the evening we watch "Cops" on TV, a program that shows live scenes of police work. The officers shown seem to be gentlemen, refraining from unnecessary force. They speak patiently, humanely, to people who are in bad shape with alcohol, etc. They do what I used to think officers do—help society. No mocking, no roughness.

Tonight on "Cops" an officer persuaded a boy, about eleven years old, to climb down from a high wire fence in a city. The boy was despondent, saying he hated people. The officer told him we all have our times when we hate people, and walked the boy back to his grandmother. "We're here to help people, that's what we're for," he said when the woman thanked him. "I'll tell you, if we're not helping people, we shouldn't be here."

It stung. That's so much like what I've told the officers here. The voice of that TV cop stays with me: "If we're not helping, we shouldn't be here."

September 10

By Rachel

CO Brenda let me out of my cell to help with cleaning this morning. I had just finished the sink when she came back in and asked the girls if they'd be willing to do some work for the Sheriff's Department. The job consisted of putting a one-page insert into the county's tour guide magazine.

We agreed to do the job. A sergeant and two trusties (inmates who work for the jail) came in with boxes of magazines. Brenda and the sergeant explained how to do the work. No one mentioned my double lock, so I got busy, along with four or five other inmates.

A short time later Brenda called to me from the office door: "Rachel, the boss says you can stay out, as long as you're willing to help, and behave."

We worked on the magazines until late afternoon, and did a total of twenty-two boxes, each with 250 magazines.

At the gym today I called to Joe to say hello. An inmate in Joe's former spot answered, "Joe isn't here. He said to tell you he moved, down to the first floor."

"Why?" I asked. "Was he bad?"

CO Christian was in the gym. He explained to me that Joe was moved to an open block, where people don't get locked into individual cells at night. "He gets that for not making any trouble," he said.

September 11

By Barbara Lyn

My visit this afternoon was fabulous. Miriam sat with me the whole half hour, and my little nieces and nephews climbed over the table for turns to sit on my lap. Kyle sang to me, "Bar-bar-a, Bar-bar-a," and I sang back to him, softly: "Ky-le-e, Ky-le-e." Once I looked back and saw one of the guards smiling. Maybe he was thinking of the "no singing" rule. Or maybe, for a moment the innocence of a child surmounted the magnificence of his uniform.

Then back to cell life. The girls seem to use the 'sh' word in almost every sentence. Tonight as the ladies were getting ready to play a card game, they found the table still cluttered with insert sheets we'd been putting in the magazines. "Get this sh - - off of here," Gwen said.

"Gwen, not *everything* is shit," I said, as I gathered up the offending papers.

Sally gasped. "Ah, Barbara swore! I didn't think Barbara would swear!"

"I didn't mean to," I said, laughing. "I just wanted to remind Gwen you don't have to use that word all the time."

Sally continued her feigned disbelief. "Barbara, I've lost all respect for you, I didn't think you'd swear!"

"Well, it's not the first time I've said the word," I said. "At home we have lots of cows, and there's something that really is called that."

The girls could hardly stop laughing.

By Rachel

This morning I was unlocked again, and helped with the magazines all day.

As we worked, Barbara and I talked with two new inmates who came in last night. Both of them are nice women, and will be leaving soon. They had heard about our case, and couldn't believe we were still here. I told them I could barely get away from farm duties for two hours, to come to Barbara's rally on August 16. Now I've been stuck here for almost four weeks.

CO Doreen has been cold toward us, ever since she double locked me. This morning she brought photos of her youngest daughter, and talked with the inmates about her children. I commented that the baby in the picture looked adorable. Afterward, all I could think is, how can this young woman be so cruel, and she has four small children? How, how?

Barbara and I helped Doreen carry boxes of magazines in and out of the cellblock. I talked to her about a problem I'm having with eye strain, my back surgery ten years ago, and my chiropractic program. Doreen said I could have my family send the chiropractic pillow for me, if that would help. She said Lt. Belson would let me have it.

This evening CO Louise treated us with hot buttered popcorn for the day's work. We also had a big supper of chopped barbecue steak, buttered potatoes in their skins, red beets, and peaches. Some of the girls gave us their extra vegetables, so we feasted. As usual, I gave Barbara my piece of cake.

September 12

By Barbara Lyn

Our 28th day. I feel worn, but peaceful.

Last night as we were getting ready for bed Rachel began to sing from the book, *Songs of Praise.* I knelt on the floor beside her bed, sharing her book, and joined in singing "Revive Us Again," and "It's Not an Easy Road." We sang softly, so it wouldn't disturb the others. Their TV was loud.

Then we started reminiscing about the days and the hours before we came to Mayville on August 16–the rumors we'd heard about officials clamping down on us; the hymn we sang just before we started out for Mayville; the caravan of cars to Mayville, over the hills and dips; the silent resignation as we drove, and the relative peace and quiet as we sat on the courthouse lawn only moments before the attack.

We shed a few tears, sang more songs, then talked some more. An unconscious barrier prevented us from getting into discussion about the violence on August 16, or the outcome. We were just here—and thinking about there, and then.

It was 10:30 by the time we crawled into our meager beds, with folded towels for pillows, a thin sheet and coarse wool blanket for covers. The TV was loud and clear. A movie the girls were watching was impossible to ignore—violent noises, filthy words, heavy breathing. My muscles quivered. I couldn't block the sound, or dispel the suspense. I felt desperate. Why did this horrible movie have to spoil our peaceful evening?

Finally I gave up the struggle. Let be what is, I thought. I'll sleep later when things get quiet. Mental torment subdued, my physical discomforts surfaced. It was cold. My hip hurt when I lay on my side, my shoulder when I lay on the other side. My back side was sore from sitting.

But I fell asleep, and awoke this Sunday morning with thoughts of the peaceful evening taking precedence over the ugly things. God is merciful.

We called home. The family was gathered for worship. They sang "A Mighty Fortress is Our God" for us, with the phone on speaker mode, so we could hear all of their voices. Rachel and I pressed close to the receiver. After the song Mom told us that Miriam, Hannah, and Susan were on their way to visit.

My two youngest sisters and my daughter, I thought. Suddenly overwhelmed with emotion, I gave the phone to Rachel, and struggled to regain my composure. Susan is going to be here anytime, I told my-self. She can't see me like this. Miriam doesn't need this either. Hannah will be strong, but it wouldn't be fair to her if I were to cry—my first visit with her.

Soon we were seated in the visiting room. Our sisters and Miriam came in, escorted by an officer. As usual, two guards stood nearby.

Hannah and Susan had barely begun to share news from home with us when first one, then the other, began to cry. "I'm sorry," Susan said. "It's just hard to see you in here—your jail clothes—and all these guards."

In all our previous visits, Rachel and I had withstood the grief of the family. This time we shared their tears. Hannah held a folded paper napkin, using it occasionally to wipe tears.

"Hannah, do you have a paper in your hand?" one of the guards asked loudly. "Paper isn't allowed."

"It's a tissue," Hannah replied, lifting it above the table to show him.

Rachel turned in her chair to look at the guard. "It's for crying," she said.

"Oh, that's okay," the officer said. He quickly turned away.

Another officer came in and stayed around for most of the visit, watching our interactions unashamedly.

"Do they always gawk like that?" Hannah asked me quietly, speaking in Deutch.

The half hour passed quickly. "Time's up!" a guard barked.

By Rachel

Tonight the men out front are watching the Bills game on TV. Off and on terrible whoops and shouts come from the office. Earlier, when the COs were changing shifts, they were making noise like a drunken street gang out there. How, tell me, can these officers on the job be sitting out there for the last two hours, whooping at the Bills? Maybe they have to be on duty, and just aren't always busy. But the fact that a TV runs at a police office bothers me. Just now another uproarious holler shook our quarters, as the men cheered the Bills.

"Don't they have work to do?" asked Barbara.

"Not when there's a football game," said Sally. She's been here before.

September 13

By Barbara Lyn

Scott Humble, the attorney who visited me several weeks ago, came again to see me. I was taken to the visiting room, and we were seated.

He began to tell me about a jury trial he had watched yesterday, which ended with a guilty verdict in fifteen minutes. The reason for his visit, he said, was to tell me that the judge had appointed him to represent me.

"I'm representing myself," I said.

"When I talked to you a few weeks ago, you were uncertain how you'd prepare your defense," he said. "Don't know if you've decided yet." He paused, looking at me for an answer. I didn't respond. He said there are motions that could be made to the court, and the judge wants to make sure he offers his assistance.

"Isn't it strange that the court appoints a public defender against my wishes, at taxpayer expense?" I asked.

He laughed a little. There was an awkward silence. "I don't know what you're trying to accomplish," he said. "Aren't you looking at the smaller picture?"

"No," I said.

"The big picture is, you may be serving some hard time here," he said.

"No. The big picture is that the court system is incredibly corrupt."

"They're only trying to get through this process as expediently as possible," he said, stammering, "and I'm offering to be available to help in any way."

There was another silence. The visit soon ended. As he walked away, I thanked him for his time.

By Rachel

Soon after Barbara came back, CO Doreen called me to see an attorney, too. I walked with her to the visiting room. At the top of the stairs stood a tall gentleman in a business suit. He reached out his hand. "Rachel? I'm Pete Clark. You remember me?"

"Just a little," I said, feeling awkward. Barbara and I had consulted him on her family court case five years ago. It had been a congenial visit.

"The court appointed me to be your attorney," Mr. Clark said.

"What does that mean?" I asked.

"We'll talk about that—I'll explain that," Clark said quickly. Then he asked CO Doreen to find a place where we could visit. He spoke in a calm, authoritative manner. "Anywhere that we can have some privacy," he said. For a moment I was tempted to think that this person could perhaps help me.

We went downstairs to the jail clergyman's office, and sat across from each other at a desk.

"The court has asked me to represent you this coming Friday in Town Court," Clark began. He opened a big legal pad to a blank page, and had his pen ready. "If you don't want me to, I won't. The court is seeing to it that you have an attorney if you want one."

I paused. I knew that anything I said could be repeated to the court. "I find myself in a strange position," I said. "I have nothing personally against you. But I find it inappropriate that the court should send you to me without asking me if I want you. If I did get counsel, I'd want to choose my own." I also told him I don't know how the court can determine that I'm eligible for a public defender without getting financial information. "The taxpayers are paying for this," I said.

Clark replied that the cost was a "minimal amount." He explained that it is my perfect right not to have an attorney, but he doesn't think self-representation is a wise thing to do. "Criminal charges are serious," he said. He also spoke about getting my bail lowered and asking the court for ROR (release on recognizance).

There was silence. "I want to play it straight," I said. "I want to speak to my accusers as individuals."

Before he left, Clark showed me his empty pad. "See, I didn't write anything," he said with a smile. But he seemed disappointed.

Back in our cell, I sat on the bed. "I hope it was all right that I didn't say more," I told Barbara, who was sitting on her mat on the floor. Barbara and I realize the lawyers who came to see us today have very difficult assignments themselves. The weight of their job can be understood in reading the two-page letter Barbara got from Judge Himelein today—urging, begging, warning that she *must* get an attorney. Then threatening her with two years in jail.

Last night I was reading on Henry David Thoreau's "Civil Disobedience." Thoreau had refused to pay the poll tax, so he spent a night in jail. He says, "Must the citizen ever for a moment, or in the least degree, resign his conscience to the legislator? Why has every man a conscience then?"

Describing his time in prison, Thoreau voiced some of the thoughts I've had lately. He said he was struck by the futility of having his body locked up. "As though I were mere flesh and blood and bones…," he said. "I could not but smile to see how industriously they locked the door…. They plainly did not know how to treat me, but behaved like persons who are under-bred."

September 14

By Rachel

I'm out of double lock.

The mail came when Barbara was napping—eleven pieces. Like a smorgasbord! One from Dad—some from home. I couldn't decide which to read first. I quickly got the ones I knew Barbara would grab if she heard me doing the mail.

After reading the mail there are decisions, and important business to answer—inquiries on our dogs, plus friends who wrote and need answers about why we're still in jail.

After lunch all of us girls went to the gym, as usual. Swanee, the rec director, sat at a desk, keeping the attention of several girls. Two of them were sitting on his desk at once, feet and all. I moved to the far end of the gym to exercise.

As I jumped rope, the inmates on the next floor yelled hello to me. They're the ones in Joe's former cell, and we always say hello. This time one called, "Rachel, come here I want to ask you something." I looked up, and could see two men through the partially open blinds. "I'm telling this guy you're thirty," the man said. "Is that true? He don't believe me."

I could hear the other man mumbling, "She can't possibly be thirty—maybe twenty-two."

"I think that's personal," I said.

"Okay, I'm sorry," he replied.

"No problem," I said, and moved away to jump rope.

Later I heard one of the girls talking to the inmates upstairs about Barbara and me. The girls often stand below the men's window, talking with them about things that make a modest person stiffen. But if we move to the upper end of the gym, away from them, we're close to the rec supervisors. That's worse.

September 15

By Barbara Lyn

Yesterday I had asked Swanee for a book on New York Corrections Law. He said he'd get it, and bring it to the gym. Today I again asked him for the book.

"It's still over across the street," he said. "I didn't have time to get it."

I frowned. Swanee rarely speaks sensibly, and you can't tell if he's serious.

"You don't need it now. You're not in a hurry for it," he said, then added, "Are you?"

I've never seen a character like Swanee. He's totally unpredictable, sometimes very silly. Like mimicking me when I'm doing stationary running—coming close with exaggerated arm motions, then quickly turning around to leave. That's his announcement that it's time to go. Teenagers could act like that, but he must be nearly forty.

The behavior of Swanee and some of the other officers is so disrespectful that it can be frightening. They ignore you, and can't look you in the eye to exchange a sincere greeting. But at another instant, at their convenience, they stare unashamedly.

I was reading in my cell this afternoon when CO Brenda came in and told me there's someone on the telephone—a movie producer from California. "He wants to know if you would release the name of your attorney," she said.

"I don't have an attorney," I told Brenda. She left. A while later when she returned, I asked her who that person was on the phone.

"I don't know," she said. "We told him you don't have an attorney and he just hung up."

Later I called home and found out the same producer had called there. He told the family that jail staff here wasn't cooperating with getting him in touch with me. He had given a California phone number, for me to call him collect. I called the gentleman, and we talked at length. My concern, which I told him, is that movie sensationalism could distort the principles important to this case. He assured me his company has a reputation for accuracy, and said he has an interest in the story because of a personal experience with Child Protective Services.

September 17

By Rachel

It's court day again—the date Judge Mifsud set for Town Court three and a half weeks ago.

As the officers took me up in the elevator, Sgt. Braley asked, "So are you going to walk in today, Rachel?"

Sudden bad memories and emotions were thrown at me. I trembled, and sighed involuntarily. Braley kept looking at me. I wished I could sit down in a corner, alone.

In the waiting room, Peter Clark, the attorney who had visited me, told me the court had offered that I could plead guilty to one charge, and be released.

Soon the courtroom door opened. Clark directed me toward the door, and I walked into court with him. In the gallery with other spectators was Andy Melechinsky, who had come from Connecticut for the second time in the last three weeks. At least a dozen officers lined the corridor.

Judge Mifsud was on the bench. He didn't say hello. I looked to my right to see the assistant DA, Ronald Gibb. He didn't acknowledge my presence. Gibb spoke to the judge, saying that he has an offer here, to resolve the whole matter. I could be released today without bail, if I would plead guilty to obstruction. The riot charge would be dropped, and it would be over.

Clark, standing on my left, addressed the court. "Rachel Lapp has indicated she does not want me to represent her," he said. The judge told him he would have to stay on the case, as standby counsel.

"I want to make it clear that it's not my wish to have Mr. Clark," I said. "My choice of counsel is here today and I would like for him to come up and speak for me."

Mifsud answered quickly. "Mr. Clark will represent you, if you want it or not."

"Mr. Clark cannot properly represent me because he doesn't know my wishes," I said.

"He was appointed to you, and he will be here," the judge snapped.

"Counsel is a personal choice. You can't choose my counsel for me!"

Clark said he would have no objections to having my choice of counsel come up. The judge said no, and closed the subject. He said a trial date has been set for November 17, and repeated the plea bargain. "Do you understand?" he demanded. "Are you accepting it?"

I paused to collect my thoughts. "I just want to repeat, since lawful process has not been followed to bring me into this court—"

"Yes or no?" Judge Mifsud interrupted. "Either you accept, or you're going back to jail until trial."

"If that's what you want to do, that's your burden," I told the judge.

"Yes, that's what I want!" Mifsud said. He brought down his gavel and ordered me back to the sheriff.

Dazed, I walked out, and somehow got my handcuffs on again. Did he say November 17? Two *more* months?

By Barbara Lyn

When I arrived at the court waiting room, the door to the courtroom was open. I could hear the prosecutor talking to the judge about Dad. "Mr. Lapp has been asked to come, but refused," he said.

He explained that despite Dad's absence, he is going to make an offer for him: drop the riot and resisting arrest charges, accept a plea on the obstruction charge, settle the whole thing with "time served," and send him home.

I heard the judge say the offer would stand until the trial date.

Next they called me.

Mr. Humble asked Judge Mifsud to be relieved of duties of representing me. He also showed the judge a motion he had prepared on my behalf, asking that the entire case be dismissed because of the district attorney's failure to try me in a speedy manner.

The judge refused to look at his papers, explaining that as "standby attorney" it is Humble's duty to remain in the courtroom, but he is not to file motions except on my request. Judge Mifsud also denied my request to have Andy assist me as counsel.

Gibb then presented the plea bargain—the same offer he had made for the others, except for my County Court charges that stand as a separate case. He said the Town Court case would be forced to a full trial, if I didn't accept the offer.

"Is that a threat, or—?" I asked.

Judge Mifsud interrupted. "No, it's not a threat."

"Or is it a bribe?" I finished.

Mifsud looked angry. "No! We're talking about resolving this matter," he said. Then he repeated the plea bargain, and asked if I understood.

I started to speak, but he quickly interrupted. "Yes or no! Do you understand?"

I couldn't immediately think what to say.

"I guess if you don't answer, that means yes, you do understand," he said. "We have to move along—I have other things to get to."

In the audience, Andy stood up and walked to the rail that separated the gallery from the court. "The record should show that if Miss Lapp had not been denied her choice of counsel, she would be represented better than by any state licensed attorney," he said.

For a moment, everyone else in the courtroom was silent, and all eyes turned to him. Gray-haired, poised, and wearing a three-piece suit, he stood about twenty feet from the judge, facing him.

Judge Mifsud brought down his gavel. "You cannot address this court!" he said, his voice cracking with anger.

Andy continued. "This court cannot deprive me of my right to speak," he said confidently. "Let the record show that in this court proceeding, the judge has broken many laws."

"If I have broken many laws, so be it," Mifsud said. "Remove the prisoner from the courtroom," he told the officers.

I waved to the crowd as I went out. "Thank God the truth is infallible!" I said.

Many of the onlookers stood, some cheering and waving.

"Keep it up Barbara!"

"I will. I promise!" I said, looking back and waving as officers moved me out of the courtroom.

"Bye, Mom!" Miriam called.

The judge was yelling frantically. "This is not a cheering session! I told you people to stay seated! I'm going to have you removed from the courtroom!"

As I stepped into the elevator with three officers, I heard the judge shouting orders to remove the spectators. Just before the elevator door closed, two of the officers stepped back out. "See how it goes to clear the courtroom," one of them said. They appeared nervous.

By Rachel

When Barbara came back from court we sat on our bunk bed and talked. Tobey called to us from her cell. "I see you two in there trying to get depressed!"

We laughed. "Well, Tobey," I said, "I can hardly say it's not depressing to have two more months ahead."

She nodded. Tobey has been here longer than we have. In recent weeks we've become close to her. She is in her early twenties, determined, possessing the charm and candor we have come to admire among the blacks. She had confided in us during the extreme difficulty of her sentencing, after she pleaded guilty to selling drugs and got two to six years in state prison.

Tobey came into our cell and sat down. "I know *you're* going to get through this because you stand on what you believe," she said. "Me, I couldn't do anything to fight back these people, because I knew I did something wrong. You're doing this for the rest of us."

Tobey continued. "This is the first time anybody has ever challenged this system like you are. You're driving these people crazy. *Nobody* goes to trial on misdemeanors."

Later tonight Tobey told us that the COs ask her questions about us when we're not around. When we missed rec today, they had taken the opportunity to question her. "What are the Lapps doing down there?" Tobey said one of them had asked. "Just sitting around depressed?"

"They're probably singing a song about now," Tobey had answered.

Our phone call home tonight cheered us and encouraged us to

face the next day. Not the next two months, though. Our survival hinges on knowing we're right, and taking things one day at a time. And believing that miracles do happen—including the miracle of being able to bear two more months in this unearthly environment.

It's 1:10 AM. I've been writing for three hours straight. Everyone is asleep except CO Sue, who keeps up the routine checks on the cells every half hour.

September 19

By Rachel

In a letter to Dad, I wrote about my feelings regarding the court hearing. The longer I stay, the more rebellious I feel. I've absolutely had it with this pretense of a government. People in cages who aren't a threat to society. Others that are a threat get out without bail. People with no money for bail sit here and cry for weeks. Male and female COs alike are discouraged and aimless. Sometimes I hear them say they don't feel they're helping. I wonder what it would be like to be in their shoes—caught up in a hopeless system, inmates coming, going, then coming back. Their only hope is for the money, the honor of a uniform, and fun with friends.

This afternoon I suddenly heard sweet voices of singing coming through our window. "Barbara, come here!" I called. We stood by the window, straining to see through the cloudy canopy. We could see dimly, to the parking lot—a group of about a dozen adults and children—our family, singing. After the second song Barbara and I pressed our faces to the window and yelled, "Yeah! Yeah! Keep it up!"

CO Carole came to the gate. *"What* is going on?" she demanded.

"Carole come, you can see them!" I said.

"Don't yell," she said. "There are officers out there, and you could get in trouble."

"I'm sorry, Carole," Barbara said.

The singing outside continued. When the songsters stopped, Barbara and I stood close to the window and began to sing, "Brighten the corner where you are, brighten the corner—"

"Barbara! Rachel! Don't!" It was Carole again. "There are police cameras out there on those people, and if there was to be a disturbance, your people could get into trouble."

We stayed quiet for a while, then spoke to the people outside again, but not loudly. They were only about fifty feet from our window.

After the family left, I spoke to Carole, standing by the wire mesh that separates the cell block from her little desk. "Why can't we sing?" I asked.

"It's one of the rules written in the book. Singing is not allowed in here."

"That's nonsense!" I said. "The TV is singing all the time."

Carole and the girls laughed.

I then asked Carole, as I've asked many COs, if she doesn't ever wonder if it's right to work for a system like this. Carole answered in the same way many others have, only she wasn't angry. "How else am I to raise four children alone?" She said she believes in our cause, but has to be very careful about what she says.

We discussed with Carole the August 16 incident, and the plea bargain we were offered. "I would have had to plead guilty to 'interfering with the lawful arrest of Barbara Lyn Lapp,'" I told Carole. "If Barbara's arrest was lawful, she is a criminal. By taking the plea, I'd be agreeing to her being a criminal. I can't do that. I support her for helping Billy."

Carole looked taken aback, then answered thoughtfully. "There are very few people who stick with what they believe," she said. "They just go along with things to make it easier."

"Yes," I said. "Including yourself."

September 20

By Rachel

It's strange how a day begins. It's never normal here, but it's becoming closer to it.

At 6:15 the CO announces wake up time by bringing our breakfast on a creaking, rattly metal cart.

I stumble out of bed, and lumber out of our cell, rubbing my eyes and pushing back my hair. The cart is where it always is, about ten feet from our cell door—milk and juice on top, donuts on the next shelf. One by one we inmates take our portions and return to our cells to eat.

I brush my teeth.

All eight of us crawl back into our beds.

At 8:15 the CO wakes us for cleaning. My eyes still hurt, the toilet in the next cell is still leaking, and the girl from that cell is still complaining. "Hm-m-m, does that toilet ever *stink!* I'm going back under the blanket so I don't smell it!"

I help her to remind the CO about the leak, which has been there for weeks. The CO tells the girl to take up the wet blanket that was in front of the toilet for absorption purposes. The girl cleans the whole floor with disinfectant soap, and puts a clean blanket down.

I scrub the metal common table, then the benches that are attached to it. Boxes of tour guides, nine of them, are still around and under the table, because staff didn't bring us the inserts to finish the job. I have to push the boxes around for cleaning.

Small things like this bother people. A girl hisses. "Those ugly boxes still here! Are *they* getting on *my* nerves!" I appease her anger by finding out from the CO when we can get the inserts.

Then it's the shower curtain, badly mildewed and frayed on the bottom half. "That shower curtain!" someone yells, turning away in disgust.

A little later, a scream comes from the shower. The water is too hot—again. We laugh. Everyone knows what it's like. You never can get it the right temperature. You gasp with cold water, yelp at the hot water, frantically pushing the hot and cold buttons. But you never get it right, because the hot and cold always do, and always will, come separately. Some mornings you might be lucky, when the hot water is warm. "Is the water hot?" the others ask when you step out.

"Just right!" If that's the answer, others will take their chance to get right in. But sooner or later, another unfortunate comes storming out, declaring it's no longer "right."

.

■ CHAPTER 8 ■

Coldness

September 21, 1993

By Barbara Lyn

It's cold. Some of the ladies are sitting around with wool blankets wrapped around themselves. Rachel and I periodically get up from our writing and hop around to keep warm.

I had a visit today from Ed Reasor, an Alaskan movie producer. He is an attorney, said he had been Attorney General of Alaska some years ago.

Mr. Reasor told me he grew up in an orphanage, and at age fourteen moved to a foster home on a farm only fifteen miles from here. His former foster family had sent him local news clippings on my case, and he sees it as a quality story for film-making.

When I called home, I found out another movie producer had left a message for me to call. A third producer, the one who first contacted me, also wants a phone call from me. With three involved, it's getting complicated. It seems my stress tolerance is low when making business decisions. I get confused easily, and it takes long to calculate things. Now I have a headache.

I'm trying not to let my mental functions deteriorate. Last night I wrote until 12:30, and between Rachel and me, we sent out nine letters.

One of the COs told us recently that they keep a record of names and addresses of everyone we write to. It seems like such an invasion of our friends' privacy.

September 23

By Rachel

This evening we got the news of the birth of Joe and Nancy's new baby. The jail phone system hadn't been working all day. When we tried to call home, we could hear them, but they couldn't hear us. Finally, on our umpteenth try, one of them announced: "The Torres have a boy!" We cheered, but they never heard us.

Beth, one of the inmates who came shortly after we did, went home today. She had suffered a lot, with no one sending her warm clothing, and no money for commissary.

When the ladies leave I often remind them of the Golden Rule, telling them it goes a long way in keeping them out of trouble. This morning when Beth was leaving the rest of us were still in our cells. Tobey called to her from her cell: "And remember, Beth, when you go out there, you treat people like you'd like to be treated."

I listened in disbelief, then delight.

"Right, Rachel?" Tobey finished.

"You're right!" I said. "That goes a long way."

Later Barbara and I spoke to two Spanish girls about our arrest, and the upcoming trials. One of them said, in a worried tone, "You better hire an attorney or you'll just stay here."

The other one, Flora, said, "No! Let them go. They're not pleading, and these people will get tired of it!" Flora is serving a three month sentence because her ex-husband once sold drugs in her house. She says the police asked her to make an undercover purchase for them, with wiretaps on her. Everyone in town knows she doesn't use drugs, Flora said, and making a purchase would have made her conspicuous as a police informant, and could have put her life in danger. She declined, and for that, they brought her to jail.

September 24

By Barbara Lyn

This morning the CO brought me a big envelope from Scott Humble, with all kinds of legal arguments he would like to make on my behalf.

It's depressing. Maybe I'd be happier if I'd do like Dad does–not have a thing to do with the courts. I'm torn between that and feelings of obligation to state my position to the jury. Even if I speak, I don't know if a court-selected jury in this zoo could find me innocent. The court will accomplish whatever they want. Unless, as Scott Humble and many others would have me believe, I get involved in the game before it's too late.

Tonight when CO Louise came in I told her we have some questions about bail.

"What's your question?" she asked.

"If someone would bring bail money what would *we* have to do?" I asked.

Louise, standing outside the gate, stared at me. "If someone brings bail money, you go out—that's it."

Rachel joined the discussion. "We just wanted to know what kind of commitment we would be making on our part, as far as coming back to court."

"You'd sign the bail receipt," Louise said.

"What would happen if I didn't come back to court?" Rachel asked.

"You'd lose your money."

"Is that all?"

"Yes."

"She might be arrested, too," I reminded Louise.

"Oh, yes, they'd put a warrant out for your arrest."

"What about the fingerprints," I asked. "Would we have to do that?"

"You haven't been printed?" she asked in surprise. "Definitely, you won't be released without it, if you're here for a printable crime."

I asked Louise for a copy of a bail receipt. She brought it after we were locked in for the night. Part of it read, "I hearby personally undertake and agree that I will appear."

After reading the whole slip, thoughts of posting bail made me feel nauseated. I envisioned myself home with Miriam, in an open field. I could feel the weight at the pit of my stomach to know I would one day get in a car, drive over the hills to Mayville, and thrust myself into this dreadful, morbid court. As the bail slip says, "there to remain to any order of the magistrate and render myself in execution thereof."

No, I will not bind my soul, just to be released for material comfort. These hard, cement walls and cold bars, and even the contemptible hands of our captors, cannot enslave me. When the day comes that God sees it well for me to be free in body, as God lives, I will also be free at heart.

It's after 8:00 now, and extraordinarily noisy. There were two fierce arguments among the inmates today, one in Spanish, over a lost bracelet that had been smuggled in. CO Doreen came in and announced to all of us that if the bracelet didn't turn up, there was going to be a shakedown. We would have every single thing taken from our cells. The girls continued to argue, and the bracelet was not brought forward. But there was no shakedown.

The second argument began when a girl was insulted that another inmate didn't want to share her cell because she's HIV-positive. We were grateful for the earplugs a friend had sent for us several days ago.

We hear the jail boiler is broken, and may not be repaired for another month. It is so cold in the cells. The extra sweat shirts our friends sent for us helped, but we're still cold at night. Last night I told CO Louise that we had trouble sleeping because of the cold. She was apologetic, and brought extra blankets for all the inmates.

September 25

By Barbara Lyn

At lunchtime, CO Carole brought us some tomatoes and cucumbers—the first farm fresh vegetables we've had in here. Rachel reacted to the vegetables with exaggerated jubilance. After eating them, she danced around, pretending to be supercharged with energy. I cried over the last of my lunch because the cucumber reminded me of home.

Felicita, a sweet Puerto Rican girl, came into our cell this afternoon, and confided her problem of not being able to sleep at night. She said she's worried about her four small children at home. We talked a long time about her legal difficulties and family problems. Then I told Felicita about my family. She asked if I want to adopt any more children. I said if she knows someone who needs a mother, she should let me know.

"Yo nesecito mama!" ("I need a mother!") she burst out.

I threw my arms around her and said, "Ah! Te llevo a mi casa!" ("I'll take you to my house!") We laughed.

By Rachel

This morning at 6:45 when we were back in bed after breakfast there was a lot of noise out at the office again. It was the day for the jail doctor to make his semi-weekly rounds with inmates, and the officers were joking about getting drugs from him. One of them let out a loud yelp. "Just write out that prescription, every eight hours! I feel *great!*" he said. They roared with laughter.

One of the girls, irritated with the noise, called out, "Shut up!"

CO Sue came right in. "Who said that?" she demanded. "If you think it's gonna be quiet here when shifts are changing, you're gonna learn. This is wake up time, not time to sleep!"

Everyone in the cellblock is asleep or quiet until about 8:00 in the morning. We respect each other. But the COs have no respect.

It's unconscionable how they behave, especially after strict controls on us. A few days ago CO Brenda was in here, laughing and telling the girls she had put cooked rice from supper in Sgt. Bohn's coffee, and into his eyeglass case, too. She bent over with laughter as she recalled that she then pricked the sergeant "in the butt" with a needle, and when he and the other officers finally had enough, three of them rounded her up and handcuffed her. "With my own hand-cuffs!" she said. "They had a hard time getting me, because I'm strong!"

Brenda then walked out to the office. We heard her yell at an officer, "Get off my phone!"

"Get your a - - back in there!" he responded.

"Get your a - - away from my phone," she retorted. "You're an a - - h - - -!"

The girls all crowded around the gate to watch, laughing. Brenda came back in. "The men don't know how to handle me!" she told the girls, giggling uncontrollably.

Then one of the inmates told Brenda how she had given the police a hard time when they tried to handcuff her. Brenda and the other girls laughed. The whole thing was making a joke out of law enforce-ment, which sadly, has become a joke anyway.

Next Brenda was out in the office, booking a male inmate. The girls again crowded against the gate of the cell block, peeping through the partially open curtain. They called to the men COs. Brenda came in. "You can't do that!" she scolded the girls. She pulled the curtain between the cell block and the office, so they couldn't see.

The phone still hasn't been repaired. It's our third day without phone contact with home. The day seemed long. The TV was loud, hour after hour. Then an argument between two inmates over who could have the TV turned into a fight. The girls began to grab each other's arms. Without warning, a male CO came in to separate them. It seems so unfair that a man can suddenly invade our quarters. The quarrels and noise make me long for the peace of home.

September 26

By Rachel

This afternoon CO Carole called me to the gate. "Someone wants to talk to you," she said quietly. I followed her to the office.

CO Jim Crowell, who is always respectful, gave me a slip of paper with a name and phone number. "An attorney. He wants you to call him," he said. I recognized the name—a business friend who is also a lawyer, and now lives in California.

CO Crowell and Carole offered to let me use their phone, as ours is still down. "I'm taking her out here," Crowell said quietly to Carole, "where she can have some privacy." He showed me a phone I could use in the hall beyond the office, where the trusties have their quarters. He and a trusty showed me how to use it, then left.

I had just dialed the number when I heard a sergeant demanding, "Why is she on the phone?" Then he came over. "You have four to five minutes," he said. I nodded.

Dean, the lawyer, said he had received the letter I sent him last week. "You've got to get out of there," he said. "I'd like to talk to the judge and the DA and we'll find a way to get you out." When he continued to urge me, I asked him what we would do. He suggested bail, or a plea bargain. "For example, if this was a traffic ticket for speeding, you'd plead to a parking violation," he said. "Some small compromise."

"Dean, I can't plead!" I said. "You don't understand how far that would be from me to plead to something unrelated. I've got to stick with the truth."

After a few minutes the sergeant came over again and asked me to wind up the conversation.

Dean said if I'm not willing to plead, perhaps we're at an impasse. He was disappointed. "They'll take it to trial, and they'll get their conviction," he said.

I thanked him for his efforts to help.

When I got off the phone I noticed three trusties sitting on a cot just inside their door, watching me. "You stick with it!" said one of them.

September 27

By Barbara Lyn

On our way back from rec, I stood at the door of the gym, waiting for the elevator. A voice from a nearby cell startled me. "Dat geht si!" (In Deutch, "There she goes!")

I didn't look up. I felt tense, standing in view of male inmates, the girls around me exchanging flirtatious remarks with them. Then I heard the voice a second time, and looked to see Dad peeping out between the bars, only a few yards away. He had a mischievous look.

"Dad!" I said loudly.

A CO came up close to me. I thought he was going to rebuke me for yelling. Instead, he told me quietly, "Your dad is out of double lock now. He took the TB test and will be able to have his first visit tomorrow." Then the elevator door opened, and I had to go.

This afternoon two telephone repairmen came in, finally tracked the problem with our phone, and fixed it. We celebrated with a call home.

Tonight at eight Rachel and I got a new inmate in our cell. She had just come from a federal prison down south. The facility where she was, had three thousand women. She shared quarters with six hundred of them. She said victims of inmate violence were regularly buried behind the prison. Women already serving life terms had nothing to lose by killing, she said.

September 28

By Rachel

The gym floor was a mess today. The roof leaks, and a large area in the basketball court was wet. Some of the water had been cleaned up with blankets and mops, which were lying sloppily around. Hair from haircuts, and dirt was mixed with the water. No one seemed to care. The other girls usually don't exercise anyway.

I picked up a dirty mop and wrung it out into a pail of water that sat under the filthy leaking water fountain. After cleaning up a big puddle of water, I went to rinse my hands at the fountain. There was no water. My hands and arms were dirty, covered with hair clippings.

I asked Swanee where I could rinse my hands. He looked up from the card game he was playing with several girls. "I-i-ish!" he said, looking at my hands. He took me out the gym door, into the hall, and opened a door into a nook in the wall. There was a large basin with running water and soap, but it was so dirty I wouldn't use the soap. The whole corner was filthy. Swanee brought me a clean bar of Ivory soap, and paper towels.

It's unbelievable how dirty this place is. On weekends, inmates are housed in the gym, sleeping on cots. On Mondays the place is often littered with pieces of apples and toast and other trash. It's ridiculous, low. There are trusties who could clean things, not to mention idle COs. I've told Swanee and the women COs that Barbara and I could clean the gym. But they say only the trusties are allowed to work.

Today I hugged Mom, for the first time in six weeks. She came to visit Dad, whom we hadn't seen for five weeks. Mom had been afraid to come here, since she was supposedly under arrest when she left the scene on August 16.

In the visiting room, Dad was seated a few chairs away from me, at the far end of the long table. I reached to shake hands with him.

"Rachel, you can sit down there if you want," the CO said, pointing to the chair beside Dad. I moved to the chair, then realized what a favor it was, and thanked him.

Dad looked much smaller, thin and white compared to his husky summer appearance. He said he enjoys being with Joe and having more freedom since being out of double lock. Both of them are in an open block now, and he helps Joe with reading and writing. Dad said he went to gym today, and slept better last night.

Mom seemed weighed down. Perhaps she suffers more than any of us. She and Susan now manage the fruit stand, with the help of a volunteer. I long to help them, but all I can do is answer their business questions.

Our cellmate from federal prison is here for the second day. She says her crime was computer tampering, and she's sorry for what she did. Tonight she asked us questions about the Scriptures, and how she could better her own life. We got our Bibles, sat on mats on the floor, and talked for hours.

September 29

By Barbara Lyn

I was shocked by the chilly air I woke up to this morning. Rachel has back pain that is no doubt exacerbated by the cold. Another inmate had a seizure and fever last night, and was taken to the emergency room at midnight.

A few days ago Rachel asked Tobey, who is taking GED (General Equivalency Diploma) classes here in jail, to find out if we could go to class too. This morning the teacher sent a message through the CO that we could. We got ready, and CO Carole took us to the classroom, just down the hall from the office.

The classroom has one long table, with room for about eight students. Today's class was only Tobey, Rachel and me. Cindy, the teacher, started us with pre-tests. Both of us scored well, except on algebra.

While in the classroom, CO Carole came in and said the public defender wanted to see me. I got up to follow Carole, and told the teacher I'd be right back.

"I'll just be telling him I don't need their help," I told Carole as we walked up to the visiting room.

Carole stopped walking and looked at me squarely. "Barbara, you *do* need help!" she said, laying her hand on my shoulder. "I don't want to see this go on and on."

I hesitated, feeling in my heart that Carole was sincere. "We don't want it to go on either," I said. "I would like help—but not the kind of help lawyers give."

"Barbara, your example is so important," Carole pleaded. "What you do is what Rachel will do. I don't want to see you two in here." Her voice trailed off. "Of course it's not my business. I shouldn't be saying this, but I can't help it—there's so much at stake. Even your dad is watching what you do."

The public defenders in the visiting room were both lawyers known to me through prior dealings with family court cases, during my advocacy work with other families. I had to force away feelings of embarrassment as I greeted them, now appearing in the garb of a criminal.

They said Judge Himelein had asked them to offer legal assistance, and informed me that my trial was to begin on October 13. I told them I did not want help from their office. "I have nothing against you personally," I said. "If it were not for the precarious situation I am in now, I would like to explain my reasons. Perhaps sometime I can."

They looked perplexed.

A sergeant soon came and escorted me back down to the classroom.

Later this afternoon Carole commented that the consultation with the lawyers didn't last very long.

"Carole, I'm sorry I can't relieve your concerns," I said, "but those people can't help me. I could get out of jail with or without their help, if I'd be willing to play the game."

September 30

By Barbara Lyn

The girl who had a seizure the other night, Dee, is still here, after many unfulfilled promises by staff that they would get her to a hospital. Dee has AIDS. This morning a CO came in and gave her oxygen. Last week she showed me, in great alarm, her fingernails were coming off. Her fingers were bleeding. No one wants to get close to her. She begs to be hospitalized. We hear the jail supervisor is trying to get her released on parole, so the state, rather than the county, would be responsible for medical costs.

This morning I was unexpectedly called out to the office. Lt. Belson said Judge Himelein wanted to talk to me. Belson said it wasn't a court hearing, and it's up to me if I wanted to go. I was so curious to find out what the judge wanted that I decided to go.

Lt. Belson and CO Brenda took me up to the courtroom.

I was surprised to see a court reporter in the room, and Judge Himelein sitting up on his platform. He said he wanted to inform me of my rights before my upcoming trial, and make it clear that standby counsel was going to be available. "You can request their assistance at any time." He asked if I planned to hire an attorney for the trial.

"I don't care to answer that," I said.

He laughed a little, then explained the trial process, in some detail. "I don't know if you will be taking part in the trial or not," he said, almost as a question.

I looked at him, but didn't answer.

"Are you?"

"I didn't come here to be questioned."

"I know," he said. "Actually, what I'd like to know is if *you* have any questions."

"I guess not."

He showed me a book he had with a list of questions to ask defendants who go to trial without an attorney. "The questions are not so much to satisfy me," he said. "I know you're an intelligent person, and you understand what you're doing." He paused to look at me, then went on. "So if I were to read you these questions—there are about fifty—would you respond?"

"The only thing I can tell you is I know my rights as an American citizen."

Judge Himelein said he planned to be in Mayville every day until my trial date of October 13. "Any time you need me, or have any questions, I'll be available," he said.

"Thank you," I said.

Brenda and Lt. Belson took me back down. As we walked, they discussed Dee's illness. Brenda said Dee is good at faking. "The aches and pains are a part of the disease she'll have to live with," she said.

Belson said the judge doesn't want to terminate her sentence unless he's sure she's on her "last days."

In the office, Brenda asked Belson if he had given an inmate a towel he'd requested.

"Nope!" Belson answered arrogantly.

"You're a bully!" Brenda said, laughing. "You and Bill (Sgt. Bohn) are bullies. You enjoy being a bully!"

As I write this evening, I feel bad about the whole day. The cold-hearted talk of our captors bothers me. And Rachel said I shouldn't have gone up to court. She is upset that the judge had the opportunity to give a show of justice.

I talked to Kevin Stefan (Billy's brother) on the phone. He was at a court hearing for his father yesterday, and said the attorney for Social Services presented three options: One, put Billy in his grandmother's custody; two, leave things as they are; three, use the "atomic fly swatter approach" and get Billy back, no matter how much force it takes.

Billy is staying with relatives part of the time, and sometimes at our home. Kevin said he's generally doing well but has some difficult times. He feels left out because he's the only one who can't be home, since the rest of his brothers are back home with their father.

October 1

By Rachel

Greetings to October! First August passed, very slowly, then September, much faster. How many more months will come and go, here in this most unpleasant abode?

I've been reading Frederic Bastiats' book, *The Law*. He wrote about his country, France, in 1850, and how it had fallen. His observation of the United States at that time was: "There is no country in the world where the law is kept more within its proper domain: the protection of every person's liberty and property." However, he pointed out instances of injustices in our history, such as slavery and protective tariffs. He called these "legal crimes…, a sorrowful inheritance from the Old World."

Bastiat says that when a government gains power to confiscate property through taxation, that is plunder. This power will be used to benefit establishments that gain from the use of plundered money.

In our case, innumerable persons and establishments are fighting loss of benefit—administrators at the children's home who wanted Billy; social workers, psychologists and law guardians of Cattaraugus County. Their actions against the Stefan family all have a motive. It's their livelihood. Just like everybody who works here, they have to earn a living. The only reason these people have the power to do what they're doing is because plunder is legal in the U.S. Plunder of property, and of liberty.

October 2

By Barbara Lyn

We hear the folks at home are sick. It's painful. Just after feeling relief with news that Nancy is recovering from the flu, we hear it's Nathan, gravely ill with pneumonia. Nathan, the family mainstay. And it's harvest time.

During a visit with the family today we talked about Nathan's sickness. Mom said he'd worked so hard, without much sleep, just before he got sick. In the daytime he was heading the tomato harvest crew or filling silo, and at night he was at the computer, working on legal research and publicity for us. Mom said she feels like Job. In a letter we got from home, Lydia wrote: "Four went to jail, now four are sick."

Last weekend a friendly sergeant here tried to assure us the farm will survive until we get home. "It will be okay—you'll have the winter to get back on track," he said.

I felt a wave of bitterness. What if members of our family die before winter? These people are responsible for this struggling family, the suffering, the sickness. But they don't see it that way.

Tonight I asked CO Carole for a book by Lysander Spooner that Mom had sent. I wasn't allowed to have it because it has a hard cover, and it had been placed in my personal storage area. "It's a historical writing on jury trials," I explained to Carole, "I need it to prepare for my trial." I pointed out that I borrow hard cover legal books all the time, and keep them in my cell.

Carole brought the book. "The sergeant says the cover has to come off," she said with a sigh. Together we inspected the book. It appeared the cover could not be removed without losing the binding.

Determined to take the book to my cell, I began to pull off the cover. It tore easily, leaving the pages intact. I was delighted. But Carole did not look at all amused.

"It's no big deal, Carole," I said. "I can replace it when I get home." Handing her the torn cover, I added. "Look at this! If I were a little smaller, I'd have gotten my hands smacked!" Carole laughed. She gave me the book's cover jacket, and I wrapped it around the naked pages.

October 3

By Rachel

Sunday supper is over. As usual for Sunday, it was two sandwiches, Koolaid, peanuts, an apple, an ice cream sandwich, and cake. Okay when you need food, but not really wholesome. Usually the bread is white. Tonight one sandwich had a ground bologna spread, the other a slice of something that looked like cheese food. It had no taste, so we put hot sauce from commissary on the bread. The ice cream sandwich was so mushy you had to eat it in a cup, with a spoon.

We've been getting apples with lunch, about twice a week. They are fresh and crisp, but incredibly sour. Most of the girls can't eat them. Barbara and I eat them, puckering faces, simply because they're fresh fruit. There are many wonderful apples in the area, especially this season. Why do we get an apple so green it would sour a pie?

If jails held only criminals, they shouldn't eat really well anyway. But there are things we observe that don't make sense. Why are the fish patties we get on Fridays either so stale or so underdone, that the girls can't stomach them? Barbara and I, more active, and hungry because we don't eat junk snacks from commissary, had been eating the fish. But not anymore. Last Friday both of us got stomachaches after supper, and felt bad for hours.

And why the lack of fresh produce in here, when around the countryside farmers almost throw away fruits and vegetables in seasons of surplus? Then the jail has to dispense milk of magnesia or other laxatives, because of lack of fiber in the diet. And why are the breakfast muffins and toast drenched with margarine, sometimes soaked all the way through?

The food one can live with. There are things we consider worse, like the lack of heat in here. And the leaking toilet in one cell. Seven weeks now, with the same leak. Every morning the girls ask for a clean blanket to stuff by the toilet to absorb the water. Every day the jail has to launder that big, heavy blanket. The whole cellblock smells.

October 4

By Barbara Lyn

At lunch time CO Brenda was talking to the girls about one of the jail cooks, who she said is to blame when food isn't done right. She went on and on, fueling the girls' disdain for the cook.

Rachel and I were offended by the gossip, and retreated to our cell. "That girl makes me sick. I can't stand it," Rachel said quietly about Brenda.

"You make me miserable talking like that," I said to Rachel. "Stop it!" Recently Rachel and I had agreed we wouldn't let the COs' bad behavior get us down.

A short time later it was my turn. When Brenda brought us back from rec, a teenage boy sat in the booking room. He looked incredibly scared, and watched us as we filed past—six prisoners in dark green. I gave him a reassuring smile. The other girls were making some mildly mocking comments about how young he was to be in here. When we got back into the cellblock, still within hearing range of the boy, Brenda told us he was just sixteen. She was laughing.

Peeping through the door, one of the girls said, "Wow, he's just a kid. He'll get a good beating when he gets home."

"What's he here for?" another girl asked.

Brenda was trying to tell us, but was laughing so much she could hardly talk. She said the boy had gotten into a bubblegum machine at Quality Markets, took some to school, and the police went in and arrested him right in front of his classmates. She said one of the officers in the booking room had told him he was going to stay for two years. The boy took it seriously. "And I told him, 'Good thing it wasn't jaw breakers—I'd give you an extra year,'" Brenda said.

One of the girls made a facial expression, imitating how scared he looked. Brenda went out, laughing uncontrollably.

I felt like crying, I was so angry. I wanted to barge out into the office and give the boy some sound advice. The fright on his face told me he wasn't the hardened kind.

I buried myself in Lysander Spooner's writings on jury trial. Spooner was a nineteenth century lawyer/philosopher. He says a jury not randomly selected is a "sham and a hoax, utterly worthless for protecting the people against oppression." He also writes about the impossibility of finding justice in a courtroom dominated by a judge wielding the power to slap contempt charges on any party—counsel, witness, defendant, or juror—who might go beyond his interpretation of law.

As historical and philosophical reading, the book is immensely interesting. For gaining insight into what might happen at my trial, it is very discouraging.

October 5

By Barbara Lyn

Inside Edition finally ran our story. The inmates whooped when they saw the previews. We all watched together. CO Brenda was here in the cellblock. She slipped out to the office to alert the other officers, then came back and watched with us.

The girls jeered as pictures of COs they recognized came on the screen. When the police violence of August 16 was shown, they loudly pointed out details. One girl gasped, "They kicked your Mom!"

After the show one of the girls asked me about the scene of a young man being yanked by the head. I told them that was my brother, and the yank had given him a neck injury that caused him difficulty in swallowing for three days.

"You should press charges against the police!" the girl said.

The *Inside Edition* program portrayed Billy as living in a secret location.

"How can you keep him hidden from the police all this time?" one of the girls asked.

"Billy is not exactly hiding anymore," I explained. "But he's not allowed to go home, so friends and neighbors help to care for him."

I told the girls the best part of the show was seeing Billy. Rachel and I described how Billy was in poor shape, emotionally and physically, when he first came to us.

"He looks good now," one of them commented. Everyone agreed.

October 7

By Barbara Lyn

CO Brenda came in this morning and said the public defender wants to see me. I told her I wasn't interested. She went out, but came right back. "Barbara, could you just step outside a little?" she asked. "He just wants to hand you a paper. You don't need to get your greens on."

"I've told them already I don't need them," I said. "How many times do they expect me to say it?"

Brenda laughed a little, and left. Soon she returned, handing me a paper from the lawyer—a motion to have the public defender removed from my case because of conflict of interest.

Lunch came. As usual, we ate quickly so we would be ready in time for rec.

"Barbara, you have County Court—how about that?" Brenda called.

"What's *that* about?" I asked. "I'm not going if they don't tell me what it's about."

She said she'd find out, and came back to tell me it was about the motion she showed me earlier. I told her I had nothing to do with that.

Ten minutes later Brenda was back—for the sixth time today—begging for my cooperation. "Barbara, we have the court on the phone. They want to know why you don't want to come up."

I was beginning to feel harassed. "They don't *need* to know!" I said.

We were called for rec. At the gym, I let out my frustration by working into a soaking sweat with one thousand rope jumps and a hundred sit-ups. Then I played basketball with the other girls.

When we got back, I had a letter in the mail from Scott Humble. He advised me to make a motion to have my second trial severed from the rest of the defendants.

I took a shower and retreated to our cell to relax. Then I heard the gate open. CO Brenda walked right into our cell, apologizing when she saw I wasn't fully dressed. "Barbara, they won't leave you alone today," she said. "There's an attorney, Scott Humble, here to see you."

"I don't want to talk to him. Tell him I said, 'No thank you.'"

At 5:30 CO Louise handed me a letter through the bars. "From County Court," she said. It was a letter from Judge Himelein, saying he had appointed Scott Humble to represent me, and hopes he will be able to convince me it would be in my best interest to have him vigorously defend me at next week's trial.

That made a total of ten attempts in one day—attempts to make me use attorneys and honor the court. Why is it so important to them? Why can't they prosecute me without asking for my help?

By Rachel

From the gym windows we can see the trees fully colored, proving to those behind bars that time is moving.

I think of the seeds I planted this spring, and how they responded to our care by yielding their glorious fruits of various colors. I think of how I had to pamper the Habañero hot peppers to get them to grow, and my concern that New York temperatures would be too harsh for this tropical pepper. Would it succumb to cold nights and abundant rain? To my delight the tiny bonnet-shaped fruits appeared, and possessed the flavor and fiery heat of the ones we'd enjoyed in Belize years ago. Now the Habañero peppers are probably dead, their fruit dropped to the ground and rotting, after a fall frost.

Somehow, those peppers—their growth and death—exemplify the suffering and neglect of creatures far more important. I mourn for my family, for their suffering in illness, and the oppressive workload our absence has imposed on them. I mourn for Joe's children, and for Mom and Dad, who have to be separated.

October 8

By Barbara Lyn

Just before eleven this morning CO Doreen came in."Barbara, Rachel, get your greens on," she demanded. "The lieutenant wants to see you."

"Why?" I asked. "What does he want?"

"I don't know. Now get your greens on," Doreen repeated.

I hadn't combed my hair, and was in bare feet and shower slippers. But we followed her out.

We were met by Lt. Lawrence, Lt. Belson and another plainclothesman. Lawrence approached us, clacking his handcuffs. "We're going to take you to court," he said.

"Do we have to go?" I protested.

"Just have to go see the judge a little," he said.

I glanced at my feet. "Can I get my shoes?"

Lawrence looked at Doreen as if he feared they'd lose me if he'd allow me to go back in. Doreen said it's okay, and took me in to get my shoes.

By Rachel

Lt. Lawrence spoke kindly as he cuffed me. "It's beautiful outside, Rachel. Sunny, sixty-eight degrees."

"Yes, we saw the sun through our window," I said.

As we began to walk, Lawrence asked, "Would you like to go home?"

I looked at him in surprise.

"It's a nice day out there," he said.

"I'd go home any day!" I blurted out. "Even if it were raining!" He chuckled.

As we walked, the officers chatted about an upcoming ball game.

We got to the holding room, where we met Dad and Joe. I took a chair beside Joe, and we spoke in Spanish. "What do you think they want with us in court?" Joe asked.

I told him what Lt. Lawrence had said on the way up. "Maybe we're going home," I said quietly, trying to contain my excitement.

Barbara and Dad sat nearby, talking in Deutch. Dad said he won't go into court unless they physically force him.

"Maybe it's easier for you," Barbara said. "But Rachel and I feel we can't keep up the resistance. I just can't take it anymore to let those men handle me."

"I can understand that," Dad said.

An attorney appointed by the court, Mr. Harley, came and knelt beside Dad. He told Dad he wanted to make some motions for him in court, and pleaded that Dad allow him to help.

Dad answered slowly. "I'd like to make it easy for you. But this court has departed from the time-tested rules of honor and justice, and I don't want to be a part of the proceeding. I'm all for law and justice," he continued. "I'm willing to abide by the law. But it has to be honorable law. One of the rules of justice is that you cannot take a person's liberty away before probable cause has been established by a grand jury. I'd be happy to go to a court like that."

Harley said he respects what Dad is saying, though he doesn't agree. "I'm just trying to think if there's any place here for compromise."

He sighed. "Would you be willing to tell the court that you object to having me speak for you?"

Dad said no, and when Harley continued to question him, he stayed mute.

Then they came for Barbara.

By Barbara Lyn

I stood in front of the judge, five attorneys on my left and Mr. Gibb, the assistant DA on my right. Judge Mifsud was on the bench again.

Gibb began with a motion to the court. "I would like the case of Barbara Lyn Lapp, Jacob Lapp, Rachel Lapp, Joe Torres, and Lynn Carroll all to be tried at the same trial," he said. "These charges occurred at the same place, at the same time…. We have the same witnesses, Your Honor… and it would only make judicial sense as well as practical sense to try all of these cases at the same time."

Gibb turned to me. "Ms. Lapp, do you have any opposition to having all of these cases tried at the same time?"

I did not answer, having made a personal vow not to speak in the courtroom today.

"You're going to have to speak sooner or later," Gibb said.

The judge looked at me sternly. "If the court is to know what your wishes are, you must express yourself. If you stand there and say nothing, then the court has to make the decision for you. So I'm asking you, as you've been asked, do you have any objection?"

He paused briefly, then continued. "Hearing no opposition in silence, I'll grant the motion," he said.

"Thank you, Your Honor," Gibb said.

The four attorneys who stood for the other defendants joined in vigorous opposition to the judge's ruling, saying their clients had not yet been heard.

Mr. Humble, the attorney who was there for me, asked the judge whether he could present motions to the court. Mr. Gibb answered that he can't do anything for me unless I ask him to. Humble replied that his motion pertains only to whether the charges against me were legally supported by New York State law, and as an officer of the court, it was his duty to make that motion. A long argument between Humble and Gibb ensued.

Judge Mifsud looked like he didn't know what was going on. "Barbara, we're going to ask you, do you want this standby counsel to present anything to this court on your behalf?" he finally asked. "Now Barbara, you must address the court…."

Three times he questioned me. Finally he said, "By not saying, I'll assume the answer is no."

Mr. Gibb spoke again. "Your Honor, I would like to address one other issue before Miss Lapp goes back to jail. She has been in jail now for some period of time…. If Miss Lapp would be willing to tell the court that she would honor the jurisdiction of this court, appear in court when directed to do so, and appear for her trial on the date that's been set… I would not have any opposition to releasing her on her own recognizance."

"Barbara, do you understand what's been said to you?" Judge Mifsud asked.

I did not reply. He continued. "I want you to know that you may be released from jail today, this afternoon, if you'll tell the court that you recognize the jurisdiction of this court and that you will be back here… for your trial in November." He made no mention of my County Court trial, scheduled for next week. Mifsud added that if I did not appear he would issue a bench warrant for my arrest, and I would be subsequently charged with bail flight.

Numerous questions and discussions among the judge and attorneys ensued, some of them directed to me.

Gibb was pacing. He told the judge that his previous offer also stands—I could get out of jail by pleading guilty only to obstructing governmental administration. "Either of these offers are standing offers, Your Honor," he said.

There was silence. Attorneys sighed audibly. Gibb wiped his brow. It seemed like a long time. It was more grueling than I thought it would be to remain silent.

The judge looked strained. "It does not make this court happy to keep you incarcerated," he said. "But by your actions you remain in jail because you did not address this court or answer any questions that were asked by it."

Lt. Lawrence took me back out and handcuffed me. "Who's next?" someone asked.

"I don't know," Lawrence said. "It was Rachel before." His voice reflected a pitiful lack of enthusiasm. He looked exhausted.

By Rachel

The officers brought Barbara from court, and Lawrence said it was my turn.

"Why do I have to go, if I don't want to?" I asked, still seated.

"Could you just stand over here by the door, then, so the judge can talk to you?" Lawrence asked gently. "You don't have to say a word."

"He can come in here, if he wants to talk to me," I said on impulse, then realized I shouldn't have said it.

Lawrence hurried off, and promptly returned with an entourage of lawyers, court reporters, officers, and finally the judge in his black robe. They filed into the tiny room. Their faces looked tense, and considering the extraordinary circumstances, there was a noticeable absence of humor. The room, about ten or twelve feet square, was packed—four in green, five lawyers, two court reporters with their equipment, and as many officers as the room could hold. The judge sat on a wooden chair with torn upholstery.

Gibb explained his motion to consolidate the trials. Judge Mifsud asked me if I understood, or objected. I was silent.

"Your Honor, I hear no objection," Gibb said. "I hear no response, as a matter of fact."

"Rachel, as I explained to your sister, your silence only has the court make the decision for you," the judge said.

"That's what it has done all along anyway," I said.

Gibb then presented the ROR issue, saying I could go home now if I'd simply address the court, honor the jurisdiction of the court, and agree to come back November 17 for the trial.

Judge Mifsud repeated the offer, and asked if I understood.

"I'm not interested in making any deal with the court," I said.

"You're not making a deal," the judge said. "All we're asking you to do is to recognize this court.... It's just a simple question. Will you appear when you're so directed? ...You've been incarcerated a long time. If you want the incarceration to end, now is your time to have it end."

"I would like to go home," I said.

"If you want to state to the court that you'll recognize it... this court will see that you're released today."

"I can't conscientiously make any deal with this court."

"You're *not* making a deal," the judge snapped. "I'll ask you one more time. Do you want to recognize the jurisdiction and be released, or do you want to remain—"

"I would very much desire to go home," I said. The judge and I looked at each other for a moment.

"The court has given you an opportunity to do so...." he said.

"I'm sorry," I said. "I don't wish to cause any trouble, but I can't conscientiously cooperate."

My hearing was over. Dad's was about to begin in the same ill-adapted courtroom, when his attorney, Mr. Harley, spoke up loudly.

"Your honor... you're sitting here with my client chained to a chair in a two-by-two holding room, outside the public eye. This is a travesty! I will not be heard in this room!" He left the room, slamming his hand against the door as he went.

The judge and Gibb had some discussions about whether Harley was really representing Dad, or whether Dad was representing himself.

Judge Mifsud proceeded to question Dad, prompting another entry by Harley. "Your Honor, *I'm* addressing the court. I'm the attorney of record for my client."

"You're standby—" the judge began.

"I'm *not* standby counsel!" Harley interrupted. "Read the assignment you sent me, your Honor. I'm not standby counsel and I will not address the court in this room!"

"Jacob refuses to leave," the judge said. "What do you want me to do?"

"Then you move him, Your Honor. Stop being a tool for the prosecution!"

"I'm not a tool for the prosecution—"

"You're addressing my client. He's chained to a chair in a holding center. Are you attempting to say this is a court of law?"

"I didn't say it was," Judge Mifsud said. "I asked—"

"My client doesn't have to answer your questions. I do. And I will not address this court unless, in fact, it is *in* court. And I will not waive my client's presence."

"You want me to physically have him carried into that courtroom? Is that what you want?"

"Your Honor, as the law states, my client is entitled to a public forum."

Gibb interrupted. "Your Honor, however, the client can waive it. And in this case I don't believe he even is his client.... It is my understanding, all of these attorneys are only standby, because these people do not wish to have these attorneys represent them."

Harley said: "Your Honor, I have a letter signed by you... addressed to me, reading, 'by receipt of this letter you are hereby appointed by this Court as defense counsel....' No one has appointed me standby counsel.... This proceeding is outside the bounds of the law. My client has the right to appear in court. I have a right and obligation to address the court.... He has an absolute right to remain silent, and I have an absolute right to speak for him."

"Well, if it's going to make you happy," the judge said, rising from his chair. "Would you please bring Jacob into the courtroom?" he said to the officers.

The proceeding was moved to the courtroom. Two officers put their hands on Dad's arms, and he went in without resistance. Barbara and I listened from the holding room, as the argument continued.

"You're standby," the judge told Harley.

"Respectfully, that's a crock," Harley retorted. "My ethical obligation is to represent my client zealously within the bounds of the law. Are you preventing me from doing that?"

"He has to speak to you," the judge said.

"He stands before you silent, and he doesn't have to do a thing! You expect me to stand here while you violate my client's rights?" Harley was almost shouting. "If I'm *in*, I'm *in*. If I'm not a lawyer, I'm *out*. What am I?"

"You're standby counsel."

"Then I'm out. It's been a pleasure doing business, Your Honor." Harley walked away, then turned back and warned the judge that the proceeding could not legally continue until his client had the protection of counsel.

"I think you should remain long enough for this court proceeding," the judge said.

"Then I'm standing here as a lawyer, and I will not permit you to address questions to my client," Harley said. "Is that understood?"

"Mr. Harley advises us of all the points he chooses to make," Gibb complained, "even at the top of his voice."

Harley attempted to present some motions to the court, to which Gibb vigorously objected. The whole argument of what Harley's duties were started over.

"For you to say, 'Oh, I don't want you to exercise on his behalf, I want you to sit there quietly while he gets railroaded, that's an *offense!*" Harley said.

"Your Honor, I think this is contempt for the court," Gibb said.

"Absolutely, it is," Harley said.

"It's totally unwarranted," Gibb said.

"The only person who can stop me from [representing him]... is my client," Harley said. "For the district attorney to try and interrupt the attorney-client relationship is improper. My client is here. He's been held here since August 16. It's offensive. He has a right to be released from jail, not because he makes some little side-room deal, or he promises to be good, but because he's been held illegally for two months...."

The judge finally gave in, and allowed Mr. Harley to address the court on Dad's behalf. Harley presented legal arguments on speedy trial, accusing the court of delaying the trial for no reason. "I want to try this case now. Let's get it over with so he can be out," he said.

"Your Honor, there is good reason why this date has been set," Gibb said. "I have a trial calendar, I have other cases that have to be tried—"

Harley began to speak.

"Excuse me," Gibb said. "I did not interrupt you, nor do I speak at the top of my voice.... That is certainly a fair trial date."

"The trial date will remain," Judge Mifsud said.

Harley continued. "Note my exception.... This court has held this man in jail for sixty—Good Lord, sixty days! He has no prior history. He's a farmer, he has a crop to get in. There's no allegation in any of the People's pleadings that he did any harm to anyone. There's no allegation of injury. There's no allegation of property damage.... Just because my client, due to his particular point of view, refuses to recognize the authority of this court over his life, are you going to continue holding him...?

"These are, respectfully, Your Honor, garbage cases. Inciting a riot—was there a riot? There was not, was there? Nothing was broken, nothing was damaged....

"It's very difficult when an elderly gentleman remains in jail forgotten.... The DA says cop a plea, we'll let you out. He says, no, I'm a man of conscience—I won't cop a plea. So you have him sit. It's absurd. It's a travesty, and frankly, the real problem is, it lends credence to his claims."

By Barbara Lyn

Rachel and I were waiting in the holding room, listening to what was going on.

An officer came from the courtroom. "For a minute there I thought we were gonna have to take him along down!" he kidded with another officer, about Harley.

Lt. Lawrence came into the room. "Let's take these girls down, this thing isn't ending," he told Sgt. Braley, who was waiting with us.

In the elevator, Lawrence said he wonders if Dad really wanted Harley. Then he turned to me. "Do you think your Dad wanted him?"

I shrugged.

"He got himself a real beauty," Lawrence said. "He's really rolling in there."

Almost at the office, Lawrence spoke again. "Barbara, wouldn't you like to go home?" He waited for an answer. "It's not that much to give up. Whenever you decide, just tell the CO to contact me, and I'll see to it that we get right up to court." As he removed my handcuffs, he continued. "I don't think you'd be compromising too much of your principles. Think about it, Barbara." He patted me on my back.

Tonight on the phone we learned that Judge Mifsud had denied all of Mr. Harley's motions. Dad was taken back to jail with Joe, who had also refused the court's offers.

CHAPTER 9

On Trial

October 11, 1993

By Barbara Lyn

Eight weeks in jail, two days until my trial, no end in sight. Even if I'm acquitted I won't be free, unless Lt. Lawrence or Ron Gibb decide to drop the second set of charges.

At night I lie awake thinking about all that could take place. Will the judge make me shut up as soon as I get started with a convincing argument to the jury? Will Mr. Humble sit beside me and intimidate me when I don't follow exact courtroom procedure? So many things to ponder.

Yesterday after our visit I searched Dad's face, hoping he would have a parting wish for me. It was the last time we would see each other before my trial.

"Just look ahead to the real one," Dad said as he shook my hand. I think he meant the real Judgment Day. I think that means I should mostly be concerned about conducting myself honorably before God, so that on Judgment Day I may hear, "Well done, thou good and faithful servant."

October 13

By Barbara Lyn

Trial day has come.

My head, neck and shoulders were hurting all night. I have a cold. This morning I asked the CO for Tylenol, which makes me feel much better, but very sleepy.

At 8:30 CO Carole came to tell me the court was on the phone. "They want to know if you're going to go peacefully, and if you're going to be peaceful during jury selection," she said.

"I don't have any intentions of being unpeaceful—I never have been!" I said.

In the courtroom, the officers escorted me to a large wooden table, about fifteen feet from the judge's platform. Scott Humble, my so-called attorney, was seated at the table. He pulled out a chair for me. I sat beside him, facing the judge.

To my right, across the courtroom, was the prosecutor's table, where Paul Andrews, the assistant district attorney sat. Beyond him was the jury box, with fourteen empty chairs. Behind me the gallery was filled with about fifty prospective jurors.

Addressing the prospective jurors, Judge Himelein gave a lengthy introduction to trial procedure and jury duty. When he finished speaking, the court clerk gave me a list of the prosecution's witnesses, exhibits, etc. The judge told Mr. Humble to explain the papers to me.

I listened to Humble's explanation. Then, speaking to the judge, I said, "I would like to make it clear that Mr. Humble is not counsel of my choice."

"That's on the record."

"Also, in order that there be no confusion or pretense, I would rather not have Mr. Humble at the table here with me."

"Well, I'm going to direct that he stay in the courtroom," Judge Himelein said slowly, "on this side of the rail."

Mr. Humble left the table and sat in a chair behind me, near the gallery.

The court clerk then called fourteen prospective jurors, drawing names from a can. After the jurors were sworn in, Himelein questioned them on possible personal biases on my case. Most of the jurors said they had heard about my case in the news, but indicated they could be impartial.

Himelein then instructed the jurors on different points of law. "In order to be jurors in this case, you do not have to know anything about the law," he said. "It is my job to explain the law to you and it is your job to determine the facts.... You will follow the law as I give it to you."

"Every person accused of a crime is presumed innocent," he said. "The fact that there is an indictment that contains charges against the defendant means absolutely nothing...."

Judge Himelein continued. "Under my oath, I must instruct you on the law as I understand it to be. Under your oath as jurors, you must accept the law as I explain it to you, whether you agree with it or not."

The judge also cautioned the jurors against drawing unfavorable inferences against me because I chose to represent myself. "As a lay person, she may have some difficulty expressing herself or in framing questions during the trial, however, we shall assist her in every way we can," he said.

After the judge's instructions, it was Andrews' turn to question the jurors. He asked them if they would not be affected by the publicity, picket signs, etc. related to my case. Twice he implored them not to be biased against him, just because he stands against a person who doesn't have an attorney. "If the evidence shows… that Miss Lapp is guilty of the charges…, can you promise me you can return a verdict of guilty, and not have any sympathy and say, 'Geez, let's just give her a break?'"

"I think I could be fair," said one juror. Others concurred.

Andrews continued. "It is possible that there will be evidence presented to the effect that Miss Lapp strongly believes in what she is doing…. Is there anyone here that believes a person can be above the law because of a sincere and righteous belief that he or she is right?"

JUROR NO. 10: Yeah, there might be circumstances… maybe there is a good reason why she kept the kid there. Hey, you don't know…. I think I can be objective.

JUROR NO. 1: [You] don't know the facts until you hear them.

JUROR NO. 10: That's right, you don't.

ANDREWS: And if [testimony] shows that even though she believed she was right, but that it was still against the law, would you have a problem in returning a verdict of guilty?

JUROR NO. 10: I don't think I would have a problem with it. I would have to listen very carefully to both sides of the story.

ALTERNATE JUROR NO. 1: I'm not sure at this point. I would have to listen.

JUROR NO. 12: I believe we have to be obedient to the law.

JUROR NO. 11: I disagree. I think the person has a right to decide and sometimes he or she could be above the law, like protecting a kid.

JUROR NO. 5: Well, I don't feel that the laws are always right… but for a person to disobey the law blatantly is wrong. It seems to me there might be other channels rather than to do something illegal.

JUROR NO. 4: I think the law should be followed even though we don't always agree with it.

JUROR NO. 3: I thought the judge was going to interpret the law for us….

Andrews explained that it is the jury's duty to listen to the facts, then apply them to the law as the judge indicates. He continued. "If the evidence shows that Barbara Lapp obstructed governmental administration and conspired with another individual to commit custodial interference and other crimes along that line, can you promise me you can return a verdict of guilty?"

"Yes," said one of the jurors. "You have to go by the law."

Other jurors nodded.

"Good. Thank you," Andrews said.

Judge Himelein asked me if I would like to ask questions of the potential jurors.

I walked over to the podium in front of the jurors. "I believe the judge forgot to tell you that you also have the right, and an obligation, to vote according to your conscience," I began. "I respect the law very highly, but there is right and wrong that is sometimes not written in the law. All of this has to be taken into consideration."

I asked the jurors if they believe it is right to violate their consciences, just because the judge says something is the law. One juror said if there is a conflict with the law, the law must be changed, not violated. Another said, "I don't understand what you are saying. A law is a law. I'm not that well versed in the law. I know if the law is on the books, I have to keep that law."

"Are you familiar with the Fugitive Slave Law of the seventeen hundreds?" I asked.

"I'm not," the juror said.

"There were many people that were severely punished for harboring a slave, because there was a law against it," I said. "That law ended when jurors acquitted people, against the orders of the judge, because they knew in their conscience it was an unjust law."

Then, smiling as I scanned the jurors' faces, I asked if any of them enjoyed alcoholic beverages.

"I do," said one juror, a gray-haired gentleman. Some of the others chuckled.

"Do you know that early in the century our laws prohibited the sale of alcoholic beverages?" I asked.

The juror nodded. "Running them across the lake—yeah, my uncle was running them," he said. He and the rest of the jurors broke into laughter. The judge laughed, too.

I also told the jurors that I took great offense to the judge and prosecutor asking them detailed questions about what they know about my case. "I have no desire to do that myself," I said. "It's not my business to ask you what your opinion is before you sit down and listen to a certain case. You are entitled to your opinion. You are entitled to vote according to your opinion when you are done.... The important part is that you vote according to your conscience, and stick to what you know is right....

"I come and stand before the judge. He knows the law a lot better than I do, or you do. What is the reason for you to be here? As common citizens, you come here to relay... the conscience of the community. You have every right and every obligation to judge both whether the facts are accurate, and whether the law is constitutional, or whether it is right."

My discussion with the prospective jurors went on for forty minutes. Then Judge Himelein gave Andrews and me the opportunity to disqualify any jurors we didn't like. He said according to the law he can dismiss up to ten jurors for each side. The court clerk then gave us both a paper to write down which jurors we wanted the judge to dismiss. I sent the paper back to the judge, blank. Andrews did the same.

The jury was empaneled—eight men and four women, plus two alternates. Judge Himelein said it was the first time in his career that the first fourteen jurors called were empaneled.

We took a break for lunch, and returned to court at 1:45. This time the gallery was filled with family, friends and spectators. Several television news people were there, and asked Judge Himelein for permission to cover the trial.

Andrews objected. "Your Honor, this case has been tried in the media from the other side, and I think the presence of the camera in the courtroom would just contribute more to a circus atmosphere," he said. "I have seen the results of what happened out in Town Court, and I don't think it would be very conducive to the decorum of the court to permit that in this instance."

"Miss Lapp, do you want to be heard?" asked the judge.

"Clearly, the public coming in through the media to observe would be a part of the Sixth Amendment right to a public trial," I said.

After some discussion with media camerapersons, Judge Himelein said they could stay. "You don't go in and out of the courtroom," he instructed them. "You don't do anything to give a juror the impression that something is more important than something else. So either the cameras are running all the time, or they are *not* running all the time. You don't show any of the jurors or any of the spectators in the courtroom...."

One of the camerapersons told the judge he would have to leave at 3:30 to prepare for evening news. "You will not allow us to leave before 4:30?" he pleaded.

"I will not allow it before testimony is concluded," said the judge.

"Would it be all right if we came in the morning and when everyone breaks for lunch we can leave?"

"I will allow you to break it up to morning and afternoon blocks."

Both camerapersons left. Several newspaper and radio newsmen remained.

Judge Himelein then spoke to the spectators. "You are welcome to be present for any of the proceedings that go on…. No outbursts or noise or anything of that nature will be permitted. If anyone conducts himself inappropriately, they will be removed from the courtroom and won't be permitted back during the course of these proceedings."

He read off my three-count indictment of obstruction of governmental administration, conspiracy, and custodial interference: "Said defendant, on or about July 7, 1993… intentionally obstructed, impaired or prevented the administration of law or other governmental function… by means of intimidation, physical force or interference, or by means of any independently unlawful act, by interfering and refusing to return to law enforcement officials one William Stefan…."

"The said defendant… with intent that conduct constituting the crimes of criminal contempt in the second degree, unlawful imprisonment in the second degree and custodial interference in the second degree be performed, agreed with Donald Stefan to engage in or cause the performance of such conduct. In furtherance of this conspiracy, the defendant intentionally aided Donald Stefan in intentional disobedience to the lawful process or other mandate of Cattaraugus County Family Court… by helping Donald Stefan interfere with the aforementioned custody of William Stefan by hiding him and refusing to return him to the lawful custody of the Cattaraugus County Department of Social Services.

"The said defendant… knowing that she had no legal right to do so, took or enticed from lawful custody one William Stefan, a person entrusted by authority of law to the custody of another person or institution."

Judge Himelein told the jury that these are the allegations the People will attempt to prove. "They are allegations only at this time," he said, "and the defendant is presumed innocent."

He concluded with these instructions: "I admonish, order and direct that you are not to speak among yourselves, or with anyone else upon any subject connected with this case....

"You are not to read anything about this case in any newspaper, magazine or any other publication. You are not to watch or listen to any news programs concerning this case....

"You are not to visit or view the premises or places where the crimes were allegedly committed....

"You are to refrain from taking notes during the course of the trial...."

Following Himelein's speech, Mr. Andrews addressed the jury with his opening statement.

He told of the Family Court order that placed Billy Stefan in the Bradford Children's Home. "He was then taken away from custody," Andrews said. "He still remains, who knows where. But on July 7 of this year, proof will show that he was at Barbara Lapp's residence and that she refused to hand him over."

Andrews then spoke of the Constitution versus state laws, and the citizens' duty to comply with these laws. "I hope at the end of the case you will have a better understanding of the child abuse laws, what the procedures are, how people work within the system. I hope you don't go into the jury room with the impression that it is us against them, that the system is impersonal and corrupt," Andrews said.

"I will expect that proof will show that Barbara Lapp could have obstructed governmental administration by refusing to hand over Billy Stefan; that she did indeed conspire with Donald Stefan to take Billy away from the legal custody of social services, and that she did indeed take him away, and that, therefore, was custodial interference...."

After Andrews concluded, Judge Himelein said I could give my opening statement.

"Obviously, Mr. Andrews feels that I broke the law and is going to try to prove that I did," I began. "I want you to know as we start here that I do not deny, and I will not attempt to hide, any of the facts of the case. The truth as it stands in my actions also stands as my only defense today, and it stands before God. I have a firm belief that honesty is the best policy, and it will go a long way in preserving community peace. And I will not betray the trust of my fellow citizens by becoming involved in any untruth or dishonesty."

I told the jury that ever since my arrest three months ago, it is my position that I did not break the law, and that my arrest was unlawful. "That's based on my understanding of my constitutionally guaranteed right to freedom to exercise my conscience," I said.

"I have been in the courtroom twelve times since I was arrested; I have not yet faced my accusers; I have not known, before today, what the nature and cause of the accusation against me is; I have not had the opportunity to face a jury of my peers—all of which is supposed to take place before a person is deprived of liberty.

"For this reason, I have maintained that the court does not have jurisdiction in the case, and actually, I present myself in a pretty awkward position to be here and to be speaking to you. I do it because I have a trust in you as fellow citizens, and I value the opportunity to face you and not just the government system that I believe has been very unjust in this case....

"I don't intend to be able to match the words of the prosecution and the judge. They have a lot of experience in handling the legal system, using the so-called law to their benefit.... [A]nd I do not believe in legal games being played over the backs of children and human rights."

I presented to the jury some background on my family, our farming enterprises, and my adopted children. "It has a lot to do with the principles of love and respect that I was brought up with that led me into the situation I am in now....

"I experienced throughout life that if you respect others, that you will receive respect in return. And I still firmly believe that this kind of respect benefits society in general, even if it means going through something very unfortunate as I have here.

"[My family has] always, as long as I can remember, had an open door policy where we have a large farm house and we have taken in children or adults that were in need—whether it was a teenager that had been kicked out of his house, or whether it was physically handicapped people from foreign countries...."

I gave a chronology of my own family court case, my outreach to other families, and finally, Billy Stefan's plight. The jurors listened attentively, faces solemn.

Then Andrews called his first witness, a Social Services attorney. Upon questioning from Andrews, she described in detail Child Protective Services policy, family court procedure, and the agency's efforts to keep families together. "During the period in which the child is in [Social Services] care, we're providing visitation, we're providing services to the family, doing everything we can to fix whatever it is, so the child can go home as soon as possible," she said.

"[O]nly the really serious cases end in court," she continued. "The sexual abuse cases, the serious danger cases involving children that have been injured severely by their parents. When I say severely injured—broken bones, serious bruises—that sort of thing."

She said the law requires the agency to find the most homelike setting for children removed from their home. Institutions like the Bradford Children's Home are generally used for children accused of crimes, truancy, running away, and other kinds of disobedient behavior. "Frankly, places like that are extremely expensive," she said. "They run well over a hundred dollars a day. Some of them go as high as $100,000 a year...."

She spoke for nearly an hour. Court was adjourned at 4:00.

❋   ❋   ❋

I got back to my cell with Rachel, just in time for supper. Exhausted and aching with fever, I couldn't eat much.

I lay down for a nap, but sleep evaded me. For the third time today, I asked the CO for Tylenol.

Rachel read to me from Psalm 37. "Rest in the Lord and wait patiently for him: fret not thyself because of... the man who bringeth wicked devises to pass. Fret not thyself because of evil doers."

October 14

By Barbara Lyn

This morning the first witness was Chuck Talbot, the CPS case worker who had handled the Stefan case.

"...[I]t is my job to receive and to respond to any and all reports called into the State Central Register in Albany," he said, "and to check on the safety of children in the home...."

Andrews questioned him about his initial contact with Billy Stefan, the day after his father allegedly beat him.

"William Stefan... was very, very afraid of me," Talbot said. "It took time to calm this child. Upon first seeing Bill, it was noticed that there were numerous scratches on his face and his ears. Bill did, after a time, show me there were multiple bruises on his back, legs, arms, where he had been struck by a belt and a fist."

Talbot described general procedures used in Child Protective Services cases. "The Bradford Children's Home is just another vehicle to try to place this child back into his regular home," Talbot said. "It allows the families a chance to work on the problems in the homes and to follow the orders of the judge."

"How would you categorize William with respect to his mental ability?" Andrews asked.

"William is slow," Talbot said. "He has approximately a 61 IQ—very charming young man, pleasant, very impressionable—he's a good kid."

After Andrews completed his questioning, I cross-examined Talbot. "[In] how many different institutions were Billy and Tom placed during their year in Social Services care?"

TALBOT: I am not really certain.

LAPP: One or two?

TALBOT: There were several.

LAPP: More than several?

TALBOT: Between the two of them, I would say two or three.

LAPP: While you were supervising this case, were you aware that… Billy and Tom, were being heavily medicated in these institutions?

TALBOT: I'm not in the position, ma'am—I don't know what constitutes heavy medication.

LAPP: But you knew they were getting medication?

TALBOT: They were, yes.

LAPP: How many times did Billy and Tom attempt to run away from Social Services care and return back to their father?

TALBOT: I know of two.

LAPP: Did Billy once receive medical treatment for beatings that he received while he was in Social Services care?

TALBOT: Where? I have no knowledge of that.

LAPP: How many times did you see Billy during the year he was in your care?

TALBOT: At the initial months of the case, I would say at least fifty.

LAPP: You said Billy is a good kid. Do you have any explanation why he landed in a secure facility like the Bradford Children's Home, where there were a lot of children who had delinquency problems?

TALBOT: It's where they placed him. They felt he needed that type of environment.

LAPP: If he's a good kid, why wouldn't he have been okay in foster care or some other kind of environment?

TALBOT: I can't answer that question.

I returned to my table and sat down. Andrews walked up to the witness stand again.

ANDREWS: You indicated you had no knowledge of Billy being beaten… or hear any reports that he had been beaten?

TALBOT: Are you referring to the Bradford…?

ANDREWS: Wherever.

TALBOT [hesitating]: I'm sorry?

ANDREWS: After he came in the care of Social Services?

TALBOT: No, sir.

Judge Himelein turned to me. "Do you have any other questions you would like to ask [the witness], Miss Lapp?"

"I guess not," I said. "He's lying."

"Objection, Your Honor!" Andrews said.

"I'm sorry," the judge said. "I didn't hear. I thought she said no." Then he turned to the jury. "Disregard that statement, ladies and gentlemen."

Andrews' next witness was a social worker from the Bradford Children's Home. She explained in detail the home's policies.

"Did you medicate across the board the kids that come in?" Andrews asked her.

"...We have a very strict policy about medicating children. We only offer children medication when we have the parent's consent, or, if the child is over fourteen, we have the child's consent."

The social worker said that shortly after Billy's admission to Bradford, she set up a treatment plan, with goals that included Billy returning to his family. "He did well in the treatment program," she said. "He was progressing nicely."

"Was he on any medication at any time during this period?"

"The only medication he was on was... a topical ointment for a skin rash."

She told how Don Stefan took Billy out for lunch, on April 20. "I requested that as soon as they were done eating lunch that they come back to the Children's Home.... And the family left for the restaurant, and I have not seen Billy after that."

I chose not to cross-examine the social worker. Questioning her on Billy's mistreatment at the home would give her the opportunity to deny knowledge of it, which could jeopardize my credibility. Besides, Billy had not expressed a clear memory of receiving drugs at that institution. I didn't want to press a point I couldn't prove.

After the social worker, Sheriff Jerry Burrell was called. He told of his discussion with me at the Cattaraugus County jail on July 7, when Don had just disclosed Billy was at my home.

BURRELL: ...I asked if in fact she was going to be willing to deliver William to us.

ANDREWS: What was her response?

BURRELL: Her response was that we could talk to him but we could not come on the property.

ANDREWS: What happened then?

BURRELL: Very honestly, that puzzled me, that particular statement.

And I recall that I told Miss Lapp that we had a warrant for William…
and that we were responsible for taking him into custody.…

ANDREWS: Is this warrant still in effect?

BURRELL: Yes, it is.

ANDREWS: What would you do as an officer if you saw Billy Stefan
today?

BURRELL: I would comply with the order and take William into custody and deliver him before the court as directed.

I cross-examined Sheriff Burrell.

LAPP: You noted that it was strange that I indicated you could see
William but you couldn't have him. You didn't have a property warrant, did you?

BURRELL: As I recall, you stated we could not come on the property.…

LAPP: Was that strange that I said you couldn't come on the property, if you didn't have a warrant?

BURRELL: I don't know if it was strange. It was unusual.

LAPP: No further questions.

I returned to my table.

Andrews quickly stepped toward the witness stand. "Why was it
unusual?"

"Because I'm—I don't know if I have ever been told that we couldn't
come on to execute a warrant, when in fact we informed the party of
a lawful warrant."

Lt. Buchhardt was called. Uniformed and armed, he walked to the
witness stand, and was sworn in by the bailiff. His testimony consisted
mainly of a chronological account of the July 7 standoff at our farm.

"When we were coming down the road, approaching the Lapp
farm," he said, "as we pulled up we noticed there were over thirty
protestors in front of the house… and channels four and seven of the
news media [were] on the other side of the road.… Barbara Lapp
arrived shortly after that… and she told us that under no circumstances would William be turned over to us."

ANDREWS: What was Miss Lapp's demeanor during this time?

BUCHHARDT: She appeared to us that she was very angry that we
were there.… She was advised that we had a copy of the writ of habeas corpus [warrant]. And she just plain advised us there was no way
we were going to enter her property and take William Stefan.

ANDREWS: Why didn't you proceed on the property to take William
Stefan?

BUCHHARDT: There were over thirty protestors on this property. Many of them were women. Many of them were children. We felt it would turn into a violent confrontation where we would actually have to push, shove our way in there, and we figured that it was not going to be in their best interest, William's best interest, and our best interest to go in there and take this child by force.

ANDREWS: Even if you had a search warrant for entry to the premises, would you have done so?

BUCHHARDT: If I would have had a search warrant... I would have gone in. Personally, I did not feel that was going to be a good idea on that day.... There was a lot of farm equipment that was moved up close to the roadway. What I believe was going to happen, that if we went in there to try to take the child by force, that the farm equipment was going to be brought and placed blocking the roadway.

ANDREWS: Was that one of the other factors you considered, in addition to the presence of women and children?

BUCHHARDT: That threw [in] a whole new scenario.... The next thing that you would have had to do there is bring in a large amount of tow trucks and wreckers to move this equipment so you could leave the property.

It was my turn to question Buchhardt. We exchanged a friendly greeting before I began.

LAPP: Being an officer of the law, do you have police knowledge of the laws of New York State and the United States Constitution?

BUCHHARDT: I have a fair knowledge of it.

LAPP: You mentioned there were thirty protestors in front of the house.... Is it against any laws to have women and children in your front lawn?

BUCHHARDT: No.

ANDREWS [looking at the judge]: Objection!

JUDGE HIMELEIN: [No reply.]

BUCHHARDT [answering the question again]: Definitely not.

LAPP: Given your knowledge of the law, is it against any laws to have news media at the home?

BUCHHARDT: No.

LAPP: Given your knowledge of the law, was it against any laws for us to ask you not to park on our property?

BUCHHARDT: No, absolutely not.

LAPP: Did you at any time show me any documents or warrants that would have required me to do something—an order of some type?

BUCHHARDT: The only order we had with us was the writ of habeas corpus signed by Judge Nenno.

LAPP: And who was directed to act on that?

BUCHHARDT: We were directed to act on that, to take William Stefan into our custody and place him back in custody of the Cattaraugus County Social Services.

LAPP: Did you believe that I should have acted on that order that was directed to you?

BUCHHARDT: It's a lawful order. In my opinion, yes.

LAPP: It was directed to you?

BUCHHARDT: That's correct.

LAPP: Did that have any relevance as far as to what I was required to do on that day?

BUCHHARDT: I don't know what you were required to do. The requirement was for us, that the writ of habeas corpus gave us legal right to take William Stefan into our custody....

LAPP: You didn't have a property warrant, did you?

BUCHHARDT: I had a writ of habeas corpus, yes. I did not have a search warrant to go in and enter your property, if that's what you are asking me.

LAPP: No property warrant?

BUCHHARDT: No, I did not have a property warrant.

LAPP: Were there any verbal orders—did you direct any verbal orders toward me, as far as something that I was supposed to do that day?

BUCHHARDT: No—no. We had one discussion where you asked me what I was doing there.... and you told me you would not turn him over to me.

LAPP: Did I violate any orders in saying that?

ANDREWS: Objection! That's a factual issue for the jury.

JUDGE HIMELEIN: Sustained.

LAPP: You indicated you were concerned about violence if you were to go in and take Billy?

BUCHHARDT: I was concerned over that, yeah. I was not concerned for my life, but I felt there would have been some type of violence if we would have tried to enter your property and try and remove William Stefan, yes.

LAPP: What led you to believe that the farm vehicles there were to be used to obstruct your exit?

BUCHHARDT: The way they were all placed to go across the roadway. You had several trucks, tractors and there was a baler, hay wagons... and it appeared to us that this equipment was going to be used for blocking the roadway....

LAPP: It *appeared* to you?

BUCHHARDT: Yes, it appeared to me, yes.

LAPP: That was an assumption?

BUCHHARDT: That's an assumption on my part, yes, that's correct.

LAPP: Was the public roadway blocked at any time?

BUCHHARDT: No.

LAPP: How many hours were you at our place, at our farm?

BUCHHARDT: Between five and six hours, I would say.

LAPP [nodding]: Uh-huh. How many times did I talk to you during that time?

BUCHHARDT: There were a couple times.

LAPP: Three or four?

BUCHHARDT: I would probably say something like that, yeah.

LAPP: What was the nature of those conversations—aside from the first one that you mentioned?

BUCHHARDT: You asked me if I wanted anything to drink. I can't remember what the other conversations were, though.

LAPP: Did I at any time ask you what I could do… to end the stand-off?

BUCHHARDT: You told me I could leave.

LAPP: Aside from that?

BUCHHARDT: I don't remember any other conversations.

LAPP: Were you aware that Billy's family was also at the home?

BUCHHARDT: Yes. Yes… I believe it was William's brother that was there.

LAPP: Were you aware that Billy was not my property, or that he was not in my custody and control?

BUCHHARDT: No. I felt that he was in your custody and control.

Rex Rater was called next.

ANDREWS: Did you happen to be involved on duty on July 7 of this year?

RATER: Yes, I was.

ANDREWS: Did you have the occasion to meet Barbara Lapp?

RATER: Yes, I did.

ANDREWS: Do you see Miss Lapp here today?

RATER: Yes, I do.

Rater looked at me from twenty feet across the courtroom.

ANDREWS: Can you point her out?

RATER [pointing]: The lady sitting over there with the blue outfit on.

HIMELEIN: The record should reflect that the witness has identified the defendant.

Rater described entering the scene of the standoff, and speaking with the Cattaraugus County officers. "And Barbara Lapp immediately came over in the roadway where we were, along with one of her sisters, and held up—had a recording device, a tape so the conversation could be recorded. Her sister was taking photographs. Then the news media started coming over...."

Rater detailed his discussion with me. "We were trying to decide basically what to do next," he said. "Did we have the right to go on the property, that sort of thing. It was also an assessment because of the large number of people there...."

ANDREWS: What was the final decision?

RATER: There was conversation between myself, Cattaraugus County Sheriff Burrell, my sheriff, Sheriff Bentley, district attorney's office, on what the strategy should be.... [I]t was my advice to Sheriff Burrell and Sheriff Bentley because of the large number of people and the intensity of the situation that for the time being we back off so that there wasn't any confrontation and nobody would get hurt. And they in fact complied with my suggestion, and we left....

ANDREWS: Did you feel intimidated through this period?

RATER: Yes, I was.

ANDREWS: From what?

RATER: From the situation.... I knew there was a lot of emotion involved with the case... and I was afraid from the number of people there and their carrying signs, and their energy and excitement at the moment.... Quite truthfully, there were a lot more of them than there were of us, and we didn't want a confrontation.

Andrews' questioning completed, I walked over and stood in front of the witness stand where Rater was seated.

LAPP: Good morning.

RATER: Good morning.

LAPP: When you came to my house on July 7, were you aware that Billy didn't want to come out of the house?

RATER: I really wasn't aware what his position was at the time.... All I know was there was an order to produce him....

LAPP: Were there any orders directed toward me personally to produce Billy?

RATER: No. Only to a police officer....

LAPP: Given your position in law enforcement, do you have basic knowledge of the laws of New York State and of the U. S. Constitution?

Rater: Yes, ma'am, I do.

Lapp: To your knowledge, is there anything against the law for having fifty people on your front lawn—women and children?

Rater: Not at all.

Lapp: Holding signs—is that against the law?

Rater: No, ma'am, not as long as it's not bothering anyone, and it's not violent.

Lapp: Having the news media there—that was not against the law?

Rater: Not at all, but it was intimidating—but it was intimidating, and I believe that was the basis of the question.

Lapp: Were you armed when you were there?

Rater: Yes, ma'am.

Lapp: Was anybody around the home armed, around my home?

Rater: Other than the police officers, not that I know of—other than carrying the posters—not that I saw.

Lapp: Were you aware at the time that it's against my religious beliefs to be armed or use force or violence on anyone?

Rater: I never had any discussion with you on any of your beliefs, so I wouldn't have known that, no. I did stay in the public roadway, though.

Lapp: You did stay on the public roadway?

Rater: Yes, ma'am, because you didn't want us on the property. In fact, I parked the car in your driveway. You asked me to move it, and I did.

Lapp: Was that a reasonable request?

Rater: Yes, it was, and it was complied with.

Lapp: Did the fact that… there was an order for you to pick up Billy—did that obligate me to take any action?

Rater: Yes, ma'am, it did.

Lapp: In what way?

Rater: Well, we all have to abide by the laws… even though we don't always agree with them. I am obligated to follow the orders that are handed down… by the courts, so I believe you were obligated, yes.

Lapp: An order that is directed toward you—what obligation would that bring toward me?

Rater: It's authorizing me to secure this young man, Billy Stefan. You, as a citizen, it doesn't authorize you to pick him up, but if you know that there is an order for this young man to be returned to Family Court, yes, I believe there is a definite obligation for you to comply with that order.

Lapp: Even if no one asked me to comply with that order?

Rater: I don't think someone has to come and directly ask you. If you know the order exists, then there is an obligation, yes, in my opinion.

LAPP: Interesting opinion.

I returned to my table. The final witness was Stephen Riley, a Social Services attorney from Cattaraugus County. He described Family Court procedures in great detail, and addressed the Stefan case specifically.

Andrews questioned him about Don Stefan's admission of physical abuse.

"Often times when you have both a criminal and Family Court proceeding going on," Riley explained, "you sometimes make a plea bargain to get rid of... the criminal court in order to get a Family Court disposition, because Family Court has a great leeway of power as far as ordering counseling... and reuniting the family, where the criminal court's basic goal is to put people on probation or in jail...."

Riley talked about Social Services and the court's efforts to locate Billy. "It had us quite upset, at the least," he said. "Suddenly we have a child in our custody and he's missing and we have no idea. Especially when we thought we had him in a fairly good place."

He spoke about my frequent appearances at Mr. Stefan's court hearings. "At a certain point... we got a phone call from the Sheriff's Department that supposedly Mr. Stefan was going to reveal the whereabouts of Billy Stefan," he said, "and that Barbara Lyn Lapp was going to be at the county jail, and all the media in the world was going to be there.

"It's kind of interesting how media has been involved in this matter. We were under the impression that when Mr. Stefan would announce where Billy was at, we would be able to go and get him. At least we thought—it was nothing clear cut...."

It was mid-afternoon when Riley completed his testimony. I knew Judge Himelein would offer me a chance to cross-examine him. I looked at my notepad, scribbled with questions I had jotted down during the hour that Riley had spoken. Suddenly a feeling of weakness and nausea came over me. My mouth felt hot and dry.

"Judge, could I have a little break," I asked. "I'm not feeling very well."

Himelein quickly granted my request, and called a recess. Several officers escorted me to the little waiting room, where I used the sink to splash cold water over my face.

The officers asked me repeatedly if I was well enough to proceed. I assured them I was, and they relayed the message to the judge. As we walked back into the courtroom, I met Judge Himelein, clad in a long black robe, returning from his break.

"Are you sure you want to go on, Miss Lapp?" he asked, as we stood face to face in the corridor. "We could adjourn."

"Yes, I'm sure—I feel much better."

Approaching the gallery, I scanned the faces in the crowd—friends, family members— Miriam, Susan. Their smiles looked forced. I turned away from them to face the judge, and sat down.

I questioned Stephen Riley on Family Court practices such as allowing hearsay into evidence, and at what age children are allowed to testify.

Riley said he doesn't like to put children on the witness stand. "It's heartbreaking to myself because often times a kid will break down and cry and it's traumatic.... That's one of the reasons they have made the lower standard [of evidence] as far as hearsay exceptions, to be able to use statements that a child has given to a worker or psychologist...."

"If the family wants to be reunited, does an admission of abuse often help to accomplish that?" I asked.

"I'm—an admission of abuse—no, not necessarily an admission of abuse," Riley stammered. "It can help in starting the psychological counseling.... Until the person admits or whatever, there is no sense in them going to counseling." Riley's explanation went on so long that the judge had to remind him he was "getting a little far afield from the question."

"As an attorney, do you sometimes tell parents that if they admit to abuse they will have a greater chance of having their children returned to them?" I asked.

Riley denied that he would do that, but alluded to it by saying that if a family really wants to get together again, an admission can help to get it over with. I continued to question him, focusing on Family Court's exclusion from due process rules such as trial by jury and speedy trial. His answers were verbose. Several times the court stenographer asked him to slow down.

Referring to Don Stefan's family court order, I asked Riley if he knew I believed the order was unconstitutional and illegal.

"I would say that probably it would have been your belief, however, I don't think that—" He paused. "You had only one side of the story, that's what you based all your actions on without knowing fully well what was going on with the total situation. And that's wrong."

"But it was well understood… that it was my belief that this particular order was not valid because of constitutional violations in the court
order?"

"In working with both criminal law and family law, a person—"

I interrupted. "That's not what I asked."

"I'm answering your question," Riley said, then turned to the right
and looked at the judge.

"Objection sustained. Answer the question that she asked," the
judge said.

The stenographer read back the question.

"That was your opinion," Riley said.

"Yes. And that was understood?"

"I never talked to you. I only read the one petition you submitted,
and I would gather… that that was your opinion."

The prosecution's testimony concluded, Judge Himelein turned to
me. "Are you going to call any witnesses?"

"No."

Himelein said court would reconvene tomorrow at 10:00 for summations from both sides, and his final charge to the jury.

By Rachel

Evening again. I was disappointed that the trial wasn't over. I wish
Barbara could rest. And the family at home—some are sick, and hardly
have the time and strength to attend the trial.

Barbara and I talked a lot. She took more Tylenol, and I massaged
her. She feels hot. She rested a couple of hours, but could not sleep.

The girls here are good to us. They showed concern for my anxiety
today when Barbara was gone. When Barbara came back from court
for a break, they crowded around her for news. Once Barbara told
them of her cross-examination of the officers. One of the girls said,
"You're gonna be my lawyer!"

Another girl said, "No! You can't have her. You know why? She's
gonna be *my* lawyer!"

When Barbara left for court again, a chorus of voices rang from
the cellblock: "Get 'em, Barbara! Go Barbara! Give 'em h - - -!"

6:00 PM. Doreen took Barbara to the office for a phone call with
News Channel 35, from Erie, Pennsylvania. Barbara said the reporter
wants to interview her tomorrow before court starts. He said he ran
the story for the first time yesterday, and got a lot of phone calls.
People consider her a "sacrificial angel," he told her.

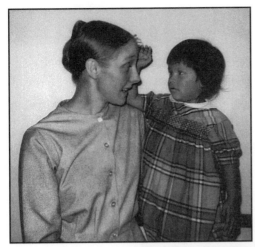

Barbara Lyn Lapp with newly
adopted daughter, Miriam. (1985)

Rachel Lapp
with one of her
purebred Norwegian
Elkhounds. (1984)

Jacob and Barbara
(Sr.) Lapp with a
granddaughter. (1984)

Barbara Lyn, her daughter Miriam, and sister Hannah, caring for their cows.
Lapp homestead in background. (1992)
Photo by Janice Barrett/ *The New York Holstein News.*

Joe Torres relaxing with his children. The children are, left to right, Naomi, Lelia, Magdalena, Ethan, and Joselle. (1992)

Barbara Lyn addresses a panel of New York State officials, regarding problems with Child Protective Services. (1990) Photo by Bill West/ *The Evening Observer.*

Sheriff's officers waiting to take Billy Stefan into custody—across the road from the Lapp farmhouse. Lt. Robert Buchhardt on right. (July 7,1993)

Billy with his aunt, Diane Moran, just after police left the Lapp residence. (July 7, 1993) Photo by Alpha Husted.

Barbara Lyn escorted to Charlotte Town Court by Lt. Andrew Lawrence and a uniformed Chautauqua County Sheriff's deputy. (July 13, 1993) Photo by Barry Bedford.

Members of the Lapp family seated around the table at lunch. Nathan Lapp in left foreground. (July, 1993) Photo by Dennis C. Enser/ *The Buffalo News.*

Picketers protesting Barbara Lyn's incarceration are driven away from the county jail by sheriff's deputies. (July 12, 1993) Photo by Bill West/ *The Evening Observer.*

Tom Stefan, Barbara Lyn, and Rachel during the demonstration in front of the county courthouse two hours before the sisters' arrest. (August 16, 1993)

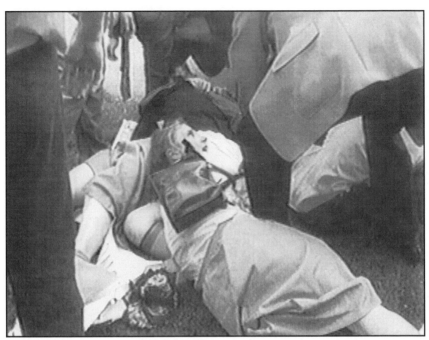

Barbara Lyn, Rachel, and their mother clinging together on the courthouse lawn as plainclothes officers try to take Barbara Lyn into custody. (August 16, 1993) Photo from video.

A sobbing Miriam escorted away from the crowd by a friend, during her mother's arrest. Other supporters look on. (August 16, 1993) Photo by Sheryl Christy.

An officer charges after Barbara Lyn's mother, as she tries to reach her daughter. (August 16, 1993.) Photo from video.

Chautauqua County Sheriff John R. Bentley yells, "I've had enough of you!" as he slaps a video camera filming the melee. (August 16, 1993) Photo from video. *(Hand in right foreground.)*

Deputy Gary Giambrone separates Nathan Lapp from
his father Jacob (center) who is in handcuffs. (August 16, 1993)

Jacob Lapp in handcuffs, as officers remove Lynn Carroll Bedford, who is
embracing him. Rachel (left) under arrest. (August 16, 1993) Photo from video.

Barbara Lyn escorted to court by Sgt. Rex Rater (right) and Lt. Lawrence. *WGRZ TV.*

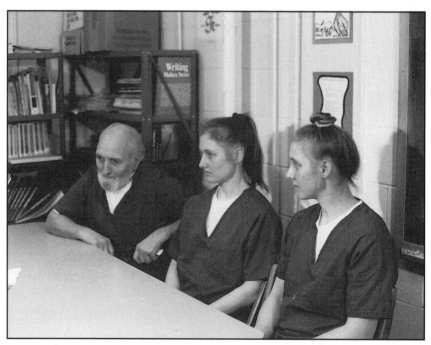

Jacob, Rachel, and Barbara Lyn during a media interview in jail. Photo by John Mikula.

Miriam at the entrance of the Chautauqua County Jail in Mayville, going to visit her mother.

Nancy Torres and four of her children in the waiting room of the jail where they visited her husband Joe.

Andrew Melechinsky (left) and Charles Gardiner in the Lapp dining room, preparing a writ of habeas corpus petition for the prisoners.

Billy Stefan in the Lapp kitchen, helping to make cookies

Barbara Lyn at her first trial. *WGRZ TV.*

A picketer's sign in front of the county courthouse in Mayville.

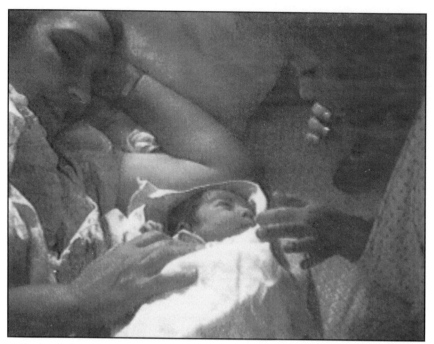

Benjamin Joseph Torres became the newest member of a fatherless household six weeks after Joe's arrest. Big Sister Naomi on right. Photo from video.

Lynn Carroll Bedford (right) with her youngest child Sparkelynn and husband Barry, after her release from jail in February 1994.

Dale Kepner from Fathers' Rights Association of New York presents
Barbara Lyn with an award for "defending the cause of children's rights."
Photo taken in jail, from video by Paul Waldmiller.

Celebrating Billy's 16th birthday and reunion with his father.
Left to right: Susan Lapp, Dennis Cimo (Chairman of the Mayville Five
Committee), Billy Stefan, and his father Donald Stefan. *The Arcade Herald.*

The "March on Mayville" organized on behalf of the
prisoners drew two hundred participants.

Relatives and
friends of "The
Mayville Five"
watch the jail
doors, awaiting
the prisoners'
release. (April
15, 1994) Photo
by Bill West/ *The
Evening Observer*

Barbara Lyn
and Rachel step
through the doors
of the Mayville jail
into freedom.
(April 15, 1994)
Photo by Bill West/
The Evening Observer.

Barbara Lyn greets Billy outside the walls of the jail. Looking on are Dennis Cimo,
Jacob Lapp and Donald Stefan. (April 15, 1994) Photo by Bill West/ *The Evening Observer.*

Susan, Rachel, Barbara Lyn, and Miriam admire a portrait of Donald Stefan with his sons, presented to the Lapps by the Stefan family. (April 15, 1994)

The Mayville Five on the Lapp farm. Left to right: Joe Torres, Rachel Lapp, Jacob Lapp, Barbara Lyn Lapp, and Lynn Carroll Bedford. (May, 1994) Photo by Jack D. Benson.

The Torres family in front of the Lapp farmhouse. Left to right: Naomi, Nancy with Benjamin, Joe with Lelia, Magdalena, Ethan, and Joselle. (May, 1994) Photo by Jack D. Benson.

Barbara Lyn still welcomes children in trouble with child protective agencies. (Summer, 1994)

Below: Members of the Lapp family on a hill above their farmstead. *Left to right:* Melissa, Lydia, Miriam, Barbara Lyn, Hannah, Barbara (Sr.), Nathan, Jacob, Rachel, and Susan. May 1994. Photo by Jack D. Benson.

■ CHAPTER 10 ■

Verdict

October 15, 1993

By Barbara Lyn

Dave Belmondo from *Newswatch 35* interviewed me before court this morning, up in the visiting area. An officer sat listening all the while.

After Dave turned off his camera, he said quietly, "This is crazy." Then, preparing to leave, he asked, "Your gut feeling, how will the trial end?"

"My feeling is, I'll be acquitted. But I don't dare place my hope on it."

"Are you prepared to serve time?"

"I can't be—but I know I'd get the strength to bear it, just as I have up to this point." My voice broke as I finished.

"Do you pray in your cell?" he asked.

"Yes," I said. Tears prevented me from saying more.

"This is crazy!" Dave said again. As I went down the stairs with CO Carole, his cameraman called, "Good luck, Barbara!"

※   ※   ※

"Miss Lapp, you may address the jury," Judge Himelein said.

Notebook in hand, I walked to the podium. The judge asked me to use the microphone.

I thanked the jurors for tolerating my lack of skill in the courtroom throughout the trial. "I apologize if I made anything confusing for you," I said.

Then I began my closing argument. "I'm sure you noticed that I didn't call any witnesses on my own behalf," I said. "There are several reasons for that. First, I'm not disputing the basic facts in the case.

Yes, I did have Billy Stefan living in my home, and yes, I was aware that Mr. Stefan had violated the court order when he took the child from the boys' home….

"The other reason that I didn't [bring witnesses] was I felt the prosecution witnesses had brought my points out so clearly, in that there had never been any orders directed toward me to bring Billy Stefan forward. Nobody ever told me to, verbally or in writing, and the courts never ordered me to.

"The third and most important reason that I didn't bring witnesses is simply because I don't feel comfortable working in this court or doing anything in this court. The court forced me into this trial in a manner that is so repugnant to American law's guarantee of liberty that I probably shouldn't have participated in the trial at all. I did, however, because I felt a compelling desire to motivate you as jurors, as my fellow citizens, and to give you the benefit of hearing my side of the story, and help to make you feel more comfortable in drawing your conclusions."

I asked the jury to consider the testimony of the Family Court attorneys and Child Protective Services case workers. "[It] was noticeably elaborate in justifying their system, and the way they say they keep families together…. Yet, when it came down to questioning them on a particular family, they had nothing to show for it—nothing except a family that was brought to such a point of distress that teenage boys were trying to run away from Social Services… [and] that the father of these boys was willing to go to jail for four months to help save his boys, to help get them freed and prevent the family from being ruined altogether.

"I think that, in itself, is a loud cry as to whether it's true what they were saying, that they do, in fact, rejoin families as soon as they can. It's my contention that they don't. And I believe that goes back to the constitutional issue… of the Family Court not permitting parties to have trial by jury in open court… and have their choice of testimony on their behalf. There again, the attorneys [who testified], even though they are purporting to support the law, made every excuse to overlook the law for the sake of convenience….

"I would also mention that if the confidentiality laws they say they need to protect the children with are working so well, I want to see the evidence. In the last twenty years since the Family Court Act was established, there has never been a [greater] increase in child abuse, domestic violence, decay in family….

"That's exactly what happens when law is abandoned for the sake of convenience. We can expect results like that. Also noticeable [in testimony] was that Family Court judges take an oath to uphold the Constitution. Yet they are not ashamed to say they violate several of these constitutional requirements for the sake of making the system work more perfectly.... That's why I asked you in the beginning, two days ago when you started here, 'Is the judge above the law?' I think not....

"As I have told you before, any laws that stand today must be in conformity with the Constitution. And it's not the proper function of law to regulate one's conscience or opinion or even manner of doing things, as long as that is not conflicting with somebody else's right or liberty....

"In case it seems or appears that it was extreme for me to do what I was doing, I just have to tell you again what I know about Billy, because it all goes back to him and why I took him in....

"As you have heard, Billy was a somewhat disadvantaged child, and had, in the year he was in Social Services care, been moved approximately seven times. Many of those places were institutions where he was heavily drugged.

"I know that the witness we had from the Bradford Home said that there were no drugs administered there, and I believe that. But in the eight months prior to that, while in Social Services care, he had been put in numerous institutions and had been drugged so heavily his family could barely get him to respond at times. He had gotten into severe behavior problems, all of which he had never experienced before when he was at home with his father and brothers.... Problems were, in fact, created by the very system that was purporting to protect him."

I told the jury of the Stefan family's desperate pleas for help, and of Billy's progress, emotionally and physically, since he came to our home. "I don't have any regret for what I did for Billy," I said. "If I would have abandoned him just as he was recovering from a year of devastating insecurity, if I would have abandoned him the day the sheriffs arrived at my home, that would have been cruel. If I would have forced him to walk into the hands of the officers who were ready to remove him from my home and take him back to where he was most afraid of going, it would have been nothing less than criminal on my part...."

"From what I hear, Billy spends some days enjoying himself at my farm. I talked to him on the phone a few nights ago. He had a lot of pride in his voice when he told me about a joint work project that he had been doing with my family and his....

"Another point. I'm not the only one that was helping out Billy. There were a lot of people involved.... Are we all criminals? This was a community standing up against an unacceptable action of the government in depriving a young man of his liberty....

"It's not against the law for somebody to come and stay with you for awhile. And if it is, why wasn't I or someone else similarly charged for Billy's brother, Tom? He was also in Social Services custody at the time.... He is still in Social Services custody, legally.

"Why did they pick Billy? Why did they pick me? If they say 'the law is the law,' where was the law for Tom? He was a year and a half older, slightly more capable. They knew they couldn't force him to do something he didn't want to do. They tried it on the more helpless, the more vulnerable.... I won't tolerate that....

I explained my decision to reveal Billy's whereabouts at my home, and Billy's opposition to the disclosure. "I expected the authorities to act with enough mercy that they wouldn't just pick him up," I said.

I reminded the jury once more of their historical right to judge the law and the facts, and their duty to act as a safeguard against government oppression.

"Consider, when you make your judgment, whether society would be a better place to have me jailed for two years," I said. "I would love to go home and perform my duties in the community, to be a mother to my daughter. But I don't want that to be your major consideration. I want you to make a judgment that is agreeable to your conscience.

"If your decision, or if your judgment, should cause me to serve a jail term, I would then have to turn to my trust in God as my assurance that at the final Judgment Day I will hear, 'I was naked and ye clothed me, a stranger, and ye took me in....'"

I choked up in tears before I could complete the Scripture reference. Turning from the jury, I walked to my table and wept silently. I could hear sniffling and muffled sobs from the people in the gallery. Officers and lawyers were all around me. I had never felt so alone.

Paul Andrews approached the jury. "May it please the court, Miss Lapp, members of the jury, good morning," he began. "I would also like to thank you for your patience, your time.... It's not an easy job. You are experiencing firsthand the culmination of 200 plus years of existence as a nation under the Constitution, and the tensions that may result in between the federal government and various state governments....

"I tried to show you some background of some of the people that were involved in the system. These are people like you and me. These are people who care. These are people who believe in our system and who try to make it work. They have to follow rules and laws—laws that are passed by us…. These people that testified have to follow these laws, in particular, Article 10 of the Family Court Act, which has for its purpose the protection of the child.

"Now, I think if you read the U.S. Constitution, this is a fabulous document. I agree with Miss Lapp in this regard…."

Andrews gave a lengthy historical overview of the Constitution, the process of legislation, and the people's duty to obey the laws. "Otherwise, a system of courts without public confidence and acceptance is but a paper tiger," he said. "Even though we may have perceived ourselves to be victims of the system, have cause to complain about its inadequacies, have cause to complain or perceive maybe an unjust situation here and there, if we lose our confidence in that system, if we fail to work within that system, there is no system…."

"You can take Miss Lapp's argument and her justification in what she has done and extend it to many other situations. Example…. If I say I don't believe in obeying traffic laws—well, think to what extreme, what the result would be if you apply that logic. It's easy. It is so easy to sit back and criticize the laws that do come into existence…."

"[T]hese laws are made to promote the safety of our citizens, the health, the good order and morals of the community as a whole…."

"Miss Lapp indicated in her opening statement that she did not believe in legal games being played with children, which I would suggest to you, that is essentially what she was involved in. She was keeping Billy Stefan on the premises. She was playing her own games, serving her own interest and getting media attention for her group…."

"Imagine placing Billy Stefan in a situation like that, in the midst of all that turmoil. What do you think, if you were… caring for someone… trying to do as much as you can to get them reunited with the family, that person is taken away when good progress is being made? Maybe, maybe, he would have been reunited with Donald Stefan a short time after that. We'll never know…."

Andrews handed the jurors copies of the court orders against Don Stefan. "Review them," he said. "This is what it is all about, ladies and gentlemen—a signed court order with the provisions contained therein…. You heard testimony that Miss Lapp knew of these provisions.

"I think you may have perceived from Miss Lapp an intense distrust of the system. I would say she's very principled in her beliefs. I respect those beliefs. But I would say that principle—there is a fine line between being principled and being just plain stubborn for one's own personal motive, whatever that is…. 'Do things my way, or we don't do them.'

"She's made some revelations or indications to you as to her staying in jail. Suffice it to say, all due process, everything that is accorded to anyone else charged with a crime had been accorded to her. She's refused to cooperate. She still holds the key to the cell in her hand.

"Miss Lapp said in her opening statement… she had a strong feeling the accusatories were overblown. Well, I don't know if she really got into discussing with Mr. Stefan his admission to the abuse in Family Court there. I don't know what Mr. Stefan told her, but she apparently didn't get the whole picture.

"She's making a big deal of saying, 'Oh, no. No demand was ever made on me.' Well, look back…. [O]n July 7, the conversation with Sheriff Burrell…. [T]he sheriff telling her, 'We have this warrant, produce Billy Stefan.' This warrant is addressed, yes, to the sheriff, constable, police officer in the State of New York. 'Where is he? We want him.' 'You can't have him.'

"Listen carefully to the elements that the judge will give you. I submit to you, Barbara Lapp is guilty of, number one, obstructing governmental administration on July 7. And the officer is trying to get Billy Stefan, pursuant to this warrant, which is based on the Family Court order. She interfered with that duty. She refused to return him to the law enforcement officials.

"I submit to you that there is sufficient evidence, as well, to show that she intentionally aided Donald Stefan in disobeying the lawful court order, by helping Donald Stefan interfere with the court order and with the custody of Billy Stefan.

"Listen carefully to the judge's charge as it pertains to accessorial conduct… because there is certainly liability of Barbara Lapp here in knowing. She knew she had no legal right to help and to take William Stefan from the Bradford Children's Home….

"Remember, when we first spoke with each other, you indicated that if the evidence showed that she did indeed violate the Court order, you wouldn't hesitate to return a verdict of guilty….

"There is one thing that Barbara Lapp said in her opening—something to the effect that the court and the district attorney used the law to their own benefit. I disagree strongly with that. I have done my job in presenting everything I could to you. The court is doing its job. Nobody has been above the law because of a sincere belief that what he or she is doing is righteous if that interferes with other people. That's the whole question here, ladies and gentlemen. Is Barbara Lapp above the law?"

Andrews told the jury to take the copies of the court orders to the jury room. "Consider carefully," he said. "But I would urge you to just view the evidence that has come in there. I suggest to you that you will then find that Barbara Lapp is not above the law."

When Andrews finished, Judge Himelein began his charge to the jury. "Ladies and gentlemen, it is now my duty to instruct you on the law. First, I want to thank you for the concentration and attention you have given to this case throughout the trial. You have been selected for one of the most important duties of citizenship, to pass judgment on the conduct of one of your fellow citizens, to determine the guilt or the nonguilt of the defendant, Barbara Lapp. It is a duty that requires the utmost fairness, honesty and courage…."

"You, as jurors, are the sole and exclusive judges of the fact," he said. "On the other hand, I am the sole and exclusive judge of the law….

"My instructions to you on the law must be accepted by you whether you agree with them or not. If you have ideas of your own of what the law is… it is now your duty under your oath to cast aside your own ideas… and accept the law exactly as I give it to you."

He then read the three laws I was charged with violating. After each charge, he read four or five different "elements" to each of the laws. The elements consisted of descriptions of my alleged actions on July 7, as applied to the laws I supposedly violated.

"If you find that the People have proven beyond a reasonable doubt each of these four elements…," Judge Himelein said, "then you must find the defendant guilty. On the other hand, if you find that the People have failed to prove to your satisfaction… any one or more of these four elements, then you must find the defendant not guilty." He repeated this instruction after reading each of my alleged violations. It took him about 45 minutes to read all his instructions and charges to the jury. Then the jury was sent to deliberate.

❋   ❋   ❋

The trial is over. I'm sitting at the small metal table in my cell. Nothing I say or do will make any difference to the outcome.

There are no words to describe the feeling. I don't know why I sit down to write—as though the pen moving across the paper might lift some of the weight from my chest.

One part of me is assuring me peace and comfort, another is gripped with pain. I have a strong desire to be free from these bonds, and an even stronger desire to be at peace regardless of what happens. It feels like a literal fight going on within—peace rising up, then fear battling it down, as if with a club.

CO Doreen called me to the gate. "They need you back up in court," she said. My heart was pounding wildly. A verdict this soon? The jury had been in deliberation for only twenty minutes.

Outside I met two court officers. "It's just a question from the jury," one of them said as he handcuffed me.

In the courtroom, the jury was brought in. Judge Himelein announced he had a request from the jury for copies of the warrants and copies of the three separate charges against me. Himelein said they could have the warrants—a writ of habeas corpus warrant on Billy, and a court order against Don Stefan—but not the charges.

"May I speak?" the jury foreman asked.

"Yes."

"The reason we want them, is so that we can take each [charge] one by one."

"I understand that. But I don't have the discretion to do that," Himelein said. "That's just one of the rules, that you can't take the charges with the list of elements into the jury room."

Upon the jury's request, he then reread all the charges and elements for them.

The jury returned to deliberate, and I was taken back down to my cell.

Less than an hour later, I was called again. In the tunnel to court, I suddenly found myself humming a tune. The words of a hymn danced in my heart, in concert with the tune: "My God and Father while I stray, far from my home on life's rough way, Oh teach me from my heart to say, Thy will be done."

I don't know why God chose that murky tunnel as the place to speak to me. Maybe He was telling me He'd be with me in the darkest places.

This time the jury's question was on the charge of obstruction. The foreman asked to have the charge read again. The jurors listened attentively as the judge reread the law and all the elements. Then they went back.

I walked out of the courtroom, escorted by officers. Scott Humble stopped me and leaned close. He said he thought it was a good sign that the jury's question was on only one of the three counts, possibly indicating they had already dismissed the other two counts.

4:45 PM. I was called for a third jury question.

In the courtroom, I watched the jurors' faces as they filed in. They looked concerned. Some of them looked at me, eye to eye, as if trying to connect the person with the charges.

This time they asked to have the elements read back to them, on all three of my charges. They also asked the judge if they could take notes.

"'No,' is the short answer to that," the judge said, then explained that state policy does not allow jurors to take notes during a trial.

The foreman of the jury pleaded: "There are so many parts to each of these [charges] we have trouble remembering exactly the wordage of them.... We're in disagreement on some of the parts of it...."

The judge told them he would read all parts of the charges for them, as often as they needed. For the sixth time today, he read the elements of my alleged offences: "That on July 7, 1993, the defendant refused to deliver William Stefan to the legal custody of the Department of Social Services.

"That in so doing she prevented or attempted to prevent a public servant, deputy sheriffs, from performing an official function.

"That she did so by means of intimidation, physical force, or interference.

"That the defendant intentionally prevented or attempted to prevent a deputy sheriff from performing an official function.

"If you find that the People have proven, to your satisfaction, each of these elements, then you must find the defendant guilty.

"On the other hand, if you find that the People have failed to prove... beyond a reasonable doubt, any one or more of those four elements, then you must find the defendant not guilty...."

He went on until he had read a total of thirteen different elements, on the three separate charges.

Several of the jurors seemed to be bursting with questions. One of them whispered something to the foreman, who then asked the judge to define, in laymen's language, the writ of habeas corpus the police had the day they came to my house to pick up Billy. "What is the power of it and the mechanics of it?" he asked.

"A writ of habeas corpus can—well," Judge Himelein stammered. "It can be different things depending upon the context in which it is used. You might have to be more specific."

JURY FOREMAN: Well, the questions that we're discussing, would a deputy have to announce that he has the writ in order to execute his duty?

JUDGE HIMELEIN: Would a deputy have to announce that he has such a writ?

JURY FOREMAN: Yeah.

HIMELEIN: In order to—

JURY FOREMAN: Execute his duty that he was to pick up the child. Would he have to say, 'I have a writ of habeas corpus here requesting that I pick up this child?'

HIMELEIN: This type of writ is issued to the police officer, or any police officer…. If he were to see the object of the writ, he would be free to take that person.

JURY FOREMAN: Without showing it or proving that he had it on him or anything like that?

HIMELEIN: In terms of the officer's right to execute the writ, yes.

JURY FOREMAN: Would he have to show it, or say that he had it on him?

HIMELEIN: No. I mean if, for example, the officer knew a writ had been issued, obviously a writ could not be issued to any police officer in the state. And if, for example, every person in a police department wouldn't necessarily have a copy of the writ, but the knowledge that it was issued to any police officer would allow that police officer to take possession of the body of the person named in the writ, if they were to find him.

Several jurors looked at each other, nodding, smiling slightly. Some still looked confused. "Are we allowed to ask a question?" one of them asked.

"Well, it's supposed to be done through your foreman," the judge said.

The juror whispered to the foreman. Others leaned toward them, listening.

The jury foreman spoke again. "Does [the writ] authorize a police officer to go in and take the subject by force, if necessary, without any consideration of harm to anybody or anything? If I was the officer, would I be allowed to say, 'Well, I'm going to do it anyway, and go do it?'"

"Well, I think the legal rule is that they would be entitled to use whatever force is necessary to execute the writ," the judge said, "but that there are certain prohibitions in New York against, for example, the use of deadly force or things like that. They certainly wouldn't have the right to use deadly force on anyone to execute it without, you know, the reasonable anticipation of it being used on them. I mean—and there are certain practical aspects to that."

"I guess we're ready to try again," the foreman said.

"One more question," said one of the jurors. He whispered to the foreman again.

After conferring with several different jurors, the foreman said, "What he is asking is, is the defendant legally obligated to comply with the writ, when the deputy shows up and says why he's there?"

The judge hesitated. "I think," he began slowly, "if I were to answer that, I would probably be invading your province. I'll think on it, but it seems to me that is something you will have to answer."

The jury left the courtroom to continue deliberation.

Judge Himelein looked uneasy. "Do either of you wish to be heard on that colloquy?" he asked Andrews and me. "That is somewhat unusual to have questions like that, and normally I would consult with the parties before I answered them."

"I would say it's the first time I've been involved in such an exchange," Andrews said. "I was just wondering about the last question that was posed."

"Well, I would anticipate that you two might have widely disparate requests for the way I answered that question," Himelein said.

Andrews spoke. "...Obviously, it would be the People's position that whenever an officer is involved in an official capacity, that there should be full compliance and cooperation with such a request."

Judge Himelein still looked worried, his normally genial expression gone. "Miss Lapp, do you want to be heard on any of those questions?" he asked.

"I don't think that's anything for anybody besides the jury to decide," I said, referring to Andrews' answer.

"Well, I will think about it while they are deliberating, too," Judge Himelein said. "Okay."

As the officers took me back to the jail, they discussed the jurors' problem. One of them said he'd give anything to listen in on their discussion.

Less than fifteen minutes after I was back in my cell, CO Doreen called again. I was startled.

"This is it," Doreen said as she took me out. I repeated it to Rachel.

This time as I walked through the tunnel I had no comforting messages from God. "Lord God Almighty, Lord God Almighty," my soul was uttering, in tune to my steps. It seemed I was not capable of completing any prayer. I felt as if I was being swept along.

When I got to the courtroom, the gallery was almost empty. I saw

officers and lawyers, the chairman of our legislature, and a few supporters. No family members. They probably didn't expect a verdict
this soon. The eyes of TV cameras followed me as I walked in.

I sat at the table, barely conscious of what was going on around
me. Then I observed the expressions on the jurors' faces as they filed
in. They looked serious—not as enthusiastic as when they had come
for questions. Maybe they had decided to find me guilty.

After the jurors were seated, the court clerk stood up. "Members
of the jury, have you agreed upon a verdict?" she asked, in a town
crier voice.

The foreman rose. "They have."

The clerk continued, in the same monotone: "How do you find in
the case of the People of the State of New York versus Barbara Lyn
Lapp on the charge of obstruction of governmental administration
in the second degree?"

"Guilty."

On the charges of custodial interference and conspiracy, the jury
foreman said "not guilty."

After the verdict, the judge reduced my bail from twelve thousand
to one thousand, and set sentencing for November 8. He thanked
the spectators "for their courtesies during the trial, and their behavior in an emotional case like this one."

Nathan came into the courtroom, just as I was leaving. He looked
confused.

Four media men stepped forward to the rail along the gallery. "Any
comments?" Miss Lapp, one of them asked, his microphone pushed
forward.

The officers behind me stopped, giving me time. I wanted to speak,
but no words came to mind. There was too much pressure, too much
exhaustion. "I'm sorry, but I can't comment right now," I said.

"Are you going to post bail?" a reporter asked, his pen positioned
on a notepad.

"Probably not."

October 16

By Rachel

Barbara and I were both stirring all night. I felt physically weak
and depressed this morning. I read the article in the newspaper about
Barbara's verdict. It made me feel sad to see the comments from a
juror. He said they had "no doubt" about convicting her on the one
charge. I guess I had allowed myself to believe there would be people

of courage on that jury. We have reason to believe there were some who cared.

I read a few verses from Romans 8: "Who shall lay anything to the charge of God's elect? It is God that justifieth."

Barbara got called for a visit at 10:30. She told me she's not sure about going, she is crying too much. I told her maybe it's good to sometimes cry with others, and handed her some tissue to take along.

When Barbara got back at eleven I was sitting at the little table, reading the Bible. She sat across from me, and told me about the visit. "I told Mom about the beautiful words of the hymn that came to me in the tunnel yesterday," she said. "But then it made me cry to talk about it, and Miriam started crying, too. It's not fair to Miriam—" Barbara dropped her head into her hands and wept.

I succumbed to tears. We sat at the tiny table, face to face, sharing our grief. Then Barbara lay on the bed and I sat down beside her. A towel hanging from the top bunk provided some privacy.

CO Sue brought our lunch in. I couldn't think of eating. I went to get my Bible from the table where Sue had put our food. Accidentally, I moved a paper plate, and it slid off the table. I caught it as it fell, but all the potato chips scattered over the floor.

The other girls noticed, and fell silent. "Oh my!" I exclaimed at my clumsiness. Dee groaned sympathetically and came to the door. I knelt on the floor, holding the plate with hot pizza and brushing the chips off a folded blanket by the table.

I apologized to Dee for my tears. "It's a hard day for us," I said.

"I'll help her," Barbara said cheerfully, getting out of bed. We looked at the mess and laughed. "Now we have to eat off the floor," I said, laughing. Then I was crying.

"You're gonna get yourselves sick," Dee said painfully. She came and put her hand on my back.

Barbara picked up the chips and ate an orange. We gave the remainder of our food to the others and lay down to rest.

CO Sue called us from the gate, to get our mail. "They're sleeping," one girl told her. Sue came in quietly and put the mail on the table. She came over and pulled back the towel that draped from the bunk where I was resting, arm across my face. "Just checking to see if you're okay," she said.

"I'm okay," I said.

9:00. We're locked in for the night, and I'm writing again. Dee checked on us a few times after supper, asking us if we weren't crying anymore.

"We're done now," I assured her, "and tomorrow we won't cry."

"We never see you like this," she said. "You're always happy and dancing around. I want you happy again."

October 17

By Barbara Lyn

Yesterday I didn't write. I was sure if I'd try to put my feelings on paper I'd cry more. Today I'm able to talk, but still confused. How could I reach such a depth of sorrow?

It simply is a dreadful feeling to be found guilty by one's own countrymen, after having served the community for many years. The fact that the verdict was spoken by a jury, supposedly unbiased, added to the pain. In facing them those three days of trial, I felt they were more my equals than the judge, prosecutor, and officers.

As I grieved yesterday I thought much of the prophets and saints of old. Jesus and St. Paul were never acquitted. Yet comfort evaded me. At times I wondered if the stress of the trial had damaged my mind. When I tried to rest, court scenes replayed themselves in my mind, like horror movies. Jurors' faces came up close. I hadn't slept much all night. I abhorred my mat on the floor. In the same spot it had been during the rough nights before the trial, it bode evil. Every small discomfort tormented me. I watched the hours pass on the clock, and for the first time since we were here I felt boredom.

This afternoon I slept for two hours. Then Rachel made me do algebra for an hour. This evening I sent a letter off to Dad and Joe, and one to Miriam.

The family visit today gave me the final boost I needed. I started to view the conviction as something that needed to happen to make our mission complete.

By Rachel

A morning of peace dawned, like sunshine following a violent storm. I feel as peaceful as I have ever felt. Barbara is a convict, but only because the DA and the judge and police could not stand under the light of her love toward humanity.

Barbara and I talked a lot about how Judge Himelein handled the jury's final question. Himelein first told the jury they must take the law as he explains it, then refused to give them the legal definition of the habeas corpus writ in question. He told them the officers could use any amount of force except deadly force to execute the writ. But he didn't tell them that the writ, without a warrant, had no legal value on our property, nor against Barbara. There is no doubt that the way Judge Himelein answered the jury made them come back with the guilty verdict. He and the DA convicted Barbara, not the jury.

There were times throughout her trial that I thought Barbara's light shone so brightly that even the vilest person, even her most evil enemy, might soften. But we see more clearly than ever that people can be truly blind. It's a good lesson for us, so we don't think we can, or should, change them. That isn't our job. Our job is to clean out the evil within ourselves, so our light and love can truly shine, so that others in need of light and love can grasp it. When they desire our help, we freely give, not so that we can be thanked, but so that God's law of sharing can be fulfilled.

CHAPTER 11

Survival

October 18, 1993

By Rachel

The cell block is beautifully lit with afternoon sun in the west window. TV is turned low. The other girls are napping, or quietly playing cards. I just finished giving poor Dee a back and foot massage. She has a new lump on her neck. Today she has pain all over.

CO Sue, who recently told us we are not allowed to enter each other's cells, found me in Dee's cell, massaging her feet. She looked at me sternly.

"Dee is having a lot of pain," I said. Sue's expression softened, and she said it was okay.

At the gym today, CO Jim Crowell brought the jump rope for me, after he heard me ask Swanee where it was. I went to the far end of the gym to jump. Soon Crowell, in his uniform and leather boots, came over with another rope and tried jumping, too. He kept getting tangled in it. Once the rope dropped onto his head and just hung there. We couldn't help smiling.

Swanee and a couple of other COs stood at the opposite end of the gym, watching us jump rope side by side. They were laughing.

"How is the cut you got on your head?" I asked Crowell. Carole had told us he'd been assaulted by an inmate.

Crowell said it had healed. "I didn't know you knew me," he said, stepping closer.

I told him we'd noticed his name tag before. After a pause, I said, "We don't have many friends in here. I can tell you that."

Crowell, who is serious by nature, seemed concerned. "I would hope—even though it's not a nice place to be," he said, fumbling for words, "you can at least feel you're treated well here."

I stopped jumping rope to listen. Crowell continued. "I don't know about the other officers, but I've never heard anything bad said of you—at least not among the blue-shirts (COs)."

"It's all so unreal to us here," I said. "We look at someone and say hello, but it's like we're nobody."

As our conversation continued, we talked about Child Protective Services and Barbara's trial.

"What about your trial next month?" Crowell asked. "Are you going ahead with it?"

"It seems as though they're going ahead. I have no choice," I said.
"You have no choice?"
"You mean as far as taking a plea bargain?"
"Yes."
"I've been offered a couple of deals, but I can't in good conscience take any of them."

"You feel if you'd plead to that one charge, you'd be admitting to something you didn't do?"

"Yes. I'd love to go home, but I feel I can't face the world if I say an untruth."

Crowell nodded. "I guess you're learning a lot," he said. "I understand you're a writer. Maybe sometime things will be written about this."

"It's my sister Hannah who is the writer," I said.

Swanee and the girls were leaving.

As I left, Crowell said, "Thank you for your concerns."

By Barbara Lyn

I was called out to see a probation officer this morning. CO Sue took me to the jail classroom to meet with him. He introduced himself as Ted Leonard, and said he was here for a routine post-conviction interview, so his office could make a recommendation to the court for my sentencing.

"Do I have to take part in the interview?" I asked. "I don't really want to give information for the court."

He said it was not a requirement but my cooperation could help influence the judge in a positive way. "It will also provide the court with a permanent record of your side of the story," he said.

"I'd like to talk to you, but I'm not sure if it's a good idea," I said. "Could I have fifteen minutes to think about it, and make a phone call?"

"Certainly," he said. "I'll come back in a little while."

After calling home, I decided I would speak to Mr. Leonard. He came back, and we met upstairs in the visiting area. Questionnaire and pen ready, he started by asking my date of birth and Social Security number, then names and address of my parents. It gave me a strange feeling to give personal information, for the first time since I came to this institution. When he asked for names of my siblings, I hesitated. "Isn't that an invasion of their privacy, to have their names on my probation report?" I asked.

"You don't need to give that, if you're not comfortable with it," he said.

He asked about my educational background.

"Eight years, home school," I said.

"Have you taken a GED?"

"I've been working on one since I'm here."

"Could I write that down?" he asked.

"I don't think it's significant."

He seemed puzzled. "I won't write it down if you don't want me to. But why don't you think it's something positive?"

I told him I've studied a lot since I've been out of school, and am proud of being self-educated. "I really didn't need the GED. I'm doing it just to pass the time, and because I enjoy studying. I scored 12.9 on the pretest."

"This will certainly give a favorable impression to the court," he said, jotting down my comments.

I mentioned that my lack of influence from public schools may have to do with my being in jail today. "I was taught to think independently," I said.

He began to write again. "That could help the judge understand you better," he said. "So your upbringing had to do with you not being aware of government limitations?"

"No, that's not what I meant to say," I said. "I understand government limitations well, and I have no problem conforming to rules of orderly society. I've been driving for fifteen years without a traffic infraction."

Mr. Leonard then questioned me about the incident at my home when police came for Billy on July 7. I emphasized that I felt a strong moral obligation to help Billy, and did not know I was breaking the law. I told him it is my belief that the jury found me guilty only because the judge misled them on points of law.

When Mr. Leonard was done he allowed me to see his report. The information was accurate. But it stung to see in writing my violations of the law. I sighed. "I was brought up with a high respect for law officers," I said. "My parents didn't even like us to call officers 'cops.'"

"Why?" he asked, taking up his pen again.

"They viewed it as disparaging—a little like calling a black person 'nigger.'"

Mr. Leonard got up to leave. "How many days have you served?" he asked.

"Nine weeks today—guess that's sixty-three days."

Back in the cellblock, Tobey was telling Rachel what she'd overheard when she went to court. An officer had asked Sgt. Rex Rater how I conducted myself in court. "She broke down, finally," Rater had said.

"Good!" the other officer said.

Then they asked Tobey, "What's she doing down there now?"

Another girl said when Rex Rater arrested her, he had said, "You're wearing the famous handcuffs of Barbara Lyn Lapp."

October 20

By Barbara Lyn

I asked to see the jail doctor this morning, because of an earache and cough I've had ever since the trial. Dr. Gleason prescribed only cold pills, which I'm not too happy about. I thought he'd give me antibiotics.

We have a full house here again. A businesswoman from Jamestown came, and went again today. Also, a well-educated working woman came in to serve thirty days for DWI.

We see injustice among all—police picking up unsuspecting people, judges imposing high bail and arbitrary sentences. Many of the offenders do need punishment. But the system is unpredictable, unfair, and with seemingly no standard. Certain judges are known to be really harsh, certain officers mean. "Making deals" with the court is commonplace. Favors are openly spoken of.

Two of the girls were sentenced to state prison today, and will leave soon. One is Dee, the sick girl. She was so upset when she got the news.

Dee had a seizure again tonight. Rachel got to her bedside first and placed her hands on Dee's back, keeping her from hitting the metal wall. Then Sgt. Melson and a CO who is an EMT came in, and asked Rachel to move aside. We had to stand back and watch Dee convulsing, as three COs stood several feet from her bedside, offering no assistance.

By Rachel

Our family says they're making grape juice today. I am imagining the crowd—all the children gathered, pulling grapes from their stems; Lydia bent over hot kettles and purple-stained cloths; others filling the half-gallon jars with the rich juice.

In the mail today I received my second package of "Revita," a liquid nutritional supplement sent by the family. But CO Sue told me I'm not allowed to have it.

"I'm using it already," I told Sue. "It was approved by the doctor when it first came in last week." I showed her the jail doctor's note and another approval note by CO Carole, signed and dated. "I was using it on my chiropractor's recommendation, before I came in," I said.

"What is it?" Sue asked, eyeing me suspiciously.

"It's a protein and mineral supplement that replaces medications I've taken in the past," I said. "It's important because of low thyroid and blood sugar problems I've had."

"It's not a protein," Sue said, continuing to stare at me. "Lt. Belson read the ingredients, and he said there's not even protein in it."

"Spirulina is the main ingredient," I said. "That's rich in protein."

Sue took the approval notes I'd given her, went out, and returned a short time later. "I'm only a messenger," she said. "Lt. Belson says you can't have it."

October 21

By Rachel

I spent the afternoon thinking and making notes for our possible trial next month. I still tend to believe it won't materialize. By our trial date on November 17, the ninety-day statutory limit for trying a person imprisoned on misdemeanor charges will have expired. But maybe they'll go ahead and take us to trial, even against their own laws.

After reading some material on the meaning of "judgment by juries," I started to make notes, then just sat around. Sometimes I feel my ability to think is diminishing.

This evening I picked up the Bushell book again, and read where the jurors on William Penn's trial were imprisoned for refusing to give a guilty verdict, as instructed by the English Court. Appealing their imprisonment, their lawyer successfully contended that juries do have an obligation to judge both law and fact. He says you can't separate law from fact. It's an extremely interesting argument in the wake of Barbara's trial, with that actor of a judge trying to tell the jury to judge only the facts.

Tobey left for state prison. She was informed at midnight that she's leaving, then left at 4:00 AM. We hadn't expected her to leave so soon, and certainly not at night. Carole explained later that they generally transport prisoners without prior notice, to avoid possible confrontations or interceptions on the way.

It is so empty today. Tobey was here when we came, and she was indisputably the boss. Very frank-speaking, she'd order the others to turn down the TV, or pick up their feet when walking in sandals.

Tobey left a letter for all of us. Her message to Barbara and me was to keep our chins up. "It's okay to cry, but not too long," she wrote, and, "Treat others like you'd like to be treated. I remember!"

By Barbara Lyn

I broke out in hives this afternoon, some hours after taking the cold pill Dr. Gleason had prescribed. Don't know if that's what caused the hives, but this evening when CO Doreen offered me the cold pill again I declined taking it. I showed her my inflamed elbows. Doreen asked if I'd ever had hives before. I told her I hadn't.

The itching got progressively worse, around my knees and elbows. I wrapped up my pant legs and rolled up my sleeves. My skin was fiery red. The other girls urged me to call Doreen.

"Doreen, these hives are driving me crazy," I said. "Do you have anything I could put on them?"

"There's nothing to do for hives," she said. "I know because my daughter gets them." She went out, but came back a little later. "Sometimes Benadryl helps," she said. "I'll leave a note for the nurse to get some in the morning."

"What about rubbing alcohol, or something to help cool it down?" I asked, stepping desperately from one foot to the other. Doreen ignored my suggestions, but spoke about the possible causes of hives, and repeated that there is nothing to do for them.

The girls gave me baby powder to put on the hives, but it didn't help much.

October 22

By Barbara Lyn

Dorine's shift ended at eleven last night. Louise came to our cell and asked how I'm feeling. "I could get you some calamine lotion," she said.

"I'll try anything," I said.

We heard Louise explaining my problem to the sergeant on duty, and she returned shortly with the lotion. It gave instant relief. She also brought me some cough syrup, even though the doctor hadn't prescribed it. She had heard me coughing, and seemed concerned when I told her it was keeping me from sleeping.

An hour later, just after I'd fallen asleep, I woke up with severe itching on my wrists and ankles. It was a fiery pain, hardly distinguishable as an itch. I jumped out of bed in near panic, grabbed a wash cloth and wet it with water. But the wet cloth applied to my ankles only added to the misery. It felt like my skin was boiling.

I frantically slapped more calamine onto my ankles and wrists. In the meantime, a heartburn-like pain in my stomach was getting worse and worse, radiating from breastbone to backbone. I paced the floor, flopped down on my mat, and jumped up again. The chest pain became so bad I couldn't feel anything else. Finally I hung onto the rail of the bunk bed, called Rachel, and collapsed onto my mat on the floor. Rachel wanted to call Louise. Gasping between words, I begged her to rub my back first.

Rachel's touch brought almost immediate relief. By the time Louise came in I was okay. Rachel told me I have to get up and tell her what happened.

Louise was very concerned. "Have you ever had pneumonia or pleurisy?" she asked.

"No," I said. "I never had an allergic reaction before, either."

She said she was going to tell the sergeant (A.J. Melson) what happened, and they would take me to the emergency room if I didn't feel better soon. Rachel rubbed me all over, and I fell asleep.

This morning CO Carole is in. She tells me jail staff would like me to go to the hospital. I don't want to. I feel exhausted, but not terribly sick. My cough is bad, but the hives are gone. Seeing a doctor would be reasonable, but ER would be stupid. I dread going out in a police car with who-knows-who, in greens and handcuffs.

Carole gently tried to convince me I should go. I told her I'd like to see my own doctor, and my family would pay the bill. She said the sergeant won't allow that, but would let me see the jail doctor at his private office, about six miles from here. I finally agreed to go.

They got an appointment, and Carole took me to the office, where I waited for my ride. A CO brought an oversized parka for me, and we headed toward the outdoors. For a moment I thought the handcuffs had been forgotten. Then he drew them out from under his coat. "I won't shackle you, but I have to use the handcuffs," he said apologetically. He put them on loosely, then asked if they weren't too tight.

We walked outside. It was my first step into fresh air in almost ten weeks. The CO opened the back door of the police van, where I was separated from the driver by wire mesh.

At the doctor's office, Dr. Gleason gave me a quick checkup, and prescribed antibiotics and cough syrup. He said the allergic reaction may have been from the cold pill.

On the trip back, I conversed with the CO about last night's high wind, and the leaves left on the trees. Then he asked what nationality my daughter is. He said he had seen her in the visiting room, and told me he and his wife had adopted twin boys from the Philippines. The rest of the way back to jail we shared experiences about international adoptions, foreign languages, and bonding with adopted children.

October 23

By Barbara Lyn

Yesterday was Miriam's fourteenth birthday. I trust God will help her see the rewards of patience and resignation, as He has mercifully shown to me.

It's honey extracting day at home, and my mind is with Susan, knowing it is a long, tedious job. It had been my job alone for fifteen years. But last year, for the first time, Susan had helped me. Maybe God knew she would need the skill.

This afternoon an inmate with an injury on her foot complained to Sandy, an alternate CO, that her bandage was slipping and her foot was bleeding. She said CO Sue had changed the bandage, and did a terrible job. I inspected her foot, and told Sandy that the bandage needed to be secured. Sandy agreed, and brought in all the necessary first aid materials.

"Are you going to do it?" she asked me.

"I'd like to, if you let me," I answered, knowing the job involves handling scissors and other items inmates are not usually allowed to have. Sandy said I could, and the patient nodded agreeably. Everyone watched as I swabbed the sores with Betadine, put on compresses, then wrapped her foot smoothly with gauze. Rachel offered advice on how to get it tight. Several girls commented that it looked like a professional job.

"I shouldn't tell you this now," I said, "but I got my experience wrapping cows' feet."

"Oh, she's just another veterinarian!" one of the girls said. They laughed. They call the old jail doctor a veterinarian whenever they don't like what he does.

By Rachel
This morning it was my turn to do the cleaning in the common area. I took a scrub brush and cleaned along the front of the cells. I thought of Mom, how she used to have us scrub the washboards on Saturdays, when we were younger. In here it's not washboards. There's a metal frame that's bolted to the concrete floor, with ceiling-height upright bars welded onto it.

The girls laughed at me as I scrubbed, down on my knees with the big plastic brush—rags, cleaners, and a bucket of soapy water beside me.

"I'm doing my Saturday cleaning," I said.

"I think she's bored!" exclaimed Irma, one of the inmates.

I burst out laughing. It was partly true.

October 24

By Rachel
This was a lovely, sunshiny Sunday. We opened our window as far as we could, which is only a few inches, and breathed a mild fall air. Outside we could see the sidewalk and a few feet of lawn. Leaves, even though they're brown, looked beautiful, as they responded to the gentle push of the breeze and danced in the grass. But the very best was the pure, radiant sunshine pouring through our canopied windows. It sent a message of goodness that transcended the suffering of confinement and the godlessness of our environment, to lift our spirits into communion with the One who created the sun's ray.

Every Sunday a minister comes to the jail to give a half-hour service. Today, as usual, several of the girls went to church.

"Aren't Barbara and Rachel going?" CO Sue quietly asked the other girls.

"No, they don't like our church," one of them answered.

Barbara and I have told the girls we prefer to study the Bible by ourselves, because we feel that in today's religions there is too much pretense instead of practice.

October 25

By Barbara Lyn

It's ten weeks today. In two more weeks I'll be sentenced. Is this just the beginning, or is it near the end?

Rachel asked Carole if she thinks any of the COs would be interested in signing a petition for leniency in my sentencing. Carole said some years ago she'd sent a letter to a judge on behalf of a Spanish woman who had accepted a plea deal involving years in prison, not understanding English. When Sheriff Bentley found out Carole had written the letter, he called her out to see the judge, and told her she'd lose her job if she ever did that again.

Carole is the only one of the COs who appears to have her heart in making the girls comfortable. She spends time in the cellblock, talking to each of us. When there are arguments among the girls, she handles them in a motherly way. Some of the younger female COs seem more concerned about showing off their uniforms and their figures than catering to the needs of the prisoners.

Last night I was coughing a lot, and Carole kept offering me cough syrup. Each time I told her I'd rather wait until bedtime. About 10:00 I got an uncontrollable coughing fit. I looked up to see Carole standing at the door, cough syrup in hand. "Enough is enough," she said. Carole doesn't waste words, and everyone knows when she's serious. I took the medicine.

I didn't write my diary yesterday, as there was letter writing to catch up on. We get letters every mail day. It helps so much to be reminded that we are not forgotten. When I get out, I hope never to neglect doing for others what has been done for me.

October 26

By Barbara Lyn

In school, we're doing some chapters in science–bacteria, viruses, cells, etc. It is interesting, but I find the instructions, both by the teacher and the books, an insult to practical education. Some of the questions in the textbooks don't have answer choices that one can be certain is the right one. Rather, we are told to guess. They call it "analysis" or "inferential comprehension."

It seems to me this type of schooling encourages nonconclusive solutions, creating an "anything goes" attitude. The teacher tells Rachel and me we take too much time trying to be certain on answers. But I can't help it. When I went to school there was one right answer, and if not properly chosen, the teacher's red mark would mar the page.

In our cell this afternoon Flora showed me pictures of her family. Three of her daughters are in foster care, and one of the COs who works here is the foster father. He and his wife want to adopt them, Flora said. Police arrested Flora when she refused to help them with an undercover drug project. She said she believes her arrest had to do with a plan to terminate her rights to her children.

I have come to see the drug laws and their administration as cruel and unjust—a monstrous government money-making business with no benefit to society–probably a whole lot of detriment. A few nights ago a woman and her husband were both brought to jail. The woman is a decent person who holds a job. She told us they used a small amount of marijuana for relaxation and pain relief. Their fourteen-year-old daughter, who reported the drug use at school during a drug prevention class, is now at home without parents.

By Rachel

We got some beautiful photographs of a rainbow today, sent by the family. In one picture, the rainbow shone its gentle colors over our home. More than ever, I believe in the promise of the rainbow. I know God is good because He has helped us endure something that didn't seem possible—in jail ten weeks now, and contented—a contentment that is often mixed with grief and physical discomfort. He has also sustained our family against odds we could not have imagined; through illness of a severity we had not heretofore known; through burdens of work and burdens of mind greater than they ever before experienced.

They survived. The worst of their farm workload is over, the fall harvest nearly done. Soon cold and snow will enable them to have more time to rest. Their bodies are healing from the pneumonia that hit a few of them. Tonight, speaking to them on the phone, their strength is apparent.

October 27

By Rachel

I spoke to the jail doctor today, and told him I'd like to get permission to use Revita, the nutritional supplement. He said I must be healthy because he isn't often asked to see me. "It's not a life and death matter, is it?" he asked.

I said it isn't, but explained the health problems I'd had prior to my success with the Revita. I showed him the package, but he wasn't interested enough to look at the ingredients. I explained that the main ingredient is water because it's in liquid form. A couple of minutes later, still looking at the box, he asked, "What is it, pills, or a powder?" He's extremely forgetful, because of his age, I guess. He must be in his eighties.

October 28

By Barbara Lyn

Last night I worked on an article about my trial, and wrote until almost two AM.

After breakfast and cleaning this morning, I went back to bed and fell into a deep sleep. It was about 8:00 when I heard CO Brenda calling, "Barbara, Rachel!" Before I was fully awake, she was saying, "From now on everyone is going to have only one blanket." We gave her the one extra blanket we had, which we usually kept folded as a cushion for the metal seat at our table. Brenda went around gathering more blankets from all the other girls.

A new lady came in last night, making a record twelve for our cellblock—three in each cell. Then three more came in today. Looking around almost makes me laugh. People of all shapes, colors and sizes are scattered over the floor in the common area. There are too many to fit into the cells. With no fans or ventilation in here, body odors are marked.

By Rachel

There's a small hole in the corner of the security screen in our cell window. We noticed it when we moved to this cell, a few days after coming to jail. Occasionally the other girls come into our cell, receive contraband from someone outside on the sidewalk, and quickly leave again. Once I observed a girl receiving a small black package through the hole. Sometimes we see them huddled together in someone else's cell, sharing a cigarette.

Barbara and I feel bothered about the smuggling, but decided not to report it. "Snitching," as the girls call it, is not tolerated in the cellblock. Lately we told the girls we wished they wouldn't do that. Dee was unhappy about our disapproval, and did it anyway.

Yesterday CO Sue came in, checking all the windows in our cells. She told us they were going to board up the bottom portion of the windows outside, and put plastic over everything for the winter. Coming into our cell, Sue inspected the hole in the window. "How long has it been like that?" she asked, looking at me sternly.

"Ever since we've been here," I said. "We don't appreciate it. You mean you didn't know it's there?" She said she didn't.

"We were going to report it when we leave," I said, speaking quietly because I felt some of the girls were listening. "Saying something now could get us in trouble."

"Do you see people come in here?" asked Sue. I looked at her, but didn't answer. "Okay," she said.

After Sue left we talked to the girls. They said a girl who was here before us had made the hole in the screen. "All the COs know about it," one of them said. "Sue don't needa act like she thinks it was y'all!"

Then last night at 11:30, as we were preparing to bed down and everyone else seemed asleep, CO Louise came in. "How big is that hole in your window?" she asked. I went over and examined it.

"About one and a half inches."

Louise unlocked the door and came in, checking the hole. "Oh, it's bent outward now," she said.

"It was that way," I said.

Barbara and I discussed it after Louise went out. We began to realize what a pretense it was, and the message of distrust Louise was giving. She knew about the hole before. And it was necessary to question us at midnight?

If the COs mistrusted us yesterday, tonight is different. It's lockup time again, but they left our door open. Three new girls who came in had to set up cots in the common area, because of overcrowding. When Doreen locked the other cells for the night, she asked Barbara and me if she could leave ours open, so the girls in the common area can use our toilet. Of course we were amenable to the plan, in fact we were honored. I said to Barbara I'm surprised they chose our cell. They're probably concerned about trouble in here, with fifteen inmates in an area made for eight. When it's convenient for them, they show they trust us.

October 29

By Barbara Lyn

This afternoon a lady got a surprise announcement that she's going home. She had three weeks left on her sixty-day sentence for switching vehicle licence plates. We're glad for her that she can leave, but the whole thing is so crooked it stinks—the jail gets full, the public defender starts making phone calls to judges, and people get out, even if they were sentenced. A few other girls here are expecting early release because of crowding.

We finally got arrangements made for a chiropractor, Dr. Freling, to see us here in jail. He brought his portable table and other equipment, and set it up in the jail classroom. Before he gave us our adjustments, Dr. Freling asked questions about our arrests and injuries on August 16. He said he knows many of the officers who work here, through his practice. After some discussion about our case, he said, "I see you're not the ordinary criminals."

Back from our visit with the doctor, we stood in the office, waiting for CO Carole to open the door to the cellblock. Sgt. Stage, a friendly officer, greeted us. "Are you behaving yourselves lately?" he kidded.

"I would say we are," I said with a smile. Lt. Belson, the jail supervisor, was there too.

Just as we turned to go into the cellblock, he said, "Rachel, would you do some stamping for me?" Rachel looked at him, a questioning expression on her face. "I have a couple thousand pamphlets that need to be stamped," he said.

Rachel looked at me.

"What does it say in them?" I asked.

Belson didn't answer right away.

"Free the Lapps," Carole said.

"It's about Family Court," Sgt. Stage teased.

"Support Child Protective Services," Lt. Belson said, a smirk on his face.

I made a face, almost laughing.

Sgt. Stage changed to a serious note. "It's about safe driving." Belson confirmed that's what it was about, and we said we would do it.

Rachel then asked Lt. Belson why he doesn't let her have the Revita the family sent for her. He said he would consider it, but he doesn't usually allow non-prescription products to be brought in.

CO Brenda came in this evening and asked Rachel and me to give up our jail towels for a few days, since we have personal ones that were sent by the family. She said the jail is fuller than it ever was before, and they're short on towels. We get laundry service just twice a week, and now have only two towels each that must do for hands, hair and twice-a-day showers.

Tonight they didn't put any cots in the common area. We're locked in now, with four in each cell. There are mats all over our floor, leaving hardly any space to walk.

We hear the sheriff is having an addition built to the jail to alleviate overcrowding. Unless things change drastically, the new part will soon be full, too. Carole says that when she started working here seventeen years ago, there were only fifty people in the jail. Now it's almost two hundred.

October 30

By Rachel

At 10:00 this morning we were anxiously waiting for our mail. CO Sue had closed the curtain across the door between the cellblock and the office, and we knew she was working on it. They have to log the mail, open it to check for contraband, and take the stamps off.

One of the girls, Irma, peeped through a crack in the curtain, and reported that Sue was out there, glasses on, reading mail. One by one the other inmates watched through the crack and confirmed it. "Barbara, Rachel, come see," Irma said, restraining her normally boisterous tone. A vibrant Puerto Rican girl, she often leads the other girls in prankish, sometimes off-color behavior.

Standing near the wire mesh, we joined the other girls in peeping. Sue sat still at a desk covered with mail, reading. Minutes went by. Finally she turned, put a letter back in an envelope, took another letter out, and began to read again.

"That's illegal!" Irma declared. "Reading our mail—that bitch!"

"That's why she always be late with the mail!" another girl said. "We needa report it—all of us!"

"It's the Lapps' mail she's reading!" someone whispered, still peering through the crack in the curtain.

I stayed to watch for a while. Finally I went back to making our beds, shaking my head and smiling to myself in disbelief. "Even Rachel is smiling," Irma said excitedly.

"Sue!" Irma called in an urgent voice.

"Just a minute," Sue answered.

The girls giggled. Sue came in. "Is the doctor here?" Irma asked.

"Yes."

"Do we have mail?" Irma asked.

"Yes."

"You're not reading our mail, are you?"

"You know I'm not allowed to read your mail," Sue said.

"Are you reading it?"

"No." Sue went out and closed the curtain tightly. A minute later she returned with our mail.

Barbara and I were called out for a visit. Entering our quarters after the visit, we were hit with the stench from the cellblock. This place is awfully dirty, with no ventilation. It's stinky—four toilets, one leaking, thirteen people. If it were up to Barbara and me, we would open the windows more. But it's cold, and the other girls complain when we do that.

Irma told us Sue had come in when we were gone and said Irma would be punished for embarrassing her. Tomorrow she wouldn't get her mail until 3:00, Sue had said. Irma was upset. She said she's going to report it to Lt. Belson. The other girls supported her, vehemently maintaining that it's a crime to read inmates' mail, and the COs are only allowed to remove the letters from their envelopes to check for contraband.

At three when CO Carole came in, the girls greeted her happily. Soon they began to question her about rules for checking mail. Carole said she never reads mail, simply because other people's things are none of her business. "But are you allowed to?" Irma persisted. Carole said the COs do what they want.

The girls began to speak up loudly. "We're not putting up with it!" one said. "We're gonna report it to the lieutenant."

"Even Rachel and Barbara saw it!" said another.

Irma told Carole of Sue's threat to punish her.

"That's wrong! She can't do that!" said Paula, a dynamic, well-spoken black woman. She insisted we must all stick together and make a complaint.

Carole went out. The uproar continued. Barbara told Paula, above the din, that she'll check corrections law to see if reading mail is allowed. She would ask Swanee to get the book for us.

I spoke to the rest, who were still fuming. "Before we report it, we need to find out what's allowed," I said. "Let's cool it a little, 'till Barbara finds out."

Everyone quieted. Some nodded. "Yes, let's do that."

October 31

By Rachel

This morning we got visits from the family, with lots of children. CO Austin, who was supervising the visit asked me if we celebrate Halloween.

"We don't," I said. "It's a little—silly, I guess."

"Would you object to me giving the children a pack of lifesavers?"

"Oh no, that would be fine!"

Shortly before it was time to go, CO Austin came over and asked the visitors, "Anyone object to me giving the children lifesavers, in honor of Halloween?" Nancy smiled and said it's okay. He handed each of the wide-eyed children a packet. They all said "thank you," hardly suppressing their delight.

At two this afternoon the girls were getting restless. Scattered out on the floor by the TV, they conversed noisily. Barbara left our cell to speak to them. "Hush!" she said, bending down to their level. "Let me tell you a plan—it's something different." The girls fell silent. "At 3:00 let's all go inside our cells, hang sheets across the front so others can't look, and see who can make the best costume. We'll have 'till four to work on it."

Their faces lit up. "Yeah! Cool!"

"I know what I'll be!" The girls began to whisper and giggle. "Can we start now?"

At three we shut our cell gates and stretched bed sheets across the front by tying the corners around the bars. Barbara and I worked on our costumes as fast as we could, but the others were done before us. They stood outside the gate, nagging. "Y'all done? It's five 'till four!" We knew dinner would come at four, and worked frantically on final details. The last step was tying on Barbara's mask, using strands of colored string from worn-out hair bands. Then we pushed open our sheet-covered gate.

"Here they come!" The girls began to shriek and shout with laughter. We looked around to see Irma dressed as a gypsy, Paula as a ghost, and another girl as a mummy. The latter was a sight, her arms, legs, and entire body and head wrapped in toilet paper.

Barbara and I wore masks made of Styrofoam lunch plates we'd saved up for weeks, and hair we saved when we got our hair cut three weeks ago. My mask had eyes accented with terry hair bands, a banana tip for the nose, red toothpaste with hair stuck on for a mustache, and eyebrows of hair stuck on with "squeeze cheese" as glue. Barbara wore a plate hat with a hole in the top, her long hair standing straight up through the hole, stabilized by a new pencil and rubber bands.

The girls went wild. "Barbara, Rachel, we're gonna surprise Carole!" they said. "Let's stand by the gate!" The five of us stood by the fence, silent.

Carole, bringing a girl back from a visit, stepped through the curtain. She looked at us, retracted a step, and blinked her eyes. "Oh-h-h!" she said. Then she threw back her head in laughter.

Carole went back out. "She's bringing a CO in!" the girls said excitedly.

I panicked and ran into our cell. I wasn't particularly well covered, with plates strung around me for a blouse of sorts, and more plates hanging around my waist as a skirt.

"C'mon Rachel," the girls begged. "He can't see anything!" When Carole came in with the CO, I stepped out for a moment, then fled to seclusion again. Barbara and I were glad it was over. We trashed our outfits and had supper.

After supper Irma came to our cell and said Carole wants us to dress again, for Sgt. Paul Stage to see. I frowned in disapproval. "Just one more time, Rachel," Irma pleaded.

"Again? We already threw our things away," I told her.

"Ple-e-ease?" several girls begged. "Paul is coming. We'll do it for him!"

"But I can't, I don't have much on!" I protested. They said I could wear clothes under my costume. Finally I said, "Okay, we'll do it just for you." We retrieved our costumes from the garbage bag, dressed, and waited for Sgt. Stage. He didn't come. Carole came in, exchanged a few words with one of the girls, and went out again.

"She's getting Dale!" the girls said.

"Oh, Barbara!" I said quietly. "That's CO Austin! I just told him at the visit we don't celebrate Halloween."

We couldn't escape. CO Austin stepped inside, smiled, and said, "Happy Halloween!"

After shedding our costumes again, we sailed the plates around the room like Frisbees. The girls and Carole said never before had anything like this happened in the Mayville jail.

Barbara claims I instigated the insanity a few weeks ago when I suggested we save our paper plates. But I'm sure she mentioned it first, when we got haircuts, and she saved our hair.

November 1

By Barbara Lyn

It was an awfully noisy day. CO Jim Crowell was in and out of our cell for several hours this morning, trying to remove the damaged screen from our window. CO Sue spent time in here helping him, and started arguing with the girls. "From now on, *nobody* will be allowed to enter anyone else's cell," Sue said. "If I see anyone doing it, I'll press charges."

"We *always* go into each other's cells—every day!" Irma protested.

"This *will* be enforced," Sue said, amid shouts from the inmates of "bullshit" and worse.

"This is *my* room!" another girl said. "You telling me I can't ask somebody in?"

"There have been people (inmates) here who requested we don't allow it," Sue said. The other girls eyed Rachel and me suspiciously.

"This is *our* house!" Irma shouted at Sue.

"This is *not* your house!"

"If it's not our house, why are we cleaning every day? Okay, I'm not cleaning no more!"

Others joined Irma. "Let's all stick together and not clean. They can't double lock us all."

The girls' mood didn't get any better as the day wore on. The phone was down again. "That f - - - - n' phone," one of them said. "We haven't had any calls! I'm getting out of here!" Dee, the girl with AIDS, came out of her bed, cursing and calling the other girls bitches.

Next Sue called one of the girls for court. "County Court—right now! They're waiting." The girl scrambled to dress.

"That stupid judge across the street—he don't know nothing!" another girl said.

"We don't have a thing to do with what the judge says," Sue answered, evoking more insults.

CO Crowell was in our cell. I stayed at the common table, trying to read the newspaper. At the height of the noise, Crowell walked past. We looked at each other and he rolled his eyes.

After lunch Crowell finally got the tool he needed to complete his job on our window. The screen is now gone, as well as the knob for opening the louvers.

Tension let up after shift change at three, when CO Doreen arrived. She prudently stays uninvolved with the girls' disputes.

This evening it got loud again. This time the girls were joking and laughing uproariously—for nearly two hours. It started after supper when Tamara sat on Paula's cake by mistake. Tamara, a black woman in her early forties, keeps the others' attention with her outgoing manner and lewd language.

CO Doreen, sitting outside our fence at the small desk, was talking with Tamara, and joked that she had seen her before, when Tamara was "on a mission" (drug dealing). Tamara began to laugh uncontrollably, and soon got the others going with jokes about drugs, alcohol and more. You'd think they had some in here, the way they were acting. The noise was deafening.

I retreated to my cell, but Rachel stayed at the table, writing. Tamara stood by the table holding a writing pad, still laughing and talking loudly. Rachel bent close to her and said quietly, "Tamara! Do some writing now. Come on."

Tamara started to write, talking the words out loud.

"No, no, Tamara. Not like that," Rachel told her gently. "You don't talk while you're writing." Tamara complied, and began to write. CO Doreen, observing the exchange, leaned back in her chair and burst into laughter.

November 2

By Rachel

I got an irritation in my throat and chest yesterday, after the girls used an aerosol spray disinfectant in our cell. I coughed until midnight. It was cold, too. Since they worked on our window, the louvers aren't closed tightly, and a draft comes in. Finally I got up and put on more clothes—extra socks and a long-sleeved undershirt, besides my sweat shirt. Still shivering, I spoke to the part-time CO when she came in. "Sandy, it's cold in here."

"Do you have two blankets?" she asked.

"No. No one does. They took them last week when they needed them for others."

Sandy said she would turn the heat up. A short time later I fell asleep, and slept until morning. When Sandy brought our breakfast, she asked if I had gotten warm.

"Yes," I said. "Thanks for getting us heat."

"The basement is always cold," Sandy said. "We turn the heat up, then it gets too warm upstairs. They're supposed to have extra blankets down here."

Marita, a shy teenage Guatemalan girl who came in on drug charges last week, went to court today. She was told she could get six months in jail or five years probation. We talked to Marita, and she told us she came to this country with her Guatemalan boyfriend last summer. Together, they saved $2,800, picking strawberries, tomatoes and other crops for local farmers. They planned to return to Guatemala with their savings before Christmas. Marita said neither she nor her boyfriend used drugs, but they boarded in a house where others did. They were arrested, along with other residents of the house during a drug raid, their savings confiscated as drug money. They have no relatives here. It's so sad, I could cry.

By Barbara Lyn

I've been trying for weeks to get a law book I need for researching my obstruction charge. But Swanee is the only one who can get it, and he doesn't cooperate. Yesterday he told me he can't find it, and suggested I ask my lawyer for information. Today I again met him in the gym.

"I still need that book," I said.

"It's buried under somebody's mattress—don't know where."

"I don't have any other way of getting legal materials."

"I don't either," he said, looking straight ahead.

"What am I supposed to do?" I asked.

Swanee finally said he could get the book from the library across the street, if I'd give him the section number of the law.

November 3

By Rachel

After supper tonight I was getting ready to go rest. My head and chest were hurting from the fever that started yesterday. Then CO Sue returned for our empty dishes. Paula was still eating. "Paula, next time the food comes, you come up first in line," Sue chided. "You're always done last."

"Geez, Sue, I did come up first!" Paula said in her usual frank manner. "Don't you remember? You said, 'What's the hurry?' And I told you I was hungry."

The girls burst into howling laughter. Sue wasn't happy about the joke being on her. She continued to scold Paula for making her wait.

"Jesus Christ! Not even my mother tells me how fast to eat," said Paula. "You're going to make me fat!"

One of the girls laughed so hard she started choking on her food. I ran to her rescue and lifted her arm.

"Tomorrow you're turning the TV off over supper, so it doesn't take you so long to eat," Sue told the girls. She went over to Paula, who sat at the common table, still eating. Putting her face close to Paula's, she scolded her for swearing.

"You have to respect me!" Paula said. "I'm just trying to finish my meal."

"I don't have to respect you!" Sue yelled, her face inches from Paula's.

Paula turned away. Sue took Paula's face with both her hands, and forced Paula to look at her. Both of them were yelling.

"Shut up!" Sue said.

"You have no right to touch me!" Paula said. She ran into her cell in tears, leaving her plate behind.

Speaking loudly in English and Spanish, the other girls jeered at Sue and accused her of being a "big mother." Sue went out to the office. Her husband, Sgt. A.J. Melson was on duty. She soon came back, and ordered Paula out to talk to the sergeant.

We could hear Paula telling Sgt. Melson the whole story. She ended by saying, "Sue manhandled me!"

For the first time, I felt obligated to speak up for one of the girls. "I think we should support Paula in this," I told the others.

CO Sue came back in. "Is there anyone here that wants to come and be a witness for Paula?" she asked. "She says I manhandled her."

"I'll go," said Irma, stepping forward.

Sue opened the door. "Come on," she said.

"I'd be willing to go," I said. I looked at Tamara, and she also stepped forward.

Sue suddenly backed out of her invitation, locked the door and went back out. Moments later she brought Paula back in. Paula was crying. "Sgt. Melson said I could do more time for lying," she said.

Sue talked to the girls. "I was just joking with her," she said. "I'm trying to tell Paula she did nothing wrong." Sue continued to talk, trying to get justification from the girls.

"I'm willing to give my opinion, Sue," I said, standing by the door of my cell. "I don't think there's anyone here that will support your pushing Paula like that. I think it was immature of you."

"I didn't ask for your opinion!" Sue said. "You're not in this, Rachel."

"Okay," I said.

Irma reminded Sue that she *had* asked for our opinion only a minute earlier.

"I was just fooling around," Sue said. "I didn't even touch her."

"You did, Sue," I said. "You took her face in your hands."

"Rachel, if you know so much, why don't you get a job as a CO?" Sue left the cellblock. "I'm a CO," she said as she locked the door.

November 5

By Barbara Lyn

I was in and out of sleep all night, too cold to be comfortable. The CO brought an extra blanket for Rachel, because she's sick. Her temperature was 102.4 last night.

If accepted as a fact, the constant discomfort of cold is more easily borne. You lie down, cover yourself as well as possible, then try to shape your makeshift pillow—a folded sweat shirt—so that it supports your head and neck a little. You think about the day, communicate with God, and sometimes venture into anticipation of days to come.

Then, just as you begin to drift into subconscious thoughts, the cold creeps up around you—furtive quivers moving from one part of the body to the other, tormenting you just enough to keep you from drifting off into sleep. Trying not to rebel against the cold, you force away thoughts of how nice it would be to be able to get another blanket. You think of the clothes the family promised to send, but your thoughts are more about the warmth of caring ones who are mailing the clothes than about quieting shivers. God sends messages from above like, "Let not your heart be troubled." Finally you fall asleep.

It's lonely doing things without Rachel today—just Emma and me for school. At rec, CO Crowell asked, "Did I hear Rachel's sick?" All the COs are concerned about Rachel, especially because she refuses to take medicine. CO Brenda brought Louise in to see her last night at shift change. Carole had a sad face this morning when I told her Rachel's lung condition started when we were so crowded in here.

Rachel's fever broke today. But she is coughing incessantly. I massaged her back, and read to her from the Bible.

Today is quiet and normal. We have three in our cell again. And everyone is going into each other's cells again—even when CO Sue was here. She didn't say anything.

CHAPTER 12

Sentence

November 7, 1993

By Barbara Lyn

Yesterday in the mail I received more warm clothes sent from home. As CO Sue inspected the contents of the package, she asked if I was getting ready for winter. Receiving new clothes just before sentencing probably gives that appearance. Only God knows.

Last night I dreamed I'd been sentenced to banishment in the woods up behind our pond. I was happy though, because I could have regular contact with the family. I was figuring out survival techniques, including a pit I was going to dig to fill with sawdust and ice from the pond, for refrigeration next summer.

CO Jim Crowell is putting the security screen back up on our window, so we'll be able to open and close the louvers again. He needed help to hold a screwdriver, and let me help for a few minutes. Handling the tools was exhilarating. I can't describe the craving to do normal, constructive things.

It's midnight now, as I finish writing for the day. Rachel is coughing so much she can't sleep.

I told Carole that ever since our extra blankets were taken we've been cold at night. She said they used to give two or three blankets each during the winter, and brought us extra blankets again.

November 8

By Rachel

Every time I lay down last night I coughed violently. There was a strange gurgling deep down in my lungs, and I hurt all over. Louise offered me cough syrup, but I declined. I sat up against the concrete block wall our bunk bed is bolted to, and hours later drifted off to sleep.

At 1:30 I awoke with a severe itch in my chest, causing me such desperation that I'll never forget. I jumped up heaving and gasping. Finally, when I could draw enough breath, I coughed until I almost vomited. The itch is still there this morning. I'm exhausted.

By Barbara Lyn

Eighty days in jail. In a half hour I'll stand in front of Judge Himelein to hear how much he wishes to punish me. Even if he believed I was a criminal, he could say I've served enough time already. But vengeance could call for a sentence of up to one year.

CO Sue came in and told me the officers are here. It was a half hour earlier than scheduled, and I was still in white cell clothes. I had hoped to get my real clothes for court. Turning back to our cell, I told Rachel, "I'm not going to hurry. First they say ten, then they come at 9:25. That's not the way I keep appointments." I didn't care if Sue heard me.

I went back to talk to Sue. "Am I getting my clothes?"

"You don't get your clothes for sentencing," she said.

I dressed in greens and combed my hair. Sue waited patiently.

I sat by a window in the court waiting room, observing the traffic and activities below. Scott Humble came in. "You look happy today, Barbara," he said.

It hadn't occurred to me that it might not be proper to have a contented look on sentencing day. I had struggled hard to get this demeanor.

Mr. Humble handed me the probation report and sentencing recommendations, and asked if he should stay around while I read it. I told him I could read it myself, and he left. Attached to the report were several "Victim Impact Statements," naming Sgt. Rex Rater and Social Services Commissioner Ronald Hackett as victims to my crime.

In Rater's statement, he said, "Barbara Lapp should learn from this case that future interference [with court orders] will not be tolerated. I have questioned that she has in fact yet learned a lesson."

He wrote he was recently involved in a case where a man and woman were jailed for refusing to bring their children into Social Services custody. "And the children revealed to their law guardian that they had spent much of the summer and subsequent time at the Lapp farm. All occurred at which time there was an order for the kids to be in DSS custody."

What Rater said is a lie. I know the family. They did spend time at our home, but it was the year before they were taken into Social Services custody.

Rater's statement ended with this: "Barbara Lapp should receive additional time in jail because of her persistent disregard for court orders on DSS/Family Court matters."

Ronald Hackett, in his sentencing statement, said I interceded in a child custody matter, apparently advising the father to remove the child from the Bradford Children's Home. "Ms. Lapp was in evidence both at court proceedings and in television and print media, advocating the violation of court orders and lawful proceedings," he wrote. "In final analysis, the real victims of Ms. Lapp's activities are the child who may never recover from the trauma of both being seriously abused and then the object of the media circus orchestrated by Ms. Lapp, and the Child Protective Services and court systems whose lawful proceedings and orders have been both ignored and violated with apparent impunity."

The probation report, which was written by the man who interviewed me several weeks ago, was generally favorable. But he wrote that my "potential problem area" is the fact that I don't see anything wrong with what I did. The recommendation was "jail time."

I was called to the courtroom, and stood in front of the judge. Paul Andrews was on my right. For the first time, there was no defense attorney on my left.

"Good morning," Judge Himelein said.

"Good morning, sir," I answered.

Himelein asked if I'd read the probation report. "You have the right to make any kind of statement before sentence is imposed," he said.

"I don't have much to say," I said, "because the court hasn't honored the truth to this point, so I don't expect the court to honor the truth today." I then read a statement from an early American Quaker man who was heavily fined for harboring slaves: "Judge, thee hasn't left me a dollar. But I wish to say to thee and to all in the courtroom that if anyone knows of a fugitive who wants a shelter and a friend, send him to me and I will befriend him."

I told Judge Himelein I feel as the Quaker man did. "What you, Judge Himelein, decide to do today—whether you wish to give me a slap on the wrist, or whether you wish to keep me in jail for a long time—will make no difference.... There is nothing you can do that will close my heart, and there is nothing you can do that will cause me to close the doors of my home to the needy.

"In this case, the law has been abandoned so that vengeance may be executed. For that reason, I don't think that the courtroom here is a place where I can adequately defend myself, or even put myself in a position of having any say with sentencing."

I paused, looking at the judge squarely. "You have an intelligent mind, and God gave you a conscience," I said, "and it's up to you what you make out of this."

Glancing downward nervously, Himelein began to speak, then stopped. "Well, I don't want to cut you off," he apologized. "Is there anything else you want to say?"

"No."

"I—as I am sure you know," he began, stammering. "I have received a great deal of mail and letters on your behalf, written by people throughout the community.... There is also a petition here," he said, holding up a thick stack of papers. "I didn't count the signatures, but it allegedly has a thousand and some signatures."

He paused, putting down the stack of petitions. "And I will tell you that this is not an easy case to be sitting here on," he said. "I certainly—I think that I am almost—I'm convinced of your sincerity in what you believe in. There was one thing that happened at the trial that made me question that a little bit. It was when you made some allegations as to Billy being drugged at the children's home, and the trial testimony was that the only medication he received was for some skin rash—and I did have some concern about that."

"I never said he was getting drugs at *that* children's home," I said, forgetting I hadn't intended to defend myself. I couldn't stand him publicly insinuating that I was dishonest.

"Then maybe I misunderstood it," Himelein said.

He continued. "I agree with some of what you told the Probation Department in terms of the merits of the charge.... On the other hand, I know something about the history of the case. And I wish that some of the statements that those children made to people over the years could be publicized. Unfortunately, they can't. I do note that it came out during the trial that Mr. Stefan had admitted to an abuse petition in Family Court. According to everything I have seen, the child was doing fairly well at the children's home...."

"We are a nation of laws, not a nation of people. And if we start letting everyone decide what laws or what court orders they are going to obey and not obey, I think that bodes ill for our future."

Then Judge Himelein read the sentence: Six months in the county jail, plus a ninety dollar court surcharge, payable within thirty days of my release.

"Six months," I told my anxious cellmates as I stepped through the gate. Sue brought a calendar and helped us figure my release date. She said they routinely take off one third of the sentence for good behavior, so I could go home by mid-December. That doesn't include the possibility of additional time for the other charges we're facing.

In our cell tonight, Rachel and I discussed the sentence. We had never heard of any sentence close to this on misdemeanor charges, for the dozens of people who have been in and out of this cell block. Some felons serve less than this.

November 9

By Barbara Lyn

Early this morning Brenda came in with the jail cook, Mary, who apologized profusely for several incidents in the last few weeks when the girls had been served poorly. Once they had run out of macaroni and cheese, and we got cold sandwiches instead. Once we were served chicken patties that were partly raw. Mary promised that from now on the ladies' block will be served first, instead of last.

We don't know what prompted the apology. Last week Rachel and I had publicized a three-page complaint on jail conditions. We had listed health concerns such as cold, overcrowding, and confinement with a dying AIDS patient, but had not mentioned food.

This afternoon I sat on a mat in front of the TV with three other women, watching the Phil Donahue show. I suddenly wondered what Mom or my sisters would think if they walked into the room. In a lop-sided sitting position, my one knee was propped up with my hands wrapped around it, the other knee resting on the leg of the woman beside me. My back was used by the woman next to me as a prop for her back.

The show we were watching was about black/white racial tensions. The women leaning on me were both dark-skinned. Now and then we made casual comments about the show.

I was enjoying the comradeship of so-called criminals—people I would never have associated with before—people I love because we share the distress of being behind bars, and share in the need for human companionship while cut off from acquaintances in the real world.

November 11

By Rachel

Last night I coughed for hours, until I was hot. Finally I took cough syrup, but it didn't help. I didn't sleep much.

I'd thought I might skip writing my journal. But that would hurt. To not write would dishonor the day.

Sick for eleven days now, in these dingy quarters. I went to rec for the first time in ten days, but was too weak to exercise. I have trouble with my mood—feelings of disgust for the place, and the complete lack of reason on the part of those who put us here. It's so awfully noisy.

Carole came in at three, after taking a few days off. The girls celebrated her entrance with greetings of, "Ca-ar-ole! Ca-ar-ole!" and even called her "Mommy." She spent a lot of time conversing with them, individually and in small groups.

Tonight a tall rough-speaking girl who came in a few days ago asked me for a massage. I followed her to her cell and instructed her to lie down on her stomach, on her mat. "This is how I do it," I said, beginning a slow, vigorous rub of her neck, shoulders and back. "If you don't like it, just let me know."

"I like your massage."

"How do you know?"

"Tobey told me you give good massages."

We spoil the girls a little. They know we share willingly, so they ask for things. Sometimes they return them, sometimes not. "Do you have candy?" "Can I borrow a carbon paper?" "Can we have two soups? We'll give them back Sunday."

Tonight Barbara gave away some hard candy I had been using for throat lozenges. I didn't want that given away. To make matters worse, she lent out a package of soup after we were already low.

By Barbara Lyn

I conversed with Carole about my sentence. She was disturbed with what she read in one of the newspaper articles, that I may not be paying the court surcharge. "Is that true?" she asked. "You wouldn't let that stand between you and your freedom, would you?"

After speaking to Carole, I went into deep thought. I need to ask myself whether refusing to pay the surcharge could be just for the sake of stubbornness. Even Henry David Thoreau, who may not have been as committed to godliness as we are, spoke of the need to examine his own motives in noncompliance with government rules.

I must pray for wisdom. Can God be honored if I give Judge Himelein ninety dollars, so I can walk on free soil? Or is it free soil after I have given of the money with which God blessed us, to satisfy the vengeance of an evil system?

November 12

By Barbara Lyn

I felt depressed when I woke up this morning. Not so much about our present discomfort, but imagining life on the outside. It will never be the same again. I remembered my last weeks on the outside, after all the publicity, when I couldn't go to town anymore without being noticed. Most of the looks and greetings were from kind folks. But I never knew when I might be arrested.

There may be more jail time ahead, too. An inmate here who used to be a legal secretary said you get an indefinite jail term if you don't pay a court fee.

This afternoon was wild, with fourteen girls contributing to noise, laughter, and unthinkably dirty jokes. We noticed some kind of conspiracy going on, and soon smelled cigarette smoke. Then nasty arguments broke out. I heard mention of "smoking crack," and looked up from my writing. One of the girls came over. "You writin' your journal?" she asked.

"Yes."

A few minutes later she said, "Hey, Barbara, it's okay to write about us smokin' crack, but don't write my name."

"I'm not writing about you," I said. "I don't know what's going on in here this afternoon, and I don't want to know."

She apologized for the noise. "Yeah, Barbara, that's what f - - - - n' crack does to the mind," she said.

Rachel and I are worried about being questioned by the COs. We don't want to inform, and don't feel it's our duty to jeopardize our own peace and safety. We've heard someone in here has a lighter and a razor blade, too.

By Rachel

My chest is improving, but I still couldn't sleep lying down last night. At 3:00 this morning I finally asked CO Brenda for hot water. She brought it, along with an apple/spice tea bag with camomile. I sipped the tea slowly. Then, sitting on my bed, I leaned against the wall again, and fell into a comfortable sleep.

This afternoon we had our second visit with Dr. Freling, the chiropractor. When we got to the classroom, he'd already moved tables and chairs to one side, and set up his own table. He joked that he thought he'd better do it before we get there—they might charge us with riot if they saw all of us doing it.

Dr. Freling noticed my skin was yellow. I told him they wouldn't allow me the Revita supplement that contains minerals, for my thyroid. "The jail supervisor won't recognize it as necessary, because it's not medicine," I explained.

"That's ridiculous!" he said.

The doctor used a vibration tool to massage my entire back. Then he adjusted my spine at various points. Returning to our cell, I put my earplugs in, went to bed, and slept soundly for three hours. It was the first time in ten days that I was able to sleep lying down.

November 13

By Barbara Lyn

CO Louise came in, after a few days off, and discovered our roommate had an extra blanket. "Someone's been giving extra blankets when I'm not here," she said. She took the blanket. "There's a hundred eighty people in the jail. Nobody's gonna have two blankets." She looked around our cell, and pointed to the one on Rachel's bunk. "Does anyone else have two?" she asked.

"Rachel has two because she's sick," I explained, "and there are a few others who have two also."

"By the end of the day everyone will have just one blanket," Louise said as she went out.

At our visit today Dad mentioned there aren't many days left until the trial. He had a little smile on his face.

"Are you admitting you're getting anxious about it?" I asked.

"I'm thinking about it," he said, pretending not to be bothered by the thought. He said an inmate asked him if he's going home next Wednesday, after the trial. "I don't know," Dad had replied, "but I'm going home with honor."

It does wonders for us to see Dad and Joe at the visits, even though we talk very little.

Sgt. A.J. Melson escorted us back to the office after the visit. He is a man I would rather never see again. It was he who ordered his men to change me into greens when we came here. The threats and the force were totally uncalled for. They could have treated my refusal to change just like they did Dad's refusal to take the TB test. Double locking is the usual disciplinary measure for failure to comply with rules. A.J. Melson is a wicked man to take part in such a shameful act. It remains a torment I can hardly push aside.

November 14

By Rachel

I've been reading FIJA (Fully Informed Jury Association) material and other info on jury rights and duties—preparing myself mentally to face trial. It would be good if I didn't look at it too much as a trial. A bogus court is assaying to try us according to their bogus laws. Whether they can come up with a conviction is not a matter that should gravely concern us. It does, though, even if we wish it wouldn't, because it involves our physical comfort. The outcome will dictate whether we stay in jail longer, or go home.

Realizing our tendency to want comfort calls for a straightforward mental review of why we're here and what we want out of life. Not for anything would I have traded my place here to cause Billy suffering. The deals the court offered for us to go home smacked of bribery. There was no temptation. So if we all could just be a little more patient, we could see that even though jail is nasty, it's the best in comparison with all the other options. Jail is good because compromise is worse.

Our growing numbers made headlines in here again. We are eighteen. That's an all-time high number of female inmates in the history of this jail. Only eight of us have bunks.

It's warmer outside, and stuffy in here. We opened our window and got whatever sparse air would come through the board nailed on the outside. The two girls sharing our cell agreed the fresh air was good, though chilly. But a tall, aggressive girl from another cell came in and closed our window. When I protested, she said she's cold.

After lunch I cleaned out our commissary box—a cardboard box we store under the bed—because of problems with ants in our food. I discovered a candy bar was missing. Sorting the contents of the box, I had temporarily left some things on the common table. A cellmate told me quietly that she'd seen Emma, a very heavy, quiet woman, take a pack of peanuts from the table. Others had previously accused her of stealing, and they openly degrade her for being fat and lacking hygiene. But I hadn't imagined Emma would do that to us. Just this morning when our once-weekly commissary order arrived, we'd given Emma a bag of pretzels and two soups. She has no money to buy things. A few other girls shared things with her too.

I should talk to Emma about the peanuts, but don't want to do it in front of the others who already despise her.

November 15

By Barbara Lyn

This morning a sergeant came in and sealed the leaking toilet in the cell next to ours. He also checked the one in our cell that just started to leak.

A little later, our toilet went berserk, flushing by itself nonstop for an hour. The toilets here flush very loudly. Added to that was the noise of fifteen inmates and the TV. Some of the girls said they're "losing it."

Then Louise called me to the fence and showed me a computerized sheet. "It's an order for fingerprinting, on the charge you were convicted on," she said. "We'll probably be calling you out for the fingerprinting sometime today."

I didn't answer.

A short time later Louise came back. "Barbara!" She had to shout to be heard above the noise of the flushing toilet. "You can get dressed now. The sergeant wants to get that fingerprinting done right now, before it gets so busy out there."

I tried to think I hadn't heard what she said. Without answering, I went back in the cell and woke Rachel, who was taking a nap. "They're asking me to go out for fingerprinting," I told her quietly. "I don't feel like going."

"I wouldn't go voluntarily," Rachel said.

Still in my sweat suit, I went back to the fence where Louise was waiting. "Louise, did you tell me to get my greens on for fingerprinting?"

"Yes, I did," she said, scowling as she looked at me from head to toe.

"I have a problem with that," I said. "I don't want to go out there for fingerprinting."

"What do you expect them to do, bring it (the equipment) in here?"

"They don't need to fingerprint me."

"Pardon *me?*"

"They don't need my fingerprints."

"Are you kidding? There's an order here for fingerprinting—the FBI needs it for their files!"

"That's their problem, not mine."

"Are you telling me you're refusing to be fingerprinted?"

"Yes."
Louise left.

By Rachel

About an hour after Barbara declined to be fingerprinted, Louise returned. "To those of you who have been here awhile," she began, as if making an announcement.

Barbara and I were the only ones who have been here long. We went to the door of our cell to listen. She said we are to sort the belongings in our cells, and send them out to personal storage, or home. Everything remaining must be put in boxes.

With all the books, mail and legal work we've collected, we weren't sure how we'd comply.

"I can bring you two or three boxes if you need them," Louise said.

After rec I asked Louise, "You want us to start sorting right now?"

"Yes. I want you to clean the top bunk so it can be used for sleeping." She gave us one cardboard box. It was an impossible task.

We use the top bunk as a shelf for personal belongings. Barbara prefers her mat on the floor. The sheet metal bunks sag slightly, and give off a pop like a gunshot when you move on them. Our cellmates don't want the top bunk for a bed either. We share the shelf space with them.

We looked at the top bunk. At least twenty books, stacks of legal papers, mail, neatly folded clothing, and towels were on it. Our books included four very large GED books and two big lawbooks.

"No one wants to sleep on the top bunk anyway," Barbara said to Louise.

"There's too much stuff up there—it needs to be cleared," Louise said.

"Well, I guess we'll need a couple more boxes then," I said.

"What's in *those* boxes?" Louise asked, pointing to the ones under the bed. We pulled out the three small boxes—one for commissary, one for dirty laundry, and one for stationery.

"We won't be able to get everything in these boxes," I said.

"You'll have to make do," she said.

I felt angry. After three months we had collected a few belongings, and we knew just where to find things we needed. But we set to work, sorting and categorizing. Hours later we gave Louise a few small boxes, mostly mail, to send home. She came in to inspect our cell. "What about those things?" she asked, pointing to the clothes, books and mail that remained on the top bunk as before.

"We figured we could put those down on top of the other boxes, if anyone wants to use the bunk," Barbara said cheerfully.

Louise thanked us and left.

"It isn't even true what you told her!" I scolded Barbara. "You know we'd need more boxes to do the job like she told us."

"I figured we could deal with that when the time comes," Barbara said.

Barbara had succeeded in allaying the tension with Louise. But I thought she took the easy way out, and it upset me.

"What was the point—her telling us to clear our shelf?" I asked Barbara. "We *didn't* even! The big stuff is still there."

"Well, I've noticed the other girls' cells look different," Barbara said. "They're neater, with things in boxes."

"Of course!" I exploded. "They don't have an intellectual existence here! They live off TV and dirty talk. We have stacks of books and important papers!"

Barbara had a little smile. "That's exactly what Louise doesn't like," she said. "They don't want us in here keeping our minds bright, doing our own legal work."

Out in the common area, I heard the girls saying, "Hi Carole!" My breath involuntarily eased out. The "Louise day" was over.

I read more on jury trials tonight. Our trial begins tomorrow night. I feel a burden in deciding what to say, and what not to say at the trial. Sometimes I don't know if anything will be right if I plan it ahead. Yet I won't be able to do without some notes. Barbara acts like she's just going to sit back and listen to me talk. She had her turn, she says.

CHAPTER 13

Five Trials in One

November 16, 1993

By Barbara Lyn

I'm a little nervous about court coming up tonight—singing hymns to myself, trying to make myself believe I'm not worried.

I feel almost comfortable with my plan of not participating in the trial. Dad's "sermon of silence" theory is on my mind. Yet I carry some guilt, knowing it will be a letdown to others involved if I make no defense. The Lord will lead. So far the notebook I will carry with me tonight is blank.

In the court waiting room, Rachel and I sat side by side. Dad and Joe came in. Later the officers allowed Lynn Carroll to come in too, though she is not a prisoner. We five defendants conversed—some Deutch, some Spanish and English. The mood was relaxed.

Dad was wearing jail greens. He had refused his clothes sent from home, in protest of coming to court. "Where do you get your nice clothes?" he asked me, teasing. I was wearing a dark gray wool skirt and black blazer. Rachel wore a blue plaid skirt and light blue blouse.

After a while officers directed us into the courtroom, to a large wooden table. We all took our places. Lynn's attorney sat beside her. Five other attorneys, appointed as standby, sat on chairs behind us, near the gallery. The attorney who had vociferously defended Dad during a previous appearance was now replaced by an elderly gentleman who looked sleepy.

Judge Mifsud spoke. "Jacob Lapp and Joseph Torres, it is my understanding that you do not want to be in this courtroom. But you must be in this courtroom in order to be tried. You have to be here. If you decide not to be here, if you're disruptive at any time… we will remove you…."

"Jacob, are you going to sit there quietly?" Mifsud asked. "Do I have your word on that—or will you not answer me?"

Dad sat at the table looking down, silent.

"You refused a standby attorney, so I am asking you—will you please answer me?"

Still no response from Dad, Mifsud said, "I'll assume that you will be sitting quietly then." He asked the same questions of Joe, who also did not respond.

Judge Mifsud then addressed the group of potential jurors who sat in the gallery. He explained our charges, and instructed them on duties of the jury. He said the trial would last one to three days, and asked if anyone had family or business matters that would hinder full attention. The court clerk then called seven names—for a six-member jury, and one alternate.

After they were seated in the jury box, the judge and the assistant DA, Ronald Gibb, questioned them about personal knowledge of our case. All of the jurors said they had heard of us in the news.

"Do any of you know the district attorney prosecuting this case?" Mifsud asked.

One juror raised his hand. "Personal acquaintance," he said.

"Do you think this would in any way inhibit your sitting on this jury?"

"No, I don't think so."

Upon further questioning, two jurors said they had sons-in-law in the police force, two said they knew Lt. Lawrence and Sgt. Rater, and two said they had already formed opinions on our case through reading the newspaper. One said he didn't like some of our statements.

Gibb questioned further. "What you read so far… does it tend to make you think they're either guilty or not guilty?"

"Yeah," said one juror.

"Is your opinion stronger than a guess?"

"Well, it's quite strong—I'll be frank."

Another juror, when asked if he had any sympathy for the defendants, said he once had a foster child. "I've seen the system get out of hand real quick," he added.

After Gibb's questioning, Judge Mifsud said, "Barbara, you may go first, if you like."

"No questions," I said.

"Jacob?"

(No response.)

"I'll assume by not answering, it's no," the judge said. "Rachel?"

"No."

"Joe Torres?

(No response.)

"Lynn Carroll-Bedford?"

"Yes, your Honor, I'd like to," Lynn said. She walked up to the podium, introduced herself to the jurors, and questioned them at length. Her questions were diverse, ranging from family and community interests to knowledge of the Constitution. "Did you know that George Washington was a criminal?" she asked one juror.

"No, I didn't."

"Did you know he was arrested for treason?"

"No, I didn't."

After her questions, Lynn wrote down the names of several jurors she wished to disqualify, including the one who said he is a friend of the prosecutor. She gave the paper to the judge. Judge Mifsud said the law requires a vote be taken among her co-defendants, and a majority need to agree on Lynn's choices. After some discussion among us, Mifsud asked for a vote. Dad and Joe remained silent. Rachel also refused to vote. Mifsud said he could not remove the jurors.

Gibb asked him to remove the juror who had said he's seen the system can get out of hand. Mifsud told the juror to step down, and the court clerk called a gentleman from the gallery to fill his spot.

A jury of six—four men and two women, plus one alternate—was sworn in. Judge Mifsud asked them to return to the courtroom at ten in the morning.

The foreman of the jury, a plump, elderly gentleman wearing heavy glasses, raised his hand. "I have to work tomorrow," he said. "Who am I going to get to work for me tomorrow?"

"I'm sorry, Bob, I'm sorry," Mifsud said. "It's too late. You must appear. The trial's tomorrow, Bob.... I can't excuse you now. I'm sorry."

By Rachel

9:45 PM. Back from court. I went with courage, but hearing the judge and prosecutor instruct and intensely question the jury, then watch them disqualify the juror I liked best was disturbing. And when Lynn wanted to disqualify the juror who said he was a personal friend of the DA, they wouldn't let her. Then, at the closing, the judge said he wants us and the DA there at nine and the jurors at ten. Why can't the jurors hear everything we can?

Now I really should make some court notes. But I'd rather just lie down and sleep.

November 17

By Barbara Lyn

I got up before five this morning, and started writing down thoughts from my pre-dawn waking. As of last night I had only one sentence written on my note pad, and no idea if I'd speak to the jury today. Rachel didn't tell me if she would either, but I saw her making notes now and then. We did not share our notes, nor discuss what we were going to do. It seems we can't, as though the plans for court are a sacred province. Maybe it's because these really aren't plans, just thoughts.

We know Dad would rather not have us talk at all. We discussed that in the court waiting room. I respect his idea of remaining silent.

Rachel and I scribbled feverishly from 6:30 to 8:30 this morning, then rushed to get ready for court.

Court began with Lynn making motions, and demanding a separate trial because of lack of cooperation from her co-defendants. Judge Mifsud denied the motion. "I have no control whether they cooperate or do not cooperate with you," he said.

Behind us, the gallery was now filled with spectators. Our family members sat in the front row, just beyond the rail. Mifsud had banned media cameras from the courtroom.

The jury had not arrived, so Judge Mifsud called a recess. Rachel and I walked to the waiting room with Lynn, no officers following. Lynn told us she thinks she'll do as we are doing, and not participate in the trial any more. Dad and Joe soon joined us, and we talked more.

It was strange to walk and talk without surveillance. Returning to our table in the courtroom, we stopped by the rail to greet supporters. Several friends reached out for handshakes. Miriam came so close I could have hugged her. I held her hand.

The courtroom was congested with officers and lawyers. But no one stopped our quiet communion with family and friends.

Judge Mifsud came back. "Let's have order in the courtroom," he said.

We took our seats at the table.

"For the people out there, the spectators," he said. "I must caution you that when the defendants come in and out of the courtroom, that you do not wave or make any noise; you sit there quietly, and there's no communication between you and the defendants. I know you're excited to see each other, but if that continues, then I'll have to remove you...."

The jury was brought in, and Gibb began his opening statement. He detailed the charges against the five of us. "[E]ach of them started fighting, pushing, shoving," he said, "doing whatever they could, hanging onto Barbara Lapp, intertwining legs and arms, laying on the ground... to stop her from being taken....

"Now, you might imagine, what would a reasonable person do if some sheriff's deputies came out with a warrant to arrest somebody...? Would you jump on them and fight with the sheriff's deputies, lock arms and lay on the ground and scream at the top of your lungs? I don't think so."

After Gibb spoke, it was my turn to address the jury. I explained why we are not participating in the trial. "Considering that the desired result of this proceeding should be that of justice and of upholding law, I have to say that it cannot logically be accomplished here. We have a case here of a prosecution taking place on the complaint of several police officers, without the consent of the people...."

I told the jury of the plea bargain we had been offered several months ago. "We only had to admit to wrongdoing on one of the three charges," I said. "In other words, the prosecutor said, 'You weren't rioting, you weren't resisting arrest. If you just agree that you were obstructing governmental administration, you can all go home....'

"We turned down the judge and the prosecutor's offer.... We would love to go home. We have families. I have a child. All of us have deep community involvement. We chose to uphold the truth above personal comfort and freedom...."

I explained the definition of jury, as intended in the Constitution— a group of twelve people who judge the facts, as well as laws applying to a case. "The judge and the prosecutor have both told you that you will be judging only the facts, and the law is up to them," I said. "That's not the real definition of jury.... [If jurors] have no say in the law, then I could essentially be judged by a judge or a computer system. That's what your minds are for; that's what your judgment is for; that's what your conscience is for....

"I'm sorry if my nonparticipation should make it hard for you or anybody else in the courtroom, but my regard for sacred truth and my respect for law and honor is too high to get into this argument today."

By Rachel

I enjoyed listening to Barbara talk to the jury. It relaxed me. I kind of wished it wouldn't end. I hoped the judge would call Dad and Joe next, but I knew if he did, Dad and Joe wouldn't respond, and that would give me only seconds more.

Then he didn't call Dad and Joe—he called me. And it was time for me to make up my mind what I wanted the jury to hear. My notes, hastily scribbled on my pad just before court were going to be cumbersome. I decided to start without them.

By Barbara Lyn

Rachel walked up to the podium. She told the jury she was not comfortable with presenting a defense in this court, after having been in jail for three months, and seeing the court's continuous violations of due process rights. "I feel that it's like skipping over A, B, and C, and suddenly coming up with D and trying to proceed.... It's very obvious to me that justice can't start right here....

"I believe in law and I believe in an orderly society where people live together and respect each other. And I'm willing to be judged by my community; I'm willing to be held accountable for my own actions; I'm willing to have people judge me and tell me if whatever I've done is correct. But I'm not willing to be called a criminal and to be punished for something before I've been heard....

"They can't just have an officer tell me that I have disobeyed the law, like they told me when they... were taking me to jail. One of them said, 'You broke the law; you went too far.' But I feel that *he* broke the law, and that *he* went too far. Okay, so if there's a controversy here, what is the proper way? What is American law? What is justice?

"Justice means that people of our own community have to be consulted to settle the dispute to decide whether the law may have been broken, establish probable cause and to see whether it's a case that can be brought to full trial."

Rachel also described the plea bargain. "It was like the DA was saying, 'Well, I'll do you the favor of dropping the two charges, you do me the favor of pleading to one....'

"I consider that a bribe. I consider that to be dishonest. I don't play like that. And second, when I checked over what he wanted me to plead to, there were untruths on the paper. They were things I didn't do....

"Everybody told me, my friends told me, 'You've got to get this thing behind yourself—plead out, say you did something so you can go on with your life.' And I thought, what kind of a life is that going to be for me? How am I going to go out and face the world... and look back and say I said something that I didn't do?

"I've been offered numerous ways of getting out. The last time they said they would let me out on my own recognizance if I—again, here's the deal—'You agree to drop your challenge to the court, we'll let you go, we'll let you have some freedom until trial.'

"I don't feel at all comfortable about being here and trying to offer a defense of any kind.... [But] I had the feeling I should come up and speak a few words to you because I don't believe you especially enjoy being here either, and I don't think that you're here by your choice, or that you have any guilt or responsibility for the fact that I'm here....

"You're going to be hearing some laws and it's going to be necessary for you to decide.... not only whether the facts were committed, but whether the law was appropriate.... There's instances where all of us, I believe, will find that we think a certain law is basically a good law, but there's instances where we'll be ignoring it for the sake of another person, or the situation. You could imagine yourself walking down the road, say, past a property where there was a 'no trespassing' sign, and you saw a child walking through the field. Suddenly you saw a dog attack that child. What are you going to do? Are you going to stand there by the sign and say, 'I can't enter the property?'

"I'm just reminding you that it's totally, *totally* inappropriate for them to tell you that you have no say in the laws, because law is what governs our behavior every day. We have to take an interest in these, and you have to keep in mind that laws are sometimes passed by a legislature, unfortunately... for the benefit of their own political buddies rather than for the benefit of the people....

"I think Lynn Carroll asked you last night, if slavery was the law right now in 1993, would you be for or against it. Well, that really was the case back in the mid-eighteen hundreds where slavery was justified by law. And the fugitive slave act prohibited people from helping slaves to escape. There were people who had enough of conscience, enough of strength, and enough of belief in human rights that they violated that [law] and helped slaves to escape....

"Juries were brought in on these cases, and juries began to acquit these people even though they had disobeyed the law. Because it was an unjust law. And there are going to be cases like this as we go through our lives, where there are unjust laws."

Rachel mentioned how Joe, who works on our family farm, brings his children to work with him. "My nephew is strong for his age and loves activity," she said. "He is ten years old, and he came with his dad and helped—picking squash or sorting tomatoes—whatever he could get his hands on…. He deserved to be given some compensation for what he had accomplished. The law forbids me, as an employer, to give him anything for his work. Should I perhaps go to the legislature, make an appeal, go to the court, have that law changed? How many years would he have to wait in his house… for the law to be changed to say that he can come to the farm and help his father?"

The jurors faces looked thoughtful. Several of them nodded slightly. In the gallery, directly behind Rachel, a dozen or so high school students had come in to watch the trial as part of a social studies project. They were listening in rapt attention.

"I could have sent my nephew home," Rachel went on. "I didn't do that. I praised him for his efforts. I realize that there are too many children today who don't have a place to go to occupy themselves in a worthwhile way…. You see it all over. You see it on TV. You see it in the news—young people who have nothing to do and they're out there stealing things and mugging people. This boy has the potential of becoming a gentleman…. I'm not going to wait for a court to say 'you can come to my place to work.' So he does work."

Rachel paused. Across the room from her, I was sitting at the defendants' table. "Rachel!" I said. "You broke the law."

Rachel looked back at me in surprise. Gibb, several feet behind her at his table, shifted in his chair. The officers in the courtroom—some seated, some standing—were smiling.

"I'm sorry," Rachel said, turning back to the jury. "I just admitted that I broke the law." Some of the jurors looked alarmed, almost sympathetic.

She continued. "But that's just the point I'm making to you, that you most certainly must judge both the law and the facts today."

Rachel told the jurors of her shock in seeing the lack of character among law enforcement officials here. "I mean, when I was being arrested—I've never been arrested in my life before—it was frightening," she said. "…They were bringing me in and they had my wrists bent in to my arms, and I was in such pain I was virtually in shock. I was wedged between these two officers—these two male officers—" Rachel faltered, and took a deep breath. "And one of them used the four letter 'f' word on me… and I said, 'That was a pretty nasty word,' and he said, 'I didn't say anything.'"

The deputies who stood in the courtroom exchanged uncomfortable glances.

Rachel then told the jurors that since coming to jail, she has asked different officers how they feel about us being in here. "The common answer is, 'It's my job,'" she said. "I'd like to converse. I'd like to understand what they mean, what they have against me, because I don't want to be an offense to anybody.... I asked one of them one time, 'Well, what do you think of the situation, about us being here...?' And he said, 'I don't.'

"Thomas Edison said once that there's only about five percent of the people that really think. And he said there were ten percent of them that *think* they think, and the other eighty-five percent—they'd rather die than think."

There was muffled laughter from lawyers and officers in the courtroom.

"And I'm going to include the district attorney and the judge in that too," Rachel continued. "I think they are like that. I don't think they're using their minds quite yet.... I think they should think.... I really do.

"And I guess I would hope that you would think... and that you would use common sense, because we really need it today. Thanks."

By Rachel

I had spoken for almost an hour. Returning to the table, I took a seat between Barbara and Joe. They greeted me with placid smiles.

Gibb stood up and spoke. "I have sat here in silence, extending to both Barbara Lapp and Rachel Lapp the courtesy of letting them continue...," he said, almost whining. "They have grossly misrepresented the law as it applies in this case, and the duty of the jurors. Had they been attorneys, I would have stood up much earlier, but I did extend them the courtesy because they're not attorneys and they may not know the error of their ways."

Gibb continued. "They have also grossly misrepresented the plea bargain offer... and the opportunity to be released on their own recognizance. Nobody asked them to give up any rights, or any arguments they would have had against this court or against the jurisdiction to this court...."

"Excuse me!" I said, calling from across the courtroom.

Gibb slowly turned his head and looked at me over his shoulder. "Can I finish, as you finished?" he asked, his voice tight.

"You better say the truth," I said. "I can hear."

Gibb rephrased his description of the ROR deal, more accurately, then complained further about our statements. "Rachel chose even to testify, instead of giving an opening address."

Judge Mifsud said he had allowed me to finish, only because I was speaking on my own behalf. "For me to deny her to say exactly what she said, again, she would accuse this court of denying her proper rights as she did before." Turning to the jury, he said, "I agree with the district attorney. His objection is sustained."

Lunch recess was called. The four of us prisoners got up, walked to the rail and exchanged a few words with the family. Hannah stood close to the rail. "You sounded beautiful," she told Barbara and me.

"No visiting," said Investigator Ecklund, a tall chubby officer with a boyish look. He began to gently push us on. A half dozen officers lined up by the rail, blocking Hannah.

"Why don't you let me in to take their place for awhile?" Hannah asked the officers, pressing close to the gate. "I'm no better than they are."

"I'll bet you'd like it down there," Ecklund said.

We four inmates walked on with the officers, piled into the elevator, and returned to our cells for lunch.

Court resumed at one. Lynn began her opening statement with a detailed sequence of events on August 16, in the hours before the melee broke out. The judge stopped her, and told her she was testifying. Lynn conferred briefly with her attorney, then addressed the jurors again, telling them that her due process rights were denied last night during jury selection.

Gibb rose from his chair. "Your Honor, could we have a sidebar with counsel?" He walked up to the bench. Lynn and her attorney followed. Leaning their heads together, Gibb and the judge talked quietly. We couldn't hear what they were saying. Neither could the jury.

"What's the secret?" I asked. "Some can hear, some can't."

Gibb turned his head and looked at me with a stony glare.

Dad spoke up for the first time since the trial began. "Is this a public trial?"

The attorneys continued their discussion with the judge.

"Secrets!" I said.

A minute later Lynn spoke to the jury again. "Ladies and gentleman, it becomes very apparent... that I am being totally denied my Constitutional rights as a citizen of the United States," she said. "I'm sorry, I can no longer participate in this trial." She returned to the table and sat down with the rest of us.

Gibb called his first witness, Lt. Andrew Lawrence. He told of their attempt to bring Barbara into the courtroom on August 16, with descriptions of the melee—some of which were exaggerations and un-truths. "As we approached the group, two or three of the people tried to push me before I ever saw Barbara Lyn...," Lawrence said, "and Barbara Lyn must have been either sitting on the ground or kneel-ing, because she popped up in front of me in the middle of this group...."

"[W]hen she got up, she took a step or two back, and I grabbed her right hand with my left hand... and I told her that I had a warrant for her in my pocket and we had to go into the courthouse."

"Did she, or did she not resist your attempts to take her into the courtroom?" Gibb asked.

"When I first had her hand, she was pulling backwards.... I told her, 'Barbara, this is ridiculous; somebody's going to get hurt here. You tell these people to knock it off or stop this.'"

"Was there any response?"

"When I had first taken her hand and said that we had to go in the courtroom, she said loudly—for her, because usually she's very soft spoken—she said, 'I know who you are,' and then when I asked her to have the people back off, she just shook her head no and said something to the effect of, 'They can do what they want.'"

"What happened from that point on?"

"I was trying to hold on to her, and people got in between us and would try to separate us. The pushing became more intense, and be-cause of the terrain, we ended up kind of between the sidewalk and the curb where the bank is fairly sharp. The footing was poor there to begin with, and people began to fall down in this tug of war.... I had fallen once, Barbara had fallen..., her sister Rachel was wrapped around her and intertwined with the officers...."

Lawrence said Lynn then came. "She yelled continually, 'What are you doing, what are you doing?' And all we were trying to do was handcuff Barbara Lyn and get her into the courthouse. I think the purpose was really to excite the other group and to make a lot of noise."

"Now, in all of your years as a police officer, have you ever seen anything quite like this?" Gibb asked.

"I worked eighteen and a half years in uniform... and I got into a lot of situations with big groups of people... but as a rule, I could talk my way through that.... I think the thing that was a little bit unique about August 16 was so many people physically got involved and at-tempted to hinder us from our jobs."

"Again, did you warn these people repeatedly to back off?"

"Absolutely.... From the time that this first began until the time that we left, we repeatedly told them to disperse, 'get out of there,' 'back off,' 'knock it off.' Terms such as that.... I distinctly remember Joe being pushed back and asked to leave or whatever, and every single time that an officer would try to push him back, he would come right back into the middle of this whole thing. He was a constant irritant."

When Gibb completed his questioning, Judge Mifsud, turned to us. "Cross examination there? Barbara?" She did not answer. He looked at me. "Rachel? Joe Torres? Jacob?" We all remained silent. "Lynn Carroll?"

Lynn rose from her chair and faced the judge. "For the record, I am unable to proceed, for I have been denied due process under the Constitution and the New York State law." She sat down again.

Sgt. Rex Rater was called next. He too characterized their attempt to apprehend Barbara. "...There were approximately twenty to twenty-five [people].... The people were visibly excited, some of them angry, and started shouting."

"What did you do at this point, if anything?" Gibb asked.

"The situation kept intensifying. I lost sight of Lt. Lawrence for awhile, trying to keep sight of Barbara. I was grabbed and shoved by people, and I tried to make my way through to her by pushing people, parting people out of the way.... I recognized Joe Torres, who shoved me two or three times...."

"What did he do to you, specifically?"

"Grabbed me by the shirt, pushed, shoved, in order to keep me back from Barbara."

"What happened at that point?"

"At that point I got further into the core of people, closer to Barbara.... and I felt a hand on my throat."

"Felt *what?*"

"A hand on my throat. I looked at the other end of the arm— realizing when all this happened there's a lot of pushing, shoving, confusion, people yelling things.... At the other end of the arm was Jacob Lapp.... I broke loose from his hand on my throat, and at that point I was struck twice in the face with an open hand by Jacob Lapp."

"What did you do then?"

"Continued to try to get Barbara. Jacob Lapp was—there were probably three people in between he and I, and he was at arms length so he couldn't get a good hold, couldn't reach me very well. At this point, somebody in the crowd shoved, and a lot of people were knocked to the ground.... Lt. Lawrence, who was laying on the ground, looked up at me and said, 'Help Sgt. Pett get the handcuffs on Barbara Lapp.' Sgt. Pett, I found him and he was lying underneath Barbara Lapp, attempting to put the handcuff on her."

"I take she was resisting?"

"She was."

"And her sister, Rachel, was still holding onto her?"

"Yes."

"Trying to stop this arrest?"

"Yes…. Things seemed to be escalating at that point, with people falling to the ground, people shouting and people obviously excited…."

"Let's catagorize this as a violent environment. You, yourself, were grabbed by the throat, you say?"

"That's correct."

"And you say you were hit twice?"

"Yes, in the face."

The next witness, Sgt. Tyka, said he and others watched from the steps of the courthouse as Lawrence and Rater went out to arrest Barbara. His account was more accurate. He said he heard Lawrence say to Barbara. "We have a warrant for your arrest, please go with us into the courtroom."

"She didn't comply?" Gibb asked.

"She did not."

"Did she resist in any way?"

"She just stood there."

Another officer, Sgt. Pett, made up a wildly exaggerated story about Dad and Joe. "As soon as Sgt. Rater and Lt. Lawrence got close to the main group," he said, "I saw Sgt. Rater spin around, and I saw Jacob Lapp grab him by the throat and slap him across the face a couple times."

"Can you point out the person that did that, in the courtroom, please."

"He's in the prison greens, he's got a white beard, approximately sixty-five years old."

"Can you continue?"

"At that time when I observed him grab Sgt. Rater, I moved toward them, and I pulled his arm off Sgt. Rater's throat. At that time, I got him into a handcuffing position…."

"Why did you have to do that?"

"He got Sgt. Rater around the throat."

"What happened next, if anything?"

"At that time, I observed Mr. Torres having a bear hug around Lt. Lawrence, with his arms and shoulders.... I grabbed Mr. Torres and swung him back from the crowd. At that time he came at me and he proceeded to punch my lower stomach with his fists, three or four times...."

After Pett's testimony, Gibb called several cameramen who had filmed the melee for television news. Their video tapes, which had been subpoenaed by the district attorney, were entered into evidence.

Then court was adjourned for the day.

By Barbara Lyn

Sitting in court this afternoon while five different police witnesses said unbelievable lies was not easy. Nor was it easy to make my opening statement to the jury this morning. But I felt confident.

The court atmosphere was strangely neutral. Noticeably absent were usual formalities such as "All rise," or "The honorable court is now in session." The bailiff, officers who took us to and from jail, and five standby attorneys sat around the courtroom, as if watching a show.

Tonight I feel sorry for the judge. Six times today he offered to let us examine the witnesses. One by one, we answered not a word. I also feel sorry for the many people who lied today, under oath. They must have been desperate to cover their sin.

November 18

By Barbara Lyn

When we got to the courtroom we noticed several large television monitors stationed in the middle of the room. One was turned toward the jury box, one toward the defendants' table.

The first witness was Sgt. Joseph A. Gerace, a senior identification and photography specialist for the Sheriff's Department. He identified the videos that had been entered into evidence yesterday, then operated the video equipment and began to play the tape for the jury. The attorneys and we five defendants viewed the tape from another screen. Both screens were positioned so that people in the gallery could also see them.

Controls in his hand, Sgt. Gerace stopped the picture repeatedly, identifying for the jury different members of the Sheriff's department and all of the defendants involved in the melee.

After the video, Gibb called Jim Fox, the Evening Observer reporter who had been present at the melee. Mr. Fox, in his upper sixties and hard of hearing, said he had worked full time as a reporter for forty-five years. He was assigned to cover happenings at the county courthouse, court politics, and county government.

Gibb asked Mr. Fox to describe what I did when officers came to arrest me.

Fox began his testimony, grotesquely distorting the account. "She... had fallen to the ground—apparently thrown herself down behind this wall of supporters and friends...."

"We've seen the video that was taken by a couple of the TV professionals," Gibb said. "It shows people falling down; it shows people lying on the ground. Was there anything... unusual about that that you noticed from time to time?"

"They seemed—the people who were doing the falling down and so forth—seemed to be doing it carefully within range of the cameras for the best possible effect. It was—had a very organized look to it."

At our table, we listened in disbelief. Rachel emitted a hiss. Dad and Joe laughed. I leaned forward on my elbows and buried my face in my hands.

Gibb continued. "Did you see the police officers do anything that you would consider to be excessive force during this entire event?"

"No. On the contrary, I thought they were rather restrained."

"Did they ever swear at or curse at or do anything like that to these people?"

Fox shook his head. "Politest riot I ever saw." He said he saw a man fall down at least twice, without anyone pushing him. "He rolled down the tree lawn, which is angled toward the gutter, and was laying there in the gutter pushing his head against the rough curb stone without anyone doing anything to him."

The next four witnesses were individuals who had viewed the melee from the courthouse. One of them was Judith Claire, an employee at the State Supreme Court office, who said she watched from a second story window. She described Ken Bellet, the gentleman with a cane. She said every so often he would "sort of throw himself on the ground, and his legs would come up in the air over his head."

Another police witness was called. Then court recessed for lunch.

On the way down for lunch, a tall middle-aged officer handcuffed Rachel. He had some difficulty attaching them, as he transferred her note pad from one hand to the other. Her folder, pen, and note pad were in disarray. As she struggled to reposition them, the officer helped her.

"Have you ever tried this?" Rachel asked him.

He chuckled. "You mean holding on to something? Yes."

She looked up at him. "No! I mean holding on to something when you're in handcuffs!"

The officer laughed, embarrassed.

Our friends in the cellblock greeted us eagerly, and asked what went on in the courtroom. They jeered when we recalled Jim Fox's account of people falling down intentionally. Most of them had seen short clips of the melee on TV and knew it wasn't true. "Didn't the jurors see the video?" asked Carla, a former legal secretary.

"Yes."

"You're gonna be acquitted! You'll just come down, get your clothes, and go!"

Carla also told us she had been in court, and overheard the district attorney discussing the Lapp case. "Mayville hasn't seen this much publicity since the eighteen hundreds," he said. Carla said the DA commented that in a way it would be good if we were acquitted, to restore some trust in the system.

Right after lunch CO Brenda came in and asked me if I wanted a news interview. I went with her up to the regular visiting room, and sat across the table from the reporter, a young man who writes for *The Olean Times* and also works in radio broadcasting.

Regular visiting was about to begin, and male inmates began to line up along the table beside me. The reporter glanced about nervously. He positioned his microphone and began to ask questions.

The COs were trying to keep the noise down. "I'll close the door to the gym, Barbara," one of them said. Another CO radioed Lt. Belson, the jail supervisor, and asked for better accommodations for the interview.

Belson's voice came back on the radio, terse: "There is no other place."

One of the COs suggested we move to the far end of the table. We did, but five minutes into the interview when all the inmate's visitors filed in, it got so noisy we could hardly continue.

"Can I get back there with her?" the reporter asked a CO. He got permission to go to my side of the table, but was blocked in, as visitors were now seated along the narrow walkway where he had come in. "I'm coming over," he said, handing me his recording equipment. He held on to the top of the barrier running over the four-foot-high visiting table, and jumped over. We moved to a bench behind the visitors' chairs, and sat side-by-side for the rest of the interview.

During the afternoon court session, more police witnesses took the stand. One of them was Sheriff Bentley's son, David Bentley. Another, Deputy Lewis Snyder, testified that when he came on the scene the group was "very tumultuous—sixty or seventy of them." He said he started to pull people off the officers, "because there were people on the backs of each of the officers."

Sgt. Darryl Braley also testified. His responses to Gibb's questions about the melee were brief and to the point. He described noise and chanting by our group, but not the physical fighting other witnesses had depicted. It was refreshing to hear an accurate account of Dad trying to block Sgt. Rater before the melee began. "I saw Jacob Lapp's hand go into Rater's face and throat area, at the time they approached the crowd," he said.

Gibb's final witness was Sheriff John R. Bentley. Apparently in his mid-sixties, about six and a half feet tall, he was brought to the witness stand flanked by several court officers. His face looked long and haggard.

Bentley said he had been called to the front lawn of the courthouse around noon on August 16. Gibb asked him what he saw and heard.

"Well, there was a big commotion and a number of people shouting and screaming and we were—we were involved in effecting an arrest."

"What arrest, specifically?"

"They were—the officers were—attempting to take one of the Lapps into custody." Faltering between words, Bentley gazed straight ahead, speaking in a monotone.

Gibb looked uncomfortable. "Now we've had testimony, Sheriff, that your officers had a warrant for the arrest of Barbara Lapp. Can you please describe for the jurors what the duty is of a deputy when he has a warrant and he sees somebody?"

"Your duty as a deputy sheriff or a police officer is to effect the commission of that warrant, to execute the warrant…, to effect that arrest if we're able."

"Did you have any personal contact while you were there with any of these defendants?"

"Yes, I did."

"Who is it that you had contact with?"

"I can't think what her name is. The person over there in red."

"Lynn Carroll?"

Bentley nodded his head. "Lynn Carroll was attempting to prevent Mr. Lapp from being taken into custody…," he said. "There was a lot of shouting and screaming and, as I say, she was—we were attempting to go take her—or him—into custody, and she was resisting that effort violently…."

"Did she also resist her own arrest?"

"That's what I say, she resisted her own arrest as well as the Lapp arrest."

"Did she do this, Sheriff—in both cases, what was she doing?"

"Well, she—well, she was clinging to Mr. Lapp and shouting, screaming…. And her own arrest the same way, she was—she was under—trying to put her under arrest and trying to stop this resistance…." The sheriff's voice was faltering markedly. He looked tired.

"Thank you," Gibb said. "No further questions for this witness." Bentley was escorted from the courtroom, and Gibb told the judge he had no more witnesses to call. The prosecution rested.

Lynn approached the bench and presented the court with several motions for dismissal, which Judge Mifsud denied. She then asked to take the witness stand. She had prepared her own questions.

"Tell me about your children. How many do you have?" Lynn asked, then answered: "I have seven children." With many questions and answers, she gave a background of her involvement with Child Protective Services, her contact with our family, and her position as secretary of VOCAL.

"How did you spend your spring?" she continued.

"Picking asparagus in an asparagus field at the Lapp farm."

"How do you know Joe Torres?"

"I know him from picking asparagus with him."

"Do you know Nancy Torres?"

"Yes, she's Joe's wife."

"How well do you know the Torres family?"

"I was present at the birth of their last child."

"How did your day start out on August 16, 1993?"

Lynn then told of her ride to Mayville with me, the assembly in the court parking lot, and the events leading up to noon. She said she had spent the morning in the courtroom, and came upon the melee scene—a lot of people on the ground, Nancy, eight and a half months pregnant, screaming with her hands over her mouth, and five officers on top of Mom. "I started screaming in just a terrible rage, 'What is going on here?' I had no idea what had happened before or what was happening then," she said.

Lynn testified of the confusion and hysteria in the group, and people coming to each other's aid. She demonstrated how Lt. Lawrence had pulled her head back with his fingers in her eyes and nose. She said after he let go, she was stunned, and could hardly see.

Lynn told how she had run up to Dad, demanding why he was being arrested. She showed how she wrapped her arms around him, and how she was removed from him by officers who twisted her hands and arms.

"Were you struggling at this point?"

"There was no possible way anybody could struggle in a hold like that."

"Did you, at any time, struggle or try to move away from Officer Giambrone or Officer Snyder while they were handcuffing you?"

"No, I did not."

Lynn's testimony completed, Judge Mifsud told Mr. Gibb he could cross-examine.

"Lynn Carroll has had the opportunity to read her entire life story to the jury," Gibb said. "I have no questions for her about the facts."

The judge called a twenty-minute recess.

During the break, we stood by the rail. Friends and family members moved up from the gallery. We shook hands with them and hugged them. Hannah climbed over the railing and joined us in the courtroom for a minute. Mom and Dad spoke at length over the rail. Today is their forty-fifth anniversary. Nancy passed the baby over for Joe, and I held him too. Officers stood nearby, but did not interfere.

After the recess Lynn requested the videotape be shown again. As Sgt. Gerace held the controls, Lynn asked to have the tape stopped at numerous points, pointing out to the jury scenes that corroborated her testimony.

Gibb then asked Gerace to move the tape to a point where Lynn came on the scene. "Now the two Lapp girls, Rachel and Barbara, they're on the ground here, intertwined?" he asked, pointing to the picture.

"Yes," Lynn said.

He asked her why she was standing so close. "Why weren't you back on the sidewalk somewhere?"

"Because I saw people on the ground getting terribly abused. I certainly wasn't going to run away."

"Did you hear the officers testify that at this point you were interfering with the arrest?"

"The officers lied."

Gibb asked to have the film moved to the scene of Lynn with her arms around Dad. "Why are you holding on to Jacob Lapp?" he asked.

"Because after what they had done to me, I couldn't imagine what they were going to do to him."

"So you decided to interfere?"

"No, I didn't decide to interfere. I decided to go up and put my arms around a man I loved as my father."

All testimony completed, court was adjourned for the day. Judge Mifsud said we would resume in the morning at nine, with summations and jury charges.

On the way down Rachel talked to Dad about Jim Fox's testimony. "I'm not completely surprised," she said. "Some of the things he's written lately have been funny."

"But it's worse under oath," I said.

"Without a conscience, an oath means nothing, I guess," Dad said.

Rachel told Dad of numerous complaints we heard recently on the inaccuracy of Fox's news accounts. Lynn had told us that after Fox testified, another person from the media met him in the hall and was heard telling him, "Lies! How could you stand up there and say those things about them?"

■ CHAPTER 14 ■

"A Different Drummer"

November 19, 1993

By Rachel

We're going to court again, for the fourth day. In a way it's nice, getting out of the cell, walking with Dad and Joe, and seeing the rest of the family in the courtroom.

The trial has been a tremendous strain, though. We're not getting enough sleep, with preparations for court, writing diary, and discussions with inmates.

One of the girls told us she went to court yesterday, and overheard the officers joking about the trial. "They're showing movies in county court, if you wanna go," one of them had said. It's so terribly unfunny—those videos. Do they love what they did on August 16?

On the way up to court they didn't have handcuffs for all of us, so I just followed the stream of people down the hall. I was walking briskly along, when a short, husky officer stepped out to block me, handcuffs extended. He began to put them on, as everyone else walked ahead.

"You know I don't need those," I said, not really politely.

"You know I have to put them on," he retorted.

By Barbara Lyn

Seated in the courtroom, we waited for the jury to arrive.

"We'll now come to order," Judge Mifsud said.

The bailiff opened the courtroom, and the jurors began to file in. Gibb hastily stepped toward the judge. "Your Honor, before you bring the jury in," he said, his voice urgent.

"Excuse me, hold up a minute," Mifsud said, waving toward the jurors and the officers who were bringing them. "Take the jury back out, please."

When they were out, Gibb began to speak. "Your Honor, unfortunately I have to bring up a matter that has come to my attention yesterday after the trial." He told the judge that members of the "Barbara Lapp supporters" had been handing out a pamphlet called, "True or False: When You Sit on a Jury You Have the Right to Vote Your Conscience."

Gibb showed the judge several copies of the pamphlet—a one-page yellow paper, folded in thirds. He said he had picked them up at the convenience store across the street. He produced an affidavit by a man who said he had been handed a copy while eating at the diner. "If people are handing this out to jurors, they are clearly tampering with these jurors and trying to influence them to do something that is outside the law," he said. He asked Judge Mifsud to question the jurors whether they had seen the pamphlet, and tell them this is not the law. Gibb then handed copies of the brochure to all of us and our standby attorneys.

Lynn approached the bench, the yellow brochure in hand. "Your honor, it does state the law in here," she said.

Inside the folded paper it said, "Why do most judges tell you that you may consider 'only the facts?'" A 1972 Court of Appeals ruling was cited, describing jury veto power as an "...unreviewable and irreversible power... to acquit in disregard of the instructions on the law given by the trial judge."

Judge Mifsud looked at the pamphlet, then told Lynn he can't tell if it's the law or not the law without looking it up. Lynn said it could be verified by resources available within the courthouse, and asked that she be allowed to check the wording, then come back and read it to the jury.

The courtroom turned into a frenzy. For a while it looked like there could be a mistrial. The five standby attorneys, some who had earlier in the trial fallen asleep, came to full attention. They leaned together, whispering. District Attorney James Subjack came in and conferred quietly with other attorneys.

Gibb looked very unhappy. "Your Honor, as you know, it is your job to charge the law...," he said. "If we allowed that in every case, we wouldn't have any system, we wouldn't have any organization; we'd have chaos. The jury is to follow the law as given by the judge.... The pamphlet in general simply says you should judge the law and the facts and vote on your conscience. That is not the law, as Your Honor knows. They are to use the law as Your Honor gives it to them. This defendant should not be reading any law whatsoever to this jury...."

"Your Honor," Lynn said, "...It wouldn't be proper for me to read the law. I'm not the judge. You are, and you are responsible to read the law and be fair and impartial.... What I ask for you to read is the law. As I said, I can go look it up if need be."

"It's not necessary to look it up," said Judge Mifsud. "It's my job to give the jury the law... and I will not accept instruction from the defense side or the prosecution side. In your closing statements, I caution you to make sure you do not deliver to the jury what the law is. I will do that."

"Are you going to read the law?" Lynn asked.

"No, it is denied," Mifsud answered.

Finally the jurors were brought back in. Judge Mifsud asked them if they had seen the yellow flier. All of them said they hadn't, and Mifsud asked us to proceed with summations. I was called first.

I apologized to the jurors for not participating in the trial, and told them it was "the test of my lifetime" to sit there quietly. "Partly because it's very difficult to say nothing when you see things said about yourself and others that aren't true," I said. "And probably the hardest part was to say nothing when the judge spoke to me. I can only hope that at some point, in a different circumstance, I will have the opportunity to show the judge that I do respect him as a person. I cannot, I do not, respect this court setting and the way it was brought about...."

I told them it was a compelling necessity to deal with matters of conscience, and a child in need, that led me to take this position of noncompliance.

Rachel also gave a closing statement. "I deeply regret that you've had to hear some things that are untrue from some of the witnesses," she began. "I also regret very much, for your sake and for the sake of our community, our entire nation, that some of the facts of the case have been kept from you. Numerous times there were small groups huddled together whispering things that you couldn't hear.... I think it's a terrible insult to your ability to discern all of the facts surrounding the case, and to know all of the laws that are being applied.... And there were cases when you were sent out, including this morning, where there was discussion in here about matters that were extremely relevant to this case—"

Judge Mifsud interrupted. "Rachel, your closing statement does not include what happened in the court. Your closing statement should be in reference to why you're here and why you're charged—not what went on in the court prior to the jury being in here. It was not for the jury to hear…. So therefore, I do not want that brought up in front of the jury."

Turning to the jury, he said, "Disregard what she has just said about incidents that happened this morning."

Rachel went on. "I feel that it is extremely relevant what I just mentioned, because I think one of the reasons that I'm here is because juries over the years have been stripped of their power to… take into consideration all evidence surrounding all cases."

"Your summation is not to discuss what juries have or have not been," Mifsud said. "It should be pertaining to the acts that were performed in front of the courthouse on August the 16th, of which you are charged…. You do not give a history of what juries have done or not done, and whether they were legal or illegal in your eyes. *I* will give the law, as *I* see."

"I understand that," Rachel said. "And I understand that the reason I'm here is because of the incidents in front of the courthouse and because of the incidents that led up to that…. And for me, if I were to be sitting on a jury, I would want to know the truth surrounding the circumstances."

"Excuse me, Rachel," Mifsud said. "What is before the jury are the charges placed against you in town court. Two misdemeanor charges, and that is what they have to know. You were arrested in this town, charges placed against you, and these are the charges the jury is hearing now…. And I want you to keep within those parameters and discuss that and that alone."

"I understand that," Rachel said. "I understand also that my actions that day were extremely pertinent to the circumstances surrounding a child that was in need. And that's what I am telling this jury; that there are circumstances that do affect a person's actions, and I think that's very relevant."

"It is not relevant because you are not charged with bringing a child here," Mifsud said. "You are charged with the two charges that are placed against you and that's what this jury—"

Rachel interrupted. "I'm charged for actions regarding the defense of a child that wasn't able to speak for himself," she said.

"Well, *that* would be the basis?" Mifsud asked. "I could say you went and performed a burglary because you were hungry. That doesn't make the burglary legal…."

"That's right, burglary would be wrong, and I think all of us in here know that would be wrong to harm or damage another person's property," Rachel said. Turning back to the jury, she continued. "I don't have a desire to refer to the laws. I've told you before I'm not a lawyer, and I don't understand all of the details of the law. But I understand there's an old saying, 'Don't get set before you get the setting.' And I'm telling you the setting of this case is extremely important, and if we're going to be disregarding that, it's impossible for us to know what really took place and why."

"You are bringing up another reason why you came to Mayville, and this court really doesn't care why you came to Mayville," Mifsud said. "This court has the charges against you for your actions here, and that's exactly what we want to hear...."

Rachel again told the jury that certain facts surrounding the case had been withheld from them. "I mean, all of the spectators, many lawyers, many officers in here listening to these facts. You are excluded. That's a great insult to your ability to discern.... And I'm sorry about that. Thank you."

As Rachel returned to the table, some of the people in the gallery were smiling and nodding.

Lynn went up next. "When you find me innocent, that means that I did not lie," she said. "That also means the police, sheriff, etc. who testified against me were lying."

She continued. "I want to thank you for your time, for your patience, for your ears, for your mind, and the conscience that determines good from bad, right from wrong, righteous from evil. I stand here before God and man and affirm I never, under any circumstances, with intent, broke any laws...."

"You could close your eyes right now, and I could be George Washington on trial for treason against the government." Lynn then gave the jury an overview of the founding fathers' rebellion against taxation and tyranny.

When she concluded her speech, Gibb began his summation. "This case is not one that's about child protection or children in need. This case is very specific. It only covers three charges...."

Gibb spoke about his police witnesses. "These were not rank rookies that were sent out to handle this situation. These were veteran police officers. Knowledgeable police officers.

"Now this is not a trial just between police officers and these five defendants. I think from what I've heard, they would like you to believe this is the system, the government, the police against the citizens."

Referring to the video evidence, Gibb said. "I want to caution you, if you do, in fact, look at the video again… there was only part of the action caught on the video. We needed the other witnesses to tell you what you couldn't see on the video. And a lot of that has to do with each of these defendants, and obstructing and rioting and resisting….

"Mr. Jim Fox also took the stand. He's a newspaper man. Been in the business for many years. He's there in a unique way to observe what's going on and report it back to you and to me and to the defendants—who apparently think it's funny…. He told us how people were apparently playing to the camera; falling down when they weren't even pushed. And he said he saw no excessive force by the police. Now, he's not a policeman. Why would he have an ax to grind?"

Gibb emphasized the testimony of his "civilian witness," Judith Claire, who watched the melee from a second story window of the courthouse. "She testified that she saw no excessive force by the police. No fingers in the nose, no fingers in the eyes, no weapons, no mace, no punching, no kicking….

"Not one officer, not one civilian witness agrees with Miss Lynn Carroll's description of the events. Nor does the video show it the way she describes it. What all these witnesses do talk about is the organization and the apparent planning of these five defendants and this group…. These people all cried victory as we were hauling Barbara Lapp into the courthouse. 'We won, we won,' they were applauding…. Apparently they thought whatever they planned went well….

"Ladies and gentleman, I don't think you believe that's the way this government works. I certainly don't. These defendants, each one of them, they are marching to the tune of a different drummer. They are not marching with us into the 21st century; they are marching backward out of the 20th century, through the 19th century and back into the 18th century…. They justify their behavior in the name of liberty and constitutional rights. But, in fact, what happened in front of the courthouse is not grounded in liberty nor constitutional rights. It's simple bullyism. Might makes right… and we cannot tolerate that kind of behavior….

"And because I feel the evidence is so overwhelming in this case, I'm asking that you find each of these defendants separately guilty of all of the charges against each of them. I truly believe it is time these defendants got a wake-up call…. The time is now, and you can send the alarm. And I'll wait for your verdict. Thank you."

Judge Mifsud called a recess. As usual, we made a trip to the wash room, then returned to the rail and spoke to the people in the gallery. Suddenly Dad climbed over the rail, walked to the third row of spectators, and sat beside Mom on the bench. Muffled gasps came from onlookers. Officers stood nearby, but didn't say or do anything. Dad, in his jail greens, looked perfectly innocent as he quietly communed with Mom for a minute. Then he came back to the rail, and as noiselessly as he had left, climbed over the thigh-high rail and returned to his place at our table.

"You must listen to the laws that I tell you, and follow them," Judge Mifsud instructed the jury. "Remember, you have taken a solemn oath, or an affirmation, to follow the law as I tell you, no matter what you personally think what the law is or should be...."

Mifsud read our charges and explained to the jury which charges applied to which defendant. The obstruction charge, he said, applied to all five of the defendants. "In order to find any defendant guilty of this crime, the People are required to prove... the defendants attempted to prevent the arrest of Barbara Lyn Lapp by laying on the ground, pushing, shoving and fighting with members of the Chautauqua County Sheriff's Department...."

I couldn't believe what I was hearing. I wasn't accused of "pushing, shoving and fighting," and certainly not of "attempting to prevent the arrest of Barbara Lyn Lapp." The other defendants were. None of the witnesses said I was pushing and fighting, and no video evidence showed it. My alleged crime was refusing to go with the police. I looked at Gibb, sitting at his table. He didn't seem to have noticed the judge's error.

Judge Mifsud read the resisting arrest and rioting charges, then concluded his instructions: "If you find the People have failed to prove to your satisfaction, beyond a reasonable doubt, any of these elements, then you must find the defendants not guilty."

I felt dazed. It appeared to me that Judge Mifsud had just required the jury to find me not guilty.

The jury was escorted from the courtroom. Their job now was to delineate fourteen charges and sixty elements of law, as each pertained to the five of us.

1:30 PM. We're in our cell, waiting for the jury verdict—the second time in five weeks for me. I can't escape feelings of fear. I told Dad that, when we went up for a jury question just before lunch. "Think of St. Paul in his bonds and torture," he said. Dad didn't look like he was afraid.

In our cell, I showed Rachel a copy of the poem, "Stone Walls Do Not a Prison Make."

"If I'm convicted, this is going to be my concession speech," I told her. The poem, sent to Rachel by a friend early in our stay here, has been an inspiration to us. I quickly scribbled the verse on a piece of paper, folded it and put it in my dress pocket. Then I made a copy for Rachel. "We'll read it together," I said.

2:10. We were called back to court, just one hour after the jury had taken the video into the jury room. The officers didn't tell us whether it was the verdict, or a question.

In the courtroom, the left side of the gallery was packed with lawyers and officers. On the right side were several dozen friends and family members.

We four prisoners sat down at the table, and Lynn joined us.

"Has the jury reached a verdict?" Judge Mifsud asked.

"Yes, we have, your honor."

"Will the foreman please rise?" asked the court clerk. "How do you find in the case of the People of the State of New York versus Rachel Lapp on the charge of obstructing governmental administration?"

"Guilty."

Rachel was found "not guilty" on resisting arrest. Lynn was also found guilty on obstruction, and acquitted on resisting and riot. My verdict was guilty on obstruction and resisting, not guilty on riot. Dad's was guilty on obstruction and riot, not guilty on resisting. Joe was found guilty on all three charges.

After the verdicts were read, Judge Mifsud thanked the jury for their hard work. "The Town of Chautauqua appreciates it, and so do I," he said. "You're excused."

The four men and two women rose and walked from the jury box. Rachel and I stood up. We took the papers from our pockets, and facing the spectators, began to read in unison: "Stone walls do not a prison make—"

"Order in the court!" Judge Mifsud said loudly.

"Nor iron bars a cage," we continued.

"Barbara, Rachel, you must be silent!" The judge slammed his gavel.

"Minds innocent and quiet take this for an hermitage—" We were still reading, voices elevated, as the jury filed out of the courtroom.

"I'll have you removed," Mifsud yelled. Four or five officers quickly moved in, within inches from us. But they didn't touch us.

We went on reading: "If I have freedom in my heart, and in my soul am free, angels alone which dwell above, enjoy such liberty." The officers around us stood still, arms dangling at their sides. Even the judge had fallen silent.

In the gallery, our supporters smiled broadly. Rachel made one clap with her hands. Then the whole crowd stood up and applauded.

Judge Mifsud's face was distorted with anger. "Would you please clear the courtroom of all those people out there clapping?" he said to the officers. They went toward the gallery, but our supporters had already begun to walk out. Rachel and I went to the rail and waved to them. I reached to hug Mom, but four officers blocked me. "No, you're not coming over here," one said. I quickly moved to one side, grabbed a hug from Mom, then held Miriam's hand and kissed her.

"The defendants, please refrain from going across the bar there," Mifsud said. "And sit down, please!"

We stayed and watched our loved ones file out. "Rachel, please take a seat! Barbara, please take a seat," the judge yelled. We went back, stood near the table, and watched in silent reverence until almost everyone had left. Then we sat down.

A few supporters remained seated in the gallery. They said they had not contributed to the noise, and would not leave. "Remove those people from the courtroom!" the judge called to the officers.

"If you want 'em out, *you* do it," an officer muttered.

Judge Mifsud finally said they could stay.

Court in order, Mifsud set sentencing for December 8, almost three weeks away. Then he revoked Lynn's bail, and remanded her to jail.

"Your Honor, I'd like to put in an appeal," Lynn said, approaching the bench with her lawyer.

"You're not filing it with me," Mifsud said, waving his hand. "I'll see you in court for sentencing." Officers handcuffed Lynn and led her from the courtroom, toward jail. Her eight-year-old daughter watched from the gallery. Suddenly an anguished cry pierced the courtroom, and a family member quickly carried the hysterical child out the door.

By Rachel

All of us were escorted to the court waiting room. While they handcuffed the others, I stood at the window and stared out. I expected at any moment to hear officers speak to me, or feel them get my wrists.

The elevator opened, and everyone went in. "Are you going?" an officer asked. He motioned me forward, and I walked in.

It was nice to go without cuffs. Last out of the elevator, I walked fast to catch up with Joe—just convicted on all three counts. "I hope you don't feel bad," I said, laying my hand on his shoulder as we walked.

"Why would I feel bad? I feel good," Joe said.

By Barbara Lyn

The trial is over and my jail time could be long. The others could go home in December, as state sentencing guidelines give six months as maximum for first-time violators of the obstruction law. That's four months, counting good time, and that time would be up by the sentencing date in three weeks.

It's hard to think of a year in here. The stupidity of the conviction bothers me. One can't help wish that at least one person in that group of jurors had taken to heart some of the sayings of honesty, liberty and truth we sowed. But the Lord knows when and how truth is planted in people's minds. If truth had sprouted in this group of people, perhaps it would not have had the chance to expand to others. Maybe if we had we been acquitted today, others wouldn't have seen the reality of terrors that threaten our communities. In this way, the truth may spread and grow.

November 20

By Rachel

It's the first post-trial day, and the first day with Lynn. I'm exhausted.

We talked a lot with Lynn. We pulled our notes from past to present, memories ditto, and shared until we screamed, laughed and cried.

I feel a little sad today. One thing that continues to hurt me is how we had to treat Mifsud and the officers in court those days. I do think Judge Mifsud brought it upon himself to have us in his courtroom. He ignored a totally valid legal argument from day one. But it was sad to ignore him every time he called our names—worse since he's an older man, and I love him as a senior citizen.

As far as the officers, society needs protection, and they sometimes work hard for us. How can I show them I recognize and appreciate that? Maybe I never can, to this class of people. I don't know why they don't at least refrain from using swear words in our presence, ugly ones. Do they think we're not hearing?

Will God ever allow us to get together, all of us, and discuss what happened, with these people? Or are they completely past the point of reasoning? There are some, like Lt. Runkle, who seemed to watch us intently at the trial. For a good reason? Or just for sport? Does he believe Dad choked and hit Rex Rater? Maybe I shouldn't care. But he's my neighbor—I've conversed with him and his wife and children at their home.

November 21

By Barbara Lyn

I had a beautiful pep-talk home this morning. Mom said they are settling together as a family, accepting the good they have left, and feel generally more encouraged since the trials are over. I share in the same post-trial relief.

Later we got a visit from the family. Miriam seemed resigned to me being in jail for a long time. "You could still come out by summer, couldn't you, Mom?" she asked. "Some other people are in jail longer than that—like all their life."

We learned this morning that Sheriff Bentley is in the hospital. It was said he had a stroke, within hours after testifying against us in court. It's a shock. After the trial, Rachel and I had laughed about how poor his testimony was. Now I feel there is no room for humor, or bitterness. To think what that poor man must be suffering, and what his end would be like. I wish I could talk to him.

This afternoon we asked CO Brenda how Bentley is doing, and what happened. She said they don't know what's wrong with him, but it's not a stroke or a heart attack. She said he hadn't been too well in the last weeks.

The atrocities of the trial bother me. But I'm distancing myself from the possibility of appeals. I've read pages and pages in law books on appeals to court decisions. It's a technical game that has nothing to do with justice, or guilt or innocence.

The appeals courts will not uphold the most important arguments against our convictions, these being the court's failure to acknowledge the jurisdictional challenge, failure to use grand jury process, and trial by six instead of a real trial by jury—meaning twelve impartial people to judge both law and facts. The higher courts are not about to destroy their own power by ruling on these essential elements of justice—not any more than King John was about to sign the Magna Carta, which would take his power and put it into the hands of the people.

The appeals court might uphold issues such as the judge's failure to properly read the elements, and his refusal to allow certain jurors to be removed from the panel. But these are the kinds of technicalities also used by murderers and violent criminals to go free. I want to go free because I am free, owing to the fact that I've never harmed anyone.

That's not the only reason I don't want to argue my case in appellate courts. If I lost, as I likely would on purely constitutional arguments, that decision would be used as law in countless future cases, stripping more people of basic God-given rights.

Our system of writing laws based on the opinion of judges is wrong in itself. The Constitution guarantees a system where only legislatures can pass laws and only juries can apply them. Laws cannot be based on the opinion of some appellate judge. The failure of our government to recognize this is precisely the reason the obstruction, resisting, and rioting laws could so handily be used against us. Can I risk contributing to strengthening these powers, perhaps broadening the meaning of these laws into prohibiting even passive resistance to police powers? And suppose I would win on appeals because of Judge Mifsud's foolish errors. Then I'd have to subject myself to another trial. The court never got permission from the people to try me in the first place. Now I put myself in the position of asking for a new trial?

■ CHAPTER 15 ■

Looking Home

November 22, 1993

By Rachel

We are getting back to schedule, and determined to answer our pile of mail which threatens to usurp our eating and writing space on the tiny table in our cell.

After lunch CO Louise came in and told us we had to move. She needed to vacate a cell for Lynn, who would be double locked because she refused to take the TB test.

We had expected Lynn would get locked, but hadn't thought they'd move us from the spot we've had for almost four months. Long-termers like us are never moved unless they ask.

Paula and Carla, whose cell is across the block, called over and invited us to move in with them. It was crowded there, with Emma, an extremely large woman, already sharing the cell with them, her mat placed on the floor by the doorway. But we were grateful for the invitation, and began to carry our piles of bedding, books, and other belongings into their cell. We stacked our cardboard boxes in corners and dropped our mats on the middle of the space left on the floor.

Louise came in to announce rec time. "Rachel," she said, coming close, "after rec one of you'll need to move over here." She pointed to the cell next to us. "They have just three, and you're five."

A few minutes later I waited with Louise at the gym elevator. "Do you realize it would be pretty hard for Barbara and me to separate?" I asked her. "We share everything—our commissary, legal papers, books."

"I know it's not easy," Louise said. "If you can work something out for one of the others to move, that's okay. But I can't make them move. They were there first."

"Then why did you move us from our cell, if—"

Louise interrupted. "Life isn't always fair, Miss Lapp."

At the gym we spoke to Carla and Paula, our new cellmates, about the problem. "We're really crowding you," Barbara said.

"It's none of Louise's business," Paula hissed. "It's stupid! The cell across from us had five—those Spanish girls that wanted to be together. But if she doesn't like it, Emma can move."

Back from rec, Louise followed us to our new cell. "What did you decide?" she asked.

"Guess we haven't decided for sure what to do," I said. "But Barbara and I are staying together—don't know what the others wish to do—"

"What?" Louise said. "One of you is going to move *now!* You may as well decide who, and get your things. I've talked it over with the sergeant—he said that's how it has to be."

Neither of us answered, and Louise left.

"They can't separate us," I said to Paula and Carla. "If they move me, I'll run right back."

"They'd have to double lock us both," Barbara said. "Then we'd be together. There's no way they could put us in separate cells—it's too full in here." We laughed, despite the tension.

Our cellmates cheered us. "Louise doesn't know what she's getting into," one of them said, snickering.

Tamara called from the next cell. "Don't be messin' with Louise. She'll come with the guys and have you chained to the bed." Tamara's voice was even, almost prophetic. "I know—I been here before."

Barbara called home and spoke to the family. "If we don't call tonight, you'll know we're double locked," she told them.

We tried to untangle our belongings, but it was hard to concentrate. Barbara showered and I washed some clothes at the sink.

Louise came back in and called Barbara to the gate. "Here's your mail," she said, pushing several envelopes through the bars. She promptly left again. The girls giggled. Louise hadn't even looked in our cell to see if we'd moved.

More than an hour passed. Louise came again, this time with a new inmate. She put the girl in the cell next to us, the one she'd ordered us to move into. She stopped at our cell. "We have another girl here now, so you may as well stay where you are," she said. Barbara and I were reading, and didn't look up.

At 4:00 Carole came in. She strode to Lynn's cell. "You're leaving," she said, handing Lynn a bag with her clothes. Carole explained that a County Court judge overturned Mifsud's decision, and reinstated Lynn's bail pending sentencing.

"Can we have our room back?" I asked Carole.

"You and Barbara are going in there—and Emma," Carole said, pointing to our former cell. Her voice was strained.

Emma has been caught stealing things from other inmates, is greatly overweight, and has hygiene problems. No one wants her as a cellmate. I asked Carole if she knew Emma has always been in the other cell. She repeated her instruction.

"Didn't I tell you?" Tamara proclaimed loudly. "Louise put Emma in Lapp girls' cell 'cuz she don't wanna be messed with! I been here before. I know Louise and them whiteshirts!"

Soon the whole block was in uproar, the girls telling Carole how unreasonable Louise was. Tamara yelled, "Louise, she'll *never* back down!"

Carole's only words were, "Listen to Tamara!"

We're back in our cell. Emma is quiet, and doesn't have many things, which is a blessing. We helped her settle in, then spoke to her. "You must not take our things," I said. "If you want something, ask us. We'll share."

Emma nodded. Later this evening when I got off the phone I told Emma I'd spoken with my mother and sister about her. "My mother said she thinks we'll get along," I told her, putting my hand on her shoulder. "My sister said to tell you that stealing is a bad habit. Every time you do it, the habit gets stronger." Emma nodded. "So it's a deal? You won't do it?" Emma agreed.

At 8:30 as Carole locked us in for the night, Tamara called over, "Good night, Barbara. Good night Rachel!" She went on, saying the names of each girl in the block, at the top of her voice. The others laughed, as Tamara crawled into bed, pretending to sleep. The TV was loud, the laughter louder.

"Good night, Lapp Girls!" another girl said, then shouted the names of each of the others. They laughed uproariously.

Carole stopped at our cell door, grimacing at the noise. Smiling, I told her, "It's okay—we don't mind the girls. It's nothing compared to what we had in here today." I began to tell her about Louise's attempt to move us.

"Don't let it bother you," Carole said. "It was just a power play." I breathed a sigh of relief. Carole had been so tense this afternoon. Barbara and I were afraid she felt bad about us. "The whole thing about moving you over there—it was creating a problem," Carole said. "It's one thing when there *is* a problem. But to *create* one?"

Carole said when she arrived at three, Louise had told her about the incident, and instructed Carole to move one of us as soon as the new girl got bail. "I told Louise, 'Now wait a minute. It's 3:00. It's *my* shift now.'" Carole said they were still arguing when the phone rang, and it was the judge on Lynn's case. "So *now* is there a problem?" she had asked Louise. "Those two can just go back where they were." Louise then insisted that Emma move with us.

November 23

By Barbara Lyn

Rachel and I were both sleeping this morning when Louise came into our cell. I woke up to the noise of her radio crackling, and saw her standing by our table, reading a verse I'd mounted on the wall. The poem says:

> *I live for those who love me, for those who know me true.*
> *For the heaven that shines above me, and awaits my spirit, too.*
> *For the wrongs that need resistance,*
> *For the cause that needs assistance, and the good that I can do.*

Louise looked at our table full of mail. Then she inspected our window screen, which had recently been repaired. She left, without speaking.

Later when we were coming back from school CO Brenda told me to wait in the office as she took Emma and Rachel back into our cell. I was puzzled, and scared. Brenda came back. "Barbara, you don't need to answer a word, if you don't want to," she said. "But Louise and Sue and I have noticed the screen in your window is being worked on again. We know it's not you. Do you have any idea who might be doing it?"

"I don't have a problem with answering," I said. "I don't know anything about it." Brenda assured me no one suspected us. She asked if I would let her know if I see anything. I told her we'd be afraid to say what we know about others. "We're not here by choice–we're confined with these girls, and if anyone were to get angry there would be no way of getting out of their way."

Brenda seemed understanding. "That's why I talked to you here," she said. "You can tell the girls we were just talking about your case. They don't need to find out what we talked about."

As soon as I got back in the girls crowded around. "Where were you?" they asked. I told them what we'd talked, and that Brenda wants me to report it if I see anyone messing with the screen again. "I'm not going to talk behind your backs," I said. "But it would make it really hard for me and everyone else if you do anything to that screen."

The girls were adamant no one had touched the screen since it was repaired. We all went to the cell to look. The screen had a little bulge in the corner—exactly as it was when it came back from repair.

By Rachel

In the gym today the heat was turned up, as it has been lately. "Does it have to be this warm?" I asked Swanee.

"Does it have to be this warm?" he repeated.

"It's so warm over by the situp boards," I said.

"Don't go over there!" Swanee said. "Rachel, it's so cold in here in this gym," he said, drawing his arms to his chest in mock distress.

I laughed a little, then tried again. "It's so warm, when you're exercising—"

"Don't exercise!" he interrupted.

Swanee and most of the girls sit and play cards the whole hour. They think it's cold.

We heard from a private source that Sheriff Bentley may have a brain tumor, or Alzheimer's disease. A newspaper notice about Bentley said he's in satisfactory condition at WCA Hospital; according to his family, no more information will be available to the public.

November 25

By Rachel

Brenda served us turkey dinner with pumpkin pie and whipped cream for lunch, in honor of Thanksgiving. The girls complained that they can't be thankful in jail. When all was quiet, Barbara said, "Look at it this way: We do have a lot to be thankful for. We have food, warm blankets, healthy bodies." Some of the girls concurred, others went on moaning.

At gym we could see the beauty of the day from the windows, though from our immediate view the sun shone only on the indurate structures of town, and on the sheds and vehicles of the sheriff's department. How lovely that sun is! It also shines on our family at home, and on the natural beauty of their country dwelling. The Scripture says, "He maketh His sun to rise on the evil and on the good." (Matthew 5:45.)

We received a list of the names of nineteen officers involved in our arrests on August 16. The list was acquired by Ken Bellet, who was injured that day. He is filing a federal lawsuit against the Sheriff's Department. I feel troubled about the suit. I hope our family does not get involved. Some of the officers named on the list used proper restraint the day of our arrests. I don't think it's fair to hit them with the same blame as the aggressive ones. In a way, the suit could be beneficial, to make even the lower ranking officers think about being part of such a disgraceful action. But it hurts me. They probably won't trust talking to us now.

November 26

By Rachel

This afternoon we were called out to see a probation officer—first Barbara, then me. I met Mike Sheffield, a young dark-haired gentleman, in the jail classroom. We sat down on opposite sides of the table. "I was at your farm last summer," Sheffield said. "Bought some Swiss chard from your sister. I took the whole three-foot row."

I smiled, thinking of Susan cutting the luscious, green leaves.

Sheffield explained that it was the Probation Department's job to get information as input for sentencing. "You don't need to say anything," he said, "but what I'd like to have are your feelings about what took place August 16, and what led up to the incident."

I told him I felt uncomfortable with talking, as what I say could get back to the judge. Sheffield admitted that was true. I explained that we have refrained from communicating with the court, because we feel that important laws were overlooked in bringing us to trial.

"Your sister didn't want to fill out the forms either," Sheffield said. "But she did give her feelings about the case. For instance, why do you think the officers arrested you?"

After a pause, I said, "I guess I'd like to ask that of the officers involved that day."

"Do you feel bad about what happened?" Sheffield asked.

"I feel *very* bad."

"Why?"

"I consider myself an orderly, productive member of society, and I don't want to be the cause of disruption," I said. "I also feel bad because before this we had a good relationship with the Sheriff's Department. We were brought up to respect officers."

"Why did you come to Mayville?" Sheffield asked. "Obviously you wanted to show your support for Barbara Lyn."

I hesitated.

"Do you think there's a better way of addressing this?" he asked.

"Yes. I'd like to be discussing this directly with the officers that arrested me."

Sheffield leaned over and looked at the papers he'd brought. One of them was signed by Sgt. David Bentley. "You'd like to talk to this— David Bentley?" he asked slowly.

"I don't know who arrested me," I said. "No one spoke to me." I leaned forward on the table and rested my head into my hands.

Sheffield was silent, then spoke again. "I just wish I could get a little more from you." He looked at the sheet of paper with his jottings. It was less than half full. "I feel it would be to your benefit to explain things from your point of view. This is your chance to tell your side of the story."

"If I talk now, and give the court information, I'd be letting up on my original challenge to the court's jurisdiction."

"You're probably right on that," he said, rubbing his forehead. "If I were in your position, I'd probably do the same."

I told Sheffield about Barbara's visit with Probation after her previous conviction. "You're saying if I cooperate, it will be to my benefit," I said. "Now Barbara did cooperate, and got an excellent report. Yet at her sentencing, Probation recommended jail time." I looked at him. "You know what I mean?"

"I know exactly what you mean," he said, looking uncomfortable. "You see, we also have to talk to the officers involved. And the judge doesn't always follow our recommendation. Don't know how it turned out for your sister."

"They gave her maximum, under state sentencing guidelines," I said.

Sheffield nodded. Finally he put his notes aside, drew out a form, and asked me additional questions. I didn't answer much, and he filled most of it out himself—address, job, etc. Then he packed his papers into his briefcase and we sat back to wait for CO Brenda to come unlock the door.

"When I was at your farm, your sister mentioned you had another garden where she could get more Swiss chard," Sheffield said. "You have more than one place?"

I began to explain the layout of our farmland. But he didn't seem to be listening.

"Your sister said something about 'if we continue in the business.' Is there a chance you won't?"

"You mean if we'll start up the fruit stand next summer?" I asked.

"Yes," he said, eyeing me with anticipation.

"Yes, there's a chance. It depends on how long we stay here. Probably at this point if I'd get out soon, we'd be okay. You see, I'm the manager of the fruit stand and—"

"O-oh," he said quietly.

I continued. "When we were arrested in August things became extremely chaotic at the farm. We didn't know if we'd make it. Barbara has managed the dairy herd for eight years. Now my younger sister is trying to handle it."

"She has her hands full," said Sheffield. "You think—there's a possibility you'd lose the business as a result of what's taken place?"

"It's possible. Right now we don't expect that."

Brenda came to take me back. Sheffield and I shook hands as we parted.

November 28

By Barbara Lyn

I just finished writing a long article about our trial, and a short one for *Family Alert*. Writing is hard work, with a jail mind that works slowly, and with incessant noise and distractions.

When I'm writing, I think of how a lot of religious writings from our history were written by people in prison. These writers, persecuted for their faith during the Reformation years of the sixteenth century, were under physical conditions much more severe than ours—dungeons, cold, darkness, chains, hunger.

The morning was quiet until about 10:00 when Tamara received word on the phone that her nephew had been stabbed. A lady she knew was responsible, and was on her way here. Tamara started using unimaginably violent, obscene language, describing what she would do to the woman when she got here. Hours later, the woman was booked. Tamara loudly announced to the CO that she would kill the woman if she came in. "My nephew's fightin' for his life and that f - - - - n' bitch'll be fightin' for hers!" she shouted.

The sergeant came in to talk to Tamara, and asked her if there was going to be a problem if they brought the woman in. She responded in the affirmative, declaring her combat capabilities, boasting that she didn't care what would happen. The sergeant left. The CO didn't even try to stop her outburst, and it continued for over an hour. The woman wasn't brought in.

We have been told on other occasions that the COs are afraid of Tamara. She holds the upper hand among the inmates, too, with explosive accusations, while keeping the majority on her side with her easy laugh and vulgar jokes. She has the seniority here in age, and also through experience—she's spent a total of one and a half years in this facility over a number of years. Anyone who wants to know about jail schedules, food menus, or the personal lives of the COs or sergeants asks Tamara.

Last night we watched drug raids on the "Cops" program. Police were shown smashing in the door of a residence, then ravaging the whole house—overturning furniture, going through the refrigerator, confiscating guns, throwing men down and leaving them lying handcuffed on the floor as they continued their search. Children screamed and cried, while mothers were questioned, and threatened by police of losing their children. Finally, a little package of white stuff was found, and the men were hauled off to jail.

"That's exactly what they did at our house," Marita, the Guatemalan girl, told me quietly.

"If that would be New York, they would've taken the ladies, too," another girl said.

November 29

By Barbara Lyn

Tamara woke up in a bad mood, blaming Rachel and me for talking about her in other languages. We speak Spanish to Marita, and sometimes Deutch on the phone, but weren't talking about her. Then she yelled at Marita for using the noisy shower while she wanted to sleep.

The woman she was threatening still hasn't come in. On the way back from school we heard she's in the trap, and the COs were talking of double locking Tamara so they could bring the woman in. A little later Tamara was called out to talk to the sergeant. She came back, laughing. They didn't lock her, and the other woman didn't come in.

Last night after we were all locked in, Licia, a petite Spanish girl, threw her plastic cup across the floor to a girl in another cell who needed it. The cup didn't make it all the way across the twelve-foot area between cells. In the opposite cell, the girls stretched their arms through the bars, but couldn't quite reach it. Rachel got one of her shower sandals and shot it across the floor, hoping to hit the cup and move it within reach of the girls. The sandal missed. Others started aiming for the cup with their sandals, too. Soon a dozen sandals lay scattered on the floor.

We got worried. CO Sue would come in for her half-hour check any time. Laughter and near hysteria followed, as inmates shot their possessions out under their cell doors, trying to move the stranded articles into reach of the cells on the opposite side.

Occasionally an article was retrieved, and muffled cheers went up. One of the girls retrieved an item by flinging her heavy wool blanket out between the bars, then dragging it back.

Flora, from the cell kitty-corner to ours, started gesturing wildly at us, pointing to the mop beside the sink near Rachel's and my cell. Rachel reached through the bars and got the mop—the tool that was needed to save us from having Sue walk in on our mess. The girls cheered.

Rachel, too naive to think of the mop as a weapon, busily put it to use, retrieving books and slippers, while Flora, who knew the mop was forbidden in the cell area, retreated to her bed, rolling over with laughter. Then Sue walked in.

Sue took the mop from Rachel, put it out under lock where it belonged, then returned to question us. All of the girls readily admitted involvement. "We didn't want to bother you to pick up our stuff," said Licia, who took responsibility for starting the whole thing.

"That's what I'm here for," Sue said sternly. She let Licia out to pick up the scattered items and return them to their owners.

Tonight, CO Carole is here. A few hours ago she called me to the office, saying that CO Jim Crowell said to bring me out. I was trembling and my face felt hot. Fingerprinting? Reprimand for last night's fun? The possibilities flashed through my mind.

When I got out, Jim handed me a court paper. "I was told to personally serve this to you," he said kindly. I thanked him, and came back in, feeling foolish to have been overcome with fear.

The paper, a notice from the county Law Department, requires me to appear before the county attorney on December 17, regarding "a certain claim" I supposedly filed against Chautauqua County. I don't understand it. Did I somehow become joined in the civil suit against the Sheriff's Department? I called home. The family didn't know anything about it either. Maybe it's a belated response to the "Jurisdictional Challenge, Counter Complaint and Claim for Damages" I filed after my first arrest.

By Rachel

When I was reading the Bible tonight, Emma asked me what parts I read. I explained the difference between the Old and New Testaments, and read a few passages with her.

We've gotten along well in our room, the "Motley Four." Marita, a small, quiet girl who speaks only Spanish; Emma, an American Indian who's three times her size; and two Caucasians who speak English, Spanish, German—and spend an inordinate amount of time writing.

Marita, who knows little English, talks and laughs with Emma, who knows no Spanish. Emma is better accepted by the clan lately. We had a sweat suit and comb sent in for her, told her she's *not* to steal, and in full trust we leave our cell door open for her when we go out for rec. Emma has become a person. "You going for a bike ride, Emma?" one of the girls good-naturedly asked her the first time she saw Emma wearing her sweat suit.

"Yep!" said Emma, laughing.

December 1

By Barbara Lyn

At our visit this afternoon Joe said Magdalena (his four-year-old) told him he shouldn't have helped me, so he wouldn't have gotten arrested. I looked over at her, cuddled into her daddy's arms, one finger in her mouth. "You have a very good daddy," I told her. "Your daddy loves you, and he helps others, too."

She nodded, then took her finger out of her mouth just long enough to say, very seriously, "Daddy helped you."

"Yes, Lena, that's true," I said, my eyes stinging with tears. "The police shouldn't catch people for helping each other." Her expression was so full of pain.

We got back from our GED test at 8:30. Tonight we did three categories of the test, and we'll finish tomorrow night.

One category, "Literature and Arts" was particularly interesting, since a lot of the essays and poems are from old classics that have a moral message. One poem by Marianne Moore, (1966) was entitled "Silence." It was about an old man who said the "most superior person" is silent in some circumstances, especially in the most emotionally charged ones. Dad came to mind, with his silence in court.

Social Studies was a subject I didn't like, because the textbooks were miserably slanted toward upholding the power of government over the people. One essay about the U.S. Constitution gave an account of the colonial court case of John Peter Zenger, which established freedom of the press. It upset me that no mention was made that this landmark Zenger case was won only because a rebellious jury refused to follow the judge's instructions.

December 2

By Barbara Lyn

We didn't get any mail today, which is the first time in our 108 days here that there were no letters on a mail day, except for the first few days. Another first today was an uncontrollable woman who was supposed to be brought into the block. She got violent in the booking room. Our curtain was open, and we could see part of the scene through the window of the office door. The woman was crying and swearing, while CO Brenda shouted at her and tried to restrain her. "I won't put up with you swearing at my lieutenant!" Brenda yelled. Standing behind the woman who was seated, in handcuffs, Brenda grabbed her long hair and yanked her head back, then sideways. There was a crash, as the woman pushed a computer off the desk with both her feet. Brenda and several male COs wrestled her to the floor and shackled her.

"You're breaking my arm!" the woman screamed.

"I will," a male voice said.

The woman was put in the trap. Shortly afterward we heard Brenda in the office, laughing loudly with the men as they talked about the incident. Later Brenda came in and recounted the story to the girls, laughing as she repeated the woman's profanities. She showed the girls her little finger where the woman had bitten her, taking off one of her long, perfectly painted nails.

Coming back from a visit this afternoon, Sheriff Bentley walked just ahead of us down the steps. At the bottom, he held the door for us. I looked up with an appreciative smile. He stared right past me. I believe today was his first day back on the job since he was hospitalized. It is said he's awaiting surgery for a brain tumor.

We completed our GED tests, and gave our teacher, Cindy, a final thank you. Throughout the course, we've been somewhat critical of the schooling. Occasionally Cindy teased us that we came just because we were bored. We assured her tonight that we had received some benefit from the education.

Cindy asked how long we thought we'd have to stay here. Rachel said she expected to be out next week, after sentencing. I told her I could get more time because of my other sentence.

"They can't keep you forever," Cindy said.

December 3

By Rachel

"No laundry today," Brenda announced this morning. Laundry dryers have been down for ten days now. It wouldn't be so bad to hand-wash if we had detergent, or lines to hang our wash. We launder—all twelve of us—with floor disinfectant mixed with shampoo or ivory bar soap. Then we hang the clothes across the top of the open door, or between the bars, where it takes all day to dry them. Hanging them on the ten-foot-long heat duct near the ceiling works better, but some of the COs won't allow it.

This morning I washed my clothes and hung them on the heat duct. CO Brenda came in again. "Whose clothes are these?" she demanded. "You can't put them there!"

I took them down, then told her we are hardly able to get our clothes dry otherwise.

The other girls chimed in. "We've been doing it—Louise doesn't say anything," one of them said.

"We haven't had laundry service for two weeks!" said another.

Brenda listened, then turned to me. "Is that true—no laundry for two weeks?"

"No," I said. "It's a week today for greens and sheets, and no personals since last Friday."

Brenda agreed to let us use the heat duct.

December 4

By Rachel

On the phone, Mom told us they had learned from an article in the paper that our sentencing was postponed two weeks. We could hardly believe it—just when we thought we had only four days left.

I read the Scripture, "Be not overcome of evil, but overcome evil with good." (Romans 12:21.) I think there are subtle ways in which one can be "overcome of evil." Like longing so much for home that we lose sight of the big picture. Or serving this prison term with self-pity, and harboring a dread of further evil.

It's evening now. No flareups from the masters or the prisoners today, unless you count Tamara, who is filling the house with an outrage right now over some of the women not showering properly, or frequently enough. She's also insisting some are urinating in the shower, and using all kinds of words to describe them—and the smell in here when people don't stay clean.

December 6

By Barbara Lyn

Sixteen weeks today. Rachel and I celebrated by cleaning our cell, every inch of it–ceilings, bars, cement wall, and two metal walls. Louise gave us a folding chair to stand on for doing the ceiling. She said she's not supposed to let that chair come in here, but she would do it this time. "If you take responsibility," she warned.

"You know they ain't gonna hurt nobody with that chair!" Tamara scolded.

We had a good time. Without even thinking about it, I was singing as I worked.

7:00 PM. Erica, a tall, athletic girl who lives in the cell across from us is making us laugh. She's telling the others she plans to talk to the judge when she goes to court next week.

"You think you're gonna talk to Judge Spann?" one of the girls said.

"You try that, you gonna be shut up in a hurry!" said another.

"Your Honor, I wish to have a few words before my sentencing," Erica said, pretending to be standing in front of the judge. "If I would have had any idea I'd be charged with escape when I got out of the police car, I would never have done it. You know, Your Honor, I've never been arrested before, and didn't have any idea what it was like."

Erica stood poised, speaking in an articulate, formal manner. The rest of us were almost bursting, trying to restrain laughter. "And you know what else, Your Honor," she continued. "I've been getting some education from the Lapp girls in jail. And I'm not pleading guilty to *nothing!*" Erica burst out laughing, and so did the rest.

We lost our wall posters this afternoon, when Louise came in and ordered them removed. It started when she noticed a girl in another cell had a half dozen letters and photos on the wall at the head of her bed, pasted on with toothpaste. "You're getting carried away with stuff on the wall," Louise said. She told the girl to take them down, then marched over to our cell. "You have to take those down," she told us, then left. We had two eight by eleven sheets of paper on the wall above our little table. One was the poem, "I live for those who love me," that Louise had read before. The other was a verse from Psalms.

I took them down, but saved the favorite poem and put it back up when Louise's shift was over.

By Rachel

Monday is often a day of roller coaster emotions for the girls. County Court is in session and inmates go to hear their fate. Poor Marita went to court today and pled guilty to a minor drug possession charge, in exchange for being released. After she'd gathered up her blankets, given away her commissary, and given us all goodbye cards, she was told to wait. Jail staff told her they'd have to make a phone call about her immigration status, and said that she might be sent back to Guatemala. I skipped rec to be with Marita as she waited. I called home a few times to discuss with the family the possibility of them giving Marita a home until her boyfriend gets out of jail, so she wouldn't be deported to Guatemala alone.

Finally Louise brought the bad news—there was a "detainer" on Marita from immigration. Bobbi Trimmer, the public defender who often visits the girls' cellblock, came in to speak with Marita, and I translated. Bobbi said Marita is now a federal prisoner, and must wait for a hearing from immigration.

December 6

By Barbara Lyn

Yesterday I spoke by phone to a radio talk show host from Florida. He said he wants to include our case in his radio program, and asked for background. One of the things I told him was how Mr. Miner, our county's commissioner of Social Services, became enraged in front of the county legislature last year, regarding public criticism I had brought against his agency. "It is preposterous, it is misleading, it is a lie," Miner had told the legislators, adding that he is at the point of needing to be restrained by his staff and attorneys, to prevent him from being more aggressive against me.

Today as I walked back from a visit, I was startled to see Mr. Miner in a room off the hallway, sitting at a table with Sgt. Gerace. Worse yet, a few minutes later when our chiropractor came we had to walk right past their table to get to the nurse's room. I looked up to say hello, and he returned the greeting in his ready-made voice.

The brief encounter with Miner struck me with a rush of unpleasant memories—his cold refusal to listen four years ago when I was falsely accused of child abuse, and the more recent disdainful public remarks he made about me.

Only eight months ago we had videotaped a meeting where Miner spoke, then we delivered messages to the public regarding the inhumane practices of his agency. Perhaps he's happy now that I'm in jail.

I gave CO Carole a second copy of our December newsletter, *Family Alert,* with my article on the trial in it. She took it eagerly, saying Cindy, our teacher, had seen her copy, and asked to take it.

The thirst for knowledge thrills me. Who can guess how much each additional day of our stay here will accomplish in reopening the system's clogged channels to justice? This work is like cleaning out the barn gutters, picking tomatoes in rain and mud, or pushing a stranded car out of the ditch. It's messy. But there'll always be time to wash up later.

December 8

By Rachel

Today would have been sentencing day. On November 19 when Mifsud set the date, it seemed then like an immeasurably distant time—probably only because the time I'll spend here is coming to an end.

In a letter, my little nephew wrote, "Come out of jail soon." But the adults at home are guarded in their expectations. Their notes to us say things like, "Is this the last time I'll write to you?"

I read a 1991 article by Nathan Stoltzfus, entitled, "Dissent in Nazi Germany." I was surprised to learn that even under Hitler's tyrannical rule there were successful protests in Germany. During one of these, hundreds of German women protested their Jewish husbands' confinement by clogging the streets and screaming at the gates of the prison day and night for a week. Whenever the armed guards threatened the protestors with gunfire, they would scramble for cover, only to return within minutes.

A top Nazi official explained why the Jewish spouses of these protestors were freed: "A large number of people gathered and... took sides with the Jews. I ordered the [Gestapo] not to continue Jewish evacuation." Stoltzfus wrote Nazi officials feared loss of support, and "the high morale needed for waging the war."

This was a time when people were executed for as minor an offense as telling an anti-Nazi joke, when they acted singly. The writer says these protestors' actions were successful because they were "broadbased, nonviolent, and overt."

I used to think Hitler got his power only by instilling fear, through violence. But the article pointed out that he first gained the support of the people. In *Mein Kampf,* Hitler wrote that "mass popular support was the distinguishing characteristic of the Nazi Party." He was not seen by most people as a bloody, feelingless character at that time. He had his plan. Get the people's support. Become a good person in their eyes. Accomplish that, and you can get away with murder.

Who else except persons already looked on as "good" could get away with what Himelein and Mifsud did? Or Rex Rater and other officers who lied?

I wish people who think of our protests here as futile would look at the example of the German protestors. Freedom in this country is not as far gone as it was under Hitler's bloody regime. Yet today people are too cowardly to speak and act. They should be clogging the streets on our behalf. If they don't, do they think there will be anyone left to speak up when this tyrannical government comes after them?

December 9

By Rachel

A hard-boiled egg I had put on our windowsill came up missing this morning. I mentioned it to Emma right away. She said quickly, "I don't eat eggs—I don't like them," and turned away.

Later we noticed some of our soup packages had disappeared. The others heard us talking to Marita about it, and told CO Brenda, who came in and loudly admonished the group. "You better think it over, and confess!" she said, addressing everyone. "If somebody doesn't show up with those stolen things, *everybody* is going to lose phone privileges. And there will be no commissary this week!"

The block burst into an uproar, most accusing Emma of being a thief. They were very angry that we would all be punished. I translated for Marita.

Brenda went out, then came back in. "So whoever did it, come out with it now! There'll be a shakedown of this place."

I told Brenda there were no witnesses, and there will be no proof. "We don't want to press something without evidence," I pleaded.

But no one else was satisfied. Brenda left again and Tamara launched a storm of profanity and violence. "I'll beat the sh - - out of that fat bitch!" she screamed. Others yelled at Barbara and me, saying we have to "stop being so nice."

In a quieter moment they did listen as Barbara told them, "The truth will come out. But sometimes we can't know right away."

Emma was crying. Finally she said she did it. Brenda said they can't double lock her because it's too crowded.

Barbara and I sat slumped over our cell table, exhausted. Emma lay on her mat on the floor sniffling. Minutes passed. "Emma," I said, "we've tried to help you. Why did you do this?"

"I didn't take you guys' soup!" Emma said. She claimed she had admitted it only because everyone thought she did it, and pressured her to confess.

December 10

By Barbara Lyn

I'm working on an essay on drug laws. It's a strange topic to choose, but not so strange after sharing living quarters with so-called drug criminals for four months. I see the cruelty of laws that are used to send police bursting into people's homes, arresting the innocent and guilty alike, keeping the innocent in jail until they admit they're guilty, and never teaching the guilty anything other than how to manipulate the system.

We haven't gotten a newspaper in here for several days. Swanee told us we won't be getting it anymore, because Lt. Belson said it was getting too expensive for the jail to provide every cell-block with a newspaper. Tamara, who has been in and out of here for five years, says they've never been without a paper before.

This morning Teensie, one of the inmates, announced it was her birthday. Since I'm not inclined to say, "Happy Birthday," I wrote her a note and put it in a tiny envelope. I colored sunshine on the outside and a picture of a rose with a thorny stem on the inside. "To pick the rose, the hands must first get scratched," I wrote. Then I dropped it on her bed, where folded clothes lay in place of a pillow. Later she came to the door of our cell.

"Come in, Teensie."

"Just wanted to tell you thank you for that note. It brightened my whole morning."

Emma is happier again, too. Rachel and I played "Memory" with her and the others.

I worked until past midnight to make three hand-printed copies of my 500-word article on drug crimes. When I was done my hands and fingers were in cramps. The pen callous on my middle finger is starting to look like a tumor.

December 11

By Barbara Lyn

It's very cold in here. Louise said they're having trouble with the boilers. She brought extra blankets. Even with all my clothes, I'm shivering as I sit at the table writing. My nose is so cold it's stiff, and my toes are cold, inside my shoes. There's no way I could get warm in bed, so I'll stay up dancing and rubbing my thighs.

I told Rachel I'm not going to shower. "It's too cold."

"Come on, get yourself in there," she scolded. "You'll feel warmer afterward."

Finally I made up my mind. Shivering and wrapped in a towel, I was ready to run for the shower when I saw one of the girls standing at the sink trying to tap hot water for her coffee. "It's cold!" she declared, holding her hand under the tap.

It was too late to turn back. The shower, I found out, was no warmer than the tap. I tried not to scream, drawing in long breaths as the water hit me. I was in spasms by the time I came out.

"Now I'm going to make you do it," I told Rachel. She did, with just one scream.

December 12

By Barbara Lyn

At this morning's visit Dad told us he's working on writing an article, "Guided By Thy Word," about his experiences leaving the Amish society. Dad has wanted to write that for many years. I wonder if that's why God allowed these extra two weeks in jail, to give Dad time to write.

It's 10:00 PM now, and we're locked in. Erica, across the block from us, just finished reciting her newest piece of rap poetry.

"Lapp Girls, y'all gonna like this one—it's about the jail," Erica said before she started. "Um—some words won't sound good—but you just have to plug your ears for them."

Erica was exactly right. The song, titled "P.O. Box 128," (our address here) had some good lines about being "in jail, without bail," and the judge saying, "You'll stay there 'till summer." It had some disgusting words, too. But we couldn't help laughing.

December 13

By Barbara Lyn

In the gym today, Rachel and I played our first basketball game. We kept making mistakes that hurt our teams. But the other girls were patient.

The girls are good to us. "The Lapp girls have very hard muscles," Erica told a new girl today. She asked us to show our arm muscles.

"Wow!" the girl said, when Rachel and I pushed up our sleeves and flexed our muscles. "Aren't you glad they aren't violent?"

"Would y'all come to my house in Dunkirk sometime?" Erica asked. I told her we would. Later she asked Rachel if we haven't seen a certain character on TV. We didn't know who she was referring to. The girls were flabbergasted when we said we don't have a TV in our home.

"They never watched TV before they came here," Emma told them.

"Y'all have electricity? Y'all have a telephone?"

"Yes, we do."

"You ever seen a live fight?" Teensie asked.

I thought for awhile. "I don't think so. Just pretend ones, like when my brother and my brother-in-law try to wrestle each other down."

"She never seen a live fight!" Teensie announced.

"No, they're not that kind of people. They're clean people—they stay away from all that bad stuff," someone else said.

"So y'all must think we crazy," Teensie said.

"No, you're not crazy," I said. "Most of the time you're very nice."

The girls laughed. "She said, 'most of the time,'" one of them giggled.

December 14

By Rachel

CO Doreen called me for mail this morning, then turned to a drawer and pulled out a box of Revita. "You can have this," she said, hastily handing me the box. She turned and went.

I'd thought it might happen. My chiropractor who started me on Revita a year ago, and Dr. Freling had both contacted Lt. Belson recently, urging him to let me have it.

This evening Emma went to court. The CO didn't let her wear her street clothes, because everyone knew she was coming back. Shortly after she got back, to our surprise, the CO brought her clothes and told her she's going home. She had received a phone call from the judge.

Two months ago the same judge had sentenced Emma to a year, upset with her for a huge unpaid telephone bill. He is employed by the phone company. Emma's lawyer had told her it was a conflict of interest, and a different judge was going to re-sentence her. Tonight it was the same judge, and he just plain let her go! Never heard the likes. No mention was made of restitution.

A few weeks ago a sergeant here told Emma she's not leaving until she pays Carla for food she stole while in her cell. But she left tonight, a thief. Barbara and I hugged her goodbye.

December 15

By Barbara Lyn

One week until sentencing. Now is the time to prepare ourselves, and resolve to be as St. Paul said, content in whatever state we're in.

Rachel and I spoke of possibilities this morning, like me being in jail until March, or even August of next year. I would be happy if the others could go home.

We got a bunch of letters from the children this morning, with photos of them in school and doing farm chores. Rachel showed the pictures to the other girls. "They look happy—are they?" one of them asked. It's hard for them to believe there could be happiness in the lifestyle we adhere to, with no parties, no TV or Christmas celebrations, and staying completely away from careless relationships with men. It seems to baffle them. But they listen, sometimes commenting on the happiness we have, compared with their own constantly alternating highs and lows.

"I'm gonna come to your farm sometime for some fresh meat!" declared Teensie. "Can I bring my kids for a weekend? We could sleep on the floor."

December 16

By Barbara Lyn

Tonight CO Sue brought a letter from Judge Himelein, with the two "Victim Impact Statements" which I had read before my sentencing. The statements had been withheld in a previous request I had made for the probation report. I thought I'd never see them again.

Himelein's letter was friendly. He signed, with a handwritten note at the bottom: "Sorry it took so long—I just returned to Chautauqua County today."

Himelein has been a most distressing character. He is responsible for my arrest and incarceration. He has maintained a professional poise throughout, which sets him apart from other top players in the game. Sheriff Bentley, the prosecutors, and Judge Mifsud all lost their tempers at one time or another. Himelein has been tolerant, almost tender. Yet with his pen and his power he has exercised the utmost in impudence. If I were good at expressing myself, I'd write a whole volume just about him. If I would not restrain my feelings, I'd say I hate him.

December 17

By Barbara Lyn

At 10:00 this morning Louise called me for a hearing. "It's about that lawsuit you have against the county," she said. I was as confused as I'd been ten days ago when I got the notice.

Louise took me to a small room on the first floor. Mark Wines, an attorney for the county, was there with a court reporter. She asked Wines how to title the proceeding.

"Jurisdictional Challenge," he said.

Then I knew what it was about. That was the title of the claim I had filed after my first arrest. Five months and two trials later, they were finally responding.

Wines said I would be questioned under oath regarding "the extent of injuries and damage" mentioned in my claim.

"I'd like to have two witnesses, or one witness and a tape recorder present before we proceed," I said, "since I'm not represented by an attorney." I had decided in advance I wasn't going to answer questions in private.

For a moment Wines seemed stumped. Then he argued lengthily that we have a court reporter, and I don't need witnesses. "I would not object to you having another person here with you, but… I do not wish to have this proceeding recorded." He urged me to proceed.

"Well, I've stated my stipulation—either two people or a person with a tape player. It's up to you."

Wines said that because of my request, he was unable to proceed. He said he did not believe I am entitled to witnesses or a recorder, but promised to check into it, then reschedule the hearing. He warned that I would lose my claim against them if I did not comply with his terms.

By Rachel

Our sink faucet is making trouble again. When we press the button to get water, it keeps running, making a whining sound that annoys the other inmates. We tried to deal with the problem by not pressing the button too hard, by pulling it, jiggling it, or by kicking the stainless steel sink until our feet hurt. We even tried yelling at it. Finally we shut it off, climbing up on top of the main sink and pulling a lever near the ceiling.

8:30 PM. Teensie just encountered a block on her phone when she tried to call home, and was very upset. She has four small children at home. Teensie is intelligent and well-groomed, has a dynamic personality, and is capable of very colorful language. This time she refrained from letting words fly. Then, turning to the shower, she exclaimed how bad the curtain looked.

I explained that the curtain had been brought in this afternoon, in a new plastic bag, nicely folded. "At least it's clean," I said. Teensie looked at me, then at the curtain. It did look awful. The bottom portion of the off-white canvas was black with moldy blotches, and strings of material hung off a torn seam. "Maybe we could laugh at it," I said.

Teensie scowled. "I'd rather frown," she said. "It's better."

There was a short silence. "Teensie, have you ever heard the song, 'You Can Smile?'" I asked. She shook her head. "But we can't sing it now," I said, "because sometimes when someone's upset, they won't like it."

"Yes, we can sing it now. I want to sing it now!" Teensie said. She began to sing, "You can smile, you can smile," on a made-up tune.

Barbara and I sang the chorus of the song:

You can smile; when you can't say a word, you can smile,
When you cannot be heard, you can smile,
When it's cloudy or fair, you can smile anytime, anywhere!

Everyone fell silent, as we raised our voices above the noise of the TV. "Go ahead," they said when we stopped. We sang the rest of the verses.

December 18

By Rachel

At 8:00 AM we were sound asleep, when we heard the bi-weekly call: "Laundry!" Inmates from all four cells came to the cart in the middle of the cellblock, picking out greens, towels and sheets we had sent to be washed several hours earlier.

Everyone was getting back into bed, when I noticed Teensie standing by our cell door. "Can you sing that little song for me?" she asked.

I looked to see if she was serious. "You mean about smiling?"

"Yes, I need it."

"Oh yes. I guess so," I said, rubbing my face. "I'm a little sleepy, but I'll try." Barbara and I sang a few verses.

When we stopped, Teensie had a big smile across her face. "Y'all make me smile," she said. Then we all crawled back into our beds and fell asleep again.

By Barbara Lyn

At the visit this morning Dad said the COs had told him my article on drug laws was printed in the *Buffalo News*. Later, when CO Doreen brought us a copy of the paper, we saw it in the Op-Ed page, headline reading, "Washington's Continuing War on Drugs is an Abject Failure." An editor's note at the end of the article read: "Barbara Lyn Lapp, who was found guilty in connection with a disturbance stemming from a child custody case, wrote this article from the Chautauqua County Jail."

The girls asked to have the article read aloud, and turned off the TV so everyone could hear. Rachel read it, and finished amid clapping from the girls.

In my article, I had written that I am ready "to condemn the whole government anti-drug crusade as a boondoggle." But I was surprised by the girls' reaction, as I had not mitigated the wrong of using drugs. In my closing paragraph, I had called all drug users fools. But they got a glimpse of reason and caring that can be found nowhere in the current insanity of so-called deterrents to drug use.

8:00 PM. Erica is doing her post-lock-in antics, first dancing, then dangling her long dark arms out through the bars, face pressed against the bars. In a mournful tone, she makes up her own little rhyme: "I'm all alone—wish I had a bone."

I climbed the bars on our door, straight across from her cell, and mimicked her tune, "Wish I had a home."

December 20

By Barbara Lyn

Some things aren't real. Can't be real, won't be real—until they become reality. Some things you shouldn't try to imagine—like tomorrow being the last day Rachel would go to rec with me. Or not seeing Dad and Joe when I go for a visit.

It's evening now, and Rachel just got off the phone. She's all fired up, because she discussed with the family how and when she'd meet them if she got released. She said she'd jump right over the rail in the courtroom—she wouldn't be a prisoner anymore. I reminded her our fingerprinting isn't done yet. She'd still be in prison garb, too. They usually don't let people wear regular clothes for sentencing.

By Rachel

I called Nancy, and spoke to her and five of her six children. They seem to be taking things normally, yet with feelings of suspense, like we also have. Nancy said the children didn't have the best of days. Some were edgy, some cried for Daddy. I spoke to Magdalena, but she would not discuss Daddy, or the crying.

December 21

By Barbara Lyn

This morning we got a letter from Mom. She wrote: "These last couple days our thoughts want to dwell on sentencing day—wondering if our loved ones will be relieved from this present suffering of being deprived from family, church and necessities of duties…. Let us trust that this trial does bring us all closer to God, so as to better understand God's righteousness, God's love toward us whether we are bound or free."

Our cellmate, Marita, left for a federal holding center. For the first time in more than two months, only the two of us share our cell. It's a sign from Above, we're convinced—timed exactly one day before we learn our fate at sentencing. Either God is allowing us this privacy to share our final moments alone before Rachel is taken from me, or He's ending this chapter of our life in jail altogether—giving us time to help each other put the meaning of the last four months in proper perspective.

Erica came to our cell and asked to see Rachel. She had in hand a blue checkered head scarf Rachel had lent her a few days ago, and an elaborate request: "Lapp Girl, that hair band—I was wondering if I could keep it because—because—let me see how to put this. So when I'm walking down the street, and I see this person I'm mad at, and ready to kill him, I'll put my hand up on top of my head and I'll feel the headband, and I'll think, 'Lapp Girls!' You know how y'all are for peace and harmony and don't hurt no one? And that headband will remind me, and I'll never do those bad things." Erica paused. "How does that sound?"

"It sounds pretty good," Rachel said. "I was going to give it to you, since I might be leaving tomorrow."

"So I can have it?" Erica was exultant.

"Yes, it's for you, for a memory of P.O. Box 128."

CO Sue stopped to talk at lockup time, and mentioned tomorrow's day in court. "What do you think will happen?" she asked.

"Rachel expects to go home," I said. "But my sentence could be starting all over. My first one just finished a few days ago."

"Whatever time you served already, they have to count in your sentence," said Sue. "They always count time on another sentence."

"I won't be coming back 'till tomorrow night," Sue continued. "In case you do go home, I just wanted to tell you good luck, with your family—and that."

I thanked her, then turned away in tears. It's hard to imagine Sue really caring. The whole thing hurts so bad—thinking of leaving—never having learned to trust each other.

The conversation with Sue makes us think that staff knows something about us all going home. It confuses my resolve to face more time here.

It's bedtime. My head hurts. But God understands it all.

By Rachel

I feel exhausted and sore from sitting, at the end of this maybe-last-day in Chautauqua County Jail. Thoughts flood over me and memories that seem to start from August 16. All my court appearances go through my mind, the conversations I've had with staff, lawyers, judges. The trial, yes, the trial. The many times when I thought I might go out, then heard, "Back to jail."

It seems this review of life in jail is causing release of many different chemicals in my brain. I find it very difficult to say what I really feel. It's a mixture of almost every emotion there is. I think I'm going home tomorrow.

CHAPTER 16

■   ■

One Year

December 22, 1993

By Barbara Lyn

The day that's been evading us for weeks has finally come. I greeted it before I fell asleep last night. I took my Bible to bed and read for consolation. "Though I walk through the valley of the shadow of death, I will fear no evil…." (Psalms 23:4.)

8:30 AM—a half hour to court time. CO Doreen came in. "Would you like your clothes for court?" she asked. I said we'd like to, but didn't expect to get them.

We have often seen COs bring clothes for other ladies going to court, when everyone knew they were going home. Does this mean we're going? My heart pounded as I dressed.

As we were walked up to court, the mood of the court officers was somber. There were six of them, just for Rachel and me. We met Dad and Joe in the waiting room, another officer with them. During the ten minutes we waited, they left our handcuffs on—Dad's and Joe's behind their backs. Not a single word was spoken to us. Lt. Belson's mouth stayed drawn in a tight line. Ecklund's normally boyish expression had changed to strange-looking lines etched over his face. Rater had a glazed stare, his arrogant grin missing. Even his chin was not upturned as usual.

We heard the judge bellowing orders to the spectators inside the courtroom. "No greetings, no waving, no standing," he said, "Anybody lifts a hand, you'll immediately be removed from the courtroom."

Rachel was first to see the judge. Only a minute after she'd entered the courtroom she returned to our little waiting room, a forced smile on her face. "He gave me a year," she said quietly—in Deutch to me, and to Joe in Spanish. An officer approached her with handcuffs, then hesitated. "Are you going back down?" he asked.

"I guess so," Rachel said.

"Well—what did the judge say?" he stammered.

"He gave me a year," Rachel said. The officer handcuffed her.

I was called next. Escorted by several officers, I walked into the courtroom. More officers lined the walkway, directing me with military-style hand motions. It looked like fifteen to twenty of them. I waved to the thirty-some supporters in the gallery. "Hello, everyone!" I said.

"Go on!" said an officer behind me. On my left, officers lined up so I could barely see the people.

Gibb was already at the bench, standing in front of Judge Mifsud. I approached, and he made a quick beckoning motion, directing me to stand beside him.

The judge's tone was not friendly as he read my sentence: One thousand dollar fine for the obstruction charge, plus a ninety dollar court surcharge. "You have ten days to pay the fine," he said. "On the second charge of resisting arrest, you're hereby sentenced to one year in the county jail." In almost the same breath, he said to the officers, "Will you please remove the prisoner?"

Walking past the spectators, I said, "They haven't convinced me I'm a criminal yet." I waved my arm at full height. Officers pressed onto me.

Back at the jail, the COs searched our faces. Only minutes before they had wished us luck. Doreen unlocked the gate to our cell block. "What did you get?" she asked.

"A year—for both of us," Rachel said.

A little later I returned our clothes to Doreen. She sighed and let her shoulders drop. "I can't believe this, Barbara. I thought I was going to be giving you your clothes to keep this time."

Rachel soon announced to the girls that we were going to lose our business, and won't be able to have a fruit stand next year. Even with "good time" we wouldn't be out until April. Carla looked shocked. She said there has to be a way to keep the fruit stand. She suggested her brother could help out.

The whole cell block seemed shaken. Paying huge fines while still in jail is unheard of. "My judge gave me thirty days to pay just five dollars!" Erica exclaimed.

By Rachel

I'm still not comprehending that we're just halfway through our stay in the pen. After talking to the girls, I flopped down on a mat and declared I want to go home, then said to whoever wanted to hear, "I'm going home now." I even ate an orange, skin and all, in memory of the day I got a year in jail.

"Rachel's going crazy," some of the girls said as they watched me eat on the orange like an apple.

We spent time putting our boxes of meager possessions in order under our bed. We went to rec—to the gym I'd thought I wouldn't see again. We were called for visits with family and friends. Dad and Joe had gotten the same sentence. Everyone was subdued. Nancy was crying. Her children were loving and composed, sitting with their father and us on the prisoners' side of the table.

It's a day of many changes. Flora and Erica moved in with us, to clear a cell for Lynn, who was also sentenced to one year. She is double locked again, because she won't take the TB test.

Erica reminded the girls in the other cells they had promised to sing, "You Can Smile" for us if we didn't go home today. They did a beautiful performance that indeed made us smile—until CO Brenda came in scolding us about the noise, saying she can't hear on the phone.

Barbara and I are talking about new goals. More diligent study, better schedules. "You have to get a notebook and study English vocabulary," I told Barbara. Both of us are getting books for that, as well as new clothing to stay more comfortable. We're going to try to improve our health, too. Barbara has to get a lotion for a facial skin problem. I've resolved to be regular with exercises. And I'm going to try to get more nutrients by eating orange skins sometimes.

December 23

By Rachel

Jail life didn't change. CO Brenda and Teensie started the morning arguing again. It began late last evening when Teensie blew up at Brenda, after Brenda had snubbed her for asking to have the curtain pulled so she could use the bathroom. There's one cell here that can be seen from the office when the curtain is open, and a man was being booked. Brenda had told Teensie it was "bullshit" to want the curtain closed, "like anybody's gonna look in here." A hot, vulgar argument ensued.

This morning Brenda left Teensie double locked, and stood by her cell watching, in silent taunting. Teensie blew up again, threatening to assault Brenda and "get me a new charge."

A little later when Brenda opened the cell to let Teensie's cellmate out, Teensie pretended to lunge at her. Brenda jumped, apparently in fright, then began to swear at Teensie. Teensie laughed, but Brenda was furious.

After Brenda went out I told the others that it was wrong of Brenda to do what she did to Teensie last night. Everyone agreed. Erica and Flora supported Teensie too, but they stayed silent, as they are to be released today. It made for a rather tense breakfast. Some didn't eat.

I was trembling. I felt I should tell Brenda she was wrong in treating Teensie like that. But it's terribly hard to speak up when things are already tense. Then Brenda surprised us by telling Barbara and me that we would be put in the double locked cell with Lynn. Brenda said we could ask whenever we wanted to get out. I began to seethe.

Brenda was coming in and out of the cellblock, serving, working on papers, and letting some of the girls out. Finally I spoke. "Brenda, we are of the understanding that if a person doesn't take a TB test, she has to be isolated," I said. "How can you put us in with Lynn?" I mentioned that my father had been isolated for two months.

"I didn't know you'd be afraid to be with Lynn," Brenda said.

"It's not that we're *afraid* of Lynn," Barbara said. "It's just that we know what the rules are."

Brenda said she'd talk to the sergeant. When she came back, she moved Lynn to another cell and locked her up alone.

The issue of Brenda's injustice to Teensie was still on my mind. Finally I got the courage to speak. "Brenda, I have to tell you, I think you brought a disgrace on this place with what you did to Teensie last night," I said. "There are a lot of girls in here that heard it."

"And there's a lot of people out in the office who heard what was said in here," Brenda retorted.

"Yes," I said. "You know I don't like bad language. But you started it. Privacy is a right."

"That may be your opinion, Rachel," Brenda said, her voice trembling. "But this really is none of your business. If you want to keep this up you'll get your share of the punishment too!"

The whole room was quiet. "I don't believe in bad language," I said to the girls, "but I believe people should respect each other."

From her locked cell, just a few feet away Teensie responded, "I won't use any more nasty language."

Soon Louise took over the shift. Erica and Flora left, hugging their friends goodbye. I told them to listen to God's Word. Erica responded that she can't do evil now because she has this (touching her scarf) and she would remember the "Lapp girls."

"I hope you'll not only remember us," I said, "but also our God, who is watching us and you at all times."

"Word," she said.

When the girls left, Teensie spoke from her locked cell. "You know how y'all say it's wrong to use these words, but *where* in the Bible does it say you can't say sh - - and f - - -? It's just a slang way of expressing ourselves." Tamara and another girl chimed in, agreeing.

I pondered their questions for a moment, then said, "I'm not telling you what you have to do. I'm not your judge, God is. But I believe if you would read in the Bible you would see that Jesus does require us to be moderate with our language and to speak words that are for edification."

Louise came in, and spoke to us about our sentence. "No one here expected it," she said, shaking her head. "I was talking to a sergeant upstairs, and I was saying, 'If they'd have it as a law, then give everybody the same.' I've seen people with Class C felonies doing only months."

"I know," I said. "We see it."

Louise said our sentence is the result of a small town's officials not having enough to do. She also said we need more women in public office.

"You think so?" I asked.

"Yes. The judge did whatever he felt like, to control you," Louise said. "That's the way men are. You see how men don't like cats? It's because you can't tell a cat to come, and be sure it will come right away. You can't control a cat."

"I don't have any particular problem with men," I said. (Louise chuckled.) "But I just wish there would be a return to justice."

I told Louise about the fines. "Joe's family has nothing, after him being here for four months," I said. "They're afraid of losing their house."

Louise said she understands, as her family had to take out a loan just to pay taxes.

"I have something else to ask," I told Louise. "Is there any possibility of us getting something to do here? Anything—like cleaning the office, or hall—just to occupy ourselves."

Louise sighed. "Carole and I have been trying for years to get permission for female inmates to work," she said. "It's like hitting a stone wall." But she promised she'd try again.

A little later Louise called Barbara and me to the fence. "Would either of you like to go up to the chest clinic to interpret for Lupe and her husband?"

Barbara said I should go, since my Spanish is better than hers. I was excited. This would be my first outing. I grabbed my Spanish/English dictionary, and followed Louise to the office, where we waited for a guard to take me to the clinic across the street. Swanee was hanging around the office.

"What are you waiting for?" I asked casually.

"Lunch. That's what I come to work for."

Louise said she'd have Barbara put my lunch aside.

"No problem," I said. "I'm not here for the food."

"Good," said Swanee. "Then I'll get your sub."

I turned to Louise. "Actually, I don't have much trouble with the food here. The worst thing is the lack of fruits and vegetables."

"The problem is, most of the girls don't care for them, and they'd get tossed," Louise said.

"I know. But what about having them available in commissary?"

"They wouldn't sell."

"They wouldn't? Well—what about dried fruit, like raisins or prunes?"

Sgt. Bohn, sitting at his desk, had stopped his work to listen. I had a purpose in bringing this up. We heard there will be a new list for commissary soon, when we get moved to the new section of the jail. Some of the girls have complained that commissary has no healthy options—five kinds each of hard candy and candy bars, three kinds of cookies, pretzels, snacks, coffee, tea—no juices or dried fruit.

"We used to have fruit," Louise said. "We had to quit. The men used it to make wine."

I made a face, and looked down. "But raisins?"

Sgt. Bohn spoke. "It didn't work. They were making wine with them."

"They come up with anything, Rachel," Louise said. "Even with the oranges and apples they've done it."

Swanee joined the conversation. "Mix fruit with bread, sugar, water, let it set. It tastes like turpentine, but it'll get you drunk."

Another CO, Dale Austin, came to the office. He gave me a very big, old, denim coat with paint splattered over it. Then, to my surprise and embarrassment, he produced handcuffs. "Oh, I won't run," I moaned as he put them on.

"I know," he said.

We stepped into the world, into bright light. I was overwhelmed. The goodness, freshness, light. "Oh—the air," I said, taking a deep breath. I wanted to stand still, to think, to absorb, to pray. I put my head down into my cuffed hands for a moment, then followed Austin along a sidewalk banked with snow on both sides.

"So you're staying 'till April?" Austin asked.

"I guess so. I was rather surprised—don't know if I'm comprehending it yet."

"We were surprised too," Austin said. "None of us expected it."

We entered another building, then the nurse's office. I sat facing Lupe, still wearing my handcuffs and huge coat. CO Austin stayed in the room with us. The nurse asked Lupe several medical questions, and followed with instructions for her. Improvising a few words and using some I'd learned just recently, I managed to translate. Then we went to another room, where we met Lupe's husband and the doctor.

"I'm Dr. Burke," said the man seated in the chair as we walked in. He smiled slightly. "I know your sisters well. Don't think I've met you."

I recognized his name as the doctor who'd delivered my sisters' babies. Now he sees me clad and bound like a criminal. I wanted to disappear. But I was able to forget my handcuffs as I applied myself to the job, translating for the doctor.

By Barbara Lyn

A friend I spoke to on the phone this afternoon said her son could help with work on our farm, so we can keep our business going. Rachel and I discussed it with Carla. She said we should ask Lt. Belson for permission to have Rachel's vegetable records and seed catalogs sent in, so she could place orders from here. Rachel thinks it's impossible. She says she doesn't feel like asking a favor of the staff here.

Tonight Brenda was finishing her second day of working double shifts. She looked so exhausted it was pathetic.

"What are they trying to do to you, Brenda?" I asked, "working you like this?" She rolled her eyes and sank in her chair.

"To tell you the truth, Barbara, I've told them this is it." She shook her head. "I can't take it any more." Later she came in and talked with Teensie for a long time. I didn't hear much, but it sounded as though they each made some apologies. I can't imagine Brenda quitting.

Reading in Titus this evening, I came across a verse that says we should be "subject to principalities and powers," and obey magistrates. Yet when the police came for Billy last July, I know I would have had to abandon the rest of Gospel teaching if I were to take the verse in Titus at face value. In another letter by St. Paul, he said he was a prisoner for the sake of Christ. He must have disobeyed magistrates in order to land in jail. Where did he draw the line? St. Peter once said, "We ought to obey God rather than men." Is it when man's law conflicts with God's law that we may be compelled to disobey?

My conscience seems to be telling me that handing Judge Mifsud a thousand dollars would be dishonorable. I'm not saying he can't have it. He might be able to get it by force. But then at least I would not be responsible for contributing voluntarily to corruption and lies.

December 24

By Barbara Lyn

I wonder if we'll be cold all winter. They say the heat can't be turned up enough to keep us warm in here, because it makes other areas of the jail too warm. Mom told us Dad, on third floor, sometimes gets so hot he almost can't breathe. He has to take off his shirt and put wet towels on himself. Whenever we go out, we find it's warm in the office and halls. Our concrete block walls without insulation, and the windows, are what's letting the cold in down here.

Rachel and I were called out for a TV interview with *Newswatch 35*. They're doing a Christmas story on our family. The reporter, Dave Belmondo, was the one who had covered my trial.

This was the first time Rachel was with me for an interview. It made me relax. She mentioned that the meaning of the season was peace and goodwill, and said that our imprisonment is an expression of love for children.

Dave said someone from the "inside" told him they had never before seen a sentence like ours imposed. "The judge threw the book at you," he said.

We watched the TV program at six, sitting on the floor with our cellmates. Miriam's face came on first, with the anchorman saying, "She wants her mom home, but she'll have to wait a little longer."

I was shocked to hear myself on TV saying, "I won't pay the judge— not a rusty penny." Now the whole world knows it. Really, I'm not ashamed. The judge should have known better than to ask me to pay him for prosecuting me.

Tamara just got news she could leave. We all cheered and hugged her. She wept for joy. As of yesterday, she was short a couple hundred on bail. I think the department worked something out because it's Christmas Eve.

December 25

By Barbara Lyn

Today is the day proclaimed to be the birthday of Christ. In our minds, it is another day to serve Him, but not without a reminder of the significance of His coming.

Mary, the jail cook, came in with Carole this morning, carrying a tray of homemade Christmas cookies. She said she made most of them right here in the jail kitchen. Others were donated by local churches.

We got to talking to Mary about the menu. Rachel told of her conversation with staff about getting more fruits and vegetables. "Seems awful I can't have fruit, just because somebody wants to make wine," Rachel said. Mary and Carole laughed.

A half hour later, Mary brought a small bag of raisins and prunes for each of the girls. She said she also got permission from Sgt. Bohn to add an extra fresh fruit to the women's menu once a week. The girls were impressed. "Rachel, you're gonna be our spokesperson!" they said.

We also talked to Mary and Carole about getting work. Mary said she'd like women's help in the kitchen, but the jail doesn't want men and women inmates working together. They tried it once in the laundry, and it didn't work.

At our visit today, CO Bowen, a short, older officer, asked if we wanted a whole hour, since there was no one else in the waiting room. Nancy smiled as she asked if we could still have a half hour tomorrow. The COs laughed.

"We can't do that," Bowen said, "but we'll give you a little extra today, and you'll still get the half hour tomorrow. Just because of Jacob, because he's so good," he teased. "And Joe—he's pretty good, too." Dad kidded that he wouldn't be any better than Joe, if he had Joe's youthful strength. The extra fifteen minutes—a Christmas goodwill on the part of the COs—was a beautiful gift. Better than the cookies and candy the other COs brought us.

At lunchtime we had a peaceful dinner consisting of ham and sweet potatoes, corn and apple-cranberry sauce. After lunch we were sleepy, but too cold to think of napping.

At 3:00 Louise came in with a stack of nine blankets, one for each of us. She said she'd gotten them without permission, and kidded, "What can they do? Fire me?" Louise helped the girls drape blankets over three of the windows in the block, to help keep out the cold. Our window doesn't have hooks to put up a blanket. But the extra blankets on our beds will help.

My treasure today was the first five chapters of Hebrews. St. Paul explains our brotherhood with Christ, into which we enter by sharing in Christ's suffering. "Though He were a Son, yet learned He obedience by the things which He suffered." (Hebrews 5:8.)

I've been contemplating the fines. Why do I feel so strongly it would be wrong to sign a $1090 check for Judge Mifsud? How will I feel about family members who might wish to avoid further difficulty by paying? I'm not in this for a game, or for butting heads with Mifsud. God knows my desperation for relief from separation with my family and church. But He has planted in my soul an abhorrence of hypocrisy, deceit—and above all, oppression of the poor.

I tested the strength of my feelings about the fine, by envisioning myself paying it—getting out the checkbook, reluctantly writing out the check, then signing it. Next I imagined getting an envelope. By the time I was affixing the stamp I was miserable. I did it anyway, and sealed the envelope. But instead of heading for the mailbox, I stood and stared at what I had just done—the envelope I addressed, the check inside with my signature. My own doings. One thousand dollars to enable the court to hurt more people. The final vision in my imaginary doings was myself tearing the envelope—check and all—into pieces.

Then I was sure. I shouldn't do it. Wouldn't do it. Couldn't do it. No one could make me do it. I felt peaceful. "Glory to God in the highest, and on earth peace, and goodwill toward men."

December 26

By Barbara Lyn

The jail had a sudden power failure tonight at 7:00. The lights and TV went off. The main heating system, phone, and hot water were gone too. One dim light in the hall outside the office and the small electric heater miraculously remained.

We were cold, and knew it would get colder. Outside, the windchill was twenty below zero. We each brought our mats, put them down in the common area in front of the tiny heater, and groped around in the dark to gather our blankets. Louise allowed Teensie out of lock. A couple girls stayed in their cells, too frightened to move. But we coaxed them to join us. Forming a tight circle—nine women on mats—blankets around us, we leaned on each other for warmth. Some complained, some laughed, some were afraid. Others got pretzels and passed them around. One girl was afraid something would come out of the shower, and wanted me to take the shower curtain down. We laughed, and pulled her close.

"I like it because I can't see the bars," I told the girls. "I can forget I'm in jail, and make believe we're camping."

Several girls moaned.

"These girls aren't country girls like you and me, Barbara," Louise chimed in. We hadn't known she was listening to our conversation.

"Let's tell stories about the dark," I suggested. I started by telling the story of my dark early-morning ride in a dugout on the jungle river in Belize. "It was much darker than this because there was no light at all," I told them.

Just then our last light went off, and the small heater, too. Several girls screamed. But soon they relaxed, and each one took her turn to recount a personal experience about fright in the dark.

Louise kept coming to check on us. She knew a few of the ladies were near panic. She suggested we could pray when our stories are done. A small lady who had been speechless, huddled on the outside of the circle for the last half hour, spoke. "It's time to pray now," she said.

I started the Lord's Prayer. "Our Father which art in heaven, hallowed be Thy name. Thy kingdom come. Thy will be done...." Others followed in unison. Then Rachel and I sang, "Nearer My God to Thee."

"That makes me feel peaceful," one of the girls said. Lynn followed with one of her songs, then we sang, "Amazing Grace." Almost everyone helped.

"That's nice!" someone said. "Sing it over again." Halfway through the song, the lights came on with blinding brightness. Whoops of delight filled the cellblock. It had been an hour and fifteen minutes of darkness.

Louise brought popcorn and praised us all for holding out. She said quietly to Rachel and me, "I want to thank you for your cooperation—it helped a lot." Then she locked all of us into our cells for the night.

December 27

By Barbara Lyn

On the phone tonight the family said radio talk shows are flooded with callers commenting on our sentence, with most expressing outrage about it. Miriam came to the phone to talk, but she just cried. She has the flu, and thinks she needs her mom.

Susan also told us about a *Post-Journal* story that praised Judge

Mifsud for setting a state record by presiding over our five trials simultaneously. In the article, Mifsud said he did everything in his power to see to it that the defendants' individual rights were not trampled, and commented that the convictions could be appealed. Susan suggested Mifsud probably made the unreasonable sentences to try to tempt us into appealing.

By Rachel

It makes me sad that some in my family still talk of appealing, or paying our fines. I think of the many needs in the world. We work hard to earn, always wishing for more time or money to give to those who are hurting. Wives who've lost their husbands, or husbands too ill to work. Children without parents. I think of Lynn, now in jail with us because she came to my father's aid. Her children at home, but who is to feed everyone? Is there any desire left to write out large checks to Mifsud? I'd rather starve, or freeze to death.

Lying on a mat now, I'm covered with a blanket as I write. I'm wearing four layers on my top, two on bottom, a towel tied around my head, and two pairs of socks. As long as I don't sit up, I'm pretty warm. We've told all the COs about the cold. They all say the same thing—they can't put more heat into this garage without getting it too warm upstairs. Or, like Louise said last night, "It's going to be cold, Miss, until we get this boiler fixed."

When Sue came today I said, "Sue, it's terribly cold in here. It's time for something to be done."

She opened the door and came in, saying, "It's a *little* cold, but— not bad." I told her to check my cell, which is the coldest. She claimed it was cold only because we had hung clothes on the heat registers. I had a towel hanging from one of the three registers. I didn't tell her that I'd be sick tonight if that towel didn't dry in time for me to wrap it around my head for sleeping. I asked Sue if we could have warm hats and coats sent in. She said we couldn't, and soon went out.

While eating supper tonight, I chipped a tooth. I told Sue about it. She said the jail doctor comes on Wednesday, and I must wait to get his approval for a dentist. I showed her the large chip that had broken from my tooth. Then she said I could write to Lt. Belson and ask for an emergency appointment. She also said I could see my own dentist if I was willing to pay.

December 28

By Rachel

I just got word from the CO that Lt. Belson said no to the 4:15 appointment Mom made with my dentist. He says staff will make an appointment with the dentist in Mayville, the one where all the inmates go.

I'm not enthused about entrusting my teeth to the care of someone who doesn't know me, especially one with a government job. I'm also thinking of the folly of this. I could pay, saving the taxpayers. Maybe Belson is worried about me being too friendly with my own doctor, and having him find out this jail doesn't allow dental floss.

When I wrote to Lt. Belson about my tooth last night, I put at the bottom of the letter: "P.S. We are cold. *Very* cold." This morning Sgt. Stage and CO Crowell came in, checking things out. They made a few adjustments, and put a big rotating fan up by the ceiling. It helped.

At the gym today Sgt. Paul Stage asked me if I have things in order at the farm, ready for spring.

"Well, that's a little hard to do from this position," I said. "I normally order seeds in December and January, but I can't do it without my seed catalogs and record books."

Paul said he thought they could work something out to have the books sent in here. He seemed incredulous when I said we weren't sure if we would open the fruit stand this year. "I'd be willing to help," he said. I looked at him with surprise. "Not that I agree with everything," he said. "I agree with your position, but just not with the way you're going about it."

Later Barbara and I discussed ordering seeds from jail. I said, "Let's not do it."

We don't think it would be wise to invest in crops when things are so precarious financially. "How can we, with Joe not trimming grapes?" Barbara said. "And Dad not cutting firewood—and us paying help to get our cows milked?"

December 29

By Barbara Lyn

It was a big surprise when Doreen called Rachel and me to see Sgt. Bohn this morning. He asked if we would be interested in working in the kitchen, and told us what the job required—work from 5:30 in the morning to 5:30 at night, with time off for meals and visits. Nothing could be taken from the kitchen to our cell without permission from a CO, and nothing for the other girls. "It's not something we've ever done before," Sgt. Bohn said. "But we're willing to give it a try. If it doesn't work out for you, you don't have to stay."

Rachel and I were surprised at the long hours, but agreed to start. "We appreciate you giving us a chance." I said.

Doreen took us to the kitchen, where the cooks, Mary and Blanche, showed us around. They said we should eat anything we like, including vegetables and fruits from the cooler.

With instructions from the cooks, we set the buffet table where jail staff and trusties serve themselves. Besides the stew the rest of the inmates got, the table had salad with choice of four dressings, and homemade banana bread. We were prepared to return to our cells for lunch when Mary invited us to stay. She put a little table in the kitchen storeroom.

"The sergeant said we'd return to our cells for meals," I told her.

Mary asked Sgt. Bohn if we could eat lunch with them. He said the plan was to have us go to our cells, but we could fill our plates here, then take them back. Rachel said we'd prefer to eat what the other girls eat, so there wouldn't be bad feelings.

Coming back from our first shift, Doreen asked if we got some treats in the kitchen. "No, not yet," I said. "It was enough to get my hands on some real work."

"Real what?" asked Sgt. Bohn, who was sitting at the desk.

"Real work," I repeated. "I enjoyed it." He nodded.

This afternoon Sgt. Paul Stage came into the kitchen with a big smile. "It's nice to see you working," he said. "How do you like it?"

CO Sue came in on her shift at three, and found us working. She spent time around the kitchen, watching us, and didn't look too happy.

The cooks, both middle-aged women, gave us a lot of trust, even asked for cooking suggestions. The four trusties who work in the kitchen answered all our questions about work, and where things belonged. They wanted to send extra bananas back to the cell with us, and were unhappy when Sue firmly said that we couldn't.

December 30

By Rachel

This morning we loaded breakfast carts for four different floors, then cleaned kitchen shelves, cabinets and sinks. The trusties pitched in, moving cabinets and scraping accumulated dirt off the legs of the tables with knives and scouring pads. We followed with soapy rags. Mary and Blanche said they couldn't believe how lucky they were to have us. "The guys do a good job, but they don't have the natural ability to clean," Mary said.

We hadn't eaten enough at breakfast for this type of work, and I got hungry. One of the trusties mixed up some tuna salad and offered me a sandwich. Mary brought decaffeinated coffee when she heard we liked it—and some of her homemade yogurt with pineapple.

Barbara and I were dishing out pudding for the inmates' meals when Jim Crowell and another CO came to the kitchen. "It's nice to see you in here," Jim said sincerely.

"About time we get some good people in here," the other CO joked.

Lt. Belson came to the kitchen, but didn't look at us.

The trusties treat us like dignitaries. The best part of the day was when three of them brought big coats for Barbara and me and asked if we're going outside with them.

"Who said? Who's taking us?" I demanded.

"Mary gave permission," they explained excitedly. "We're gonna unload the delivery truck, and you can help."

"Oh, yes!" I exclaimed. They laughed, then led the way—across the hall, through the jail laundry room, out a back door, and past the window of our cell. A CO supervised. We picked up boxes of supplies from the truck and carried them back to the kitchen storage.

December 31

By Barbara Lyn

The state jail inspector was here several days ago, and ordered that our little heater be taken out. He said it's against fire code. It was so cold last night I didn't sleep well, and got a sore throat. Some of the other ladies are sick too, and cursing about the cold.

We received some warm sweat shirts in the mail, sent by the family. Brenda showed us the clothes, but apologetically said we can't have them because they had buttons.

"It's intolerable!" Rachel declared. "It's inhuman!"

The inspector returned today, apparently concerned about the cold conditions he found the other day, and ordered the jail to get heat in here—but not with the spare heater. As I write, it's as cold as ever.

When Brenda took us out to work she told us they are trying to get Dad and Joe down here to work as trusties. I told her Dad says he doesn't think he wants to work for the jail. This evening the girls told us they had overheard Brenda and another CO talking about "that old man who won't accept he ever committed a crime." One of them was heard saying, "He is responsible for the downfall of this whole family."

■ CHAPTER 17 ■

Serving our Captors

December 31, 1993

By Rachel

9:00 PM and I haven't picked up a pen or a book all day. Quite a rarity for jail life. But now it's not cell life alone anymore. Now it's making normal decisions—like when to pour coffee for third floor, so it's ready when Barbara and the trusties have the plates on the cart, but not too soon, else it cools before it gets served. The COs then pick up the carts. We work closely with them, which is a change from having them order every move we make.

Maybe that's why it struck me so hard when a CO put shackles and handcuffs on me today, to drive a few miles to the dentist. I had to keep my chains on, even in the dentist's chair.

Sgt. Bohn was sitting in the office when I came back. "Did you cry?" he joked. "Did they give you a sucker?" One of the COs had just asked me to get on my knees on a chair, so he could remove the shackles. He'd done the same to put them on.

I shook my head. "If I would have cried about anything, it would have been about you putting these shackles on me. It's completely humiliating."

"I'm sorry if we humiliated you, Rachel," the CO said. "We didn't mean to. We're just following orders."

Another CO, seated nearby, said, "So were the Nazis."

I looked up in surprise. "That's right," I said.

"Depends, though, on what orders you're following," he said.

"It certainly does."

"Like if they told me to beat you, I wouldn't," he said. "This is a necessary rule, because some people here need the chains."

I contained my grief until evening. In the safety of my cell, I sat on my mat and wept.

January 1, 1994

By Barbara Lyn

What can I say but, "Welcome, New Year!" Everything God made is very good, even New Year's Day in jail. At home they sang New Year's hymns without us.

At our visit I talked to Dad about his decision not to become a trusty. "My name won't be Jake Lapp if I ever work for this jail!" he said. The guards standing nearby smiled, and Dad did too.

Back in the kitchen, Mary called us aside to talk with Sgt. Bohn about a new work arrangement for Rachel and me. Apparently the trusties had complained about us not helping with cleanup after meals, when we go back to our cells to eat. We accepted Bohn's recommendation that we now eat in the kitchen storeroom, help with dishes, then return for breaks in our cellblock whenever the trusties take their breaks.

Later we heard Mary tell CO Doreen that Sgt. Bohn had made us trusties. We thought we were just kitchen servants, getting good food in exchange for work. We ate well today. Lots of fruits, lemon tea, and the banana bread Rachel made.

Subconsciously I resist feelings of pleasure, as I work and eat. I'm still within bars and gunmen rule. And I should be doing this work at home, taking responsibility as a mother. Yet there are moments of genuine enjoyment, simply because I'm working with my hands, and making people like Mary, the cook, happy.

7:00 PM. I'm exhausted. I think I'm getting sick. We've been getting up at 5:10 for work, still going to bed near midnight. Sleep isn't so good when it's cold. Tonight Brenda gave extra mats for those of us who sleep on the floor. It helps to get us off the cold cement.

January 2

By Barbara Lyn

I took the noon shift off, skipping lunch, because of fever and a cold. This afternoon I decided to work, despite my aching. At dinner time I found an onion in the cooler, and piled thick slices of it on my cheeseburger. It made me sweat, relieving my fever.

It was the first onion I'd had in four and a half months. I wished I could send some slices up to third floor for Dad. But they'd never let us do that. We can make good things, but just for jail staff, the rest of the trusties, and us. That makes working in the kitchen sad.

In the cell tonight, it's still cold. I'm chilling with fever. I feel like another night in here could finish me off.

By Rachel

Though we work long hours away from the cellblock, our friendship with the girls continues. It comes naturally to speak to different ones of them throughout the day when we return for breaks. This morning I gave Sammie, a soft-spoken teenage girl, a massage. She had become feverish overnight, and was lying in bed very quiet. Next I spoke to Teensie about when she's going to court, and when she'll get out of double lock.

Lupe, our cellmate, told me I should rest at breaks. I said I might not wake up in time to work. She said she'd wake me. Then I said maybe it's good to write in the day and sleep at night. She responded in her delightful, emphatic manner, counting her fingers: "Tu escribes en la mañana, en el día, *y* en la noche!" ("You write in the morning, in the day, *and* at night!")

In the kitchen, Blanche mentioned that Monday is a big day for food preparations and asked me for recipe ideas. She said she tries to cook extra things because "it's court day, and the investigators come for lunch."

Blanche's mention of court day hit me. During our trial some of the officers had begun their testimony about the August 16 melee by saying, "It was Monday and we were taking inmates to and from court." I thought of the six officers who took Barbara and me to our sentencing, and the crowds more in the courtroom standing to make a wall between us and our loved ones.

Yes, I'd love to bake scalloped potatoes with a little buttermilk and cheese. Blanche thought the recipe sounded fabulous. But is it okay to cook for these tyrants? Should I just think, "If thine enemy hunger, feed him; if he thirsts, give him drink?" (Romans 12:20.)

When I sat beside Dad at the visit today, I mentioned this conflict. "What do you think, Dad?" I asked.

Dad said I should keep in mind that life is short. "These things will pass," he said. "Just do your best, and look forward to eternal life." His words were encouraging. He never referred to the good or bad, or yes or no of our work. As always, he gives his confidence.

January 3

By Barbara Lyn

Three times a day, at mealtime, Rachel and I help fill food carts for the inmates, and prepare the buffet table. Then we get in line, fill our plates, go to the storage room, and close the door—except for a crack. At a tiny metal tea table, Rachel sits on an inverted bucket, and

I find a banana box or a bag of rice to use as a chair. We bow our heads in silent prayer, then for about fifteen minutes we eat and converse in peace. No radio or TV nearby, no bad language, and no camera on us.

This evening one of the trusties told me yesterday's *Evening Observer* had a big picture of the August 16 melee, highlighted as one of the major events of 1993. We discussed our arrest with the trusties, for the first time.

Then as I took the food cart down to the women's block, I walked into Lt. Lawrence in the hallway. He said, "Hello Barbara, how are you?"

"Good," I said, walking on.

I'd like to ask him if he thinks all this was worth it, and what he thinks was gained by arresting me and the others. Maybe before I leave jail I'll ask to talk to him.

January 4

By Barbara Lyn

I received a letter from the county attorney who had wanted to question me, without witnesses present, on the jurisdictional challenge several weeks ago. He wrote he had reviewed case law, and concluded that I am entitled to have one witness present during questioning. But not two witnesses, or one witness and a tape recorder, as I had stipulated.

That's his way of closing the case, I guess. I'm not going to give up my right to a public trial just because of some quasi-court's ridiculous interpretation of case law. There's no use even beginning with a case against the county if we're not going to have a level playing field.

In other legal news, our fines are now due. What will happen next? A lien on my car? Or for Dad, on the land? Will they collect by selling the property?

Louise came today for the first time since Rachel and I started working. When she took us to the kitchen this morning she said she was shocked to hear they had us working with the men. "Some of those men, I don't even know why they ever made them trusties," she said, then mumbled something about their "animal instincts."

"We haven't had any problems," I said.

"If you ever do have a problem, just let me know right away," she said, in a motherly manner. "You don't even need to wait until the end of the shift to report it."

Louise probably doesn't realize that working with those men, however low their character, is a small difficulty when compared with our dealings with the men in uniform. True, there are some trusties who would take advantage of us if we'd let them. But they would be afraid to go too far, knowing they would either lose their trusty status, or lose our help in the kitchen. The uniformed men don't have anything to lose when they go too far. They have treated us like no other men ever did. They grabbed us at their convenience to use force on us, they stood and gawked, they used obscenities in our presence, and even helped pull off our clothes. They still have their jobs.

By Rachel

This morning's work was done early, and we had a two-hour break ahead. I was tired, with a sore throat and headache. I said to the girls, "Who will promise to call me at ten, and take the heat if I get to work late and get yelled at because you forgot?"

Carla raised her hand. I made my bed, hanging a large towel from the upper bunk to provide hiding for my head. I put in my ear plugs, and settled in.

I had fallen into a deep sleep when Doreen called. "Jim is coming in to fix your sink. Is everyone dressed?"

"Is it alright if I stay in bed?" I asked. Barbara appeared to be sound asleep in her corner on the floor.

Doreen said it was okay, and she and CO Jim Crowell came in. "Is it the toilet that's leaking?" Jim was asking Doreen. "Which button is it?"

I couldn't go back to sleep. I jumped out of bed and showed them where the problem was. When Jim went out I told Carla, "I still have an hour left. Guess I'll try napping again." I had just dozed off when I heard a two-way radio crackling and realized Jim was working on the sink again. I gave up my nap, folded my blankets, and went to the common table to write until we were called for work.

January 5

By Rachel

This morning Brenda called us to the fence and brought up the subject I feared would come. Fingerprinting. A feeling of heat swept through me.

Barbara told Brenda she wouldn't voluntarily go to be printed, but if they want to do it, she can't prevent them. I told Brenda I felt the same way.

"Does that mean you're going to just stand there, or what?" Brenda asked carefully.

"Maybe we should speak to them," Barbara said.

Brenda agreed to take us out to the sergeant. In the office, Sgt. Bohn looked friendly. He sat leaning back in his chair. A couple of COs were standing by the wall.

First we discussed a package of clothing that had arrived from home. The sergeant and COs seemed amused at the large size of some square flannel cloths Mom had sent for us to fold as head scarves. Sgt. Bohn asked what they're for, then said we could have them. I think they were worried we'd use them for skirts.

"Now we have to talk about fingerprinting," he said. "I know you don't agree with it, and you don't like it. But the state requires us to do it before you leave."

Barbara and I were silent. Bohn continued. "I don't know if it's a problem for you." He smiled. "You don't have to do anything—I can take care of it."

"Yes, I would have a problem with cooperating with this," Barbara said. "I'm sure you realize we don't agree we're criminals."

"It's not my decision," Bohn said, his tone still gentle. "It's something we're required to do before we release someone."

CO Austin, who stood nearby with another CO, added, "We have nothing to do with this. It's the court that decides these matters."

"You have the guns," Barbara said. "We don't have any say."

"We *never* hold a gun to anyone for fingerprinting," Austin said.

There was more silence, then I spoke. "What's the purpose of fingerprinting?"

"It's a requirement of the state," Bohn said.

"But what's it for?"

Bohn shifted in his chair. "Basically it's something the state requires for their records."

"So it's for putting me on record as a criminal?"

CO Austin muffled a laugh, looking down. Sgt. Bohn had an uneasy smile. "Well, I guess that could be another way of putting it," he said.

"I look at it like this," I said. "I never bothered you, or anyone else, so you shouldn't bother me either."

"We have no choice," Austin said.

Another silence. Bohn said, "It has to be done."

"In your opinion," I said.

He chuckled. "No, in the court's opinion."

Barbara told Bohn it was getting late for going to the kitchen. He left for a moment, saying he'd tell Mary we'd be late. When he returned, he relaxed in his chair again. "Well, what do you say, get it over with?"

"That's up to you," I said.

Bohn slowly got up, went to the printing apparatus in the corner of the office, and prepared the ink. The COs got numbers ready for our photos, and got information from the computer. "We don't have Barbara's social security number," one of them said. Barbara was silent. More COs came in and out of the office, keeping friendly conversation going. CO Brenda spoke to me about Marita, the Guatemalan girl, who is now staying with our family while awaiting deportation.

By Barbara Lyn

"Step over here Barb," Bohn said suddenly. Forgetting I wasn't going to cooperate, I walked toward him. He put his hands on my shoulders, and positioned me in front of the camera for the mugshot.

CO Austin was on the camera, just in front of me. I kept my eyes downcast, reading newspaper headlines on the floor. "Smile, Barbara!" someone said. The camera flashed, then Bohn turned my body for the side picture. "If you don't smile, you'll look like a convict," Austin said. Their ill-fitting comments made me smile.

Sgt. Bohn repositioned me for fingerprinting. He pressed one finger at a time onto an ink strip, then onto stiff paper. Last of all he printed the palm of my hand. Each hand was printed twice. Then they gave me a gel for ink removal, and told me to wash in a sink nearby.

"I need you to sign at the bottom of these prints," Brenda said, as I dried my hands.

Her normal manner startled me. "Brenda, I won't sign!" I said. "I'm sorry, Brenda, I thought you would know." She and Sgt. Bohn said they don't know whether the state will accept the prints without a signature. Bohn said I was excused. I went to the kitchen to work.

By Rachel

Sgt. Bohn didn't even ask me to step up for the mugshot. He put his arm across my back, moved me forward abruptly, and positioned me on the foot marks. Austin held the plate with my number in front of my chest. Bohn snapped the camera. "Guess Rachel won't smile either," he said. Then he came over beside me, picked up my hand, and moved me into the positions he wanted for printing, without speaking.

After I washed up, I asked, "May I go to the kitchen now?"

"Yes," Bohn said. "My job is done. But I don't know what they'll say about no signature."

Ten minutes later Bohn came to the kitchen. "Rachel, just wanted to tell you, the only thing you'd be signing to is that those are your prints."

I listened, nodding. He left.

January 7

By Barbara Lyn

A new girl, Vicky, came in yesterday. As soon as she came, I sensed she was not an ordinary inmate. She had a controlled, respectful manner. Vicky told us she had just graduated from a shock incarceration program in a local facility.

At the gym today, Vicky showed me all kinds of new exercises she had learned while in the shock program. She said inmates work and study sixteen hours a day and become very strong physically. She claims she was completely reformed. "They tear down all your pride, your stubbornness, then they rebuild you into a different person," she said.

We had to laugh tonight when Vicky had her first experience with our crippled shower. It's small, and when the water turns hot, then cold, you can't get away. Vicky bounded out through the curtain once or twice, then finished her shower with screams and healthy outbursts of vocabulary, minus the vulgarity we often hear from first-time shower users.

Vicky gives the others advice about the benefits of self-control. "You just think you have to curse at people when you're angry," she told one girl.

"I do what I want—no one can change me," the girl said.

Tonight we talked a long time with Vicky. She said the program taught her to shun bitterness. Not for the same reason we were taught, which is God's condemnation of hatred, but for personal betterment. She seemed to appreciate the scripture I mentioned which says, "Vengeance is mine; I will repay, saith the Lord." (Romans 12:19.)

Before dinner tonight one of the trusties brought two boxes of cake mix out of the storeroom, and gestured for me to make something. Several other trusties, standing nearby, laughed. "Willy's gonna make her bake him a cake," they said.

With permission from the cook, I made two chocolate layer cakes with vanilla icing. When I was done I learned the guys had planned that one would be for them and one for us. They are allowed to take things to their quarters, and when I told them we couldn't take one, they were disappointed. "It was a condition for working here," I said. "Sgt. Bohn said we couldn't take things back."

One of them quickly left the kitchen, saying, "I'll ask Brenda." He returned a minute later, trying to hide his delight. "She said you can," he said. Sgt. Bohn was on duty, and apparently okayed it. Rumor has it he and CO Brenda are very good friends.

We could hardly believe our good fortune in being allowed to take a treat for the girls. We cut the cake and served it in the cellblock, on paper plates.

The kitchen work has brought us relief from continuous exposure to TV and foul language. The trusties respect us highly with their language. But our existence in the workplace with our captors creates an awkward friendliness with them. Daily, hourly, Rachel and I seek discernment in our work. We talk together. We challenge our consciences. We pray for guidance.

At rec the men COs come in to play, and invite the girls to play with them. One day we all played football together. They watch us try new games, cheering at our accomplishments. Today one of them asked me to play catch with a football. I declined.

By Rachel

It was 9:30 this morning when CO Louise informed Sammi that the teacher would be ready for her at ten. Ten minutes later Sammi was still in bed. Louise came in. "Up, Sammi!" she yelled. "Teacher will be ready for you soon!"

"I'm not going," Sammi said.

"I don't think it's very nice when the teacher schedules for you, then you don't go," Louise said. "Now get your a - - up!"

"No!" Sammi said.

Louise, who had worked three hours overtime, was edgy already, and responded with a sharp tongue. Since the GED program is voluntary, she couldn't force Sammi to go.

A short time later, Louise again went to her cell. Teensie, who shares the cell with Sammi, was also still in bed. "Teensie, I want that wall cleaned up before the day is over," Louise said.

Teensie sat up and glanced around. Toothpaste smudges, where pictures had been pasted, were all over the wall. "What? That? I didn't do that," she said. "Erica did it when she was here."

"I don't know who did it. I want *you* to clean it up," Louise demanded.

Teensie was furious. "You wakin' me up outa my sleep! I didn't do it. I swear to God, I'll never clean that! You can double lock me!" Teensie had just been let out of double lock, after ten days. Louise got the key out of her pocket and locked Teensie and Sammi. Both girls were angry, locked in like dogs.

We have heard that CO Louise is working toward becoming a sergeant. Louise would be a likely candidate to fill a position where power and not justice prevails. She is the kind of person who is willing, ready, and proud to break any spirit left in a person after they get through the humiliation of being arrested and booked. Louise is like Sheriff Bentley—hard, cold, facial expression set. Yet she has an air of knowledge and professionalism. Often she is kindly and flattering, making her deceptively likable.

January 8

By Barbara Lyn

Weekend days don't go so slowly anymore like they did when we stayed in our cells all the time. Rachel said maybe the time will go fast now that we're working.

Our fears about causing friction by going out when the other girls can't, have totally dissolved. The girls seem to enjoy sending us off to work. "What's for dinner tonight?" they'll call when we leave at three for the last shift. Lupe even does our share of the cell cleaning when we're at work.

Tonight I told the girls they're getting frosted flakes for breakfast. They started suggesting things they'd like much better. "Grits!" "Applejacks!" "Oatmeal!"

"How many of you would like oatmeal?" I asked. An easy majority raised their hands. "We'll bring you some, one of these days," I said. They couldn't believe I was serious. I told them Mary said we could serve oatmeal for them if they wanted it.

Earlier today a lady in the cell next to us lost control emotionally. Rachel went to her bedside and sat with her, wiping her face with a cold washcloth as she cried out in anguish. The noise affected the others, and they began to decry the situation, telling Carole the woman needs to be in a hospital. The atmosphere became hysterical, as their loud protests blended with the wails of the woman Rachel was trying to console. Carole finally brought two male COs in to try to calm her. They took her out to the office. Tonight she seems fine. We spoke with her at length. She's a businesswoman who says she had a broken marriage, then depression problems, and had overdosed the day before she came here.

I read in the newspaper that the Erie County sheriff who stole $39,000 is in a federal prison that has no bars, no fences, no locks. It's called low security prison, and it's made for white-collar criminals with low risk of violence or escape. Doesn't sound much like jail, or punishment. The sheriff was sentenced to only four months, and gets paid for his work in food service. But I wouldn't trade places with him. I have my free conscience.

January 10

By Rachel

We've developed a nice working pattern with the other trusties. Today Barbara made three huge cakes for the inmates, and the tossed salad for our lunch. I made three hundred sandwiches for lunch and dinner. Willy usually takes care of coffee in the kitchen and cleanup in the break room. Guillermo and Jess are at the sinks, washing dishes. Steve, who's been here the longest, is in charge of inventory and getting boxes of food from the freezer.

Don't know why a person like Steve is in here. He's not jail material, it seems. He has restaurant experience, and is a big help in food decisions. He often helps Barbara and me learn new things in the kitchen. It's also hard to understand why Jess is here. I heard him talking to the others about his college courses.

When we came back from the kitchen tonight, we learned that the woman with mental problems had tried to commit suicide. Louise had found her with wrists bleeding. The COs are trying to find out how she got a razor blade.

January 11

By Rachel

I now can get a twelve-inch piece of dental floss once a day, on the dentist's recommendation. I had told him several of my teeth made trouble catching food. Today I flossed, for the first time in nearly five months. I hate to even mention how fetid the material was I got out from between my teeth. My whole mouth stank.

Some of the others want dental floss too. Louise said it's not allowed, because of a case in prison where it was used for suicide. Inmates can save it, braid it together, and use it as rope. I suggested giving a small piece and asking it back, like they do with razors for shaving. Louise said the girls could hide it and say they lost it.

I shook my head. "I shouldn't be here in the first place."

"I know," she said.

"It's ridiculous. Taxpayers paying my keep! I should be home working."

"Unfortunately, you chose to mess with the worst thing," Louise said. "Male ego."

"You think that's what it is?" I asked. "It's more than that, Louise. It's the protections they have under their laws."

Louise said she's been here long enough to know it's the male ego. I didn't say more. I can hardly believe Louise is ignorant enough to think I'll buy that. Maybe I should have told her I've observed some female ego, too.

January 12

By Rachel

10:15 PM. I just got back from a trip to Westfield Hospital to get my ankle X-rayed. I sprained it at rec today, jumping over a rope while two girls held each an end. I heard a crack, and it hurt badly. But I was able to walk. After rec I went to the kitchen to finish work.

At two this afternoon Carole called CO Jim Crowell, who is an EMT, to check it out. My foot was grotesquely swollen. We wrapped it with an ace bandage.

After work I asked for Tylenol, and lay on my bed. When I sat up the pain got worse, and I felt nauseated. CO Brenda came to see me. "Rachel, you're white!" she said. She asked permission to call the hospital. Barbara said I should go.

Brenda took me to the office. A CO approached with handcuffs, but Brenda told him they weren't needed. "Rachel's not going anywhere," she said. The sergeant agreed it was okay to take me without handcuffs.

The ER doctor said my foot isn't broken. He said I can use it as tolerable.

January 13

By Rachel

I got up at five to get ready for work, but Sue recommended I don't go. I stayed and ate breakfast with the other girls, the first time in two weeks.

Later I went to work, wearing my leather sandals from home to fit my oversized foot. After work I unwrapped it for the cook and trusties to see. The foot was highly colorful. The ankle was red and blue, with a band of deep purple traveling up my leg, changing to green and yellow.

January 15

By Rachel

I asked Mary if I could make peanut butter cookies, using some leftover butter and margarine I'd saved up in the cooler. Mary suggested weekends are a good time to make special things, as there aren't so many people. She mentioned that the sheriff isn't around, and he didn't like when the cooks made pie and cookies. Employees pay only a dollar per meal, and the sheriff didn't want them eating luxuriously, she said. When we bake, we often use surplus commodities from government warehouses—butter and cheese, honey, almond butter, prunes, and sometimes frozen fruit. Mary said she thinks the COs are greedy, wanting good food when they pay only a dollar.

Rumor has it that the county court judge across the street is ready to let any of us out, if we would appeal the sentence. In a conversation in the hallway, Carole spoke to Barbara about it. "Your daughter—you need to get home with your family," she said, a frown drawing deep lines across her forehead. She said she thinks if the two of us would take the lead in "doing something," Dad and Joe would follow. "How does your mom feel about this?" Carole asked. "And Nancy—and the poor children? Isn't it your responsibility to end this?"

After a while I joined the discussion. "People like you make the mistake of thinking that being in jail is loss of freedom," I said. "I'll tell you what real loss of freedom is. It's when you come to the point where you are afraid to say what you believe, and live it."

We explained our position in not appealing, and told Carole that the family supports us. She still looked very unhappy. "In the meantime—here you sit!" she said.

When we came back from work the girls had a party of sorts set up—for watching the Buffalo Bills game. On the table were a variety of commissary snacks. The girls had mixed hot sauce or squeeze cheese with popcorn, pretzels and peanuts, and put them on paper plates. I put a bag of hard candy out, and watched the game with them.

We snacked as we watched. I can't make sense out of football rules and teams. The game seems rough. I can't believe how people go flying through the air and hit the ground.

January 16

By Barbara Lyn

When Carole took me to work this morning she said, as if talking to herself, "Barbara and Rachel—after I got on them like that yesterday—will probably have me written up."

"Carole!" I said, and smacked her on the shoulder.

In the kitchen, Rachel and I made sandwiches for tonight's servings—egg salad and peanut butter with jelly—a total of 334. We used leftover almond butter for the third floor tray, because we knew Dad likes it—and strawberry preserves with big chunks of real strawberry. The women's tray, another priority for us, got the same as third floor.

The COs like it when food is uniformly prepared for each floor, so the inmates don't fight. As we worked on the combinations of peanut butter, almond butter and jellies left from previous weeks, Rachel and I kept getting confused, and ended up yelling at each other. We finished late, with a sigh of relief.

But the real nightmare was tonight at serving time. After all the loaded food carts including our carefully stacked sandwiches were sent up, we got in line at the buffet table for chicken wings. Then Guillermo called, "Rachel, Barbara—second floor didn't get any egg sandwiches—just peanut butter." Dropping our trays, we ran for plastic gloves, loaves of bread, egg salad and utensils.

A CO came in. "We're okay after all," he said. "We found the sandwiches on first floor."

We got our food and retreated to the storeroom to eat. When I came out for a second serving, I found Merla, the part-time cook, rapidly making egg sandwiches. "They say they need sixteen more sandwiches, eleven oranges, two ice cream sandwiches," she said.

I ran to collect the oranges and ice cream sandwiches. Rachel brought bread for more sandwiches, as Merla slapped them together, making the peanut butter ones without jelly.

A CO soon came to pick things up. He explained the whole mixup to Rachel and me. We took responsibility, and apologized. But we felt so bad, it spoiled our supper. As we finished eating, a CO came in. "Your Dad's gonna have a talk with you about those sandwiches being late," he said. He burst out laughing as he explained he'd told Dad the trusties counted the sandwiches wrong. Dad said, "That's my daughters! You tell them I'm gonna talk to them about that."

We were devastated to learn Dad hadn't gotten our sandwiches— just Merla's hurried ones. We'll never know if the COs serving the sandwiches made the mistake, or if it was ours.

January 17

By Barbara Lyn

One of the trusties told us he's expecting to go home on early release. We asked him who decides such moves. He said it's up to Lt. Belson. "You're not going to be here 'till April," he told us confidently. "They'll let you out soon." He said Belson lets people out thirty days early if they work, doesn't need permission from the judge.

We heard through the grapevine that some guy up top said he's now convinced these Lapps will never change their minds, no matter if they keep us here until April or if they let us out next week. Perhaps that idea will provide a logical excuse for letting us out early.

January 18

By Barbara Lyn

Teensie had her bail reduced, and was supposed to leave today. At rec, I told her I was going to give her a ride on my shoulders, for her last day. She ran away, but with the other girls' help and some persuasion, I eventually got her to climb up on a piece of gym equipment, and mount my shoulders. I took off at a run across the gym, with Teensie straddling my neck, screaming and pulling my hair.

In the kitchen, Alberto, one of the trustees told me quietly that Rachel's and my fingerprint cards are over on Lt. Belson's desk. "Been there a long time," he said.

"How do you know?" I asked in alarm. He said he knows because he cleans his office every day. The other trusties laughed, and stayed to listen to our exchange. Smiling, I told Alberto when he sees them again he could throw them in the wastebasket.

Later I wished I hadn't kidded about it. The reason the prints are on Belson's desk is of course because they are minus our signatures. The state would probably send them back if he sent them in. So there they stay on Belson's desk.

By Rachel

I really thought I'd get more letters sent out today, but our break time was taken up with conversations and activities with the girls and the trusties.

We were still eating supper when Louise opened the storeroom door. "Rachel when you're done, could you interpret for Lupe? Bobbie Trimmer is here, and has good news for her."

I went right away.

"Lupe might leave for rehab this week, if I can find a spot," Bobbie said.

I repeated it in Spanish. Lupe, who had an especially difficult week, began to cry with joy. She's been here over two months, no sentence, and a very poor idea of what's to happen. I hugged her, explained the details, thanked Bobbie, and went back to supper.

Back in the kitchen, I heard Guillermo say, "Thirty more weeks. I don't count days—I count weeks." I asked him a few questions about his case. He got a year for "possession" (drugs). I told him about our case. "The system's a mess," he said.

Later, Jess, shy and awkward, came to me. "Tomorrow's my last day," he said.

"You're going home? That's good!" I asked him how long he was here. He's serving sixteen days—burglary, he says. Goes to college, and seems a decent character.

Back in our cells, Sammi begged Barbara to exercise with her. Barbara talked to her while they worked, about the positive effects of exercise. Later Judy asked for a massage.

"Did you go to rec today?" Barbara asked her.

"No."

"Judy, it's part of the deal, you must go for exercise, if you want a massage."

Judy has a lot of pain from drug withdrawal, and we always tell her she needs to get exercise. Judy promised she'd go tomorrow, and Barbara gave her a massage.

I was ready to plunge into writing when I heard Carla trying to help Sammi with nutritional advice. "You explain it to her, Rachel," Carla said. Sammi, eighteen, had bulimia in the past, and still worries about her weight. "She doesn't know what foods she can have, then she feels guilty," Carla said.

I dragged my mat into their cell, and we began to talk. Judy and Lupe joined us, sitting on the mat. I shared with Sammi some problems I had in the past, similar to hers. She looked at me in surprise.

"You're so happy," Judy said.

"A lot of that comes from inside," I told them.

"I wish I could have a clean soul," Sammi said.

Louise came in and stood looking into the cell with everyone in it. The girls tried to explain that it's okay, but Louise wasn't so sure. "What's going on?" she asked sternly.

"It's a consultation," I told Louise. We continued talking. Louise went back out.

January 19

By Rachel

Lt. Belson and Jim Crowell came in to check out the heat registers, finally. I told the men there is a fair amount of heat coming from the registers, but the problem seems to be the windows and wall absorbing it all, and the eighteen-inch crawl space above our cells where heat is trapped. I suggested putting plastic over the opening by the ceiling. Jim crawled up the bars, checked out the space, and said that's where the heat is. He came back with plastic, and Brenda and the girls helped install it.

Tonight it's already much warmer.

January 21

By Rachel

Mary came into the storeroom where we were having lunch today. "Could you sit in the office to eat, and punch cards?" she asked. "I need to leave for a little while."

Staff members use tickets to pay for food. It was again a turning of tables, as we two inmates punched meal cards for our guards. Sgt. Gerace punched his own, after saying hello. Hanson, who handcuffed and took me to court many times, handed me his card, as did three or four COs. Some commented about our job.

January 22

By Barbara Lyn

In the kitchen this morning, Mary sent me to the staff lunch room about twenty feet down the hall to clean the microwave. I hummed as I worked, enjoying the freedom of being alone. CO Brenda came to the vending machine nearby for pop. She ignored me. I wondered why she looked so unhappy. Soon Mary came over, and stayed around until my job was done.

Earlier Mary had told Rachel she was leaving at noon, and would like to have us close the kitchen at 12:30. But when 12:00 came, Mary quietly told me she had been reminded she's in charge of us girls whenever we're working, and has to take us back to our quarters before she leaves. We quickly finished our work, and she escorted us back to the office, like a CO. She seemed uneasy. "Just for the extra precaution, I guess," she said.

We couldn't figure out why the sudden mistrust. Rachel had noticed Brenda talking quietly to Mary, and was sure Brenda was responsible.

January 23

By Barbara Lyn

Brenda was here again today, friendly as ever. Blanche told Rachel this morning that the orders to not leave us alone in the kitchen came from the lieutenant, and are probably a well-meant safety precaution. It's possible the lieutenant was concerned about the character of some of the men working in the kitchen. Can't blame them for being cautious.

There's one weekender I'm glad isn't here all the time. He talks too much and tells off-color jokes. Another, who's leaving this week, seems to lack intelligence and craves attention. He tries to get it by helping with whatever we happen to be working on. We've learned to deal with him with a balance of kindness and firmness, and avoid being alone with him.

"It's nice and warm in here," Doreen commented when she came into the cellblock. "To think it took them three years to figure this out!" she said, pointing to the plastic by the ceiling space. We didn't tell her it was the inmates who came up with that bit of common sense.

January 24

By Rachel

My back has been very bad since a couple days ago when I bent to lift a garbage bag in the kitchen. I woke up to my third morning of wondering just how I'd bend enough to brush my teeth and get dressed. Finally gave up on my socks, and Barbara put them on for me. I managed to put on shoes, then went to work. The cooks don't give me much time off. Seems they don't understand how much pain I have.

By Barbara Lyn

Blanche was in the kitchen today, and let us do some experimenting with new recipes. Rachel's potato patty batter turned out too wet, then her chiropractor came at serving time and she had to go, leaving me with the mess of frying them. The patties were falling apart all over the pan. Blanche had barely enough help to serve the hot dog lunch, and it was late. The third floor cart finally went up, but the CO who had taken it came back. "No fruit today?" he asked.

Instantly, I remembered. "Yes, there's fruit, but we forgot to load it," I said. I went to the cooler, yanked out a crate of oranges, counted them out—sixty-three on a tray—then filled more trays for first and second floor before returning to the stove to fry the wet potato patties. When Rachel came back I said to her, "I'm tired of this mess!" and walked away from the job.

Rachel finished the patties, dubbing them "potato flops," much to Blanche's amusement. But the serving table wasn't in shape yet, and court personnel were arriving for food. I was nervous about the guesswork cake I'd baked with leftover oatmeal and apple butter. When I cut it, I found it was soggy all the way through. Blanche sampled it and said it was okay, so I put it out on the table. Swanee came in and ate a piece, then went around advertising it. By the time we were carrying the hot food to the table, the room was clogged with officers and other jail personnel—nurses, the chaplain, the teacher. Some were grabbing up the cake, some waiting in line to fill their plates, some hounding us with questions about what we made. "O-o-o! What's in this cake?" "Potato pancakes? I'll be your guinea pig!"

Usually we prepare the food in relative privacy, then retreat to our tea table to eat while others pick up their food. When Rachel and I finally sat down for lunch I was in a sweat. "Never again a late meal on court day!" I told her.

January 25

By Barbara Lyn

Marge, a new inmate, was called to court at the same time I was going to the kitchen. In the office, she told Carole and CO Johnson she's going to tell the judge she's guilty, because she is. "I just want it over," she said with a sigh.

"Guilty of smoking pot," Johnson said. "What do you think, Barbara? How much time will she get for that?"

"I don't know," I said, not too happy about the teasing.

"Two years, maybe—that's the going rate for women nowadays, isn't it?"

"Barbara got a year for doing nothing," Carole said.

Carole and I headed toward the kitchen. I turned the corner in the hall and almost walked into a crowd of court officers, handcuffing inmates to take them to court. I stepped back quickly. Carole was just behind me, and leaned on me, laughing. She said I looked like I was afraid I'd get handcuffed. "...and you'd get up to the judge and say, 'Judge, I was just on my way to the kitchen and I landed up here!'"

In the kitchen, Freddy, one of the trusties, complained about washing pots and pans, telling another guy he's doing women's work. I ignored him. "Did you hear what I said, Barbara?" he asked.

"Yes," I said, as I swept the floor.

"Did you see all the women's work I'm doing?"

"Yes, but that's okay," I answered. "I do men's work sometimes, too. You have to be versatile."

"Like what?" he asked.

"Like tractors and cows and other farm work," I said.

Later, Sgt. Paul Stage came to the counter where I was spreading sandwiches. He said his sister is a foster parent, and has seen cases of children being shuffled around by Social Services. "She asked me to tell you she's behind you," he said. "She's ninety percent behind what you're doing. That's the way a lot of people are—they're behind you *almost* all the way."

I stopped my work. "I really can sympathize with people who don't understand the whole thing," I said. "But I look back, and try to imagine where I could have done something differently—"

Paul interrupted. "The only thing I think you did wrong was—nothing like resisting arrest—but that you didn't have a little better control of the crowd."

"I don't think you even know the whole story," I said. "It was not my intention to have my arrest physically blocked."

Paul said I should have foreseen the crowd's reaction. I tried to explain, but he kept interrupting. Finally he said, "You're all right, Barbara. A lot of people are behind you." He put his hand on my shoulder, then left abruptly.

By Rachel

Last night after work I sat soaking my injured ankle with Epsom salt, while wearing a snow-pack on my back, made with plastic bags. Dr. Freling had recommended I use snow rather than ice for my sore back, because it conforms to the body. Louise had brought the snow. "The first request I ever had for snow," she said, smiling.

Teacher Cindy brought our GED diplomas today when I was in the kitchen. I took the envelope and thanked her.

"Aren't you going to open it?" she asked. I took out my diploma. She and the cooks congratulated me. Cindy said it was the highest score she had seen yet.

This morning Marge, the new girl, said, "This place is *so* much nicer." I asked her what she meant. She said she had been here before, and the girls were always getting into fights. "I'd cry," she said, "then they'd yell at me for crying." Marge expects to do a month or more for violating probation.

"Everyone in here cries sometimes," I told her, "but we can help to make it better by being nice to each other. We're all friends here." Her eyes were wide with happiness, but serious.

The others chimed in. "Nobody fights here—we all get along."

■ CHAPTER 18 ■

"Mayville Five"

January 26, 1994

By Barbara Lyn

In the kitchen, we're shorthanded since several trusties went home. Mary told me they're going up to ask Dad and Joe again if they would like to help.

I know Dad's opinion. But inside, my heart is begging: Please come down, Dad and Joe. I'd love to cook your oatmeal in the morning, and work at your side in the kitchen.

We worry about Dad's health. Rachel said maybe she could convince him to come work by asking if he wouldn't spend some time with us before he dies.

By Rachel

We had visits from Mom, Nancy, and several friends. They told us of their meeting last night with a group of community members called "The Mayville Five Committee," who have recently organized in our support. They got together to discuss a brochure they're doing on our case. They're also doing local fund raising, distributing literature and even writing songs.

Then I talked to Susan on the phone. They had worked on the brochure all night, she said, with a print deadline today. She sounded tired. Friends are making plans for a benefit dinner for the Torres family. They plan to have a band playing songs in support of our cause.

January 27

By Barbara Lyn

Last night a woman who was being booked put up a fight. Later Louise brought her into the cell with handcuffs and shackles. She was drunk, and hollered until late in the night, when Louise finally took her chains off. The girls talked to her, and she was more agreeable with them than she was with the COs.

Today the woman seems normal, but a little nervous—double locked because of her behavior last night. She's facing felony charges now because she hit Louise while being booked. Initially, it was just a minor harassment charge. I feel sorry for her. She said she used to have a good job, but went to drinking after her ex-husband, a lawyer who knew the family court judge, gained custody of her three small children.

I was impressed with the inmates' sharing and caring for the new lady. Despite crowding and having to move around when new ladies come, the girls take pride in preserving what has become the norm in here—tolerance, compatibility and caring. We speak openly about that. I also talked to Marge about dealing with a CO she says she can't stand. "Don't let Sue's attitude get you down," I said. "Let her be what she wants to be. You don't need to be like her."

January 28

By Barbara Lyn

It's Friday. At rec I finished the last day of the week by running one mile—thirty laps around the gym. I'm in near perfect health. It's a lot to be thankful for, especially since Rachel is struggling with her ankle and back injury in the past few weeks. She hasn't been going to rec, and finally cut work hours. Mary and the boys gave her permission to take half days off until she recovers. I put in eight to nine hours some days, as the kitchen is short in help.

January 29

By Rachel

We got copies of "The Mayville Five" brochure in the mail today. It's a three-page folder with articles that cover the case, along with photos of Billy, and the five of us. The front page pictures an eagle, wings spread, holding a scroll with "The Mayville Five" printed across it. Under the heading it says, "A cause that affects every American." The insert sheet gives notices for a benefit dinner on February 12, and a rally on February 19. "Come March With Us in Mayville," the heading reads.

Reading the brochure inspires us. We salute the men and women whose minds and energy were spent for our cause. I spoke to Susan and Hannah, who are feeling the burden of the upcoming mailing spree, when it gets off the press. It will be mailed to fifteen hundred addresses.

January 31

By Barbara Lyn

Lynn was called to court this afternoon. A County Court judge reduced her sentence to ninety days, making her release date February 11. He said it's because she has children and he thought her one-year sentence was excessive.

This was not an appeals hearing, as Lynn had been led to believe. Instead, she had to agree—on the record—*not* to appeal her conviction, in order to get the sentence reduced. She would have stayed here until August if she didn't go along with the deal.

Lynn would have had an excellent chance for success on appeal, because Mifsud had forced her to be tried with co-defendants who were not putting on a defense. Simply put, Judge Ward coerced her into not appealing, just to help Judge Mifsud cover his wrong. Her hearing today was done in closed chambers.

We're glad for Lynn. She's leaving in a week and a half. However, I have no interest in engaging in covert exchanges with the court, just to get out.

Lynn said that on the way back from court one of our arresting officers, Sgt. Tyka, commented that the food in the kitchen is better since "the Lapp girls" work there. He told Lynn he can't believe how much we've changed since we work in the kitchen. "They look so much happier—they even talk to us," he said.

Sgt. Tyka can express amazement that we now appear more happy? If he were not so blind he would realize that a woman might not be too friendly or happy while locked up or being led about in chains by men.

By Rachel

Tonight we have a new roommate, Martha, a registered nurse. She had been here briefly two months ago, at the time of her arrest, and came back to serve a twenty-day sentence for writing a bad check. She was surprised that Barbara and I are still here.

We got to talking with Martha about what we see as problems with the system. She told us she was shocked the other evening when Brenda demanded she wash her hair, after she'd already showered. "I'm a professional woman," Martha said. "I just couldn't believe her telling me to get back in the shower." Martha had asked Brenda if she could wait until morning, as she has very thick hair that wouldn't dry, and she had to sleep on the cold floor.

Brenda scolded, "Don't you talk to me like that!" Martha had silently complied. Martha also told us Brenda was openly degrading

Carole in the office today, saying Carole should hang up her hat and retire, and that she doesn't have the qualifications for the job.

In here, Brenda talks about Gail, a part time CO, saying she's not good for the job, and calling her "The Fluff," or "Gail the Snail." It's hard to believe. Gail and Carole are the true leadership here, more capable of handling difficult inmates because of their non-threatening manner. Too bad Brenda doesn't learn from them rather than calling them names.

February 3

By Barbara Lyn

Rachel keeps count of the weeks since we were arrested. "Twenty-four down, ten to go," she said on Monday. I told Rachel I think ten weeks is too long to start counting down yet.

Our rec schedule changed, because of construction going on in the gym area during the daytime. We accepted the offer to go for rec from 9:50 to 10:50 PM. But it cuts into our sleeping and writing time.

Guillermo, one of the trusties, lost his job. For smuggling Koolaid up to another prisoner, we heard. They sent him back upstairs. Jail staff is strict with the trusties. A few days ago they sent one up because he didn't come to work when the other boys called him. The boys reported it to the sergeant, and we never saw him again. Today we got a new one, a cheerful Puerto Rican who appears to be a good worker.

Brenda brought us a box of Mayville Five brochures sent from home. We're giving them out to the cooks, the trusties and some of the COs. Sgt. Stage told me he had gotten one already, and Blanche said she'd picked one up at the local corner store. They're out all over the place, she said. The family tells us they're running out of the first printing of three thousand.

February 4

By Barbara Lyn

7:15 PM. I've been writing letters for the last hour. I have a list of former cellmates who had asked to know about the Mayville Five rally when it comes up. Lynn addressed the envelopes and stuffed them this afternoon when I was at work.

Our workday was long, breaks short. I'm tired, but will have to keep writing for two more hours, exercise an hour at the gym, then take a shower and read my Bible before going to bed.

Just now Rachel crashed our growing pile of mail onto the floor, and yelled, "Look at all your mail!"

"Pick out your own mail, and see how much smaller the stack will be," I said.

"You know it's mostly yours," Rachel said. "I can't even use the table anymore for writing or anything!" It has been a continuous sore spot to Rachel that I let my mail collect on the tiny cell table.

The girls gathered at our cell door to see how this "family feud" would be settled. They laughed when I remained unperturbed by Rachel's outburst. "You see, one person can't fight alone," I explained. "I'll wait 'till she cools down, then get on top."

Rachel picked up a copy of the Constitution and, with mock authority, read the seventh amendment, claiming that the value of this controversy exceeds twenty dollars, and her right to trial by jury must be preserved. I replied that the Bible says we should not take each other to law, and the Bible is higher than the Bill of Rights, so we might as well settle this between us right now. We were laughing so much we could hardly talk.

When we go to rec late, Doreen doesn't make us wear our greens—because there aren't many people around, she says. Exercising in sweat suits is more comfortable. But the COs aren't busy at night and they often stand around the gym watching us. I don't understand what kind of men they must think themselves to be, watching girls exercising, then making lewd jokes with the ones who choose to engage in unclean talk. I ignore them to a large extent, but it's disgusting.

Martha, our cellmate, moved out today when a vacancy came up. We came back to an empty cell and found a note hanging on our doorway, ending with, "I'm only across the hall." Now Rachel and I are alone once more. Though we work together, eat together and sleep in the same cell, our privileges for talking in privacy are limited, as long as we have a cellmate. As a matter of respect, we don't usually talk Deutch in the presence of other inmates.

Alone in our cell this afternoon, we discussed workplace challenges. I am appalled at the prevalence of gossip and backbiting among the four cooks and other employees. We hear there's extra tension now because they're taking civil service tests, and the outcome will determine who gets the supervisory job in the kitchen.

Seeing this reminds me of the importance of curbing our tendency to talk behind people's backs. It also makes me profoundly grateful for our parents' teachings to be open with one another. It started when we were little, and Mom would require us to say out loud what we were whispering, whenever secrecy offended another sibling.

February 5

By Barbara Lyn

I have an irresistible urge to do hard work, like handling big containers of food, milk crates, etc. But I have to be careful when the cooks or trusties are around because they seem to think the men should do all the hard work. Today I restacked a big stack of bread trays in the storeroom, without being noticed. Later Rose, the substitute cook, asked if the men had stacked that bread. "No, I did it—I put the old bread on top," I said, assuming she was concerned about rotating. "Is it okay?"

"I just wondered, because the guys should be doing that, not you," she said.

"Oh Rose, I can't help it. I love to do the hard work," I told her. "I'm used to it at home, and I miss it." She seemed to understand.

Rose has been a pleasure to work with. She's an older lady with a commanding nature. At first I felt that she was intimidating, but now that we've gotten to know her, we see she's a good teacher—and a very good cook. Rachel and I love to watch her do innovative things like putting leftover fruit juices into the sweet potatoes she's baking.

By Rachel

I often wonder just what I will do when I get out. I have an almost alarming craving to "do it again." Not to come to jail necessarily, but to defy this insane establishment. I really mean insane. I have a lust to ignore the horrible rules and regulations that cause human suffering, and to live a purified life, where actions are guided by respect and goodwill toward those the Lord created just like me.

I heard recently that Social Services is after a family we know, wanting to interrogate their children. I found myself hoping we can help, and just feeling like I could go to jail all over again. It's really awful. Jail is nasty beyond description. It's cruel, it's—it's more than ugly, it's—how can I describe the awfulness? I *hate* jail. But when I heard that the District Attorney said on the radio that he has "no sympathy for the Lapps—they could appeal like Lynn did," and we happen to know Lynn didn't appeal at all, but rather is getting out on a regrettably deceitful maneuver crafted by lawyers, it made disdain rise up inside me. Hatred for tricks, hatred for their thirst for power.

February 6

By Barbara Lyn

8:00 PM. Carole is here for the late shift. I told her we had heard from home that Dad isn't able to get cough drops, and mentioned my package of Hall's I'd gotten through commissary a few weeks ago. "Do you have any way of getting them up to him?" I asked. "Without getting yourself in trouble?" I told her about Dad's asthma, and that he now has a cold besides. She said she'd ask Jim Crowell. Later she came back and said she'd gotten permission.

Rachel had a fit this evening. She wrapped herself in an exercise mat and started walking around, purposely bumping into things and falling down. "Uh-oh, Rachel's losing it!" the girls exclaimed. Rachel appeared to prove them right by muttering, "I gotta get out of here, I gotta get out of here!" She climbed the wire mesh fence, all the way to the ceiling, and hung there with her fingers and toes. Then, like the girls do when they're feigning emergencies, she yelled, "Security!"

The girls erupted in laughter. "Oh, Rachel, you're good, Rachel!"

Carole finally came in, and found Rachel on her perch near the ceiling. She was speechless.

"I gotta get out of here!" Rachel said in a low, frantic tone. "Please, Carole, can you help me get out?" Carole looked genuinely alarmed—until the girls again burst out laughing.

February 7

By Barbara Lyn

Two seasons have passed—summer and fall, and winter is nearly over. There's an urgency within me, telling me I must be home by spring. Yet I want to be where God wants me to be. So I shed some tears and say, "Lord this is best, because you said so."

I heard Mary tell the boys in the kitchen that "Barbara and Rachel" are spoiling them. "You'll find out when they leave," she said, speaking of the sandwich job they don't like. I do it almost every morning—spreading margarine on 300-some pieces of bread and counting it out on trays for each floor.

Mary's reference to our leaving seemed to be echoed all over the place this morning. A road deputy came in when I was doing bread and butter. "Lots of English muffins," he commented about the stack on the serving table. "I like that." Then he turned to Blanche, who was working nearby. "This place'll never be the same when these girls leave. How will you do without them?"

Rachel's pizza casserole, made with noodles, brought on more comments. After dinner we noticed the huge pan was almost empty. "That stuff was good!" one of the boys said as we started dishes.

"The best meal we've had yet!" Steve said.

Jon joined in. "I hope you girls stay a long time—at least until after I go home."

Tonight as I knelt beside Judy on her mat giving her a back massage, the 6:00 news came on. "More trouble for a troubled family," began the announcer for *News Channel 7*. Then I heard something about "Linda Stefan," Billy's mother. I bolted over to the TV and got the volume up, yelling to the rest of the girls, "Be quiet!"

The news said she was arrested on statutory rape charges, for acts committed two years earlier. It was the same incident we had heard from the Stefan boys months ago. She had slept with a teenage boy at a motel room where Social Services placed her and the boys, after they were taken from their father. On TV, short pieces were shown from news files of Don in jail, and our Mayville arrests.

The women in here cheered and clapped as the news story ended. "She's the one that abused those kids!" one of the girls said. "She needs to be in jail!"

I was stunned.

Carla looked at me. "Barbara, you're not saying anything. What are you thinking?"

I could barely describe my feelings. A part of me wanted to call the news a victory. It was one step toward the truth of the Stefan boys' torment, when Social Services forced them into their mother's care. But I felt sorry for the woman in jail facing a hopelessly rotten legal system.

"Justice delayed is justice denied," I said. "That goes for her *and* her boys—*and* us." I told the girls how Social Services' testimony at my trial focused on how well Billy was doing in their custody. If Linda Stefan's crime had been known to the public at that time, they couldn't have gotten away with so many lies.

"You knew this all along?" one of the girls asked.

"Yes. Billy and Tom told us about it," I said. "The crime wasn't against them. But Social Services forced them to live with her while she had this thing going on with a teenage boy."

"Now they have you in jail—and everything you were saying was true!" one of the girls said.

Later, in my cell, I went into meditation. If this information had been available to the jury, perhaps the witnesses against me wouldn't have lied so much. But then we wouldn't have known how well they can lie. Personally, I won't look back with regrets. Truth works in marvelous ways. Sometimes we have to be patient in order for the best of it to come out.

February 8

By Barbara Lyn

Carla just braided my hair, in a "cornroll." Doing each other's hair is a big thing here. The girls style it in every imaginable way, with improvised rollers made of rolled up toilet paper, and even apply toothpaste to stiffen it. They know Rachel and I aren't interested in adorning ourselves, but enjoy trying different braids on us—which we appreciate because it keeps our hair back for working.

By Rachel

Ephesians 5:8 and 10 says: "Walk as children of light.... Proving what is acceptable unto the Lord." I'm not sure what that means, "proving" what's acceptable. Maybe it means setting an example, and proving by our actions what kind of a God we have.

It's frightful what a mockery is made out of God nowadays. It's as though people think He could be manipulated to our whims, as though whatever someone wants is okay, good or bad.

This subject came up last evening when we were talking to the girls about age. I told them it doesn't matter so much how old we are, it's most important that we're ready to face God. And claiming God calls for responsibility. "You can't just say, 'I'm going to heaven.' It doesn't work that way," I said.

Carlos, the new trusty, gets a little too wound up sometimes. A couple of days ago he was trying his Spanish with me. I believe he still thinks I know just a little. After answering him once in Spanish, I tried ignoring him. Then he suddenly asked, "Tienes esposo?" ("You have a husband?")

"Yo? No." ("Me? No.")

"Porque no?" ("Why not?")

I thought for a moment. It wasn't the proper time to discuss the subject. He was taking advantage of his Spanish, so others wouldn't hear. I changed to English. "Guess I haven't found the right one."

"Has to be white, right?"

"No, that doesn't matter. What matters to me is that the person fears God, and is concerned about preparing for eternity. Life is short."

He didn't ask any more questions.

February 11

By Rachel

We got a letter from a woman in Corning, New York. She starts, "Just a quick note to let you know that thanks to 'The Mayville Five Committee,' your story has reached Corning." She said she and others plan to car pool, and come to the rally on February 19—with groceries and donations for our families. She wrote that though she doesn't understand all the details, she is willing to join the cause on the basis that "due process has been missing."

By Barbara Lyn

Lynn went home, and Carla left for Erie County Jail for a few days. Suddenly we were at a record low of six. But tonight we had two more girls in. We're still at a comfortable one-per-bed.

Lynn and Carla were both leaders in here, and have left a void. It gives Rachel and me added responsibility to make sure everyone is happy, when we get back from work.

Teensie came back, after being out less than a month. She and her boyfriend both came in, on drug charges again. Now their poor children—four of them, aged one to five—are again without parents. I don't know when officials will realize they're the greatest fools, searching houses for marijuana, then hauling people in.

February 12

By Barbara Lyn

Our visitors today all came wearing new T-shirts, imprinted with "The Mayville Five," with an eagle and the words, "Marching to Liberty's Beat."

Joe's six-year-old, Joselle, crawled onto my lap and showed me her tooth that was so loose it was hanging out. She hadn't forgotten the family custom of having me pull loose baby teeth for all my nieces and nephews. "I saved it for you," she said. She shook with giggles when I exclaimed how loose it was. I pulled it out, amid laughter from the rest of the children. Joselle stuffed the hole with a piece of cotton she'd brought in her pocket.

Our break this morning was short, as Rachel volunteered to do an extra project of making apple pies for one of the trusties' going-home treat. Then the boys left the kitchen before the work was done, and I had to do some of their chores. I was exhausted, and felt irritated at the cook who was sitting in her office, on the phone with a friend. If she had been overseeing things, she would have made the boys help us. I refuse to put myself in the position of giving the boys orders. Yet the cooks leave so much in our hands, it makes it almost necessary—or else take on all the leftover work ourselves. I counted out 165 bananas for the three floors, dipped 165 cups of tapioca pudding, and made a salad for our lunch with two heads of lettuce, half a green pepper, half a cuke, six radishes and two diced carrots.

By Rachel

Working in the kitchen tonight, I couldn't get my mind off the Joe Torres benefit dinner going on at the Sinclairville fire hall. At 5:10 I said to Barbara, "You think they're playing our songs now?"

I washed dishes, scrubbing pots and pans until I was sweating—working as if helping at the dinner. When the dishes were done I announced, "We're still in time for chicken and biscuits. Let's all go!" I thought of our friends and family—talking, eating, wearing Mayville Five T-shirts.

Later tonight when we called home, Drusilla told us the dinner was a success, with about four hundred people served. She said when she got to Sinclairville there were so many cars she couldn't see the town.

February 15

By Rachel

Incredible, the noise level in the ladies' quarters today! Is it the lifestyle the girls are used to that drives them to turn the TV up so high, then talk and talk in horrible language? Or is it the stress of confinement? I put earplugs on, but after a while I couldn't stand them. The insides of my ears get sore. I hate sleeping with them.

With eleven inmates, Barbara and I don't mathematically have the say when the TV gets turned down. When Lynn and Carla were here it was kind of the rule to turn it low at 10:00 PM. Last night at ten I took my earplugs out. "Could you turn the TV down now?" I called to the girls across the block.

"It's not high," Teensie said. They lowered it a little, then I think they must have upped it again, as I'd barely dozed off when I realized it was very loud.

"The TV is too high!" I called.

"You better get yourself some earplugs," Teensie joked. "Some real big ones, to cover your whole head. 'Cause I watch TV late."

I went to sleep, but woke up again. It's surely my right to sleep, I thought. That's not the question though. The question is how best to keep things peaceful. I feel our relationship with the newer girls is fragile. They could say, "What privilege do these girls have to go out, then come back in at intervals and tell us what to do?"

Marge has been staying to herself a lot lately. Tonight she came to our cell, and we talked. She can't go home until May, and dreads the stay. I told her I think it's bad that no work is provided for the girls here. Marge said she doesn't think it's fair that only Barbara and I get to go out and work, that we're no different from her. She said she talked to the sergeant about it, and he said she can't work because in the past when they let women out to work they fooled around with the boys.

Another problem would be smuggling things, like knives. With Barbara and me, the COs trust us. They don't even search or question us when we get back from the kitchen. The arrangement with the men trusties is different, as they have their own quarters, and don't mingle with unstable people.

Fairness is an issue though. Male inmates are given the choice to work, based on character. Women aren't given a chance, except for us. I couldn't begin to tell Marge it's fair.

The total inmate number posted on the kitchen blackboard is 176. "Numbers are getting high," Barbara commented as the cook and four of us trusties filled plates, lined up along the serving counter, assembly line style. "I don't know how it works to use the same number of cans of vegetables for twenty extra people," Barbara said. The servings of peas on the plate looked small, as Barbara dipped from a big pot, trying to make them reach for all the plates.

The trusties discussed the overpopulation. "They got more coming in," one said. "That drug bust in Jamestown."

"Maybe they're filling up the jail so they have an excuse to let us out," Barbara said.

"Yeah," Steve said, "when the number gets over 180, they start letting people out."

February 16

By Barbara Lyn

Half a year in jail today. "It seems like half a century," I told the girls.

Rachel and I are trying to reach an agreement on how much time to spend with management in the kitchen. I'm always after her not to involve herself with extra things like preparing the special meals for inmates with dietary problems. When we first started working, the cooks did the specialty jobs. Now they seem to take advantage of our skills. The COs sometimes bypass the cooks and bring their requests straight to us. We still have to do the same amount of regular work, then we get late for breaks.

Rachel agrees we must be cautious with our involvement—because of our own need for free time, and because of the nagging uncertainty we feel on whether it's right to be dealing so closely with the COs and sergeants.

February 17

By Barbara Lyn

Last night we noticed our stamp and envelope supply was low. "It's time for a 'little miracle,'" I told Rachel. Sure enough, it came today. We got lots of mail, including a box of writing supplies and stamps from a lady in Syracuse.

Our morning shift was long—almost four hours for me, even longer for Rachel. When I got back to the booking room no one was there. I leaned against the wall to wait for someone to let me in. Sgt. Mitchell finally came, but was busy on the phone. A friendly CO came and offered me a doughnut from a box of assorted ones. I wasn't hungry. Besides, I felt like crying. I was tired, and couldn't rest because of my bed being inside some stupid locked doors. By the time Brenda came to open the gate, I felt like saying, "This is outrageous—standing here waiting to be locked in where I don't even want to go! Why don't you just let me out of here?" But it wouldn't have helped. I didn't say anything. Like I told Sgt. Stage this morning when he teased me for the umpteenth time for being too quiet, "My dad likes to say, 'Don't speak unless you can improve the silence.'"

Stage had looked thoughtful. But only for a moment. "Barbara, have you ever been married?" he suddenly asked.

"No."

"Because married women, they have to talk a lot to make sure their husband knows they're the boss. That's why they're always talking first thing in the morning."

February 18

By Barbara Lyn

Jail count was up to 187 this morning. Mary says it's an all-time high. I think we're going home today, because when the weekenders come in they'll have 190.

I have this feeling they'll get us out. Partly because tomorrow is the day of the Mayville Five march, and I think it's no small embarrassment to Mayville to be put on the map this way. Tomorrow is also the day of Mayville's famous annual ice castle event. I imagine the march will spoil their event even worse than last year's warm weather that melted down the castle. "Chautauqua County Vacationlands," as Mayville wants to be known, is home to four unwilling vacationers, in the worst way.

9:15 PM. I think I'll sleep early—if I can. A few minutes ago there was a nasty argument over racial skin color in the cell next to us, with wickedly vile language. CO Doreen handled it well. She didn't take sides or try to figure out the argument. "Give each other a little space," she said. Then she stayed at the desk to read. It's calm now. But across the room from us a new inmate who is here for stabbing is recounting what she did—in detail, and without remorse.

February 19

By Barbara Lyn

I was almost done writing my diary last night, when we heard a pop and all the lights went out. Several girls screamed. We were already locked in for the night. Rumors were going around that the place is on fire, and several minutes later when the Mayville fire sirens started, some of the girls panicked. Just then Doreen walked in with a flashlight. "There's a problem somewhere," she said, her voice tense. "I'm leaving for a little bit, and don't f - - - around!" Then she was gone.

"All the COs are leaving and we're gonna burn down!" one of the girls said.

It did seem strange that Doreen was so uneasy, but I wasn't terribly alarmed. "Do you think we'd get charged with escape for breaking out this window if the jail is on fire?" I kidded.

After a while Doreen came back. She told us a county truck that was moving snow had hit the pole with the transformer on it, out in the parking lot.

By Rachel

What a day! The day of the Mayville Five rally. We shared in the excitement, even from our hole in the basement of Chautauqua County Jail.

I felt my blood running high as noon approached. We were in the kitchen washing dishes. We knew the rally participants would be gathering on the sidewalks around the jail and courthouse. I looked at the thick, clouded windows of the jail kitchen, trying to get an indication of what the weather would be like. I couldn't see a thing. One of the trusties said he had been outside, and it was nice.

Back in our cell at 1:00, we opened the window louvers, letting the first warm breeze of 1994 flow in and add to the adrenalin already rushing in our veins. The day was beautiful, the sun bright. The sidewalk and the strip of ground outside were a welcome sight, after having our windows boarded shut for months. Sometime the board outside had fallen off, and the tape holding the plastic on the inside had begun to peel. The plastic was down just far enough so that Barbara, standing on tiptoe, had been able to reach down to the knob that opened the window louvers. We asked the other girls to come in and listen for sounds of the rally.

Sue came in. "What's going on?" she demanded, looking at the half dozen girls who were crowded around our window, arms around each other.

"They want to hear," I said. "We invited them."

Sue stood by our cell door, looking stern. "So now the plastic gets ripped off?" she asked.

"Yes," I said. "It was coming down anyway."

"One *corner* was coming down," Sue asserted.

"Yes," I said. I didn't want to argue—I wanted to listen. I'd seen an officer in gray uniform stride past, then up the hill toward the parking lot where Susan had told us they'd play for us. Was he going to keep them away?

About 1:30 I let out a yelp. "I hear it!" Music of a song, "March on Mayville," drifted in the window along with the breeze. We pressed against the window, straining to hear. We could catch only snatches of the songs, and voices. Barbara tied into the excitement by calling Nathan and Susan on their car phone, less than a block from our window. On the phone, we heard the words clearly: "Come all ye people, come march along with me, we're going to march in Mayville, 'till the Mayville Five are free! ...Barbara Lapp and Jacob, Rachel, Joe and Lynn, have never done a wrongful act, for caring's not a sin...."

By Barbara Lyn

On our way to the kitchen this afternoon we met Dad in the hall with a CO. For a moment I thought he was going home. Then I remembered he was coming down for a TV interview that was scheduled to take place in the jail classroom. Rachel and I were called, too, and spent an hour with Dad. It was reassuring to see him answer questions in his confident, simple manner. He's still the same Dad, unscathed by six months in a pen. We felt sorry Joe was not included in our clan meeting.

Tonight we watched coverage of the rally on the 6:00 news. "They've come to be known as the Mayville Five," began the announcer from *News Channel 4*. "Hundreds of citizens from Chautauqua and Cattaraugus counties staged a rally on their behalf, singing songs that were composed about the Mayville Five...."

February 20

By Barbara Lyn

At our visits today we discussed yesterday's rally. Our visitors told us the event was attended by people from hundreds of miles away, and from several different states.

As the initial excitement wears off, it's sobering to think how God directs all this. The day of our release is entirely in His hands. It seems He chose to bestow a little of His strength on us, as both events—the benefit dinner and the rally—landed on days with marvelous weather, during a winter of relentless cold and snow. Both times the weather forecast on TV looked bad—freezing rain for the dinner event, and spring rain for yesterday's outdoor event. Both times the forecast changed a day beforehand, and the predicted foul weather came a day later. Maybe God wanted us to notice His hand in the weather so we wouldn't think it was our own work that made this successful.

I was in a deep sleep this afternoon when CO Sue came in and shook my foot. "Barbara!" she said in an urgent tone. "Do you have any extra sheets or blankets?" She lifted my covers to check.

It took a moment for me to wake up. Then I called Rachel, who was asleep below me on the bottom bunk, and asked if she had any extra sheets or blankets. We had one blanket we didn't need since it's warmer, but no extra sheets. I expressed surprise to Sue that she suspected us of having extra sheets. "The other girls had lots of them," Sue said. "There are people being booked in that have no sheets. We can't let anyone have extra."

Kitchen blackboard count says 190, a new record. The trusties said Lt. Belson is coming in tomorrow to let a bunch of people out. Cellmate Judy says we're prime candidates. They can't let people out unless they've been sentenced. Probation violation inmates, which make up a large part of our population, are also not eligible for early release.

I was writing to a lady tonight, explaining why we shouldn't complain about rainy, muddy spring weather, because that is how life is born. Suddenly I had tears streaming down my face. I wanted to smell the dirt so badly—spring mud—the kind everyone likes to complain about. I wanted to feel the nastiest, coldest rain. I wanted to say, "Everything God made is very good—except jail." I wanted to get out so I could prove I would never complain about nature's ugliness again. I felt totally fed up with all the things around me that are contrary to nature: man-made disasters, man-made miseries.

CHAPTER 19

Triumph Amid Treachery

February 23, 1994

By Rachel

CO Sue just doesn't seem to be able to deal with things. She's as cantankerous as imaginable today—double locked another girl, our former roommate, for swearing at her. Sue had awakened her to demand she take a TB test.

Another confrontation arose after rec when Teensie, in her blunt manner, asked for a shower. Since she's in double lock, it's the CO's discretion when to allow time to shower.

"You don't have to be demanding," Sue chided. "If you want a shower, you have to ask nicely." Teensie kept her cool, but told Sue she was not demanding, and she did not intend to ask again, just to patronize Sue. She didn't get her shower.

This evening Blanche told us Sue had come to the kitchen crying, because of the trouble she was having with the girls. Steve, one of the trusties, said he'd heard about Sue's problems from another CO. He seemed surprised when we told him she locked one of the girls for swearing.

"Don't the men get locked for swearing at COs?" I asked Steve.

"They couldn't—there wouldn't be room for that," he said. "Just when they get in fights, throw water at the TV, urinate on the floor—stuff like that."

Mary the cook is also nervous and cranky lately. We try to follow her orders and be patient, but her moods are unpredictable. While serving this morning, she rejected a meal Barbara and I had prepared for a "no meat" guy. She replaced it with a salmon patty, which everyone dislikes. Many times this inmate, who can't have meat, gets only cold American cheese when others get hot food. This time we had given him a sandwich with two slices of cheddar, lettuce, tomato, and mayonnaise, put it on a plate, and tagged it with his name.

"He doesn't need to be *that* special," Mary said, and fussed at length about how prisoners don't need good food.

I didn't answer, but took the sandwich back, as she instructed. I knew a true vegetarian doesn't eat fish, and wondered if he would reject Mary's sandwich. A minute later I broke the silence. "Better keep that sandwich around—that guy might not take fish."

Mary fumed that he doesn't have to eat it, he can throw it away. "Can't treat everybody special," she said. "If we did we'd be treating your Dad and Joe special."

Mary's mention of Dad and Joe made me feel hot. I turned away.

Next she yelled at Freddy—a well-liked, quiet trusty—to get out of the kitchen. He works in cleaning, and had stopped in briefly. All of us felt like defending Freddy, but stayed quiet.

We have nice times with Mary, too. Like today when I used a paper towel to wipe the lard off my scraper. My thoughts far away, I accidentally threw both the scraper and the towel in the garbage. Mary happened to be right there, and looked at me, face stern. I looked at her, bewildered, and began to ask what's wrong. Suddenly I realized what I'd done, and started to laugh. Mary laughed too. "You can't get away with anything here, can you?" she kidded.

February 25

By Rachel

Today I again prepared a meal for the "no meat" guy. The others were getting hot dogs. I put cheese in the hot dog rolls, as Mary ordered, then added tomatoes, lettuce and mayonnaise, with tossed salad on the side. This time I put the meal with its label straight on the cart. Mary saw it, and fussed that it was "very fancy for jail," but didn't scold me. She was in an unusually good mood, since she's going on vacation tomorrow.

Tonight I found out the "no meat" inmate had left for state prison, and hadn't gotten the meal. There's a sad spot in my heart as I think of his nice sandwich from the other day that ended up in the garbage. And the one today—a last chance to brighten the moment of someone I'd never seen—didn't reach him.

February 26

By Rachel

The day was better with Mary gone. No complaining or pushing people around, and no disparaging remarks about inmates.

Barbara and I had a minor spat at the end of our work. When we came back to our cell, I felt discouraged and burst into tears. It's more than just our disagreement about how to finish the work so we don't get late. We got that talked out. I guess it's jail. I feel depressed. I hate jail, and I hate working for the jail. I regret we don't have enough time for Bible reading.

By Barbara Lyn

It seems I've gotten in the habit of being snappy with Rachel when our work hours get drawn out. This morning I blamed her for making us late. Merla, the part-time cook, had asked us to do extra things that are the cooks' job. It upset me that Rachel didn't tell Merla we don't usually do that. Merla sat in the office jabbering with CO Sue for a half hour, while we hurried to get work done.

Merla has been good to us. But Rachel and I are both stressed out. Besides workplace challenges, we're dealing with lack of sleep and abnormal levels of excitement. During my nap this morning I awoke with a start when I heard snow being scraped outside my window. I thought I was in my own bed upstairs, hearing Nathan's tractor scraping the barnyard drive. I couldn't go back to sleep. A few days ago I was almost asleep when CO Sue called, "Barbara, Rachel!" I instantly imagined we were being called to go home, and could hardly get my pounding heart to slow down again, though I saw Sue had only brought our mail.

February 27

By Barbara Lyn

12:30 PM. We're back from the kitchen early—not because our work was done, but because the lieutenant says we can't work with the men unless the cook is there. At least that's what CO Sue said CO Max said the sergeant said the lieutenant said.

Sue came to the kitchen to give Rachel and me the message, and found everyone quiet and busy—me sweeping the floor, Rachel scrubbing sticky potato casserole pans, Steve and Carlos cleaning ovens, Kirk and Bill wiping dishes and counter tops. Blanche had left ten minutes before.

"I want to explain this to the two of you," Sue said, her hand on my shoulder. "I hate to be the one to tell you, but the lieutenant's orders are that we can't have male and female inmates together unsupervised."

Some of the other trusties slowed their work, trying to listen. Sue seemed nervous. She continued. "I talked to the sergeant (her husband, A.J., was on duty), and he said I have to put you back in."

"Uh-huh," I said.

"It's for your own protection," Sue said. She looked at me, begging for approval.

"Whatever you say," I said. I wasn't going to pretend I agreed with Sue. The boys didn't deserve to be treated with mistrust.

Sue looked at the boys. "The lieutenant says it has to be this way— Max and the sergeant told me to tell you," she said. "They're making me look like the bad guy."

Rachel and I walked back with Sue, out of the kitchen, about thirty feet down the hall, and into the booking room. A.J., the same sergeant who had ordered his men to undress me months ago, was seated there. He had a big, friendly smile. "This is stupid, isn't it?" he said. "I would think if any of those guys would make a smart remark you'd just give him a slap on the face."

I didn't answer.

We walked with Sue into the cellblock, and disappeared into the welcome privacy of our cell. Leaning my elbows on the cell table, I let out my indignation to Rachel. "I wanted to tell him, 'Those guys aren't as dangerous as you are,'" I said. "He is the rapist, and he dares discuss with me how I might handle another man?"

Rachel smiled, assuaging my anger. "You could have said, 'Yeah, that's what I should've done to you.'"

February 28

By Barbara Lyn

Jon, one of the trusties, brought the *Evening Observer* to the kitchen and showed me a letter to the editor. He was smiling broadly. "Read it first, then I'll tell you about the man who wrote it," he said.

The writer complained about "the Lapp supporters," saying, "They act out violence, disruption of public order, assaults on police officers...."

I grimaced as I read. When I finished, I said to Jon, "Now tell me who that guy is."

"He's a Dunkirk Police officer."

Rachel and some of the other trusties had gathered to read the letter. "Maybe he really doesn't know the truth," I said after everyone had read it. We told the boys about the false witnesses at our trial, and how Rex Rater said Dad choked him and slapped him in the face.

Jon said he'd seen on the TV broadcasts of our arrests that an officer kicked someone.

A little later the boys and the cook were getting ready to serve, when Steve called, "Barb, come 'ere. We'd like to ask you something."

I went over. Steve and Jon's question, which obviously held great importance, was whether we would have accepted a plea bargain if we had been facing state prison time.

After giving a moment of thought, I said, "No, I guess I wouldn't have, because there were lies in the deal. The charges made it look like we'd attacked the police, and that's not true."

"Even if you knew you could get three to nine years?" Jon asked.

"No," I said, shaking my head. "Not if it was a lie."

The boys were silent. Then they told me why they'd asked. Both of them had plea bargained on drug charges, scared into the deal by threats of state prison time, far away from family and friends. Both said their pleas were not entirely truthful.

March 2

By Rachel

Mary is going on vacation again, this time for two weeks. She came into the storeroom as we were finishing breakfast. We talked about the possibility of early release. "Don't know if I'll see you again," she said. She wished us well, then asked, "You girls aren't feeling well today?"

"Well, Mary, there are days that are harder than others," I said. "It isn't always easy to stay on top of things."

"I thought I was the only one like that," Mary said.

Back in our cell, Sammi asked me in her quiet voice, "Rachel, how come you're going around like—" She demonstrated a stressed expression, mouth glum. The other girls were looking too. Josephine came and felt my face and said it's warm, and blotchy too. My head was hurting.

Crying hasn't helped. I don't know why my emotions are so fragile. I feel physically weak, hungry and depressed. Seems to be some of my old blood sugar problem.

By Barbara Lyn

We received copies of our probation reports today. Rachel's report said the "victim/arresting officer, Sgt. David W. Bentley," had asked the court to give Rachel "the maximum allowable jail sentence, as well as make necessary restitution." But the Probation Department's recommendation to the court was "time served."

Mine was similar. "Because the defendant is working, and has lived a lawful life until recent events, it is felt that she would not benefit from a term of probation supervision. It is felt that a more appropriate sentence would be incarceration equal to time served."

The wrath of David Bentley. The impudence of Judge Mifsud—to go against Probation's recommendation. Our passive resistance has angered people to the point they have lost their ability to reason. We saw another angry letter to the editor in the paper, by an officer. "The Lapp cult has blamed every agency in the county for their problems...," he wrote. "Yes, Barbara Lapp, you and your cult members were found guilty by the people of Chautauqua County, not the judges." He ended his letter: "The system works, Barbara Lapp. Ask Lynn Carroll. She's at home while you still reside in Mayville."

Judy went to court today, and said a tall, stern-looking deputy drove her. The deputy asked about "the Lapp girls," then said he doesn't eat in the kitchen anymore since we work there. "They could poison the food," Judy said he'd told her.

We have noticed the deputy comes to the kitchen for coffee, but never takes a meal. He always looks sour.

March 4

By Barbara Lyn

Six weeks 'till our release. We're now on official countdown. Even the children at home told me they're keeping a "days to release" chart. I finally decided I can participate in the countdown without giving up my belief that I'll be out before then.

We had a long discussion with Chariss, a cellmate, tonight. It started when she asked Rachel and me if we have boyfriends. Chariss, outspoken with lively facial expressions, had asked us the same thing when she came in a month ago. "You ain't got a boyfriend?" she demanded, after the other girls told her we're single. "You lyin'!" she exclaimed good-naturedly when I answered in the negative.

"Why? You nuns?" another girl asked. I explained to the girls that I don't have anything against marriage, but don't want a relationship with a man unless it's someone who shares my values and who I can commit myself to for life.

Chariss seems troubled. She can't easily dismiss my position as odd because her own life of promiscuity is not satisfying. "I think I have to turn my life around," she said one night, her eyes brimming with tears. She looked at me, as if longing for answers, then continued her card game with a group of noisy girls. A moment later she said, "I wish I could be like y'all."

March 5

By Barbara Lyn

There are so many mood swings and outbursts here in the cellblock lately. Sometimes I can be a buffer, often in silence, or with a smile, or with a few words. I consider it favorable when the girls cry rather than scream or curse. Or when they admit their moods, like Teensie did this morning when I came back from the kitchen to use the bathroom. They were complaining loudly about different inconveniences and personalities they didn't like. "We got an attitude this morning," Teensie said to me. "A bad one—and it ain't gonna go away."

"Okay—so I can hear more of it when I get back from work," I said as I went back out with CO Gail. Teensie laughed. As soon as we were out the door Gail laughed too. She normally takes things in stride when the girls are nasty. Today her patience was wearing thin.

By Rachel

When Gail brought us back to the cellblock after work we noticed the big curtain outside our fence was missing. "Where's the curtain?" Gail demanded.

The TV was turned high. Four of the girls were playing cards at the table. They didn't interrupt their play, except to say, "I didn't do it."

"I'm dead serious," Gail said. "If you don't put that curtain out here, there will be a shakedown."

She went out, and in a couple minutes Sgt. A.J. Melson came in and said, "We're going back out. If that curtain doesn't show up, we're coming in for a shakedown. That's all I'm saying." He left.

The girls kept on playing. I looked at them accusingly. "You mean you're having them come in here for a shakedown? And they'll go through all of *our* stuff, too?"

"I didn't do it," one said.

"Don't look at me!" said another.

A minute later the curtain appeared—on the floor by the cellblock entrance. "You ain't gotta worry, Lapp Girls," one girl said. "The curtain's out there now."

A.J. called. "Are you ready?"

"Yes."

He came in, saw the curtain, and said, "Thank you."

"You're welcome!" the girls chorused.

We returned from work after a nice shift with Rose and the boys. In the office, CO Sue looked unhappy, and said something about "the girls acting up in there." CO Bruce Wlodarek was there too. "Do you have any pull in there?" Bruce asked. I thought he was joking. I chuckled.

CO Bruce, a large heavy man who is Doreen's husband, was the acting sergeant in the absence of a whiteshirt tonight. He was pacing the floor. "Seriously," he said. "They've been giving Sue a hard time." Apparently the girls' TV had been very loud, and when Sue asked them to turn it down, one of them told Sue, "Get back out there where you belong!"

"Do you think you could get them calmed down?" Bruce asked Barbara and me.

"Well, maybe. We can lead the way," I said. We turned to go. At the entrance of the cellblock we picked up the mop bucket and cleaning supplies as usual, and took them along in.

"I'm not cleaning tonight!" a few of the girls declared.

"Why do we have to clean?" others chimed in. "Why can't we have a break tonight, like we did last Sunday?"

I reminded them it's not Sunday. "We want our room clean," I said. "We're opening our window—so brace yourself for the cold air." Barbara and I took the mop and broom and got busy.

CO Sue stood outside the fence, looking at the four girls who were playing cards. "Why aren't you cleaning?" she demanded. "Sammi! Josephine! Come on, you have to clean."

That evoked a storm of insults and profanity from the group, already so angry with Sue that they couldn't even stand her presence. I sighed, and prayed silently, "Sue, why can't you give them a minute?" Some from each cell were busy, preparing to clean. The few who were stalling would surely have pitched in to help their friends. In recent months the COs have never ordered us to clean. Six days a week we come back from the kitchen, bringing the cleanup things along in. On Sunday anyone who wants takes a break, except for changing garbage bags. Everything is orderly and understood.

Sue wasted no time going back out to talk with the guys, then came back in. "You have to clean *now*, or you'll be double locked," she said. Sammi and Josephine yelled back at Sue.

Sue went out again. I heard male voices, and looked up from where

I was wringing out the mop to see five male COs and Sue standing by the gate. CO Bruce spoke to the girls, reinforcing Sue's orders. The girls talked back. He and two others came up to the girls at the table. "Josephine, go to your room," said Bruce. She got up and went into her cell, still screaming profanities. "Shut up!" Bruce told her, then bellowed, "Shut the f - - - up!"

Josephine only yelled louder. Bruce went into her cell after her, and bearing down on her with his humongous frame, backed her up to the wall. Then he lifted his hand and said, "Shut *up!*" giving her a push backwards, hand on her shoulder-throat area. A moment later he and two other male COs were on top of Josephine on the floor of her cell, handcuffing and shackling her. They took her out to the office and put her in the trap. She was still yelling.

The men came back and ordered Sammi to her cell. She sat at the table and said she wouldn't go. They dragged her, cursing and yelling, into the cell, then proceeded to handcuff and shackle her—with considerable difficulty, since they had only handcuffs for her feet. They had her on the floor. "Don't you f - - - - n' bite me!" a huge CO yelled at Sammi. Finally they carried her out. In the office, the yelling continued.

CO Sue came back in. Teensie began to upbraid her for having caused Josephine, her cellmate, and Sammi, such suffering. Describing the force the men had used, Teensie said, "You knew it Sue! You knew they'd do that! It's your fault, Sue!" Teensie was beside herself, screaming.

I went over to Teensie's cell. She had closed the door, and stood just inside. I reached through the bars, put my hand on her shoulder, and said gently, "Teensie, Teensie."

"They told Josephine to get in her cell, and she did," Teensie said, in tears. "Why didn't they just lock the door?" She turned away and collapsed on her bed sobbing. I went in and sat on the bed beside her, patting her shoulder. "I know Teensie, I know," I said. "I saw it too."

"Sue ain't sh - -! Sue ain't sh - -!" Teensie sobbed.

"Just ignore her, Teensie. Don't depend on her."

Bruce came back in and tried to console the girls. A normally amiable fellow, he looked troubled as he listened to their complaints. "I don't have any desire to make things hard for you girls," he said. He soon went back out.

Half an hour passed. Three men, one of whom was Sgt. Paul Stage, brought Sammi back in. Sammi likes Paul, as most people do. Paul, the diplomat. He had been in our cell last August, trying to convince us to change into greens. Next they brought in Josephine, and double locked both girls into a cell they'd vacated.

The turmoil wasn't over. Every time Sue would set foot inside the block, they'd call her every imaginable name. Sammi had managed to hit Sue while in the office, and the girls loudly joked that her ear was swollen. It must have been terrible to be Sue.

Once when Sue was out, a girl with a petite frame reached through the wire mesh fence and spilled a quart jar of water that stood on Sue's desk, soaking her papers. Others put sheets of paper with obscene pictures on the door for Sue. Finally she came in and locked everyone in for the night. From their cells, the girls sang rap songs as fast as they could compose them—about Sue, and their hate for her. Every time Sue appeared the girls made unbelievably graphic assault and death threats. She didn't even try to control them anymore.

At 10:30 Carole came in, much to everyone's surprise—in her street clothing. She said Sue had gone to the hospital because she was dizzy and had trouble walking.

I don't know if my thoughts were in the line of love, but I kind of prayed that something would befall Sue so she'd never come back to work again. Sometimes wickedness is so great you have a feeling God should stop it on the spot.

I called hello to Carole, then said, "Carole, you look good in those clothes."

"Why?" she said. "Don't you like my uniform?"

"No. You know what it says on it—'Chautauqua County Sheriff's Department.'"

"I know you told me that the first day you saw me," Carole said.

"This is a low-down place, Carole," I said. "This department is low-down!"

By Barbara Lyn

Carole stayed in the cell block a long time, listening to the girls' complaints. She told Rachel and me she expects Sue will press charges against Sammi. She indicated there would be job compensation involved. We had already suspected that was the case with CO Louise, who got hit by an inmate about a month ago and hasn't returned to work. One of the cooks recently told us she had seen Louise, and she looked fine.

After Carole went out, I called over to Sammi and Josephine, who were sitting on their bed, still in handcuffs and shackles. "We're staying awake with you tonight because we're too mad to sleep," I said.

The girls giggled. They knew we usually beg them to quiet down early. It was almost eleven, and we weren't a bit tired.

Bruce and another CO came in again, and told the girls they could have their chains removed if they calmed down. Miraculously, the girls didn't fly up again. Bruce stayed in their cell after they'd removed the restraints, and talked with them, listening to them cry and speak about the incident. It brought me to tears, to hear them plead with him, explaining how Sue had managed to push them off the edge. They said they knew it was wrong for them to fly up like that. "But we're penned up, we've lost everything," Josephine said, her fair cheeks washed red with tears. "It's the only thing we have left to do—express ourselves."

March 6

By Rachel

When we left for work at 5:15 this morning, the cell block was quiet, everyone was asleep. After breakfast, CO Doug Christian strutted into the kitchen where I was making salad. "What's wrong with those girls this morning?" he asked. "Not enough cigarettes?" He snickered.

I looked up in surprise. "This morning?" I said. "A problem this morning?" I thought perhaps in the two hours since we left there had been another flare-up.

"I just chained them all to their beds," Doug said.

My heart jumped. Then I realized he was only joking.

By Barbara Lyn

After our visit today Brenda let us return to the kitchen without frisking us. She appears concerned, and almost sincere at times. Perhaps it is her age. She's only twenty-seven. Lately she seems to crave approval from Rachel and me.

Brenda spent hours in the block today, listening to the girls' complaints about last night. She seemed supportive of them, and told them the reason they become bored and frazzled is because they have nothing to do.

In the office on our way back from work, Brenda said, "Bad night last night, huh?"

"Yes, it was bad," Rachel said, then added. "It was nice of you to listen to the girls. Even if it doesn't change things, maybe it can help their immediate pain."

Brenda appeared pleased, and spoke at length about how she'd stayed with the girls for a long time, though she had other work to do. She said she'd talked to the lieutenant about getting more activities for them, like rec on weekends. We discussed the incident further. "When a person is already in a cage, how else are they going to let out their frustration, except in words?" Rachel asked.

"Yes, sometimes it's best to just let them cool off," Brenda said.

Rachel mentioned to Brenda the incident several months ago, when she had double locked Teensie for swearing. "We didn't feel that was right," Rachel said.

To our surprise, Brenda agreed. "That was one of my mistakes," she said. "When I make a mistake, I admit it."

As we ate supper tonight in our nook in the kitchen, Brenda came again to talk. She asked whether the girls are calmer now, and if we have any ideas on what could be done to help make it better for them. Rachel and I didn't answer much. I didn't appreciate Brenda's prodding, as though we had some say in this administration. I also didn't like her emphasis on inmates being "bored," when the real issue was the aggression of the COs.

In our cell alone, Rachel and I again discussed last night's episode. The girls know we believe the actions of the police are often wrong. I told Rachel maybe it doesn't work to sow seeds of rebellion with people who lack self control. Josephine, amid her uncontrolled verbal attacks on the COs last night, had declared loudly, "This jail is f - - - - d up! The law is f - - - - d up! The whole system is backwards!"

At work today we had talked to the trusties about the incident. Since Josephine was in the trap, near their quarters for awhile last night, they'd heard what she said about the system. "Everything she said was true," Steve said. "I couldn't have thought of a better way to word it if I'd tried a whole week!" He also said the girl who hit Sue on the head deserved a medal.

Rachel laughed a little. "Steve, you're not very nice," she said.

"Why not?" Steve said. "Sue's nasty."

March 8

By Barbara Lyn

I got sick last night. At 2:00 this morning I vomited for the sixth time. Finally at four, when I climbed off my bunk for the umpteenth time, my abdominal cramps were lower. From then on, it was only diarrhea. By morning I was feeling desperate with thirst, yet not able to tolerate water. CO Gail brought ice chips.

It's embarrassing to be sick in a small area like this, especially with a group of girls who raise a fuss about every little natural odor, as well as "y-u-uck!" whenever someone spits. Last night when I knew it was getting bad I announced an apology for the noises they were about to hear. "You can turn the TV up as far as you want—and you don't even need to ask Rachel," I said. No one complained.

I wrote several letters today, trying to make use of my time. I'm concerned about Rachel, because she has to work longer hours with me off. The head trusty, Steve, is also sick, and according to the rules, would get sent upstairs because he can't work. We're hoping for tolerance.

By Rachel

In the kitchen today without Barbara and Steve there were only three workers instead of five. I was flying around getting bread and butter for lunch and dinner. Across the kitchen Bill and Hank sized things up. "This will be fun," Bill complained.

"We'll be here all day," Hank said.

"Nah," I said. "We'll just all pull together and work a little faster. We'll be so efficient, we'll get done only slightly later than usual."

At noon I asked Bill if they're going to take the garbage out today. "It would be nice to get some fresh air," I said.

It didn't take more than a hint. When noon work was done, CO Roy Sobilo came to the kitchen. "You want some fresh air?" he asked.

"Well, if I can be of help."

"We'll have you carry some bags, and get some fresh air too." He said they were ready, and led the way.

It had been two months since I'd been outside. A rush of mild March air flooded into my face. I felt like worshiping. I walked with the others, carrying a garbage bag in each hand. On the way back, I wanted to run and jump, but didn't dare. My hands moved slowly up, as though to embrace the goodness of nature. Inhaling deeply, I let out a quiet "whe-e-o-oh!"

March 9

By Rachel

I heard that a lawyer Lynn consulted since her release said if people had full control of the government, that would be anarchy. I wonder how he defines anarchy. What the government did to Billy was going too far. The people took control, and ended Billy's suffering. That's anarchy? Trash those lawyers!

A newspaper story I read recently said the Erie County executive declared he would refuse to impose a new tax the feds were threatening. He stated, reportedly, "If that's a revolt, so be it. We can't take any more." The writer suggested that if all counties would take a similar stand, things could be changed. So what's so eccentric about our stand? It's just that we "couldn't take any more." Like the folks who refused a load of tea from Britain. Only we did it in a nondestructive, nonviolent way. Why is it portrayed by the system people as something so awful, terrible, unacceptable, go-away-ugly?

I told Sammi tonight I wish that I could have had enough influence on her so she wouldn't have gone off on Sue like she did Saturday night. I reminded her that there are evil people in the world, even out of jail, and she needs to learn self-control, or she'll get into more trouble. Sammi agreed. She's in such grief. She just learned she had a felony charge of assault placed on her by Sue, and may have to spend much more time here.

At gym I had overheard a conversation between Sammi and CO Dale Austin. He walked up to her and said, "Having a bad day, Sammi?" She was in handcuffs and shackles, and couldn't help with our games.

"I'm always having a bad day," she mumbled.

"Oh, so you don't want to talk to me?"

"No, I don't want to talk to *any* of you!"

"So you think we're all a - - h - - - -?"

"You *are* all a - - h - - - -!" Sammi said, her voice shaking with anger.

"If that's the way you feel, you deserve to be here." CO Austin walked away.

The cruelty, I thought. A grown man, antagonizing, deepening the pain of a girl, only eighteen. During the struggle Saturday night Sammi was telling the COs they're so and so, and one of the three or four men holding her, face down on the concrete floor, their feet on her back, said, "We know you think so. That's why you're in jail."

March 10

By Barbara Lyn

8:00 PM. Just got done talking to Mom on the phone. Hannah is very sick with pneumonia again. I worry that the family works too hard, and I can't understand why Hannah gets pneumonia twice in one winter when we never had it before. When Carole came in, I told her about Hannah's sickness. "Maybe you should tell Lt. Belson to let me out," I said. "I'm afraid Hannah will die." Suddenly I was in tears.

Carole looked sad. She said she'd call Lt. Belson in the morning. "There are a lot of people in here who think you've served more than enough time," she said, "but they're not the ones in control."

"Belson could make that decision, couldn't he?" I asked. "There's nothing binding them to make us serve the full time."

Carole said she thinks Belson would have to talk to the judge before he could let us out. I can imagine what Judge Mifsud would say. He is trying to teach us a lesson. He wants to prove that we can't be free without using their system.

By Rachel

CO Roy Sobilo offered me a job of shoveling snow this morning. He brought boots, gloves, and a huge coat. As I pulled the boots on, I couldn't help smiling. How long since I've done that, I thought. "Only thing I don't like, they're green!" I said.

We went upstairs—Roy, another trusty and I—and went out the front door. I'd never seen that area, since I never entered the jail except through the tunnel from court.

The area to shovel was a wide sidewalk stretching from the jail to the road, about thirty feet long. My work partner, a shy teenage trusty, had a good snow scraper—large enough to hold the fluffy snow. My shovel was a small, heavy, twelve-inch one—extremely slow and ineffective. The trusty said the jail has other shovels, but they're worn out.

After the sidewalk was done, CO Roy took me out beyond a small building behind the jail to shovel a path and concrete steps. He left, and I was at work alone for fifteen minutes. It felt funny to be outside without chains. If I walked away, though, I'd go to state prison for six years.

March 12

By Rachel

We learned from our family that Don Stefan talked to Lt. Buchhardt from Cattaraugus County, asking whether it was safe to take Billy out in public. Buchhardt said they aren't looking for Billy, but if they saw him, they still have the order to pick him up. Billy wants to see Barbara after his sixteenth birthday next week. He is spending most of his time with relatives now.

Brenda was on today, and spent time with the girls again, even brought them coffee and juice. She talks and jokes with them—about their boyfriends, her new jewelry, why she doesn't want children, etc. She brings them things and gives them privileges that the more orderly COs don't venture to do. Then she talks endlessly about other COs she doesn't like. We hear Brenda and Doreen want Lee Ann, the new CO, out. It's crazy to hear her in here gossiping.

Last night we heard Josephine talking to CO Carole about the law, saying she just sold drugs and doesn't need to be in jail. "It's like Barbara and Rachel say, the law should be for protecting us," she said.

Carole looked at her sharply, then at us, with a mock accusatory glare.

Later Carole asked the girls if they know what the fastest growing religion is in this country. They were making a few guesses.

"It's sic'em-ism," I said. Josephine nodded, smiling. "Go-get'em-ism," I said. "Put'em-in-prison-ism."

Carole looked at me. "Rachel don't you sound bitter?"

"Oh no. I'm not bitter at all—just stating facts," I said. "I read recently that this country has the largest percentage of inmates of any civilized country."

March 14

By Rachel

Thirty weeks in Chautauqua County Jail. The past few days have been tinged with the feeling that our release is imminent. We say to each other, "Maybe this'll be our last day," or, "We'll probably go home Monday." Then we go on with life.

We greet two new women who are escorted in by the CO. Their return gaze shows their thoughts are elsewhere. They don't like having walked into this hole. Can't blame them. It has fourteen women in it already.

Brenda announced that Gwen went home. Some others are leaving too, she said, but she doesn't know who. We felt a little excitement. But not for very long, as different ones of the girls said their lawyers are out there doing this or that for them. Bobbi Trimmer, the public defender, was in, saying something about "getting some of these girls out." Then she left.

A few of the girls were anxious, feeling sure Bobbi should let them go. "I have to get out," said one. "I have two children at home. Never been in jail before. *Never.*"

"Been sitting here for a month," another said. "It's not fair!"

In the kitchen, we did some extra cleaning and dusting. Tomorrow will be Mary's first day back from vacation. We're trying to please her. Several of the boys and Merla made comments about it being no use. At the same time they were doing extras too.

Darwin, a young man who is new in the kitchen, hasn't met Mary. But he has been warned about her disposition. "Now I'll get yelled at all day," he told me.

"Don't think the worst of a person," I said. "There's good in everyone. If we do our best, we don't need to feel bad."

Last night Darwin and I had a chance to talk as we worked. He spoke of his cousin, Alberto, who was a trusty here back in January. Darwin and Alberto are both nineteen, and were caught stealing a car. He was intoxicated at the time, says he never had been in trouble before, though Alberto has. Darwin is deeply ashamed. He got a tough sentence of one year. Alberto got out easy. He had gloves on, so they only got Darwin's prints. Darwin is a working person. You can tell the difference between the two. Alberto had that devil-may-care air.

I made potato-ham soup, for the second time. Last time I made it, CO Houser had told us vinegar is good on potato soup. Tonight when we were preparing supper I noticed he was around, so I put a small cup of white vinegar on the serving table. We were eating when I heard Houser say, "Oh, potato soup!" Then, "Where's Rachel?" He opened the door to the storeroom. "You must have known I was coming—you had the vinegar ready."

"I got one glimpse of you," I said, "and I said, 'Uh! have to get the vinegar out!'" He laughed a full laugh, thanked me, and left.

We heard Sheriff Bentley intends to return to work, though he's walking with a cane, and can't see from one eye since his brain surgery. Mood of the staff here seems to be they'd rather never see him again.

Barbara asked me tonight why I didn't write in my diary that I'd cried the last couple of days. The reason I didn't was because I couldn't explain it. I've been concerned about my strange emotions, and worry that there's something wrong with my mind. One moment I'm doing fine, then suddenly I feel like—I don't know what.

March 15

By Barbara Lyn

Tomorrow is Billy Stefan's sixteenth birthday—the day that should set him free from Social Services' control. We don't know yet if it will be complete freedom for him.

I made a card for Billy, and asked Teensie to print something on the outside, as she has a good hand at decorative printing. I gave her the words I wanted, and offered an exchange with soup from commissary. She refused to take the soup. "You always be lookin' after us," she said affectionately. "This'll be fun."

Later in the afternoon she gave me the card, beautifully printed: "To a very special person, on a very special day!" A leaf and flower pattern was wrapped around the print. It was much more than I'd asked for.

I spent my spare time today recopying a letter I've been working on for the State Commissioner of Corrections, regarding the brutality of the COs here in the cellblock the week before last. I asked Carole if she would let CO Bruce know that we would like to talk to him about the incident, and share the letter with him. Carole seems to be scared of even conveying the message. She tells us her job is uncertain these days. Sounds like she's in constant conflict with the others. But she agreed to ask Bruce if he would see us tomorrow night.

March 16

By Barbara Lyn

Today is Billy's birthday and homecoming. Rachel and I are exuberant. "It's the biggest victory since last May when Billy's pleading face came on TV saying, 'I just wanna go home,'" I told Rachel. I got goose bumps talking about it. Social Services agents had been running around like chickens with their heads off, trying to find Billy and prove to the public that he is a sick, abused boy who badly needs their help. Then Billy's own voice and face had come to be heard and seen by thousands of people, declaring just the opposite. He just needed to be home.

Now, after ten months and six people in jail, Billy is having a celebration—home with his dad. We talked to Blanche about the event, in the kitchen. "We won!" I said.

At the gym we heard the news on the radio. "Billy Stefan is home," the announcer said. I yelled at the girls to be quiet. "Four members of the Lapp family are still in jail," the announcer continued. The newscast ended on an upbeat note: "But for today it's party time!"

I started clapping. The others joined. Rachel jumped off the monkey bar, whooped, and twirled across the gym. She came toward me, right hand raised high. I raised mine, too, and we clapped our hands together.

At 12:15 I came down from the gym to make a phone call to the Stefans, as planned. At the Stefan residence they had a speaker phone so I could talk to everyone—Don and Billy, my family, the media. I heard Billy's voice, soft and happy. "Billy!" I said. "Come closer, so I can get my arms around you!" Billy laughed childishly.

6:15. The TV news stories of the Billy Stefan reunion/birthday celebration made me shiver. They showed ugly pictures of the melee last summer, interspersed with lovely pictures of Billy hugging his dad,

Susan saying this makes the whole ordeal worthwhile, and the serene faces of my sisters—at the Stefan home. By the time we'd watched the stories on channels two and seven, I felt queasy. My face had broken out in blotchy red.

I called home, and the family welcomed me so that I stayed on the phone for twenty-five minutes. The birthday event was glorious, they said, not overly festive. Final concerns about police coming for Billy dissolved when one of the newsmen called the Sheriff's Department and was told all orders to pick up Billy have been rescinded. All officers are on a "stand down" notice, officials said.

Now that the battle is over, they should let us out of jail. Like the government did with war protestors in the past. Even when sentences weren't fully served, they had to be released when the war was over because it looked foolish to keep them locked up. Oh well, this crime of "endangering the welfare of the government" is not to be compared with any others. Maybe they'll never let us out.

March 17

By Barbara Lyn

Last night I didn't fall asleep until midnight. It was cold. The heating system must have been malfunctioning, although no one admitted it.

This morning I came back from work early, hoping to get a nap. Brenda wasn't in the office, and CO Roy didn't have a key, so he suggested we hang around in the kitchen until Brenda comes.

Back in the kitchen, Mary cheerfully invited us to help bring in a load of groceries that had just arrived. We got big coats on, stepped outdoors a few feet where the boxes were stacked on the sidewalk, and carried two or three boxes at a time—down the ramp, through the laundry room, around the corner, then down the hall to the kitchen.

It was good exercise, and I got just enough fresh air to mix up my emotions again. The sun was shining on the snow outside, and it hurt my eyes. The air was clear, clean, heavenly. The thigh-length oversized coat I was wearing felt so right. But men and women wearing stiff uniforms and carrying the keys to the door have robbed me of essentials such as modest clothes and fresh air. I felt like I couldn't look at them, as I walked briskly up and down the hall, arms stacked up with boxes. Why do they smile as though they were glad to see a little delight on my face?

Sgt. Paul Stage—tall, friendly, handsome—stopped me in the hall. "Barbara, you have to raise your voice a little louder," he said, pretending to be giving important advice. I listened, not certain if he was serious. He continued. "I heard your voice on TV last night—you sounded a little too excited." He meant when I spoke to Billy and reporters from the jail phone.

"I guess I *was* a little excited!" I said.

Paul laughed. I went on walking, my thoughts in turmoil. I wonder if Paul Stage thinks I'd like advice on sounding more professional, or being a better performer? Well, Paul, you can just go with your polished suit and fake voice, and all the hypocrisy that goes with it. I'll believe in myself as God created me, and directs me. No matter how many times I'm seen and heard on TV and radio, I'm not for show.

We went back to the office. Brenda still wasn't there to let us in. I was exhausted, and there was no place to sit. Rachel went back and helped the guys unpack and stack groceries. I finally went in and sat outside the cellblock gate, at the CO's desk. Ten or fifteen minutes passed. Still no Brenda. I wandered back to the kitchen and found Rachel working. I helped a little, made some tea, and returned to the office. Finally Brenda returned.

"Brenda, we were waiting a *long* time!" I sighed, smiling a little.

"I told you I'd call you from the kitchen," Brenda said tersely.

After lunch Brenda called us for a visit with *WJTN Radio* personnel. I had known they were coming, and apologized to Brenda for not giving advance notice. She accommodated us and our visitors well, in the jail classroom.

Our visit lasted an hour. Merrill Rosen, director of the radio station, and Kathy Sortore, whom I knew through business advertising, said they came to discuss ways of getting our voice out to the public. They said public discussion on our case has quieted somewhat since the initial outcry after our sentencing. "But people want to hear from you," Kathy said. "A lot of people are wondering what's happening right now."

Mr. Rosen proposed a plan where I would give a forty-second "voice message" via jail phone, on a daily basis. Kathy said they could run it as a promo, just before the morning news. They couldn't cover costs because of business ethics, but would give the lowest rates allowable. Rachel and I were enthusiastic about the plan, but told them we would need to contact the Mayville Five Committee to see if sponsors could be found for covering the cost of air time.

By Rachel

CO Carole walked us back to the office. We waited for Brenda to lock us in, as she had the keys. When Brenda appeared, she looked very unhappy. "I need to talk to you two," she said, coming close. "We put plastic on the windows of the cells, because it's been cold. We can't be turning the heat up just because *you're* opening windows."

Barbara and I listened, wondering what had invoked Brenda's displeasure.

"And that plastic will stay up 'till we say it can come down," Brenda continued, looking straight at us.

"That's all right, until it gets warmer," Barbara said.

"Okay?" Brenda demanded.

"Okay," Barbara said.

I was silent. We'd never been told *not* to ventilate our rooms. Now she's demanding an okay that we won't tear the plastic off, when we wouldn't *consider* doing that?

Brenda had stopped talking. We turned to go in to our quarters.

"I hope they don't keep the plastic on too long," I said, "because when it warms up you can't stand the stuffiness."

"That's not for *you* to say, Rachel! That's for *us* to decide!" Brenda said.

I turned to look at her.

"That's not up to you!" she repeated. Her lips seemed to curl around her words.

I was confused about Brenda's outburst. Last evening our cell had gotten very cold, and Carole helped Marge, our cellmate, hang a blanket over the window, with tape. Just before we'd left for the interview this afternoon Marge apparently had taken it down. Did Brenda think we did it?

Brenda continued, focusing on me. "That's not just *your* house in there. You're sharing it with a lot of others. And you have to take them in consideration. Apparently the majority of the girls think you're ruling the place," she said.

Her last statement stung deeply. I knew the windows being opened were sometimes the cause of minor complaints. Probably half the girls wanted some ventilation for cleaning, and we, especially me, had kind of pushed it as a good health practice. After all, it was our room. I now wondered whether I'd overstepped that fine line between compatibility and leadership. I answered Brenda. "We wouldn't want to do that."

"What?"

"We wouldn't want to rule the place. We don't want to cause trouble for anyone. We weren't aware of problems."

Barbara was silent. Was I the big trouble-maker, I wondered. Why didn't I just say okay, like Barbara did? I felt stubborn, and angry.

Brenda opened the gate to the cellblock. "You have too many boxes in your cell, too," she said as she followed us in. "You need to cut back to two each."

"We'll try to put our things together," Barbara said calmly.

In the block, Brenda called the girls. "I've just told Barbara and Rachel that the plastic is up, and they have to be careful not to just do as they want. They have to consider others, too."

The room was silent. I tried to figure out the girls' faces. "We weren't aware there was a problem," I said. "We're sorry if we hurt anyone."

No one answered except Judy. "None by me," she said.

"Good," I said, and went to our room to get ready for another shift in the kitchen.

By Barbara Lyn

We left for work, shaken. Both of us had trouble concentrating. I didn't hear when one of the boys was speaking to me, close up, and Rachel asked where the women's silverware tray was when she had it in her hand. We laughed with the others, but didn't tell the boys until after supper that we'd been hollered at. Rachel said, "Maybe we'll lose our job in the kitchen."

"They hollered at *you?*" Hank asked. Rose, the cook, and Steve insisted on knowing which CO it was. Steve looked shocked. He likes Brenda. He'd told us once that they were drinking partners before he came to jail. Rose said now we can relax because Carole is here.

Back in the cell, Rachel asked the girls if there had been a problem with us opening windows. Several of them said it's cold when they're open. We told them we'd be more careful.

The girls didn't seem anxious to admit there was a problem. "I don't know why Brenda yelled at us," I said. "If there's a problem, we would want to talk about it." I leaned against the door of my cell.

"Barbara, you look pale," Josephine said, looking through the bars of her double locked cell. "You look like you wanna cry."

"I do feel like crying," I said, my voice almost breaking. "I don't want to be a problem to anyone. I could quit work in the kitchen, if that is causing tension."

The girls objected. Teensie came out of her cell. Speaking loudly, she said she has nothing against us. "And all you in here," she said, motioning to the other girls, "you better 'fess up about what y'all been sayin' behind Lapp Girls' backs."

Then she spoke to us. "You know how y'all be workin' and you come back here, and y'all be heated up and open windows—" She gestured as she spoke, her eyes glowing with sincerity. She went on to mention the extra privileges we get like an extra set of greens—nice ones at that—when the rest had old ones. "I'm just bein' open," she said. "I want y'all to keep workin'."

One by one the girls began to speak, spilling out their grievances. Chariss, with a towel wrapped around her, got in the shower but couldn't leave the conversation. "You have to admit it, Marge," she said, leaning out of the shower. She told Marge to tell what she'd told Brenda about us—that she wanted one of the clothing hooks in our cell for her clothing, wanted to work in the kitchen, and was cold when the windows were open.

The others began to confess what they'd discussed with Brenda, and how Brenda talked to them about us. As we talked, the complaints were ironed out. We had no problem giving Marge one of our clothing hooks, and told her we'd be more careful with the windows. They hadn't known we're required to have two sets of greens, so we can get them washed without taking off time from work.

Chariss stuck her head out of the shower again. "I have one more thing to tell y'all about gettin' along," she said. "If you have something to say, talk straight to the person, instead of behind them."

We complimented the girls for their candor, and told them we forgave them. We also told them we felt Brenda is out of place, not only in discussing things about us, but in coming in to gossip about other COs. "A professional shouldn't do that," I said. "You'll still have to deal with Lee Ann and Gail when they come. You suppose her talking them down will make that easier?"

The girls seemed to understand. Josephine told us Brenda wants us out of the kitchen. "She said it's not fair you get special privileges," Josephine said. "And she doesn't like the trouble—taking you in and out."

"Know what else Brenda told us about you?" another girl said. "She said Barbara got mad at her when she had to wait to get in today."

The other girls told more. Apparently Brenda told them of an incident in the office when she gave Rachel our package of vitamins that were sent from home. She claimed Rachel dropped the wrapper on the floor and refused to pick it up, then CO Jim Crowell scolded Rachel, but she just walked away.

Rachel gasped and shook her head as we listened. "I can't believe Brenda really thinks I was being mean," she said. Rachel explained that she'd accidentally dropped the wrapper, after finding a note from home in the package. In her excitement, she hadn't noticed the wrapper on the floor until Brenda bent down to pick it up, and Jim Crowell said, "Thanks, Rachel," with a laugh. Rachel had apologized quickly.

We spent over an hour talking. In the end everyone felt closer than ever before. "We're all in this together," one of the girls said. "And Brenda, where's she tonight? Out living it up!"

Teensie, foresightful as ever, predicted Brenda would someday find out we've talked about this, and things would get twisted.

During our long discussion CO Carole checked on us several times, but didn't stay. After everything was quiet and peaceful, she complimented the group for getting along.

CHAPTER 20

Countdown

March 18, 1994

By Rachel

A supporter from South Carolina sent us photocopied pages from a book entitled *Conscience Be My Guide,* by Geoffrey Bould. The subject is prisoners of conscience. The reading is phenomenal. The writer says: "On their shoulders they carry the burden of society, for their protest can right the wrongs of society." One of the people he referred to was a man who refused to serve in Hitler's army, and was executed. He knew he would be, but held out against the persuasion of his bishop, his army recruiting officers, his fellow villagers, and his affection for his family.

Also described was a student who challenged the tanks in Tiannamen Square. Our suffering is small when compared with these. Yet the writing brings back thoughts that have gone through my mind since we came here—thoughts that over the ages have been shared by prisoners of conscience. Sometimes these people were in prison many years, tortured terribly, chained to beds with shackles so tight their ankles got raw. One person, in his diary, wrote that on one night of torture, riveted to his bed, he was illuminated with this message: "Today less than ever have you the right to desert your post."

The meaning of this post, and the stance we have in common, may never be fully appreciated by observers. In reading these pages, there was nothing that struck me with such familiarity as one prisoner's description of the carelessness of his tormenters. Torturing people was "routine and banal," he said. They could listen to pop music throughout, then go home to wives and children. "They treat it as just a job," the writer says. "[This is] perhaps even more dangerous than the act of torture itself."

It reminded me of my observations last August and September, when I realized, as though blows had struck me, that these people in uniform don't know, don't care, and don't think. "We follow all orders, good or bad," they said. "It's my job. I have to feed my family." So it became normal to treat good people like animals. These crude characters, to my consternation, were void of conscience. It sunk in slowly. But once in, the understanding became in itself a source of strength. It explained why I had to wake each day to the sight of iron bars and uniformed guards; why the torture of vulgar language, deafening TV noise, and demeaning treatment from officers.

March 19

By Barbara Lyn

The jail is having problems with the heater again. Everyone is cold. The girls are hollering. When I took a nap, my sleep was wild, with dreams that woke me up, screaming.

With Marge in our cell, we can't turn the TV away when ugly things come on. Her TV is right against the outside of the bars when we're locked in for the night. She goes for the most violent, most lewd stuff she can find.

A few nights ago the girls were watching HBO, a cable station that the jail got in here recently. They were delighted with the new program. But it was very bad. As the girls watched, they gasped and screamed until Carole came in to see what was going on. I sat at the little cell table, writing, turned away from the TV as best I could. Laughing, the girls begged Carole to look at the screen, which she did, then jumped back, saying, "Ugh!" It was pornography. I had trouble going to sleep that night.

March 21

By Barbara Lyn

6:00 PM. We're back from work, cleaning done. The cellblock is doing well, aside from Marge claiming that she's getting things thrown at her—shoes, books, etc.

It has been really stuffy in here the last few days. It doesn't seem to bother the others as much as it does us. They ask for aerosol spray deodorizers when the odors get bad, then we choke on the chemicals. Our window still has plastic taped over it. I was going to do a half hour of exercises tonight, but it's discouraging in such a tight place.

I got the go-ahead from home to do the "voice diary" for *WJTN Radio*. Now I must get started making notes so I can rehearse tomorrow.

By Rachel

Felicita, a young woman who had been here last fall, came again this afternoon. CO Brenda brought her in, then came to our cell and squatted beside me. "Rachel, you and Barb know Felicita, don't you?" she asked. "She has let me know that she wants to kill herself. She doesn't want to live." Brenda asked, hesitating, if we could talk to Felicita. I promised we'd do our best, and offered to take her in our cell. We already had four.

Brenda moved Felicita in with us, and another girl out. When she checked on us later, she found Felicita sitting beside me on the floor, talking. Brenda looked pleased.

Carole's shift started. She brought Felicita's bedding—a stack of three blankets and one sheet, but no mat. I looked at Carole in alarm when she said the jail is out of mats and Felicita would have to sleep on the floor. Felicita looked very thin, and the floor is so cold. I knew she wouldn't sleep well at best. I took the blankets and gave Felicita my mat.

Carole looked at me, as though demanding an answer.

"I have a bed," I said. "And the floor is worse. She's not that well."

"But it's a steel bed," Carole protested.

March 22

By Rachel

Marge can't get along with any of the girls. After many failures and fights, the COs put her in our cell a few days ago. Finally things are quieter, but the problems are far from over. Marge says the girls are throwing things at her when we're not around.

CO Carole told us Judy and Marge want to get out and work. Judy has hopes of going out with the guys to do outdoor work, repairing ditches, etc. Marge wants to work in the kitchen.

March 23

By Barbara Lyn

After kitchen work this morning, I joined the girls working on a jigsaw puzzle. Another spat was going on between Marge and the others. Brenda was yelling, "I'm sick and tired of hearing these complaints!" This time the object thrown was an empty Vaseline container. The girls were declaring it's a false accusation. Teensie fled to her bunk saying she feels like "hurtin' someone." Josephine asked me where we had kept the empty container, and whether it could have fallen off the table onto Marge's bed.

We told them we'd stored it on the bars, which is not close to Marge's bed. "Where's the lid?" I asked.

Marge, lying on her mat in the back corner of our cell, searched through her blankets. Then I saw her reach to the table and pick up the lid. "Here it is! I found it in my blanket," she said.

I went to Marge and knelt beside the mat where she was reclining. "I feel sorry about what's going on," I said. "But Brenda is partly right. You have to try to find a way of getting along. You can't just retreat to your corner and not face the others."

"I did try."

"You have to try harder."

"It's not worth it." Marge covered herself with blankets, crying.

"Marge, won't you come out, so we can talk about it? I'd like to say something, and I don't want to talk behind your back."

"You can go ahead and talk—I can hear," Marge said.

"I'm sorry, Marge, I don't like to see you feeling like this." I went back to the puzzle.

A while later Brenda was in, talking with the girls in whispers about the incident. Teensie was still raving about Marge's claim.

"Teensie, calm down," I said. "I'd like to say something. I wanted Marge to come out and listen, but she doesn't want to." Everyone fell silent. I told them what I'd seen with Marge getting the lid off the table, then saying she'd found it in her blanket.

"Now I really feel like hurtin' her!" Teensie burst out. "Now I *know* she be lyin'!"

The others blasted accusations about Marge just wanting attention. Some suggested how Brenda should punish her, to which Brenda quickly retorted, "Don't you tell me what to do, that's *my* job."

"She need'a be hurt!" Teensie declared. "Barbara seen it happen!"

I spoke again. "Marge must have problems—she wouldn't act like that if she didn't have problems. She doesn't need to be hurt more." To my surprise, no one talked back.

Brenda brought Teensie some orange juice. "She's having a tough day," she said to the others. Later when we left for the kitchen, Brenda stopped us in the office and asked how Marge is doing. "I told the girls Marge has problems and they shouldn't hurt her more," Brenda said, copying my words. She also told us Marge speaks highly of us, has a world of confidence in us, and we should try to open up with her. "I'm not asking you to be her counselor," Brenda said in her best confiding tone. "That's not what you're here for."

7:00 PM. Marge is talking to us again, friendlier than ever. She even talked to the other girls a little tonight. It's amazing how this gang is run in here. New girls are often treated with mistrust and even hatred, as with the girl who was physically attacked by Sammi a few days ago, and verbally abused by Josephine. Tonight she sits on the floor, happily playing cards with both of them, Sammi playing from inside her locked cell door. If they "stand the test" and don't act too intimidated, while also not fighting back, they'll eventually be adopted into the order. I'm sure Marge could do it if she'd try. She doesn't want to be accepted, and the other girls know it with uncanny clarity.

I spent close to two hours doing puzzles with the girls today. Mainly to put myself at their level, and share in their pleasure while it was clean. But it was also for my own good. It offered an escape from my mental stress.

By Rachel

I'm lying on a blanket to write. The table is busy, and besides it's very warm. The floor is cooler. Brenda finally allowed us take part of the plastic off the window. A nice breeze comes in, but I don't dare open the window much, since Marge sleeps on the floor, and rarely leaves her mat.

We heard through gossip in the kitchen that CO Brenda has an extramarital relationship with Sgt. Bill Bohn, who is also married. Some of the girls have been telling us that is the case, and confronted Brenda about it. She laughed and said, "People say that, but it's not true. Bill spent time helping us with remodeling at the house. He's like a father to me."

Barbara recently walked into the office from the kitchen, and found Brenda leaning on Sgt. Bohn, caressing his back and shoulders as he sat at the computer, his eyes almost closed.

To me, this explains why Brenda has such control in here, and gets away with anything she wants. Her bosses, it seems, are her boyfriends. It also explains why she's unstable, and why she hated CO Lee Ann. The girls say Brenda told them Lee Ann had a "more-than-business" relationship with Sgt. Bohn, and boasted she'd gotten Lee Ann fired.

March 24

By Barbara Lyn

Brenda followed us in when we arrived back at our cells at 8:00 this morning. She stayed by the gate as Teensie broke the news that there are rumors that I wrote in a condescending way about other inmates, and that doing puzzles is the only clean thing they do. She spoke as though making an important announcement, her voice elevated and articulate. Everyone in the cellblock listened. "Whoever it was that was reading your journal, whether that was right or wrong, better get into this, because we're gonna have a discussion," she said, gesturing as she spoke.

I sat down at the table where Teensie was starting a new puzzle. Others joined in the discussion. The story was long and complicated, but it had to do with several lines in my journal that Amy, a new girl, had read over my shoulder while I was writing at the common table last night. Everyone in Amy's cell seemed to be in on the accusation. "You act friendly and smiling, then write things like that," Judy said. "That hurts my feelings."

Sammi muttered that it's all been a front, us acting like we're nice to them. "Then you go out and talk anything you want about us," she muttered. "F - - -!"

Amy, round-faced with light brown hair, stood by the door of her cell. "You wrote you had to lower your standard to help us do puzzles," she said. "You're elevating yourself. Even the Bible says you can't judge!" She retreated to her bed, cursing.

CO Brenda sat at her desk by the fence. Rachel and I were in shock. I told the girls it's no secret that I don't go along with a lot of the language and conversations the other girls engage in, and doing puzzles was something I had pleasure in doing together with them. I offered a correction on the wording Amy had repeated from my diary, but Amy, calling from her bed, insisted it was as she had said.

"Maybe I should have my mom send it back so we can see it," I said. We had sent the diary home already, as we do every evening after writing.

Amy came to the door of her cell again, and made a rambling statement about us needing to be tolerant of each other. "You act like you think you're above everyone else, like you wrote. You ain't f - - - - n' better than the rest of us!" Amy shouted, "or you wouldn't be in here like the rest of us!" She turned her back, crying.

Brenda was still listening. Rachel stood outside our cell, silent. I sat at the table, occasionally putting in a piece of jigsaw puzzle. "It's true that we're all created equal," I said. "But we come from diverse upbringings and backgrounds, and we can't expect to think alike."

As the argument continued, Teensie went into her cell and whispered a few words to Josephine. Then Josephine spoke up. "I don't know what's true in *this* case," she said, "but I don't like how Amy says things that aren't true about me and my brother." She described an accusation that Amy made earlier, about "smoking crack."

"Josephine!" Brenda said sternly. "That's not what we're discussing."
Everyone fell silent.

After a while Brenda said, "Barbara and Rachel, if you have any-thing to say, say it, because you'll have to be leaving for the kitchen." We said nothing. "What Amy said is true," Brenda continued. "We all need to be tolerant and get along."

"I'm sorry we have to leave," Rachel said to the girls as we went out with Brenda. "Maybe we can talk more later. We didn't mean to hurt you."

It was a tense day, with Judy and Amy not looking at me, and Sammi, who has been very unstable recently, avoiding us altogether. This time the damage was deep, and I couldn't imagine recovery. I felt resigned, and wondered if we might have to stop working in the kitchen. Judy and Marge have tried hard to get work, and perhaps are jealous. Amy, new in here, sees our happiness and probably thinks it's because of the extra privileges we get. They know we eat well, and only send them what's on the menu.

When I got to the kitchen, Blanche asked me if I'm feeling okay. "Your eyes don't look good," she said.

"You're too sharp, Blanche," I said, letting out a sigh. "Crazy things go on back in the cells. There's nothing to do about it, so we just shut up."

Some relief came when Josephine approached me at the gym. "Bar-bara, I just wanted to tell you I don't think you're lofty or anything like that," she said. "And I don't believe most of the others think so either. If anyone thinks you have a 'higher standard,' it's probably because they wish they could be more like you."

As the day went on, things became normal. I helped the girls with puzzles again. Chariss and I sat close, intently looking for the right pieces, while Teensie was on the phone right beside us having an inti-mate talk with her little children. Touched by Teensie's conversation, Chariss and I looked at each other. Both of us had tears in our eyes.

In the kitchen, preparing for dinner, I set a bowl of tossed salad on the table, then joined Steve across the kitchen on the serving line, filling plates. Rachel came over and told me I should have put three times as much lettuce on the salad bar.

"Oh," I said. We continued working.

"Do you and Rachel ever disagree?" Steve asked.

"Oh yes, we have our times," I answered. "We have disagreements."

"If you would have said no I might think you're not normal," Steve said. "I just don't ever see you fight or anything."

"Well, we try to be open with our differences," I said. "Bad feelings don't survive too long when they're in the open."

Back in the cell block, Amy sat writing at one end of the table, while I wrote at the other end. Amy, speaking to Marge, who was beside me, mentioned she'd had a bad day. "I got mad at Tammy for no reason—I let off on Barbara this morning—" She said she'd gotten news of a possible six-month jail sentence, and might lose her four small children permanently. "It's driving me crazy!" she said, still talking to Marge. Finally I contributed a few words about the accumulated stresses she had mentioned, and her cigarette withdrawal problem she'd told me of earlier. Then Amy asked me advice on a letter she had written to the district attorney. I read the letter with her, offering a few corrections. We conversed comfortably the rest of the evening.

Carole came to lock us in for the night. "Thanks for helping with the letter, Barbara," Amy said, as we each headed for our cells.

"No problem."

The mild headache I'd had all day changed into a smashing migraine. Carole gave me Advil.

March 25

By Barbara Lyn

The hot dogs for lunch were over-baked and dried up, because the cook left them in the oven longer than necessary. When Rachel and I came back to the cellblock Teensie announced in a town crier voice: "Y'all know what they be tryin' to do to you, don't you? They put you to work in the kitchen so you can send this sh - - back here to us, to make us be mad at you—you know, to turn us against you. Y'all know that, don't you?" She laughed, then finished, "But I don't buy that. I know y'all can't help it."

"Sometimes we feel like quitting," Rachel said with a sigh.

This whole place is crazy. A diabetic woman who has been here for almost four weeks can't get a no-sugar diet. She's waiting for a medical recommendation, I guess. So she goes hungry whenever donuts or sweet rolls are served for breakfast. Once when she ate one, she collapsed with a serious sugar reaction. CO Gail tried to get help from one of the EMTs on staff, but no one came. Rachel and I tended to her, wiping her face with cool cloths and giving her slices of an orange. She was half-conscious for hours.

Tonight Judy stopped at our cell door, handing out rolls of toilet paper. She had not spoken to us since yesterday, and looked sad.

"Judy, are you okay?" I asked.

"No, not really."

"Is it because of what I said yesterday?"

"No, it's not that," she said. "I got bad news." She said she found out she may be getting one to four years in state prison, instead of being released late May as she'd anticipated.

March 26

By Rachel

Should I feel so weary? It seems we're surrounded by evil. Right after morning shift we got our family visits, and they told us they hadn't gotten our diaries yet—the ones that had sparked controversy in the cellblock two days ago. We told the family how Brenda had acted when the dispute arose. We worried that Brenda had confiscated our mail. It was the first time our letters had not arrived home in one business day.

This afternoon we called home twice, finding out finally that our diaries had reached home. But our second-worst fears were confirmed. The letter had been delayed a day, and opened, contents slightly damaged by moisture, and closed back up with scotch tape.

As Barbara and I reviewed what we had written in those diaries we began to feel as though we'd been sabotaged. Diaries are thoughts. They're almost like part of a person. Those thoughts can be interpreted wrongly, and the wrong person reading them could spread falsehoods. Brenda can't really harm us, but I don't know how she can face us after reading what we wrote about her boyfriends. And I don't know if we'll stay in the kitchen. She might get us fired.

Tomorrow is Sunday. Brenda said she'd be back, even promised to bring pop and chips for the girls. Barbara and I know we must tell her what the family told us about the opened letter.

In the kitchen today, Mary got upset when the girls sent a complaint about lunch. They apparently thought the soup was disgusting—*very* disgusting—bad enough to use the 'sh' word to describe it. Steve found their message to the cook on a sheet of paper tucked under the tray on the empty food cart, and showed it to us. The wording was really funny, ending with, "Thank you for our continuing stomachaches." The boys got a big laugh out of it.

I was surprised, then a little frightened when Mary became angry, saying loudly to Barbara and me that from now on nothing special would ever go in to the girls.

Before we left, Mary was calmer and spoke to us about the note. We also got to talking about corruption among jail staff, and told her we're having problems with Brenda and can hardly hold up under the pressure. "If we don't come to work one day, you'll know why," I told Mary.

Mary said Brenda's control in here is well-known. She said the way Brenda fools around with the men is not acceptable, and the sheriff never permitted that when he was around. I told her what happened a few days ago. I'd looked up from my work in the back of the kitchen to see Brenda pushing a young deputy into the kitchen, and laughing uproariously. He was laughing too. A moment later Brenda had looked my way and caught me watching. She stopped laughing.

March 27

By Barbara Lyn

I had planned to ask the sergeant to confirm our release date this morning, after learning from our cellmate that jail terms are calculated at thirty days per month, and we might have a few days less than we thought. But returning from work I met a scene in the booking room that knocked down the urgency of my desire to find out. Sgt. Bohn was reclined in his office arm chair, feet propped up on the desk. Facing the TV, he looked like he was almost sleeping. Brenda, across the narrow desk, was in the same position, her legs stretched out alongside his. Three other male COs were aimlessly sitting or standing around the small room, watching TV.

Brenda got up and let us into our quarters, without saying a word.

When Brenda came back to the cellblock a while later I told her about the letter the family said they'd received late, wet and taped. She lost eye contact for a moment, then asked which of the COs took the letter in the evening. We told her it was Carole, and Brenda suggested we talk to her. She also asked which sergeant was on duty, and suggested we talk to Lt. Belson.

I asked her if staff is permitted to open outgoing mail, in cases where the content of the letter caused a disruption. She said only when criminal or suicidal content is suspected. Even then, it would need to go through the jail supervisor before a CO could open it. Brenda appeared concerned, and said she'd talk to Lt. Belson in the morning, even if we didn't. She ended by saying she wasn't quite sure of the rules herself, and would ask him about it.

Rachel described what the family told us about the envelope being wet and taped. Brenda looked uneasy. "Was there anything in the diary that was really personal, that could have been damaging if someone read it?" she asked.

I told Brenda whoever opened the letter had to be someone who was aware of the controversy in the cellblock. She agreed, and said the night CO (Doreen), or even Carole from the shift before, could have known the girls were upset about our writing. She asked when the controversy started.

"There were no problems until we came back from work at eight that morning," I said.

"Not that you were aware of," Brenda corrected. She said it was going on as soon as she got on at seven, and could have started earlier. She continued to advise us to talk to both Carole and Doreen about it, since they were on when the mail was handled. "By the time I get in at seven, the mail is all packed up, sent upstairs, and sent out," Brenda said. "There's no way I could have stopped it if I wanted to. That mail is *gone.*"

Tonight we talked to the girls about our discussion with Brenda. They were enraged about the letter tampering. "They better not open *my* mail!" one of them said. The girls agreed it would have to have been Brenda. All of them, even Amy, were adamant that they hadn't told Doreen or Carole anything about the controversy over the diary.

"Only Brenda knew, and she be doing that sh - -!" Teensie declared.

11:00 PM. All is quiet in the cellblock now. News of our mail being opened has spread all over the kitchen. Blanche is sympathetic, and the boys are intensely curious about what will evolve, asking at every opportunity how Brenda is treating us. Brenda has been one of their favorite COs. Her true colors are hidden under layers of professional and personal makeup.

March 28

By Barbara Lyn

We were in our cells dressing for work this afternoon when I heard Carole's voice. "Hey Barb? Jeff wants you over in the kitchen."

Our cellmates were excited, wondering what the lieutenant wanted with us. Rachel and I were in a blank state of mind. As soon as we got to the kitchen Merla, the cook, said, "Oh, the lieutenant wants to talk to you." She and the boys looked like they were bursting with curiosity.

Waiting for Lt. Belson, Rachel and I went around the kitchen, touching this and that, checking the refrigerator, trying to think. What did

Belson want? Was he going to release us? Or was he going to tell us this is it for the kitchen?

Belson finally came, and called us into Mary's office. "I've been made aware that you had a problem with your mail," he began. He said Doreen had dropped two letters on his desk just before she left her shift a few days ago, with a note asking him to check them out. "Apparently she was concerned that they looked altered," he said.

Belson said he also was concerned about how the letters looked, but had mailed them out that afternoon, and made a note to himself to watch for anything further. He said all mail goes out at 9:00 AM. Brenda had told us it goes out at seven.

We asked him to describe the condition of the envelopes. He said one of them was neatly closed with tape, but the other one looked damp, like someone had used a moisture roller to seal it and got it too wet.

Belson listened carefully as Rachel told him she had asked Carole for tape to close an envelope that hadn't sealed properly. But he appeared confused about the other envelope that was wet. He answered all our questions without reservation, and assured us our mail would never be suspected for contraband and should not have been opened. "The COs are not permitted to open envelopes," he said. "They'd have to contact me, and fill out the proper forms. No one contacted me." Belson said we would have every right to file a complaint. "We could get our investigators in," he said.

I asked him if he knew there was a dispute in the cellblock regarding the content of the letter that was opened. He looked surprised.

"Didn't Brenda tell you?" I asked.

He shook his head. "Has that issue been resolved?" he asked. I told him the dispute was resolved, but we still consider it an issue, since Brenda was the only CO who knew about the controversy. Belson became uneasy, and rather quickly ended the conversation, saying we should let him know if there are further problems.

This evening Carole told us the undersheriff had called her up to his office to talk about the opened letter. She was suspected, since she was the one who took our mail that night. She said the undersheriff told her, "They could press charges, you know." We made it clear to Carole that we didn't suspect her. We told her we believe Brenda did it, and why.

March 29

By Barbara Lyn

I feel tired, both body and soul. Went to bed at 12:30 this morning, up at 5:00, half-hour nap this forenoon. I dragged myself to the kitchen. Then Mary told me the sergeant left a message for me to call home. "It's not an emergency," she said.

I went back to use the phone. In the office, Brenda was seated at the desk, sorting mail. "Could I get back in?" I asked. "I need to use the phone."

Brenda didn't look up. She slapped a stack of mail down on her desk, let out a sigh, then got up to open the gate to the cellblock.

I spent much of the day somewhat numb, just plain tired of thinking—floated around the kitchen almost mechanically. Serving time came. CO Bowen, a stout older fellow who likes to tease, was standing around the kitchen waiting for the carts to get loaded, making a nuisance of himself by talking to the trusties. The boys were fussing about the sauerkraut, making every description imaginable about its taste and smell.

"I like sauerkraut, because when you grow up with eight sisters and a brother you eat anything you can get," Bowen said.

I looked up and smiled.

"You know what that's like, don't you Barbara?" he said.

"Yes, I grew up with eight sisters and three brothers."

Suddenly I was overtaken with tears. Dropping the knife I was using for chopping salad, I fled to the cooler in the storeroom, wiped my tears with my apron, and returned to my job—walking briskly so no one would notice. CO Bowen was still there. I wanted to tell him, "You stand there and talk about nice, big families, while keeping me from my father, my sisters, my daughter—my pride—and you even smile while you talk."

It took several more brief retreats to the storeroom before I had put myself back together. As I put it in my voice diary tonight, "The decay of human decency hurts more deeply than the bars today."

We got back from the kitchen and found the whole place, including our room, shining clean. "Marge," I called. "Thank you!" She was playing cards with the others.

It's nice to see Marge accepted in the circle now, after secluding herself for months. Last evening she said, "Thank you for your advice, Barbara. It worked."

"What advice?"

"Mingling."

Today Marge happily moved from our cell to her previous one, when a bunk became available there.

By Rachel

It was 6:00 AM when CO Pat Johnson came up to me in the kitchen. He spoke quietly. "I heard you want to file a grievance about a problem with the mail," he said. "Just wanted to let you know I'm on the grievance committee. I'd be glad to help you file the complaint."

We hadn't planned to file a complaint, but I began to tell him about the incident. Soon we were discussing it in depth. Barbara joined us. I told Johnson we feel we know who did it.

"Who is that?" he asked.

"Brenda is the only one who could have had an interest in that letter."

"I was told it was someone else," he said, adding that Brenda wasn't the one that handled our mail that night. He said he had been there early Thursday morning when Doreen threw the letters on Belson's desk, saying, "This letter has been opened, and I'm not taking responsibility!"

CO Johnson is a jovial person by nature. This time he was serious and professional. He seemed surprised when Barbara told him how Brenda had treated us during the confrontation about Barbara's writing. He asked how we handled that problem. I told him it's pretty hard to defend yourself about things you write in a personal diary.

"To be honest, we write things about the COs," Barbara said.

Johnson chuckled. "No doubt you do."

He promised to discuss the problem with everyone involved, including Brenda. He said they would never suspect us of contraband or dangerous schemes. "You've been model inmates, and it's not right that this should happen to you," he said. "I don't want this putting the department in a bad light. I work here. This makes me look bad."

Johnson left. We went back to work. Later we shared with Blanche, Mary, and the boys what has been happening. Steve suggested we get a good lawyer. "I know you don't believe in lawyers," he said. "But I'd like to see you scare the sh - - out of these people."

Carole told us tonight that Doreen and Brenda both met with Lt. Belson in his office, about the mail incident. She said Doreen came for the meeting, off duty, and didn't look at Carole when they passed in the hall. Carole believes they deliberately excluded her. She feels very bad about being suspected. It seems people are scurrying to the lieutenant in an attempt to be freed from suspicion. Mail tampering is a federal offense.

March 30

By Barbara Lyn

After a lot of discussion, Rachel and I decided we must let Brenda know what we've been telling others about her in regard to the letter tampering. When we came back from the kitchen this morning I asked Brenda if we could talk to the lieutenant, with her present.

She took us right to his office. As we walked over I told her we wanted her there when we discussed it, because we're concerned about how she handled the situation that morning in the cellblock. "We feel it's connected with the letter being opened," I said.

"How I handled *what?*" Brenda made a nervous, mocking laugh. In Lt. Belson's office, she sat down on the edge of his desk. "They're saying they have a problem with the way I handled their mail," Brenda said, her face ashen. "I've told them I never *touched* their mail."

"I don't want to claim anything I don't know," I began. "But we can't help making a connection between the cellblock incident and the letter that was opened." I paused, then turned to Belson. "I want you to know we feel Brenda is responsible."

"Brenda wasn't in charge of your mail," Belson said calmly. "I don't see how you can hold her for it."

"You can't say things you don't know!" Brenda said angrily. "Didn't I already tell you I did not touch that letter? I didn't even see it. That mail is *gone* before I come in!"

"Yes, that's what you told us," I said. "But you have to understand, there was a dispute about a letter I'd written. That letter was opened. And you were the only CO aware of the dispute."

"I have no reason to have an interest in what you write," Brenda said. "I know the girls have told me you're judgmental of the COs, but that doesn't bother me. You can write what you want!"

I told Brenda we were not satisfied with her handling of the cellblock dispute. "You didn't as much as tell the woman it was wrong to look at my private writing," I said.

"I think I did a pretty good job," Brenda said. "The girls remained totally polite, and Amy admitted repeatedly that it was wrong for her to look at your writing." She glared at Rachel, then me, and continued. "If you want to write personal things about people, you go in your cell to do that—that's what your cell is for, not the common table where everyone can see what you're writing." Brenda was trembling, and her face had turned red.

Lt. Belson leaned back in his chair, his mouth drawn tight. Brenda spoke again. "Personally, I feel you girls are getting away with far too much—going out to the kitchen, getting personal phone calls in the office. None of the other girls are allowed to do that, and I don't think you should be given extra privileges."

More silence. "We realize we're getting some privileges the others don't," I said. "It's been a concern to us ever since we started working that it could cause jealousy."

Belson spoke. "What they think makes no difference. You're going out to work, and you've earned that."

"We do have extra privileges," Rachel said.

"That's because you work—that's not just because you're the Lapps," Belson said.

"There are a few others who would like to work," I said.

"They *think* they want to," Belson said. "You put them over there for a day—they wouldn't last. We tried it before. Either the girls were messing with the boys, or the boys were fooling around with the girls— or they're passing notes."

Belson's normally expressionless face looked a bit more human. "In fact, I didn't expect you girls to last this long," he said. "We did it as a try. I haven't heard a single complaint—I've heard a lot of compliments."

Belson's phone rang, and he pushed back his chair to answer it. Brenda continued to talk about the inequity of the work arrangement. When Belson came back, I asked him why they didn't show us the questionable letter before mailing it. He said the letter wasn't in bad shape. "It wasn't really moist—just taped," he said.

Brenda added that it's not unusual for inmates to tape their letters. "It happens all the time."

"But it is unusual to have them land on your desk, isn't it?" I asked Belson.

"Yes. But I think I did my job," Belson said.

Brenda referred again to the letter. "It happened on the night shift—not when I was here," she said. "Carole was on that night. When I take the mail, I make sure I do my job right."

I told Belson we had given the letter to Carole with a perfect seal. "And it was on your desk in the morning, apparently opened," I said. "Carole told us she didn't do anything to it. So it had to be either Doreen or Brenda."

"You mean either Doreen or Carole," Brenda said tersely.

"No, I mean you or Doreen. And you were the only one who knew about the controversy."

"I did not touch the mail!" Brenda said again, voice raised. "I'm telling you this, and Jeff could confirm it, that I had nothing to do with the mail. I told you, Barbara, that mail is out of this place by the time I come in at seven!"

Belson had stopped talking. Rachel and I stood silent for awhile. "I'm not sure what we're going to do from here," I said. "We've been pressured from people on the outside to press charges. I'm not inclined to do that. But I can't promise we won't take this farther."

Belson said we couldn't press charges, because there's not enough evidence. "But you could have the recipient of the letter file a complaint," he said. "I'd have my investigators look into it."

March 31

By Rachel

Doreen came up to me in the office, just after Barbara had gone to the kitchen. "Rachel, you *are* pursuing this thing aren't you?" she asked. "About the mail?"

"Well, we're not really sure. As far as court action, it's not something we like. We'd rather solve it here."

Doreen told her story, spilling it out quite rapidly, describing how she felt when she found the envelopes, at 2:00 AM. "They looked bad. The one was rumpled, plus had tape. It had been opened, obviously," she said. Not wanting anyone to think she'd done it, she said she made a report on it, talked to several COs, and called Sgt. David Bentley, who was on duty upstairs. "I don't get into things like that," Doreen said. "Carole doesn't own up to anything. But there's really only one person who could have done it."

After our conversation, Doreen helped me take the cart and tray to the kitchen. We talked a little more. A question came to my mind. "Did you talk to Brenda about the letter when she came in at seven that morning?" I asked.

Doreen's expression changed, her eyes looking straight ahead. "Yes, ah—" she stammered. "I'm sure she saw it, yes."

By Barbara Lyn

Kitchen work was done early. "This time I'll get a nap, while you write," I teased Rachel. She was busy recording her conversation with Doreen. But the new evidence of a cover-up revealed from Rachel's discussion with Doreen stirred me up. I started thinking what I would say on my voice diary tonight. Then a terrible noise started to rock the jail—a jackhammer, I guess, on the outer wall of our quarters. Followed by disgruntled inmates swearing at the rude awakening.

Followed by Brenda coming in and telling them to cut out the bad words, and how it doesn't help anything to get angry about it. Which made them even madder, now at Brenda. As soon as she went out, they blew up.

"She's just a 27-year-old bitch with a badge!" one of the girls declared.

"She better not even try 'n smile at me today."

"She knows she read Lapp Girls' diary. That's why she gonna be mean now—but I don't care a f - - - about Brenda's attitude!"

"She be sayin' Gail is airheaded! *She* be airheaded!"

The girls told us they had heard Carole getting blamed for the letter tampering last night, by the sergeant and Doreen. "Carole didn't do that sh - -!" they said unanimously.

Rachel told them what Doreen had said this morning, that there's only one person who could have done it, and how Brenda and Lt. Belson had put the blame on Carole. This enraged the girls even more. "They be tryin' to set up Carole—nasty bastards!" Some of the girls were almost crying.

By Rachel

Brenda came in with a new girl, and for some reason proceeded to introduce her to all the girls, saying their names. They weren't in the mood for that, and some walked away. One girl said, disgruntled, "I don't have a name, I'm generic." She was in bed resting, as were most of the others. Marge, across the block, echoed the same.

Brenda strode up to Marge's bed. "Don't you start that attitude!" she scolded.

I heard Marge tell Brenda, "You have things on your own mind. I don't know why you take it out on me." Her voice was almost calm.

"That was uncalled for!" Brenda yelled. "Now, knock it off!"

Later today we spoke to Carole about her being blamed for the letter. She looked worried. She started talking about how Barbara and I shouldn't be here, and how she noticed "that look" on us the minute she saw us last August. "I don't know how to describe it," she said. "Your expression. Every time I locked you girls in I felt guilty. Maybe it's time for me to think really what I want to do."

April 1

By Barbara Lyn

Subconsciously there is fear about Brenda's hostility. My sleep was disturbed last night. Once Rachel woke up screaming.

Carole opened our gate at 5:15, and we started talking about the previous night's episode, when Doreen and Sgt. Panfil had verbally attacked her about the mail tampering. The girls in here had heard some of it, and said Doreen told Carole, "What are you waiting for to admit you did it?" Panfil said she belongs in a state penitentiary. Dorine and Panfil even claimed Sgt. Bohn had witnessed Carole opening the letter.

We had news to tell Carole about Rachel's discussion with Doreen, how we'd learned Brenda *had* seen the letter, after four days of hearing her say, "I never saw your mail—it was gone before I got here at seven."

Carole seemed discouraged. She said she'd called Belson and said, "What do you want me to say? Do you want me to admit to something I didn't do?" She also told him she feels like quitting; she doesn't know how she'll be able to work here with other COs who are accusing her. She spoke of the clout the others have, with Brenda and Sgt. Bohn sticking together, Doreen and Brenda covering for each other, and Doreen married to another CO.

After seven and a half months, the day finally came that we had a shakedown. I had asked Brenda, on our way back from the kitchen, if we could have an extra towel, since we'd lost one in the laundry a week ago. She said she'd look for one, then came back in five minutes. I was getting ready for the shower.

"Barbara, you have to get dressed—the men are coming in," Brenda said.

The other girls immediately demanded to know why. Brenda said it's a shakedown, which brought on more questions. All I heard Brenda say was, "Because the guys said there's gonna be a shakedown."

As soon as she went out I told the girls I know why. "It's because I asked Brenda for a towel, and told her I'd lost it in the laundry." I assured them that's all I said, knowing that the shakedown would insinuate I'd reported someone for stealing.

The girls begged Brenda for a chance to hand over their extra blankets, towels and sheets, rather than have the men come in. Brenda insisted the men ordered it, and within minutes two COs came in, with plastic gloves on. Sgt. Bohn came in a little later. They went through each cell, counting blankets and towels—digging through boxes, even checking mail. The girls busily cooperated with handing over their extras, filling garbage bags with blankets, sheets, and towels they had underhandedly collected over months.

Brenda came to our cell and announced they would no longer

allow jail towels for anyone who has personal towels.

"Oh, no problem," I said.

A large CO came to our room, where Rachel was seated writing, and I was drying my hair with a towel. "Are you two the only ones here?" he asked. Rachel said yes. He asked how many blankets we had, lifted the edge of my mattress a little, and pulled each of the five boxes out from under our bed for a moment, barely touching the contents. Rachel gave Brenda our last jail towel. The brief check of our room had yielded no forbidden material.

Sgt. Bill Bohn and Brenda came in and inspected the window screen that had been in question last fall. Then the shakedown was over, and the COs all went out, taking the things they'd collected with them.

Josephine called me to her cell. "You know they did this to turn us against you, don't you?" she asked. She said earlier Brenda had come in and told them quietly this shakedown was because the Lapp girls had a complaint about a missing towel.

"They be tryin' to turn us against the Lapp girls—and it ain't workin'!" Teensie said.

April 2

By Barbara Lyn

I wrote a letter to Dad and Joe—probably my last one. But then there have been times before when I thought it was to be my last letter to them.

Jim Fox's latest article in the *Evening Observer* was a reassurance that we're going home, though I know it was intended to scare us. They're planning to release us April 15, despite us not paying the fines, the article said. It says authorities will give us ninety days from the time of our release to pay. "If they fail to do so, they could be jailed again," Fox wrote. "The length of that term would depend on what the sentencing judge thinks is a fair 'amount per day' for them to work off behind bars."

I was standing in the kitchen eating a grapefruit this afternoon when one of the CO interns who have been training here in the last few weeks came in. "Excuse me, please," he said coming close. "My internship will be done very shortly, and I didn't think I'd have much occasion to speak with you before I leave. I admire you greatly for what you're doing."

"Thank you," I said.

He left quickly.

By Rachel

Our count on days is down to thirteen. The urges grow stronger, though we already thought them strong a month ago. I try to stay calm, because of the others here. Many of these girls have months to go. All are worse off than us—not having the comfort of a loving family, and many anxieties besides bars.

Leaving our friends here makes me feel serious, wondering who will give them cheer, who will be there to hear when they speak. To-night a girl snapped at CO Sandy when she was told to empty the mop bucket. I asked if I could do it for her. Then there was peace and quiet. When we're gone, who will care one way or another?

In the kitchen, when we're gone, who will smile when things go wrong, and say, "I'm sorry, Mary." And the boys. Who will cook their favorite dishes on weekends? I'll think so much of Darwin after we leave. Only nineteen, he's the youngest by far in the kitchen. He's the only colored person there now—a total of twelve trusties. He gets picked on a lot.

April 5

By Rachel

Susan and Mom came for a visit. We'd planned to talk about get-ting started with produce planting when I get home. Instead, we be-gan to talk about home and jail. Soon all four of us were crying. I confided to them about my recent bouts with depression. I had thought I was handling jail well, but it seems depression is something I can't change. Maybe it's from lack of sunlight.

Mom told us she cried when she went to the garden and saw the rhubarb coming up. In other springs, Mom and I had always shared the joy of watching the first sprouts break the ground. Susan told of her discouraging times with health problems.

I think it was good for all of us to share our tears. Strange, just ten days until we go home, and for the first time in our eight-month stay, I sobbed at a visit. It was so undignified—sitting beside Teensie and all the other people visiting, and of course the guards. A new CO, the intern who spoke to Barbara, sat in the chair behind us the whole time.

April 6

By Barbara Lyn

Doreen brought us the garment bags in which they stored our court clothes and other belongings we weren't allowed to have in here. We put things in boxes to send home, and saved only what we'll need for the day we leave.

As we packed our things, I saw the big yellow envelope where the officers had put my watch and barrettes after my arrest. Thinking of my watch still ticking inside almost made my mind go blank. Doreen asked us if we're getting excited.

"I'm sweating," Rachel said.

By Rachel

Sleeping isn't easy these days. Just when I'm relaxing for a nap, butterflies flutter inside. I drop off to sleep—half dreams, then dreams. I'm home. I'm hysterical, screaming loudly at every little thing. I don't remember how I got home, but I'm still in greens. A teenage boy from someone else's family seems bitter, distressed. I take my lunch and sit with him, and we talk. He cheers up. He leaves. I'm in charge of making a repair involving an old stove. I do something wrong. A woman, some authority, comes in, begins to yell and hit me. I'm on the floor, her punches hurt. I'm yelling repeatedly for help. Then I wake up.

Trusties Freddy and Wallace plan to leave the same day as us. Bill and Steve could leave anytime too, on work release. We discussed it in the kitchen this morning. Blanche said to Darwin that it will be just him left in the kitchen. Darwin looked sad.

I put my hand on his shoulder. "You'll make it," I said.

"I'll make it. If I don't go crazy."

"You won't go crazy."

April 7

By Rachel

Last night Barbara wrote a short letter to the undersheriff regarding the mail tampering, telling him we would like to discuss it with him. Brenda was on duty, responsible for outgoing mail. I showed her the letter addressed to Undersheriff Ernewein. "Does this need a stamp?" I asked. Brenda said she'd put the letter on his desk herself. "Oh, thank you," I said.

Brenda left. I wrapped a blanket around myself and read the Bible. A short time later she came again.

"Rachel? Can I talk to you for a minute?"

"Sure." I got up and went to the door.

"I took the letter upstairs and put it on the undersheriff's desk," she said. "I asked one of the deputies to accompany me, so he could see I laid it on his desk. So if anything happens, you'll know I did put it there."

By Barbara Lyn

Just before lunch Rachel and I stood by the stove, preparing food with Blanche. A tall, stout man with a white shirt and tie came up to us. "Hello," he said in a friendly way. "You probably don't know me—I'm Ernewein, the undersheriff."

He had the letter we'd sent him last night. "When did you want to talk?" he asked.

"Whenever it's convenient," I said.

"I don't like this either," Ernewein said, frowning as he tapped our letter. "I'd like to meet with you as soon as possible." We discussed with the cooks when would be a good time to leave kitchen duties, settled on this afternoon at 1:00, and got his permission to have Hannah at the meeting. Ernewein asked if we could have Hannah bring the letter along in.

After he left, Mary and Blanche said they were alarmed when he appeared in the kitchen. "He never comes in like that," Mary said. "I thought, 'Oh, the Lapp girls are in trouble!'"

When we came back from the kitchen, Lori, a CO intern, locked us into our quarters. I told her to let Brenda know we need to get out at 1:00 for a visit with the undersheriff. Brenda came in a little later. "Who told you you're seeing Ernewein?" she demanded.

Brenda led the way to Ernewein's office—up the stairs, through locked gates, past the visiting area, and down a hall with offices on either side. She didn't speak a word.

She guided us into a room where Hannah and Ernewein were already seated. "Have a seat," Ernewein said, gesturing to Rachel and me. Brenda left.

The undersheriff's office was beautifully lit with sunlight coming through a big west window. Pure glass. We could see the parking lot and village park beyond. The chairs, with arms and light padding, seemed luxurious. Our sister, wearing a homemade dress and gray sweater, was sitting next to us, momentarily making me conscious of my prison apparel.

We took no time for cordiality with Hannah. She pulled the damaged envelope from her purse, and we inspected it, together with Ernewein. He asked who we think did it, and why. Rachel and I told how Brenda handled the cellblock incident regarding my diary, her response when we told her the family had received the damaged letter, and our visit with Brenda and Lt. Belson together. I mentioned Brenda saying the girls had been "polite" during the cellblock argument. "It was *not* a polite conversation," I told Ernewein. "Not unless you call the 'f' word polite."

Ernewein looked concerned. He asked if we've had problems before with other inmates. Rachel told him this case with Amy had been the first time someone swore at us. "Actually, we're on good terms with her now. She was new at the time, and didn't know us."

We told how Doreen revealed that Brenda had seen the damaged envelope, after four days of Brenda's insisting she'd never seen our mail.

As we spoke, Ernewein occasionally made faces. "I don't like what I'm hearing," he said. He leaned back on his tall-backed, upholstered office chair. We explained that it was a combination of Brenda's hostile attitude toward us, and the enormous inconsistencies that came about during the four days of discussions with different people that convinced us Brenda had done it. Plus the impossibility of the other two COs having had any interest in the content of the letter. We said we are confident Carole didn't do it, and it disturbed us to see the blame placed on her.

Ernewein said he'd talked to Carole, and she said she hadn't done it. "I have no reason not to believe her," he said. "Carole has always been truthful with me. I've been told otherwise, but in my dealings with her, that's how I feel." He asked if it's true what he hears that we have a good relationship with Carole.

"Yes," Rachel said. "We do have a respect and trust for each other—aside from the fact that we're on opposite sides of the bars."

"What about the rest of the COs?" Ernewein asked. "How do you get along with them?"

"There are no real problems," I said. "We never expected jail to be comfortable."

"It's not like we're friends with them," Rachel added. "Friends don't lock up friends."

Ernewein smiled a little, then nodded. We told him Carole is more understanding than the others, so far as our belief that we shouldn't be in here.

"Personally, I didn't agree with the sentence you got either," he said. "A lot of people here didn't want that."

I described what I'd written in my journal about enjoying doing puzzles with the girls because it was one of their cleaner activities.

"The girls interpreted that as us saying we're clean and they're not."

Ernewein chuckled. "It's no one else's business what you write," he said.

He then asked if we ever wrote on yellow paper. "One report was that Carole was reading from yellow paper that night in the office," he said. Hannah, Rachel and I all confirmed we had used only white paper lately, and the tampered letter was white.

"What is it you want me to do?" Ernewein asked, after we had spoken for an hour.

"Mainly we want to clear our concerns that no one be blamed for something she didn't do," I said. "We feel sure Brenda did it, and wanted you to know why we feel that way."

Hannah said she thinks we would also expect him to thoroughly investigate his employees, and at least try to uncover what happened. He said he could get his investigators to look at it, take the envelope, fumigate it and pull all the prints on it.

"How can you get someone that's unbiased?" Hannah asked.

"I'm unbiased," he said. "Even though I know you probably don't think so." He asked if we could leave the letter with him. We agreed to leave the empty envelope.

"What else do you want?" Ernewein asked, a kind expression on his face. "Do you want a visit?"

Hannah, Rachel, and I glanced at each other, unable to keep from smiling. "We wouldn't turn down that offer," I said. "But it's past visiting hours."

"C'mon," he said. Rising from his chair, he led the way down the hall a few steps. "I'll get you a room here." He directed us into Sheriff Bentley's office, which obviously was not in use. There was a large desk, a wall covered with plaques, and two chairs. Ernewein brought another chair from his office. Then he left the room and closed the door behind him.

We sisters hardly knew where to start, left totally alone in a room gloriously filled with sunshine from a huge window. We had not enjoyed such privacy for almost eight months. We talked in Deutch, and even kidded about switching garb and glasses on Hannah and Rachel, so Hannah could take her turn in jail.

A half hour passed. Brenda came to get us and we walked down the hall. She unlocked a door to the outside for Hannah, then escorted Rachel and me back to the kitchen.

April 8

By Rachel

CO Pat Johnson said a friendly good morning when we left our cell early. "Just a week now, right?" he asked. Teacher Cindy also reminded us we'll be leaving soon. Everyone mentions it. First thing this morning Carole said, "This is your last Friday." I'd already whispered it to Barbara as we dressed.

In the kitchen, Blanche said she's worried about Barbara and me. She leaned close to tell me Brenda had said to her, "I'm so mad at those Lapp girls, I wish I could smash their teeth down their throats! I wish they would get the h - - - out of here!"

By Barbara Lyn

At the moment all eight of the other ladies are happily chatting in Josephine's cell, where she stays since she injured her ankle playing kickball. Long gone is the rule that we can't go into each other's cells. As rules go around here, it was forgotten. A new one was a notice from Lt. Belson, which Doreen brought in one day, calling it sh - -. It says we're to get only one bar of soap per week, handed out by the CO on Mondays. And no one will get toilet paper without turning in their empty roll. The COs continue to give us soap and toilet paper whenever we ask, occasionally referring to "that stupid rule."

In the kitchen it's the same way. There are notices on the office window from Sheriff Bentley and Lt. Belson requiring payment of one dollar per meal (for staff), including breakfast. COs are not allowed in the kitchen except at serving time. No one obeys the rules. At night, the COs get keys from the sergeants, or unlock the kitchen door with credit cards. They cook, they eat, they raid the refrigerator and even the freezer, they leave messes on the floor.

April 9

By Barbara Lyn

Poor Carole feels so out of place here with the letter incident boiling. She said it escalated since we spoke to the undersheriff. I told her we just wanted the truth to be known. She said the truth will probably never come out, with all the sticky connections in here. The Captain Van Vlack party is coming up next week, for Brenda's father-in-law's retirement. A probe into his daughter-in-law's job at this time would be an unbearable embarrassment to the department.

Carole talked about her conversation with the undersheriff several weeks ago. She said he expressed sympathy for us, and is concerned about the image of the department. He apparently hoped the sheriff would be back to bear some of the weight, but it appears now that Bentley may not be coming back to work. He's not recovering well from his brain surgery.

"You should just leave with us on Friday morning," I told Carole when she spoke again of the injustices and crookedness among staff. She said her retirement comes up in five years, but she doesn't know if she'll hold out that long.

I filled out our weekly commissary order form, for the last time, and asked the other ladies if there's something I could get for them. One by one they let me know what they could use. After that Rachel and I spent a half hour making a detailed list on how to distribute our personal belongings to the girls when we leave.

Teensie left for state prison, and Chariss went home. The remaining eight of us are longtermers. None expect to leave before we do.

April 10

By Rachel

I was tingling with excitement when I awoke at 12:45 AM. What woke me? What's that noise? Drip, drop. I went to the window. Rain! Was that the excitement? Nature speaking in my dreams? Or was it—yes! It was past midnight. Day five.

I was slicing dill pickles for supper while CO Roy waited for the carts. He asked if the last week goes slowly. I looked at him nodding.

Roy said seriously, "I'm glad you're going. We're going to miss you—guess that sounds strange."

"Yes. It's kind of hard to understand. I used to think jails were for dangerous people. Never thought jail would be a part of my life."

Roy shook his head. "I've worked here for ten years, and I've seen a lot of things. If I had a nickel for every time I could say something went wrong—but there isn't really much I can do about it."

"The saddest thing in leaving is to think that we've been here all this time, and there are many of you that know it wasn't right. But not one of you had the courage—or you might say the principle—to stand up and say, 'This isn't right, and I'm not having any part in it.'"

"Speaking of opinions," Roy said, hesitating. "There are a lot of us—but I guess opinions don't count."

"Not really," I said. "Not as long as you say one thing, and do something else. It's hard to understand. You see people who seem to be nice people, yet they're willing to lock us up."

Roy was uncomfortable. "I don't put people here. Just about every-

one that's here, it's a judge that did it. I'm just—the only way to protest orders is to not vote for him."

"That's the only way to protest a judge's order?" I asked.

"Well—I'm not willing to give up my livelihood."

"I guess in our case, we were forced to make a choice. We had to
give up our livelihood, or at least our freedom. We had to either say a
lie, or stay in jail."

Roy had to leave with the carts. He looked at me. "I admire you,"
he said sincerely.

April 11

By Rachel

CO Brenda is back, after a two-day break. Her manner with us is
hard and arrogant. It's almost scary. She's friendly with the other girls,
but won't face us unless we ask for things.

When we came back from work this evening, I asked if we could
take in the cleaning supplies, as always. *"I'll get them,"* Brenda said.

We walked in to the girls, hands empty. Then Brenda allowed a few
of the girls outside the gate to help gather the supplies, talking with
them a long time. Everyone else was waiting to clean. Later Brenda
delighted the girls with a big bag of tortilla chips and a bottle of Pepsi,
served on ice.

Our release time Friday, confirmed to the media by Lt. Belson, is
to be 7:30 AM. We also heard there are news stories coming out on the
mail tampering issue.

April 13

By Barbara Lyn

Last night Brenda carried on a horrendous party of sorts in the
cell across from us, with most of the girls gathered there. It involved
outrageously lewd behavior and talk, the girls recounting experiences
they'd had with men, in lurid detail. Screaming with laughter, Brenda
sat on the same bed with other girls who were bouncing around, dem-
onstrating the actions they were describing.

I had not seen or heard anything so horrible since we've been here,
though the girls previously had similar fits for short periods of time.
This time it went on and on, Brenda clearly encouraging it. At 10:00,
two hours after our normal lockup time, she finally locked our gates
and went out.

I wanted to cry. Not just because I was lying there unable to sleep,
or because I knew Brenda was trying to torture us. I felt it was so

pitiful what she was doing to the girls, all badly in need of a little direction in their lives. After the laughter, there will be deep pain for them, cut off from the sensual life they were accustomed to. Then Brenda won't be there for them.

This morning I announced to the boys that I was serious about cleaning out the grease trap in the kitchen before I leave. It's a much-hated, extremely smelly job. A few weeks ago when I heard it needed to be done, I said, "I'll do it—to make sure I have a really bad memory about jail."

"No, you won't," Steve said, then added, "Unless you have a cast iron stomach."

I found out today it did smell very nasty. Darwin unscrewed the top and removed the heavy cover, on Mary's orders. It was only halfway open when odors starting escaping, prompting everyone to move to the far end of the kitchen. It looked like vomit—ten gallons of it. But I got it scooped out with dippers and cups, into a garbage barrel lined with five super-strength bags. After I'd tightly tied all the bags, the boys carried it out.

I feel good about having done the worst job around here before leaving. I also managed a favor for the girls. I'd been after Sgt. Paul Stage for weeks to get a new mop bucket for the women's block. Today it finally came in. He called me out to the hall to show me the brand new equipment, along with a new broom, and gave me permission to present it to the girls.

Doreen didn't look pleased today when she told us an investigator upstairs wants to talk to us. She escorted us up to the office of Investigator Jim Hanson.

As Hanson questioned us about the mail tampering, he did his best to be objective and straightforward, or at least it appeared he did. He knew little about the cellblock incident with Brenda and the girls, and asked if we'd had a chance to tell Lt. Belson the story.

I said we did, and that Brenda had lost her cool during the discussion. He nodded. "I was told she did that when the undersheriff talked to her, too."

We described her hostility toward us. He made notes, and urged us to tell anyone who has information to contact him or Ernewein.

We expressed concern about everyone pointing the finger at Carole. He said Ernewein is forceful about it, that no one will be railroaded through this, nor will any action be taken without evidence. Hanson also told us Ernewein had met with Belson, and apparently there was "quite a discussion" about the propriety of him sending the damaged letter on without investigating how it happened and who did it. Hanson said nothing like this has ever happened in here before, and Ernewein is not happy. "There seems to be an attitude among the COs that we're meddling, and should let the jail supervisor (Belson) handle it," Hanson said. "They're a clique down there."

After an hour or so Hanson looked at his watch. "It's lunch time," he said. "Speaking of meals, they won't be as good anymore after you leave." He returned us through the locked doors and down the stairs, instead of calling the CO to take us as they usually do.

April 14

By Barbara Lyn

It was our final breakfast in the storeroom, with the flimsy little metal table that has hosted our meals for nearly four months. Tomorrow morning we want to eat with the girls.

Almost 2:00 PM. The day is rolling on, methodically. Not unlike any other jail day, except in my mind each activity ends with the significance of the end of a chapter. Our last outing in the gym. Our last noon meal. Our last noon shift. Our last baking project as a treat for the boys.

Blanche told us Brenda boasted to her that she's going to be on duty when we leave. "I'll see to it that they leave when I'm ready," she told Blanche.

I called home and talked to Susan. She said Dad and Joe had finally been fingerprinted. But a CO told them they might not go home if they didn't sign the card. "Dad told them, 'So be it,'" Susan said. She sounded scared.

After kitchen work this morning Blanche gave us each two quarters and said, "Get yourself a pop." We went to the vending machine in the hall and got Seven-Up.

I sat on a portable kitchen table, sipping pop and eating oatmeal cookies that Rachel had baked. Darwin sat at the other side of the table, doing the same. "We'll miss you girls when you go," he said. Rachel joined us, leaning on the baking table counter. We discussed Darwin's problems, and his future. He said he wants to come visit our farm when he gets out in July.

7:00 PM. "Twelve more hours," I told Rachel.

"Be quiet," she said.

We spent an enjoyable hour with the girls, dividing out our things—towels, colored pens, writing pads, terry hair bands, and T-shirts. "We don't want to take things home that remind us of jail," we told them.

We promised the girls a final breakfast with oatmeal. We would eat with them, family style, around the table, with the milk in a pitcher instead of individual servings in cardboard. I'm sure Carole will let us.

Am I ready to accept this as my final day here? If so, Lord, let it be an ending of everlasting significance, through acceptance of Your divine guidance, Your all-knowing voice which is to say when our chastening begins, and when it ends. So that in glorifying Your name for this joyful ending, I am ready also to glorify Your name when a new and heavier mission comes in need of being accomplished. "Here am I, send me."

By Rachel

We received six letters on this final mail day. One was from a woman in Minnesota who offered her home to us when we get out, if we don't have a home. Susan sent a note on a card saying, "Roses are red, violets are blue, the soil at Lapp's Produce, is waiting for you!"

When we came back from work Amy called me. "Rachel? Are you excited? It's tomorrow!" A mischievous smile spread over her face. All bad feelings between us have melted away. Last evening we leaned on each other, arms wrapped, as we talked about parting. The night before she had asked me to French-braid her hair.

I felt sentimental about saying goodbye to the gym. I wore my torn Asics one last time, did two miles jogging, and some last-time basketball hoops. I'm proud to have maintained a fit, muscular body, and remarkably good health. I asked Swanee, one last time, if he could lower the music. It was so loud it hurt my head. He grabbed my arm. "Just one more day you'll have to put up with it!" But he lowered it.

Only a few COs came to soberly tell us goodbye. Many others commented on it. "We're kicking you out of here soon," one said.

"Would be our pleasure," I replied, walking past.

"You aren't really leaving us, are you?" asked another.

I turned to face him. "We're going, as soon as you let us out."

Another CO asked, "Can I come over for lunch tomorrow?"

"We've never been known to turn people down," I said. "But you can't wear that uniform."

"These are my play clothes. I leave them here when I go."

Sgt. Stage said, "I guess I'll be seeing you next at the fruit stand."

It's evening, and the date says our last one in jail. Will I not again be locked in at eight? All the things that have become familiar to me, albeit ugly, will I now be leaving them behind? A few of our clothes that we'll need in the morning are drying on the bars above me. When I remove them, will I not again have a need to put clothing there? My feeling just now is disbelief, a lack of comprehension that this evening has arrived. When I consider how it came, how it evolved from time's passing, that draws me into contemplating the particular mystery of time itself. I'm awed. Awed that time did this. Eight months. Time made me stay to wait its passing. In the morning, time will carry me out. But it won't stop.

I've also noticed that time has no mercy for us when we challenge its chosen speed of passage. Like when I was busy with fruit stand work at home I'd have appreciated it slowing down to allow me a little catch-up. In jail, time punished me by its awfully slow movement. It also highly intrigued me when I looked back and noticed it had moved when I thought it had stopped. I realize it's guided by God, and I don't need to understand it. I just need to be submissive. As I enter time outside the jail I'd like to keep good thoughts with me about the portion of time I spent in here.

It's 10:00 PM. Barbara just called good night individually to each of the girls, and went to bed. Then she said good night to me, and started laughing. I answered, but she said she didn't hear what I said. She had her head wrapped in her towel already. I went and tried to pull her off her bunk. She yelped so loud CO Sandy came in to see what was wrong.

I just finished filling my umpteenth writing pad, with the one-thousand-thirtieth page of jail diary. I tore the final sheet off the cover of the pad, and put the cover in the trash. It's over.

■ CHAPTER 21 ■

Home

The Buffalo News, *April 14, 1994. A yearlong hide-and-seek drama that landed four family members in jail for eight months while a 15-year-old boy hid on their Chautauqua County farm ends in celebration Friday with the release of the four....*

To the authorities, this has been a case of citizens defying the law and them paying the price in jail.

"It's a case that the defendants, the Lapps, and their supporters took and made into a public spectacle, making themselves martyrs," Chautauqua County District Attorney James P. Subjack said....

To the Lapps, this has been a case of standing up for citizens' rights when the state oversteps its authority.

"We've been in here for eight months and haven't submitted to a system that we maintain is immoral," Miss Lapp said.

April 15, 1994

By Barbara Lyn

4:10 AM. At home they're milking the cows. Early, so they can come pick us up.

Carole brought our clothes last night. She said she'd try to get us out of here before her shift ends at seven, when Brenda comes in.

I am glad our Father in heaven has kept us these 243 days. Each day had a special meaning, many very painful. This day has a special meaning, in its own way. It is like the stone that Samuel called "Ebenezer," saying, "Hitherto hath the Lord helped us." (I Samuel 7:12.)

At 5:15 Carole opened our gate to go to the kitchen. We returned at six, as we'd promised the girls, with their breakfast cart loaded with eight steaming bowls of oatmeal, a tall plastic pitcher of milk, toast, juice and coffee. "Breakfast is here!" I called.

There was not enough space for everyone on the benches of the common table. Carole brought in several folding chairs, and we were seated.

"Pass the milk, please," I said. Judy gave it to me. I couldn't help smiling. Sammi passed a tray of toast around the table. Reverent smiles flickered across the girls' faces.

"This makes me think of my family," one of them said. Marge glanced at me, her eyes brimming with tears.

After breakfast Rachel and I gathered our blankets and sheets, stuffing them into garbage bags Carole had provided. We used another garbage bag to pack the belongings we had left—a few clothes, our Bibles, and last of all, our writing pads and pens.

The only item we didn't pack was the vitamins we kept in the jail kitchen. We'd left them there so we'd have an excuse to stop in the kitchen on our way out, to say goodbye to Mary and the boys. In our months of work as trusties we had observed inmates being released, always escorted quickly down the hall, past the open kitchen door. Dressed in street clothes, they had suddenly become outsiders. Sometimes a restrained voice calling, "Good-bye!" was heard as they left, but by the time we looked up, only the guards in tail could be seen moving past the door.

We asked Carole for a broom and swept our vacant cell. Then we dressed in clothes from home and stood by the gate. Carole's shift was almost over.

Carole stepped in from the office and leaned against our gate. "I'm leaving," she said. "Everything's taken care of, I think. Your names are already off the computer." She lingered for a moment, a distressed look on her face. It was 7:00, and Brenda had just come in.

We expected to be let out at any moment. Brenda came into our quarters, talked with several of the girls, picked up our sheets for laundry, and went out again.

A half hour passed. Rachel and I paced the floor and talked to the girls. Now and then Brenda came in to answer requests of the inmates. She ignored us. In the office, she and Sgt. Bohn chatted quietly.

I stood near the gate, rocking from one foot to the other, watching the office door. "Wonder if Dad and Joe will come to the booking room before they leave," I said. "Maybe they let them out already."

Judy peered out the window of the office door. "They're out there!" she exclaimed. I strained my eyes to see, but could barely identify them—beyond our wire mesh, the door, and a small window in the far wall of the booking room. The girls are practiced at identifying people in the trap, and insisted it was Dad and Joe. Rachel took her turn. "Yes!" she shrieked, "I see them! They're wearing their Mayville Five T-shirts."

"Sh-h," I said.

Rachel kept her gaze. "Dad!" she yelled. "Joe! We see you!"

I cringed. "Rachel!" I gasped. The girls laughed. Rachel and I had never yelled out there to other inmates. The other girls did sometimes, and got scolded by the COs.

Brenda came in. She glanced at Rachel with a look of contempt, then left.

7:45. Brenda walked in fast, her six-inch-long key extended. "Barbara, Rachel, time to go," she said as the key clacked into the latch. The gate swung open.

We hugged the girls. I grabbed our bag of things and went out, Rachel a step behind me. Dad and Joe were in the hallway, with a bunch of COs.

"You look like you're going somewhere," Dad said.

"We're going home. Where are *you* going?"

"Home," Joe said. The COs snickered.

Sgt. Bohn led the way. We walked single file, Rachel behind me, then Dad and Joe. Brenda and two male COs followed. I wondered why so many.

At the door of the kitchen, I stopped. "We need to get our vitamins," I said to Brenda. As I went to Mary's office to get them, Rachel shook hands with the boys, and spoke a few words of encouragement to each. I did the same, and both of us embraced Mary, who appeared to be near tears. The sergeant and three COs waited with Dad and Joe in the hall.

We returned to the hallway, went up the stairs, and around a corner. A heavy metal door with a window studded with iron bars was there. Through the window I saw a glass door, then outdoors. Sgt. Bohn unlocked the metal door and held it as we filed through.

"Thank you," I said.

One more door. Not locked. As I pushed it open, I heard the clack of the key in the door behind me.

Outside, bright sunshine, a throng of people. They screamed and whistled. My right arm flew up to greet them, fingers in a victory signal. Rachel's hands reached skyward as she yelled, "Yea-a-a!"

I hugged Miriam, then Mom. "God is so merciful," I cried, head on her shoulder.

Billy stood on the sidewalk, almost smothered in the crowd. I had never seen him in public before without the look of fear that often tainted his youthful countenance. He was smiling. I ran to him and we embraced. "Oh, Billy—it's all over!"

Nearby, Joe bent down to pick up his two littlest ones from their stroller. Magdalena, third in age, clung to his leg. Nancy was smiling, but she looked pale. It had been a tortured hour of waiting, as she and others were unable to get confirmation from jail staff whether we were still coming out.

Well-wishers and family members reached toward us for handshakes and hugs. Television cameramen pressed in. Miriam held my arm. Rachel and Dad were swallowed by the crowd.

Suddenly the April sunrise engulfed me, its glory intensified by music of a Mayville Five song playing from a nearby car. "We've marched before in Mayville, beneath the August sun…."

Members of the crowd began to move in tune to the music, their voices joining the final lines: "Come all ye people, come march along with me, We're going to march in Mayville, 'till the Mayville Five are free!"

Rachel and I were driven home in a friend's van, followed by a twenty-car motorcade. We descended the hill into the valley that cradles our farmstead. The old farmhouse came into view, it's imperfections more obvious than ever—white siding on the west side, clapboard siding with gray, peeling paint on the east, and a north porch begging for repair. It had never looked more beautiful.

A fifteen-foot banner reading "Welcome Home" was strung across the driveway, tied to the tall maple trees on either side. The buds on the trees were beginning to swell.

Rachel and I ran up the front steps to greet Lydia, who had stayed home to watch the house. Then we headed to the barn. Rachel's dogs were all over her, exuberant. My favorite old cow, standing in her stall just inside the barn, turned her head to look at us. I stroked her neck, and quietly promised the docile 1,800-pound beast I would be here to care for her.

We returned to the house. Dad and Joe had just arrived. Through the window, I spotted a band of snow, above the banks of the creek that runs through our valley. "The snow's not gone yet!" I exclaimed. "It must have been waiting for us!"

Out the door I ran, followed by Rachel and a crowd of youngsters. Joe and Dad ran with us—down the road, across a little bridge, into the field. We bent down to touch the snow, then picked some up and began to pelt each other with snowballs. More family members and friends joined in, and we kept up the snowball fight until all our faces were flushed from laughter and exhaustion.

More than a hundred guests poured into our valley. Among them were several appreciative COs, and a family of seven who had been forbidden by Social Services to have any contact with us. Our guests brought food and cheer, and assailed us with questions. Members of the media mingled with the rest, jotting notes and snapping photos.

"Let's go for a walk," I said to Miriam and a group of her cousins who surrounded me, their little voices drowned in the hubbub. Billy sat on the steps. "Come on, Bill. You can go with us."

"I go too?" begged two-year-old Lelia. I hoisted her onto my shoulders, and we started out a tractor lane that cut through the flat fields across the road from our house.

The temperature had risen to almost eighty. The sunshine fell on us with exquisite warmth as we walked toward a strip of woods on the northern side of our property. A little brook was hidden there. I'd told the children we would go touch the water with our hands.

Miriam walked on my right, arms wrapped around my elbow. A half dozen nieces and nephews scampered along, bubbling with questions. "Barbie, will the water be cold?" "Can I take my shoes off?" They ran ahead, shouting gleefully.

Billy walked in pace with me on my left, calm, almost manly. After a silence, he said. "Barbara, do you think it was worth it?"

"Worth it? You mean going to jail?"

"Uh-huh."

I knew Billy would demand a straightforward answer. "Yes, Billy," I began slowly. "You're home with Dad, right?"

"Yeah."

"That's better than being in an institution, isn't it?"

"Yeah." Billy laughed.

"You know what else, Bill? Don't you think the next time Social Services people are thinking about taking a boy away from his dad, they'll be a little more careful?"

"Yeah— 'cuz they didn't like all this publicity 'n stuff," Billy said thoughtfully. "Maybe this'll keep more kids from getting hurt."

We kept on walking, in silence, until we got to the little brook. All of us dipped our toes in the ice-cold water.

As we walked back to the farmhouse I looked around me, at the children playing, at Billy, at the trees, the hills, the endless blue sky.

In a nearby garden, Rachel and Mom, spades in hand, were digging carrots. Insulated by fertile earth and mounds of straw, the hardy roots had survived the long winter.

The vastness of our freedom and the great, gentle valley spoke of God's infinite law of mercy—a mercy that reaches fulfillment only when shared with others.

■ EPILOGUE ■
By Barbara Lyn Lapp

When books end, lives go on. And dates change.

September, 1996. Two years and five months after our release from jail, life on the Lapp farm is as peaceful as it was in the spring of 1993 before Don Stefan called. Our fines have not been collected.

Dad, approaching his seventieth birthday, is in good health. He and Mom do long-distance trucking for our produce business—besides cultivating and harvesting crops. This winter they plan to cut a hundred cords of firewood from our woods, as they do each year.

Joe and Nancy Torres have had another son, their seventh child. They named him Eben—short for Ebenezer—in remembrance of victory over the hardships they endured when their previous son, Benjamin, was born in Joe's absence.

I still milk cows, answer VOCAL calls, and counsel families in trouble with CPS. A new child was added to my family in March, when a mother I befriended through VOCAL placed him in my guardianship to avoid a foster care placement. This time the state consented.

On numerous occasions Rachel and I have returned to the Mayville jail to visit our inmate friends.

In April, 1996, we made a five-day trip around New York State, visiting prisoners in seven different state correctional facilities. All of them were men and women who had previously corresponded with me through VOCAL, and who we believe were falsely accused.

Rachel continues to manage Lapp's Produce, grows and markets fruits and vegetables, and raises purebred dogs. She also helps nurture my children—and sometimes answers the VOCAL hotline when I'm out.

❋   ❋   ❋

After we left the jail, the investigation into the tampering of our mail continued. Corrections Officers Brenda, Doreen, and Carole were questioned by Investigator Hanson. According to Sheriff's Department records, Brenda again insisted she had not seen our letter. Doreen stated there is no way Brenda could have gotten the envelope. Both women, during their questioning, attempted to implicate

Carole. But Carole told the investigator she did not tamper with our letter in any way.

As part of the investigation, the tape used to reseal the letter was processed for fingerprints. No readable prints were found. The investigation was closed on May 2, 1994.

Chautauqua County Sheriff John R. Bentley died on May 19, 1994, less than five weeks after we left the jail. At the time of his death, he was serving his seventh four-year term as sheriff. His son, John R. Bentley, Jr., was defeated in a special election held to fill his post. Sgt. Joseph A. Gerace won the county's top law enforcement position.

After our sentencing—and after our release—Judge Mifsud was questioned by members of the media and concerned citizens regarding the sentences he had imposed. "Why I did what I did, I'll carry to my grave," he said in response to one inquiry. "I won't explain to anybody why—and I don't have to!"

A law student who questioned him asked if he is generally harsh on crime, for instance DWI.

"I'm not a harsh judge," Mifsud responded. "I don't like to see people sit in jail away from their family and work." He mentioned that he had long-standing differences with our family regarding agricultural policies, and referred to our past criticism of government controls in milk marketing. Mifsud also said he was upset about the brochures on jury rights that supporters had distributed during our trial.

Months later, during a media interview, Mifsud said simply: "They (the defendants) exhausted the goodwill of this court."

In May, 1995, only six months before his term would have expired, Judge Mifsud resigned unexpectedly. His court clerk stepped down at the same time. Mifsud told the media he was resigning because of "time restraints and work schedules." But a colleague of his, the town justice who was to take on his workload, commented to the press that Mifsud's resignation was "for no apparent reason."

In September, 1994, Corrections Officers Brenda Van Vlack, Doreen Wlodarek, and Sue Melson filed allegations of sexual harassment against Lt. Jeffrey Belson, Chautauqua County Jail Superintendent. The three women, all married to officers employed by the sheriff's department, went public with their claims simultaneously with their attorney's announcement that he would file suit against Belson and Chautauqua County. Belson was suspended with pay awaiting the results of the trial.

Two other employees of the department have since joined the suit—now with five women claiming damages in excess of twenty million.

The public reacted with some skepticism regarding the women's allegations against Lt. Belson. Media reports said that Brenda, Doreen, and Sue claimed the harassment had been going on for eight years, but they did not report it for fear their husbands would "retaliate against Belson." CO Brenda told the media she "had to lie" to her husband in order to avoid telling him what was happening.

Rachel responded to Brenda's comment in a letter to the editor of the *Evening Observer*. "To lie or to tell the truth is a choice, not a compulsion," she wrote. "How do we know what choice Mrs. Van Vlack is making now?"

A federal lawsuit against the Sheriff's Department regarding the August 16 melee in Mayville, is scheduled for trial on April 15, 1997. Ken Bellet, who was injured during the melee, filed the suit jointly with Billy Stefan's aunt, Diane Moran, also injured. They are seeking over one million in general and punitive damages.

Chautauqua County District Attorney James Subjack has steadfastly refused to comment publicly on the Lapp/Stefan case since our release from jail. To one reporter who questioned him, he asked, "Isn't it over?" A director of a local radio station invited him to participate with me in a one-hour talk show about the case. He declined. Later, Subjack spoke at a senior citizens' meeting regarding crime control. My father was present. A gentleman in the group raised a question about his handling of "the Lapp case."

"That's Jacob Lapp right there!" Subjack said hotly, pointing to Dad. He refused to answer the question, and abruptly closed down the meeting.

Of all the public officials, Judge Larry Himelein had perhaps the most far-reaching involvement in the Lapp/Stefan case. Court documents show that he was the district attorney in Cattaraugus County at the time the Stefan case was ongoing there. According to attorney correspondence, he was responsible for the decision to drop Don Stefan's sexual abuse charges in exchange for an admission of physical abuse in September 1992. Later, he also served as Family Court judge in that county.

When I was arrested in July 1993, Himelein was sitting temporarily as judge in Chautauqua County. He returned to Cattaraugus County shortly afterward, but came back for my trial in November. During the trial, he claimed to have no knowledge of the Stefan case. When the prosecuting attorney asked about admissibility of certain evidence, he said, "I haven't had any involvement with the Stefan case, so I don't know what you could be referring to."

At my sentencing, however, Himelein contradicted his earlier claim. "I know something about the history of the case," he said, making reference to Don's admission of abuse.

Judge Himelein was back in his home county of Cattaraugus when Linda Stefan was arrested for statutory rape, a felony. He released her without bail. Several months later he sentenced her to probation on a reduced charge of "Endangering the Welfare of a Child"—a crime which carries a penalty of up to one year in jail.

Donald Stefan still operates his welding and repair business near his home in Chaffee, New York. Business is "back to normal," he says. His work vehicle, a converted school bus painted black, is decorated with bumper stickers and white lettering that carries messages such as, "Save your child from Child Protective Services," and "Restore the Bill of Rights with fully informed juries." The bus elicits comments and questions wherever Don drives it. Once it was the cause of a mistrial, when jurors spotted it during a court proceeding that involved a defendant falsely accused of child abuse.

Billy Stefan lives at his father's home and helps out in the welding business. At eighteen, he has his driver's license, owns a car, and stays out of mischief most of the time.

Billy speaks proudly of his accomplishments, and his goals. He takes GED classes, and hopes to get his diploma someday. He bears the mark of a survivor.

■ APPENDIX A ■

Sources of Learning

Books on CPS and False Child Abuse Accusations

Brenda Scott. *Out of Control: Who's Watching Our Child Protection Agencies?* Lafayette, Louisiana: Huntington House Publishers, 1994.

Richard Wexler. *Wounded Innocents: The Real Victims of the War Against Child Abuse.* Buffalo, New York: Prometheus Books, 1990.

Mary Pride. *The Child Abuse Industry.* Westchester, Illinois: Crossway Books, 1986.

Richard A. Gardner, M.D. *Sex Abuse Hysteria: Salem Witch Trials Revisited.* Cresskill, New Jersey: Creative Therapeutics, 1991.

Dean Tong. *Don't Blame Me, Daddy: False Accusations of Child Sexual Abuse—A Hidden National Tragedy.* Norfolk, Virginia: Hampton Roads Publishing Co., 1992.

Steven J. Ceci and Maggie Bruck. *Jeopardy in the Courtroom: A Scientific Analysis of Children's Testimony.* American Psychological Association, 1995.

Books on Jury Rights and Other Historical Freedom Principles

Godfrey D. Lehman. *The Ordeal of Edward Bushell.* Sacramento, California: Lexicon Publishing, 1988.

Frederic Bastiat. *The Law.* Irvington-on-Hudson, New York: The Foundation For Economic Education, (15th printing) 1990.

Henry David Thoreau. *Walden, and On the Duty of Civil Disobedience.* New York, New York: Macmillan Publishing Company, 1962.

Lysander Spooner. *The Lysander Spooner Reader: With an Introduction by George H. Smith.* San Francisco, California: Fox & Wilkes 1992.

Rose Wilder Lane. *The Discovery of Freedom: Man's Struggle Against Authority.* 1943.

Thomas Paine. *Rights of Man.* 1791.

Bernard Schwartz. *The Bill of Rights: A Documentary History.* New York, New York: Chelsea House Publishers and McGraw Hill, 1971.

Etienne de la Boetie. *The Politics of Obedience: The Discourse of Voluntary Servitude.* New York, New York: Free Life Editions, 1975.

Periodicals on Family Rights

Family Alert. Newsletter. Published by Chautauqua County VOCAL (Victims of Child Abuse Laws), P.O. Box 85, Cassadaga, NY 14718.

The Family in America. Newsletter. A publication of the Rockford Institute, P.O. Box 416, Mt. Morris, IL 61054.

■ APPENDIX B ■

Fully Informed Jury Association—The Yellow Flier

The following two pages duplicate
the yellow flier seized by the DA
during the trial of the Mayville
Five (page 250).

Worse, many judges and prosecutors, apparently anxious to reassure the public that they stand for law and order, do their best to select jurors they know from previous experience to be "conviction prone". Then the judge (wrongly) "instructs" them that they *must* reach a unanimous decision, and *soon*, to avoid "overburdening the taxpayers."

Jurors are very rarely informed they may vote according to conscience, even after swearing to "apply the law as given"–or told that it's better to "hang" the jury than to violate one's conscience in order to reach consensus. *These are some of the reasons why FIJA was formed.*

What is "FIJA"?

FIJA stands for Fully informed Jury Association. We are a nationwide network of jury-rights activists and groups. Our current project is also known as "FIJA", the Fully Informed Jury *Act* or *Amendment*.

As law, FIJA would require that trial judges resume the former practice of *telling* jurors about their right to judge both law and fact regarding each and every charge against a defendant. *We want the judge, like everyone else in the courtroom, to tell the whole truth and nothing but.*

Resume? Did judges fully inform jurors of their rights in the past?

Yes, it was normal procedure in the early days of our nation and before, in colonial times. America's Founders realized that trials by juries of ordinary people, fully aware of their rights as jurors, would be essential to preservation of our *freedom*. As long as juries had the final say on the laws of the land, the government would remain the servant, not the master, of the people.

Our third president, *Thomas Jefferson*, put it like this: *"I consider trial by jury as the only anchor yet imagined by man by which a government can be held to the principles of its constitution."*

John Adams, our second president, had this to say about the juror: *"It is not only his right, but his duty...to find the verdict according to his own best understanding, judgment, and conscience, though in direct opposition to the direction of the court."*

TRUE... "BUT"...

it's extremely unlikely the judge will tell you this, because the law doesn't require it.

Instead, expect the judge to tell you that you may consider *"only the facts"* of the case and you are *not* to let your conscience, your opinion of the law, or the defendant's motives affect your decision.

How can people get fair trials if the jurors can't use conscience?

Many people *don't* get fair trials. Too often, jurors actually end up apologizing to the person they've convicted–or to the community for acquitting when the evidence clearly established guilt.

Something is definitely wrong when jurors feel badly about their verdict. They should never be ashamed of their decision, or explain "I wanted to vote my conscience, but the judge said we had to apply the law as it was given to us, like it or not."

Most Americans are aware of their right to trial by jury, but how many know that *the jury has more power than anyone else in the courtroom*–and that in pursuit of a just verdict, *jurors are free to judge the merits of the law itself, its use in the case at hand, or the motives of the accused.*

If jurors were supposed to judge "only the facts", their job could be done by computer. It is precisely because people have feelings, opinions, wisdom, experience, and *conscience* that we depend upon jurors, not machines, to judge court cases.

Why don't judges tell juries their full range of rights?

In a trial by jury, the judge's job is to referee the trial and provide neutral legal advice to the jury, but judges rarely advise jurors of their rights. And judges are not supposed to dismiss prospective jurors because they admit having qualms with the law, or know about their right to judge the law and its application. But such dismissals are routine.

We can only speculate on why: Disrespect for the vital concept of "government of, by, and for the people?" Unwillingness to part with their power? Ignorance of jurors' rights? (Yes, some judges do not even *know* about the rights of jurors.)

TRUE

OR

FALSE

?

When you sit on a jury, you have the right to vote your conscience.

These sound like voices of hard experience. Were they?

Yes. Only decades had passed since freedom of the press was established in the colonies when a jury decided John Peter Zenger was "not guilty" of seditious libel. He was charged with this "crime" for printing true, but damaging, news stories about the Royal Governor of New York Colony.

"Truth is no defense", the court told the jury! But the jury decided to reject bad law, and acquitted.

Why? Because defense attorney Andrew Hamilton informed the jury of its rights: he told the story of William Penn's trial—of the courageous London jury which refused to find him guilty of preaching what was then an illegal religion (Quakerism). His jurors stood by their verdict even though they were held without food, water, or toilet facilities for four days.

They were then fined and imprisoned for acquitting Penn—until England's highest court acknowledged their *right* to reject both law and fact, and to find a verdict according to conscience. It was exercise of that right in the Penn trial which eventually led to recognition of free speech, religious freedom, and peaceable assembly as individual rights.

American colonists regularly depended on juries to thwart bad law sent over from England. The British then restricted trial by jury and other rights which juries had helped secure. Result? The Declaration of Independence and the American Revolution!

Afterwards, to protect the rights they'd fought for from future attack, the Founders of the new nation placed trial by jury—meaning tough, fully informed juries—in both the Constitution and Bill of Rights.

Bad law—special-interest legislation which tramples our rights—is no longer sent here from Britain. But our own legislatures keep us well supplied...Now, more than ever, we need juries to protect us!

Why haven't I heard about "jury rights" before now?

In the 1890's, powerful special-interest pressures inspired a series of judicial decisions which tried to limit jury rights. While no court has yet dared to deny that juries can "nullify" or "veto" a law, or "bring in a general verdict", some—hypocritically—have held that jurors need not be *told* their rights!

That is why it is nowadays a rare and courageous attorney who will risk being cited for contempt for informing the jury about its rights without obtaining the judge's prior approval. It's also why the idea of jury rights is not taught in (government) schools.

Still, the jury's power to reject bad law continues to be recognized, as in 1972 when the D.C. Circuit Court of Appeals held that the jury has an

"...unreviewable and irreversible power...to acquit in disregard of the instruction on the law given by the trial judge. The pages of history shine upon instances of the jury's exercise of its prerogative to disregard instructions of the judge; for example, acquittals under the fugitive slave law." (473 F. 2d 1113)

What will happen when FIJA becomes law?

Three good things: (1) Unjustly accused persons and their trial jurors, as well as crime victims and their communities—will more often be satisfied that *the jury system actually delivers justice;*

(2) Legislators will have access to regular *feedback from ordinary people*, sitting on juries, instead of mainly from special-interest groups and other very political sources. With better information, they can better represent the will of the people;

(3) When the laws of the land respect the will of the people, as revealed by their jury verdicts, the people, in turn, will show *more respect for the law.*

Sounds good! Where can I find some "FIJA Action" right now?

There are several current, exciting fronts: activists are working with lawmakers for passage of FIJA legislation in some states, and are attempting to put FIJA on the election ballot by *citizen initiative* in others. There are people distributing *educational materials* (including this brochure) in every state. And, whenever our budget allows it, FIJA engages in newspaper, radio, and television *advertising.*

In 1991 we named September 5th (the anniversary of William Penn's acquittal)"Jury Rights Day" and handed out brochures at courthouses around the U.S.A. It's an annual event, and you're invited!

As with any right, the right of jurors to reject bad law resides in the people, not the government—so all that is needed for people to use it is to *learn* it!

It's time to act against injustice!

● **We need to regard every day as "Jury Rights Day".** Almost every day, attempts are made to limit jury power, mostly via subtle changes in the rules of court procedure, often directly by court decisions, or by the creation of types of law which "do not require" jury trials for the accused.

● **Far too many harmless people have gone to prison** because their trial juries were not fully and truthfully informed, to the point that the U.S.A. now leads the entire world in percentage of population behind bars! More prisons are being built than ever before, and they will be filled largely with people whose only "crime" was to displease the government "master", not to victimize *anyone.*

● **Likewise, there are dangerous criminals free on the streets**—sometimes because a jury thought it "had to" acquit after being instructed by the judge, even though evidence of guilt was very clear. This type of injustice occurs much less frequently than does unreasonable or unnecessary incarceration of harmless people, even though it typically receives more publicity. But here, too, "FIJA" might help.

THE RIGHT DECISION — WHEN THE LAW IS WRONG

--TO RECEIVE MORE INFORMATION—
We'll send a free introductory information packet to you when you call 1-800-TEL-JURY, then tell (and spell) your name, address and phone, on our tape.

--TO BECOME AN ACTIVIST TODAY—
Copy and give this brochure to friends and family—or to jurors, among others, at the local courthouse.

--TO JOIN OR CONTRIBUTE TO FIJA—
Send at least $15 to FIJA, P.O. Box 59, Helmville, MT 59843. You will get both the FIJA introductory information packet and at least the next year's worth (4 issues) of our newsletter, *the FIJActivist.*

--TO TALK TO PEOPLE, NOT TAPES—
Phone Don Doig, Kathy Ballard, or Larry Dodge at FIJA National HQ: 406-793-5550. Locally, contact:

Nathan Lapp
RR#2 Box 174
Cassadaga, NY 14718

▪ A P P E N D I X   C ▪

Jailhouse Poetry

Who Decides?
By Barbara Lyn Lapp, September 2, 1993

Some things move, some things don't—some things can't.
Some people come, some people go, others won't;
Some can't.
Who decides when things move, when they don't, where people go?

I wondered these things,
Because where I stood, I couldn't go.
Nature prevented me not; the strength of my youth called,
and the desire of my heart said "go."
Move with the rest, decide where to go, and when.
Touch the beauty of creation,
Feel of the movement and charm of the day.
Smell the scent of the green in the grass and the trees,
Feel the rays of the sun on the skin.
But I couldn't.
Why?
I am chained by my hands, and bound by three men
who say they are officers of law.
At a gate nearby is an entrance to the place called court.
Around me are hard polished walls
with locks on all sides,
And three men, who when I look in their eyes,
I meet for a moment with folks of my kind—
Created by God at my equal.
But why am I bound, and they are not?
They sit, and they talk—no hint of distress.
And bask in their honor and gain.
While torn with pain, my heart breaks within,
My countenance without still serene.

For if I would break, and show all the pain,
Who knows, that might add to their feelings of gain.
Their feelings are different from mine, I have seen.
"It's only our job," they will say.
Hearts as hard as the walls, minds locked against learning,
They're just like the room and the doors.
But no.
Because God made them humans,
To enjoy the same things I enjoy—
Freedom to move and to see and to feel.

Who decides, then, if ever I'll move, or flow with
nature and time?
To love and to give as ever I choose,
And whenever the need should arise?
Might the judge,
Seated within the gate, clothed in black, encircled with luster?
Might he be the one to decide?
Or these men who hold the keys to my chains,
And on their belts jingle the keys to the doors.
Might they be the ones to decide?

My heart tells me no, that can't be.
Man alone can't lay claim to my future.
For if in their pomp and perverted ambitions,
They should decide that inflicting more pain
would change me in heart
and cause me to part
From the ways in which I have prevented their gain.
My heart tells me no, they cannot decide,
but that God who controls the created,
will cause that their ways be directed
To bring about freedom and all that I need,
At a time only He can be certain is right.

Beneath His Wings
By Rachel Lapp, December 13, 1993

There's shade beneath His wings
And healing; It's in His word, a promise
Circumstances, or people, or any other thing
Can't take that from us.
Unless we let the tempter feed our doubt
And we give in to fretting and worrying about
What people might do, or how circumstances might work out.

Beneath God's wings, I'm under lock and key
For Billy, only fifteen
For a while his father also had to be
In jail, for hiding Billy with my family.
The father now is home with his three other sons
Waiting for a judge to say Billy can come.
So we minister to Billy, 'till the family can be one.

Beneath His wings I am content because
'Tis there He's shown
That though some strut and flaunt their so-called laws
To put me down
To change the facts, to lock me up and cause me pain
That inward peace and freedom doesn't have to change
That by this exercise of love, we and others gain.

Beneath His wings I've learned
That iron bars do not make a prison
Not when hatred and deceit are spurned
And love and truth design the soul's decision
To guard these with a fervor
To employ them as a catalyst in each endeavor
To aspire to the freedom that's forever.

Four months in jail; my cell is twelve by nine
It's shared by three others
There's a day room, twice the size of mine.
But with up to eighteen in it, I've had to smother
Some of that flair I have for physical activity
And divert it to maintaining mental creativity
If I'm to stay intact in this morbidity.

Beneath His wings, this still hurts. It's not as much the keys
I'm under; nor the cellmates, but the staff
Of this jail. It hurts so bad that these
People like myself can talk and joke and laugh
While herding us, who haven't harmed, about like animals.
The pain of this breach of trust is indescribable
I need His wings each day to make it bearable.

For this it takes a love sublime.
More than I can keep. It has to come direct
From the Father's heart to mine
To help me bear the tyrants' actions and protect
From that consuming evil, bitterness
To which in human weakness I might well regress.
But no! His wings, they lift and lighten even that distress.

I've won! Because I love and do not hate.
I've won! Because the truth has set me free.
I've won, and I my consolation take,
In that I have what ever mine will be
The Sun of Righteousness arose with wings of healing.
We go forth, and grow, to all revealing.
That beneath those wings, the blessing is increasing!

(Based on Psalms 63:7 and Malachi 4:2)

■ APPENDIX D ■

Jailhouse Freelancing

Marching to the beat of a different drummer

The Mayville trial of the five men and women accused of obstructing police officers during their attempt to arrest Barbara Lyn Lapp is over.

The prosecuting attorney, Assistant District Attorney Ronald Gibbs, in his closing statement, said of the five defendants: "They seem to be marching to the tune of a different drummer."

There was a time when the most respected members of society knew that individuals choosing the tune to which they wish to march was the ultimate beauty of freedom, a freedom that the founders of our once-great country upheld as sacred.

Listen to Henry David Thoreau: "If a man does not keep pace with his companions, perhaps it is because he hears a different drummer. Let him step to the music which he hears, however measured or far away."

Thoreau speaks of individual choice with adoration; the assistant

Henry David Thoreau: He went his own way.

district attorney of Chautauqua County speaks of it with disdain. This is a time in which we, hopefully as respected members of society, must decide who we will hear.

RACHAEL LAPP
Chautauqua County Jail

From *The Buffalo News,* "Everybody's Column," December, 1993

The Buffalo News/Saturday, December 18, 1993

Washington's continuing war on drugs is an abject failure

MY VIEW

Words from Western New York

By BARBARA LYN LAPP

Surgeon General Joycelyn Elder's recent suggestion that drugs be legalized prompted a barrage of criticism from all over the political spectrum. Conservatives, who already despised Ms. Elder's liberal ideas, are ready to cry "Treason!" President Clinton, who is probably more concerned about his image than the consequences of such a legal change, lamely states he doesn't agree with everything she says.

As far as I'm concerned, the political quarreling on the controversy can stay in Washington. However, the ramifications of these laws and non-laws cannot be ignored on the home front.

After I have spent four months in a small-town holding center, I am more willing to take a realistic look at the impact government's social experimentations may have on the lives of those around me.

In my estimation, about 75 percent of the female inmate population here at the Chautauqua County Jail is related to drug crimes. Here are sample descriptions, as they have been described to me:

✓ Smoking marijuana in the living room for relaxation at night.

✓ Refusal to cooperate with police in an undercover project.

✓ Selling a small portion of illicit material almost a year ago.

✓ Having temporary residence in a house where drugs have been sold by another person.

Of course, there are also cases of hard-core users and dealers, of which few intend any change of lifestyle following their stay here, other than perhaps locating police informants and killing them.

Those who never participated in illicit activities face long jail terms because of either their denial of such acts or refusal to become informants. Their only possible release from jail usually involves a plea bargain of an admission to a lower degree of the offense, and they go down in history as drug criminals.

I am one American citizen who is ready to condemn the whole government anti-drug crusade as a boondoggle, or perhaps more appropriately, a racket. Not because of what Ms. Elders says, but because of what I've seen before my own eyes.

Are we willing to condone a war machine that leaves in its path innocent by-standers, helpless children orphaned by having their parents jailed, and countless millions of wasted tax dollars? The same machine offers a joyride for cunning manipulators who take advantage of being coddled in rehab centers or well-fed in state prisons.

Who benefits? Politicians, police forces and construction workers building jails around the country to provide more space to house more people with even more of our tax dollars.

Ironically, individuals trapped in hopeless addictions, or families suffering from the horrible effects of drug use, are usually calling for more of the same laws which have caused drugs to be a lucrative business in the United States.

I doubt if there is anyone alive today with a stronger dislike for drugs and the suffering that is caused by their use than I. Personally, I also abhor the use of tobacco, alcohol and most legally approved drugs. However, I believe that with example, education and heart-to-heart assistance, our nation would fare much better without drug laws. Sanctions against drug use by educational and employment facilities would accomplish much more than any federal law.

Of course, there will always be those fools who choose to destroy their own bodies with dangerous substances, whether legal or illegal. Just remember, our Constitution gives the federal government no authority to institute laws that protect people from self-destruction.

BARBARA LYN LAPP, who was found guilty in connection with a disturbance stemming from a child custody case, wrote this article from the Chautauqua County Jail. Send submissions for this column to My View, The Buffalo News, Box 100, Buffalo N.Y. 14240.

■ APPENDIX E ■

Letters to the Editor— Conflict of Views

GIVE HER A MEDAL

To *The Post-Journal:*

Congratulations to Norman P. Carlson on his fine article on the Lapp case, Jan. 3, in *The Post-Journal.* I don't always agree with Carlson, but I can find no fault with his deductions in this article.

I myself feel Mrs. Lapp was guilty of civil disobedience and should have been fined $3.50 payable to 10 cents a week so not to create any financial hardship on her. Then maybe she should have been given a medal for defying the system.

It's a black mark against our justice system the way Mrs. Lapp has been treated. Only criminals deserve to be put in prison, not good hearted souls like her.

Robert K. Hooker
Mayville

Disagrees with Lapp's actions

Sept 18 93

Editor, OBSERVER:

Many readers of the OBSERVER have written articles in favor of Barbara Lyn Lapp's actions. I, for one, disagree. Anyone can interpret the law to justify his or her actions.

I saw Barbara on television and couldn't understand her behavior. Why was she defying the law? Does she think she is above the law? All she accomplished was getting her family involved. Now she, her sister, her father and brother-in-law are in jail.

We are lucky to live in a country that has courts of law where disputes can be settled. The law is a rule of action or conduct established by authority, society or custom. Let us obey it.

SANDRA LOBRACCO,
Irving

Let my mother come home   Sept. 93

Editor, OBSERVER:

I would like to answer some things that have been in the newspaper about me and my family.

I am not nine years old; I am 13, but not very big because nobody took good care of me before my Mom adopted me.

Some other mistakes: Grandpa is not 65. He is 66. Grandma was not arrested, it was someone else. It's not true people were purposely falling down. The police shoved them down and didn't care if they stepped on them. And it's not true the lady officer was holding me. Me and my Grandma were holding each other hard so they wouldn't take me away.

Two proud men came marching out of the courthouse door ready to start up the riot. It wasn't true we did the rioting; they did it themselves. Suddenly, many police started barging themselves in. I was scared because I thought they were killing my Mom.

I guess Sheriff Bentley planned those things against us. He should be ashamed of himself for getting his officers ready to do that mischievous thing. It made the children very sad that they did that stuff. They hurt my Mom's foot without caring about it.

The judges were not nice to my Mom. I want them to stop being bossy and let my Mom come home. It wasn't right they put my mother in jail for not even doing a thing wrong. It makes me very unhappy. The farm animals are not feeling very happy about it, either.

One of the guards told me one day: "Your Mom's a good woman." I felt like answering: "So anyway, why would you put my Mom in jail for no reason?"

I still love my Mother and I hope every officer stops this bad business.

MIRIAM HOPE LAPP,
Cassadaga

A PLAIN TRAVESTY

To *The Post-Journal:*

8-27-93

After attending the arraignment hearing of Barbara Lynn Lapp on Tuesday afternoon (Aug. 17, 1993), I felt compelled to share my thoughts and observations concerning what I regard as a travesty of justice.

Most striking was the quiet courage exhibited by Ms. Lapp amidst the tense proceedings of a judicial system run amuck and the glare of the media. Civil disobedience has been know to extract a heavy price -Ms. Lapp appears willing to unwaveringly stand on the basic tenets of the United States Constitution, and temporarily forfeit her freedom in the process.

At one point in the proceedings, Judge Himelein alluded to Ms. Lapp's actions as similar to those of a martyr. An interesting choice of words, as the existence of a martyr is often predicated upon the existence of persecution, sometimes sanctioned by an established social institution. What message was the judge subconsciously sending with this label?

While waiting to enter the courtroom, the observed actions of one deputy sheriff, however innocuous his intentions, bolstered my negativity toward the handling of this matter by Sheriff Bentley's department. This officer, smirking to a comrade, pantomimed pulling the plug on the camera of a newsman covering the story. Perhaps he wasn't shown in his "best light" the previous day outside the courthouse during the fracas initiated by the sheriff's deputies. Whatever his reason, it was a vulgar gesture given tension pervading the courthouse.

Barbara Lynn Lapp, her father, her sister, and others arrested in connection with this custody dispute may go to trial to test their convictions. Before this is resolved, I fervently hope the secretive system encompassing family court, child custody and/or abuse cases will be exposed as the hopelessly bureaucratic and autocratic legal fiasco it has evolved into.

Larry Sweet
Lakewood

Sick of reading about the Lapp family

Editor, OBSERVER:

I am sick and tired of reading articles in the news about the Lapp family and their supporters. Their actions are those of common criminals—not those of common citizens. As far as I am concerned, they got what they deserved. They fought the law and the law won. They acted in defiance of our laws. They acted as common criminals in their actions of arrogance and defiance of what this country stands for and its laws.

The Jamestown Post-Journal investigated this matter showing the Lapp supporters choking a deputy sheriff in their last confrontation with the Chautauqua County Sheriff's Department. This was a disgraceful act.

Now the Lapp supporters are wearing purple and white ribbons. The purple is supposed to represent bruises they sustained in their confrontations with the Sheriff's Department.

I think the law-abiding citizens also should wear ribbons ... red, white and blue ... for what this country stands for and in supporting the sheriff's officers for the bruises they sustained from the Lapp supporters ... those actions shown by those with animalistic behavior.

I support our laws and the Chautauqua County Sheriff's Department. God bless them all!

RICHARD MAKUCH,
Dunkirk

This letter was written by a local police officer.

A4 Wednesday, January 12, 1994
    EVENING OBSERVER, Dunkirk-Fredonia, N.Y.

People's column

Power struggle of control by the courts

Editor, OBSERVER:

I am writing concerning the Lapps, Mr. Torres and Mrs. Bedford.

Where is justice? Where is common sense? Where is wisdom in the courts concerning this case?

I believe that the courts could have put more effort into resolving this case by reasoning together with the Lapps to reach an amicable solution to the problem when it was first known that Billy had been placed in the Lapps' care.

In some situations, the letter of the law is not sufficient to properly resolve the conflict for the benefit of all concerned. It is unfortunate that the judges in this case did not appreciate or consider that the Lapp family were only looking out for the best interest of Billy.

This case did not need to turn into a power struggle of control by the courts for if an amicable solution had been reached when this first happened, the latter would not have happened and five people would not be sitting in jail for obstructing justice, a misdemeanor, while felons, drug pushers and people of such character who are a real threat to society roam the streets uninhibited.

And how does all this animosity from the courts help Billy? It doesn't. From what I can understand the state wants to retain custody of Billy. And do what? Send him back to the Bradford home in Pennsylvania. You cannot compare a state-run institution to a loving home environment (as with the Lapps).

The children's home has hired hands. They do what is necessary, their job description. But when it's time to go home, they leave. When it's their day off, they take it. It's a job that they get paid to do.

However, in Billy's situation he was placed into the Lapps' care. A family of strong dedication to God and in their love for one another, stable, hard-working, moral. Many people pay thousands of dollars to psychologists in the hope of having a family so devoted to one another.

I pray that the courts would strongly reconsider their position on this case.

ELEANOR DeWEESE,
Dunkirk

■ APPENDIX F ■

The Mayville Five Songs

Marching on Mayville
By Ken Bellet, February 1994

[1]
The Lapps are in the jailhouse doing a year of time,
Caring for a child is the nature of the crime,
They cared for Mr. Stefan and took care of his son,
And caring for a child is the only thing they've done.

[first chorus]
Come all ye people, come march along with me,
We're going to march in Mayville, 'til the Mayville Five are free.
We marched before in Mayville beneath an August sun,
They tried to stop our voices and think that they have won.

[2]
The Judge at the Mayville courthouse has truly lost his mind;
He's sending folks to jail just for being kind;
Barbara Lapp and Jacob, Rachel, Joe, and Lynn
Have never done a wrongful act for caring's not a sin.

[second chorus]
Come, all ye people come march along with me,
We're going to march in Mayville 'til the Mayville Five are free.
But they'll never stop our voices because that can't be done;
Come march with us in Mayville, Come march and the join the fun.

[3]
We people love our freedom and free we ought to be,
But none of us have freedom for the Mayville Five aren't free.
If you believe in freedom, would you like to come?
We're marching to the rhythm of an old and glorious drum.

A Different Drum

By Ken Depledge, Kevin Anderson, Dennis Cimo, February 1994

[1]
Now these people were honest, upright and fair,
That's why Don Stefan put Billy in their care.
The sheriff had a warrant for Billy's arrest,
That's when the Mayville Five were put to the test.

[2]
Now the judge thought these people, they had to be dumb
For marching in tune to a far away drum;
A drum that still rings with liberty's beat,
With fire and truth that knows no retreat.

   [first chorus]
   A different drum played on those Plymouth shores;
   A different drum played at old Valley Forge;
   A different drum forged liberty's bell;
   A different drum beats in man's conscience still.

[3]
Men and women gathered on the courthouse stairs
Looking for justice that was no longer there.
The sheriff couldn't stand it, he cried "That's enough!"
He gathered all his deputies and said, "Let's get tough."

[4]
So they grabbed Jake and Nathan to get to Barbara Lyn,
And when they threw the women down, that's when Joe stepped in.
The judge said they broke the law, and put them all in jail,
Then tried to sell their freedom back and called it "posting bail."

   [second chorus]
   A different drum played on Galilee's shore;
   A different drum plays against tyranny's roar;
   A different drum plays at the Mayville jail;
   This drum will keep playing 'til freedom prevails.

[5]
They had the Constitution, they had the Bill of Rights,
And all they should have needed for a fair courtroom fight;
But a fair fight in Mifsud's court was not to be achieved,
Vengeance raw instead of law is all that they received.

[6]
Now the judge told the jury, "What I say is law—
Don't let your conscience guide you at all.
These people are marching to a different drum,
Now they must pay for what they have done."

[third chorus]
A different drum played at Galilee's shore;
A different drum played at old Valley Forge;
This different drum iron bars cannot kill;
To this different drum the five are marching still.

Let Our People Go
By Hannah Lapp, February 1994

[1]
Our brothers, sisters, kindly friends,
Marched out one day at summer's end;
In Mayville's streets they raised the cause
For freedom, truth, and mercy's law.

[chorus]
Oh Mayville let our people go!
What ails your minds to treat them so?
The world is asking, what's the gain?
In keeping harmless folks in chains.

[2]
The men in power's cozy seats
Conspired their peaceful plea to meet
With hate of truth and vengeance raw:
"We'll beat them up and call it law!"
[3]
They stormed our brothers, knocked them down;
Our sisters dragged and kicked and bound,
But 'mid their pain and fearful bonds,
Our people cried, "The truth has won!"

[4]
The winter moon will cast its glare
In depth of night and frigid air.
So, brethren, let your love not fail
To shed its light in dismal jail!

[5]
As winter too must yield to spring,
And storm and pain new life will bring;
The tyrants' rage will not prevail,
Where patient hope the victory hails.